D1475286

THE FATHERS
OF THE CHURCH

A NEW TRANSLATION

VOLUME 102

THE FATHERS
OF THE CHURCH

A NEW TRANSLATION

THEODORET OF CYRUS

COMMENTARY ON THE PSALMS
PSALMS 73–150

Translated by

ROBERT C. HILL
The University of Sydney
Australia

THE CATHOLIC UNIVERSITY OF AMERICA PRESS
Washington, D.C.

The paper used in this publication meets the minimum requirements of the American National Standards for Information Science—Permanence of Paper for Printed Library Materials, ANSI z39.48—1984.

LIBRARY OF CONGRESS CATALOGING-IN-PUBLICATION DATA

Theodoret, Bishop of Cyrrhus.

[Interpretatio in Psalmos. English]

Theodoret of Cyrus : commentary on the Psalms / Theodoret of Cyrus ; translated by Robert C. Hill.

v. <1   > ; 22 cm. — (The Fathers of the church, a new translation ; v. 101–)

Includes bibliographical references (p. xiii–xiv) and indexes.

Contents: v. 1. Psalms 1–72. v. 2. Psalms 73–150.

ISBN 0-8132-0101-2 (v. 1 : acid-free paper)

ISBN 0-8132-0102-0 (v. 2 : acid-free paper)

1. Bible. O.T. Psalms—Commentaries—Early works to 1800. I. Title: Commentary on the Psalms. II. Hill, Robert C. (Robert Charles), 1931– . III. Title. IV. Fathers of the church ; v. 101–

BS1430.3 .T4913   2000

223'.207—dc21

99-031556

CONTENTS

vi CONTENTS

INDICES

ABBREVIATIONS

AB   Anchor Bible, New York: Doubleday.

ABRL   Anchor Bible Reference Library, New York: Doubleday.

ACW   Ancient Christian Writers, New York: Newman.

ATD   Alte Testament Deutsch, Göttingen: Vandenhoeck & Ruprecht.

BASOR   Bulletin of the American Schools of Research.

Bib   *Biblica.*

CCG   Corpus Christianorum Graecorum, Turnhout: Brepols.

DBS   *Dictionnaire de la Bible. Supplément,* IV, Paris: Librairie Letouzey et Ané, 1949.

DS   *Enchiridion Symbolorum, Definitionum et Declarationum,* 34th ed., edd. H. Denzinger, A. Schönmetzer, Freiburg: Herder, 1967.

DTC   *Dictionnaire de théologie catholique* 15, Paris: Librairie Letouzey et Ané, 1946.

EstBib   *Estudios Biblicos.*

ETL   *Ephemerides Theologicae Lovanienses.*

FOTC   Fathers of the Church, Washington DC: Catholic University of America Press.

ITQ   *Irish Theological Quarterly.*

JECS   *Journal of Early Christian Studies.*

LXX   Septuagint.

NJBC   *New Jerome Biblical Commentary,* edd. R. E. Brown et al., Englewood Cliffs NJ: Prentice Hall, 1990.

OCA   Orientalia Christiana Analecta, Rome: Pontifical Oriental Institute.

PG   Patrologia Graeca, ed. J.-P. Migne, Paris, 1857–66.

PL   Patrologia Latina, ed. J.-P. Migne, Paris, 1878–90.

RHT   *Revue d'Histoire des Textes.*

SC   Sources Chrétiennes, Paris: Du Cerf.

StudP   *Studia Patristica.*

TRE   *Theologische Realenzyklopädie,* Berlin: Walter de Gruyter.

VTS   *Vetus Testamentum,* Supplement.

SELECT BIBLIOGRAPHY

Azéma, Y. *Théodoret de Cyr. Correspondance* I, II, III, SC 40, 98, 111, 1955, 1964, 1965.

Bardy, G. "Théodoret." DTC 15 (1946): 299–325.

_____ . "Interprétation chez les pères." DBS IV (1949): 569–91.

Barthélemy, D. *Les Devanciers d'Aquila. VTS* X. Leiden: Brill, 1963.

Bouyer, L. *The Spirituality of the New Testament and the Fathers.* Eng. trans., London: Burns & Oates, 1963.

Canivet, P. *Histoire d'une entreprise apologétique au Ve siècle.* Paris: Bloud & Gay, 1957.

Clark, E. A. *Women in the Early Church.* Message of the Fathers of the Church 13. Wilmington: Glazier, 1983.

Dahood, M. *Psalms.* AB 16, 17, 17A. New York: Doubleday, 1965–70.

Dorival, G. "L'apport des chaînes exégétiques grecques à une réédition des *Hexaples* d'Origène (à-propos du Psaume 118)." *RHT* 4 (1974): 44–74.

Drewery, B. "Antiochien." *TRE* 3, 103–113.

Fernandez Marcos, N. "Some reflections on the Antiochian text of the Septuagint." In *Studien zur Septuaginta—Robert Hanhart zu Ehren.* Göttingen: Vandenhoeck & Ruprecht, 1990, 219–229.

Guinot, J.-N. *L'Exégèse de Théodoret de Cyr.* Théologie Historique 100. Paris: Beauchesne, 1995.

Halton, T. P. *Theodoret of Cyrus on Divine Providence.* ACW 49. New York: Newman, 1988.

Hill, R. C. *St John Chrysostom's Homilies on Genesis.* FOTC 74, 82, 87. Washington DC: Catholic University of America Press, 1986–92.

_____ . "On looking again at *synkatabasis.*" *Prudentia* 13 (1981): 3–11.

_____ . "Chrysostom's terminology for the inspired Word." *EstBib* 41 (1983): 367–73.

_____ . "Psalm 45: a *locus classicus* for patristic thinking on biblical inspiration." *StudP* 25 (1993): 95–100.

_____ . "The spirituality of Chrysostom's *Commentary on the Psalms.*" *JECS* 5 (1997): 569–79.

_____ . "Chrysostom's *Commentary on the Psalms:* homilies or tracts?" In *Prayer and Spirituality in the Early Church.* Ed. P. Allen. Brisbane: Australian Catholic University, 1998, 301–17.

_____ . "Chrysostom, interpreter of the Psalms." *EstBib* 56 (1998): 61–74.

_____. *St John Chrysostom*. Commentary on the Psalms. Brookline MA: Holy Cross Orthodox Press, 1998.

_____. "Theodoret's *Commentary on Paul*." *EstBib* 58 (2000): 79–99.

Jellicoe, S. *The Septuagint and Modern Study*. Oxford: Clarendon, 1968.

Kelly, J. N. D. *Early Christian Doctrines*. 5th ed., New York: Harper & Row, 1978.

McCollough, C. T. "Theodoret of Cyrus as biblical interpreter and the presence of Judaism in the later Roman Empire." *StudP* 18 (1985): 327–34.

Mandac, M. "L'union Christologique dans les oeuvres de Théodoret antérieures au Concile d'Ephèse." *ETL* 47 (1971): 64–96.

Quasten, J. *Patrology* III. Westminster, MD: Newman, 1960.

Rondeau, M. J. *Les commentaires patristiques du Psautier (IIIe–Ve siècles)*. OCA 219, 220. Roma: Pont. Inst. Orient., 1982, 1985.

Vaccari, A. "La θεωρία nella scuola esegetica di Antiochia." *Bib* 1 (1920): 3–36.

Viciano, A. "Theodoret von Kyros als Interpret des Apostels Paulus." *Theologie und Glaube* 80 (1990): 279–315.

Wallace-Hadrill, D. S. *Christian Antioch. A Study of Early Christian Thought in the East*. Cambridge: Cambridge University Press, 1982.

Weiser, A. *Psalms*. ATD 14, 15. 5th ed., Eng. trans., London: SCM, 1965.

Weitzman, M. P. *The Syriac Version of the Old Testament*. Cambridge: Cambridge University Press, 1999.

Wilken, R. A. *John Chrysostom and the Jews. Rhetoric and Reality in the Late 4th Century*. Berkeley–Los Angeles–London: University of California Press, 1983.

Young, F. *From Nicaea to Chalcedon. A Guide to the Literature and Its Background*. Philadelphia: Fortress, 1983.

_____. *Biblical Exegesis and the Formation of Christian Culture*. Cambridge: Cambridge University Press, 1997.

COMMENTARY ON THE PSALMS
73–150

COMMENTARY ON PSALM 73[1]

A psalm for Asaph.

E HAVE ALREADY SAID that some claimed that this man was an author of the Psalms, some that he was a musician and conductor of the singers. Others, on the other hand, said David uttered these psalms, too, whereas Asaph wrote them down. Our view, however, as we have often said, is that blessed David wrote them all, which is in fact the truth of the matter.[2] Still, let everyone take it as he pleases: no harm will come therefore from taking it this way or that. Under the guiding light of grace we shall make clear the psalm's meaning.

(2) The people taken captive to Babylon were beset with many and varied calamities; but on seeing the Babylonians living a life of impiety and lawlessness, and enjoying great prosperity and good fortune while they themselves were in difficulty and hardship, they set to thinking about divine providence, reflecting and wondering why on earth godless people feel no effects of troubles but enjoy every good fortune, carried along by fair winds. [1444] The grace of the all-holy Spirit foresaw this from afar and, devising help for them and in fact for all human beings, wrote this psalm, giving clear articulation to their

1. In keeping with our remark at the close of Ps 72, whose concluding doxology Theodoret does not seem to take as an index of termination of a "Book Two" of the Psalter (an ancient division evidently unknown to him, though not to Eusebius), there is no sense here that he is introducing his reader to Book Three. The following block of eleven psalms associated with Asaph, however, raises an issue he addresses, just as it perhaps accounts for absence of commentary on them by Chrysostom.

2. Theodoret discussed the authorship of the Psalms in his preface. Aware of the role of Asaph recorded by the Chronicler, he is quite flexible in allowing for divergent views—not as dogmatic as this sentence from the longer form of his text suggests (see Introduction, section 2, and note 8 to the next psalm). He requires only acknowledgment of the Spirit's guidance of the psalm's composer (as of the commentator), whom he sees not singing but speaking and writing.

thoughts and offering elucidation of their quandary. On the one hand, then, the teaching of the psalm is applicable to all those pondering or uttering such matters;[3] on the other, it is expressed in the person of those returning and recounting their mental sufferings.

(3) *How good is the God of Israel* (v. 1). He uses *how* not in a comparative sense but to show the high degree of goodness. Now, he says it is also *the God of Israel* who shows great care. *To the upright of heart:* yet not all know this, only those employing right and sound reasoning. After praising them in this way, he makes no secret of the tumult of his own thoughts: *But my feet had come close to stumbling* (v. 2): I had come close to losing my way. *My steps had nearly slipped.* Symmachus, on the other hand, put it this way, "My supports had almost fallen away": I was at risk, he is saying, of abandoning sound and supportive thoughts, and suffering an awful lapse; *slipped* suggests as much, like pouring out, coming apart, and running under. In figurative fashion he also calls his thoughts *feet* and *steps.*[4]

(4) Then he cites the cause as well: *Because my zeal was aroused at the lawless, on observing sinners' peace* (v. 3): I became heated in seeing those living a life of impiety and iniquity, in peace and great good fortune. We see today, too, some people saying similar things against those living a life of impiety and avarice, and in their view exercising power through wealth and publicity. *Because there is no denial in their dying* (v. 4). Aquila, on the other hand, put it this way, "There is no misfortune in their death," and Symmachus, "They did not give much thought to their death." When undergoing the test of hazards, he is saying, in other words, they do not despair of their fate. *Denial* suggests

3. Theodoret, as we have noted, bishop though he is, does not often see it his role to acknowledge the generally pastoral application of the Psalms' sentiments, preferring historical and/or eschatological senses. But this psalm has a particular claim to that recognition; as Weiser remarks, it "occupies a foremost place among the more mature fruits borne by the struggles through which the Old Testament faith had to pass. It is a powerful testimony to a battle fought in the human soul comparable to that in the Book of Job." Theodoret, however, is not moved to that extent, we shall see, Job not rating a mention.

4. We have noted Theodoret's appreciation of the figurative language of the psalms; only occasionally does he feel it necessary to warn his Antiochene congregation not to be literalistic in their appreciation of such language.

despair:[5] when prepared to despair of something, we usually deny it. *And strength in their scourge.* Distress comes their way briefly, he is saying. *They are not affected by human troubles, and will not be scourged along with other people* (v. 5). Things go smoothly for them, he is saying, and they are not beset with toils and sufferings or chastisement like other people.

(5) [1445] *Hence arrogance gained control of them in the end; they were enveloped in their iniquity and impiety* (v. 6): from this they became puffed up with imposture and conceit; and not having paid the penalty for their former sins, they fell foul of worse lawlessness. The word *enveloped* suggested the extent of the iniquity in so far as it encircled them on all sides. *Their iniquity developed as though from fatness* (v. 7). Fatness, as we have often said, implies comfort and prosperity; so they committed iniquity in complete security, he is saying, as though living in such great good fortune.[6] *They passed on to their heart's disposition. They were disposed to wickedness and spoke of it, they extolled iniquity. They lifted their mouth to heaven, and their tongue went abroad on earth* (vv. 7–9): injustice against human beings did not content them; instead, they took aim also at heaven both in words and thoughts. By this he implies blasphemies against God, abuses against the people, drunken rage against the divine temple; and he said so more clearly in the forty-first psalm, "My tears became my food day and night when it was said to me every day, Where is your God?"[7]

(6) *For this reason my people will turn back here, and full days will be found in them* (v. 10). As though the God of all were saying this, the inspired word uttered it to give heart to the downcast. Despite their blasphemies against God, he is saying, and the abuse directed against us, the God of all made positive decisions in our favor, promising our return and the life prescribed

5. While modern translators of the Hebrew word have recourse to linguistic parallels to get sense, the LXX introduces a *hapax legomenon* that taxes Theodoret; the other ancient translators are also struggling with the meaning.

6. Theodoret is getting through the verses of the psalm at rapid rate, not pausing to make the parallels that the Scriptures make available, as Weiser suggested. He is not about wringing his reader's withers, concerned more to honor his promise of conciseness made in the preface.

7. Ps 42.3.

for [human] nature. From this it is clear that the psalm applies to those already returned and recounting what had transpired in Babylon;[8] it said, *For this reason my people will turn back here,* that is, to Judea. So living there they say *here,* something quite inappropriate to those in Babylon. He called old age *full days,* meaning, They will return and live to old age.

(7) Having thus shown God's promise, he reverted once again to the account of the Babylonians' blasphemies and the confusion of their thinking. *They said, How does God know? Is there knowledge in the Most High?* (v. 11). Symmachus, on the other hand, put it more clearly, "But they said, How does God know? Does [1448] the Most High have full knowledge?" Whereas God made those promises, he is saying, they formed their own idea that God does not take note or know anything of what happens. Then to show in this their impiety, he develops his own ideas: *Look at these people, sinners, prospering for ages, they gained wealth* (v. 12): in their life of lawlessness they enjoy good things in abundance, and have uninterrupted good fortune, *for ages* referring to the present life; often he calls the life of the human being *age,* "Our age in the light of your countenance."[9] *And I said, Is it in vain that I kept my heart righteous?* (v. 13). For my part, on the contrary, to see them faring well and swaggering about in their wealth, I wondered, Surely the possession of righteousness is not without fruit? *I washed my hands among the innocent:* so it was of benefit to me, he is saying, to keep my distance from those living in sin, *I washed among the innocent* implying, I kept myself innocent and had no truck with the wicked. *Scourging was my lot all day long, and in the morning my testing* (v. 14): attending to righteousness and fleeing the company of evil, I am tormented and abused every day.

(8) *If I had said, I shall give this version of things, behold, you would have been faithless to the generation of your children* (v. 15).

8. From a verse "usually considered corrupt" (Dahood) Theodoret, who cannot allow himself to appear tentative in his commentary, insists on finding confirmation of the historical basis to this psalm, showing less interest in its generally sapiential investigation of questions of theodicy, which would be more helpful to his reader, one would think. But his argument is hardly compelling, and he is careful not to complicate it by citing the alternative versions.

9. Ps 90.8 [LXX].

Abandoning the other thoughts, he is saying, I pondered this within me: Surely God has not cancelled his agreement with us? Does *You would have been faithless* mean, in fact, You would have broken the agreements made? They call themselves *children* as given this name by God: "Israel my firstborn son,"[10] and, "I gave birth to children and raised them."[11] *I came to the realization, This is hardship for me, until I entered God's sanctuary and understood their fate* (vv. 16–17). But I abandoned those thoughts, he is saying, I considered that God had allotted me trials and hardships in exacting penalty for my failings. Nevertheless I shall return, I shall see his consecrated temple and perceive their evil end.

(9) Then, thanks to divine grace, he learns this lesson beforehand: [1449] *But you put troubles in their way on account of their deceitful acts; you brought them down by lifting them up. How did they meet with desolation? All of a sudden they failed, they were lost on account of their lawlessness, like a dream when people awake* (vv. 18–20). All this happened to the Babylonians in the time of Cyrus: he took them captive and enslaved them, whereas to the Jews he granted return. Now, he was right to compare their prosperity to a dream; the unreality of the present life is no different from a dream, after all.[12] It is easy to grasp this from the Babylonians themselves: puffed up and conceited for a while as rulers of the whole world, they suddenly lost their power and fell foul of extreme servitude. *Lord, in your city you have brought their image to nothing:* the image had a brief period of flourishing. He compares the Babylonians' power, then, to an image, lasting a short time: You bring it to nothing, exacting penalty for the irreverence towards your city.

(10) *Because my heart was inflamed* (v. 21). I reasoned this way, he is saying, seething at their lawlessness. He picked up the opening thought, *Because my zeal was aroused at the lawless:* what he called *zeal* there he calls *inflamed heart* here. *And my vitals were moved.* He gives the name *vitals* to his thoughts, as I have of-

10. Exod 4.22.
11. Isa 1.2.
12. Negative remarks like this about the world in which his readers spend their lives are less frequent in the bishop's commentary than in a preacher's like Chrysostom's, but still unhelpful. (See my "The spirituality of Chrysostom's *Commentary on the Psalms.*")

ten said: despite my pious thoughts, he is saying, I was briefly led astray by their arrogance. *I was brought to nothing and was ignorant* (v. 22). Symmachus said it more clearly, "But I was without understanding and sense":[13] I had this experience out of ignorance, not recognizing your judgments. *I was like a brute beast before you. I am ever with you* (vv. 22–23): but I shall no longer have this experience, nor bring myself to make any inquiries or busy myself with the arrangements of your wisdom; instead, like a beast I shall follow your decisions, in this way not likely to be cut off from your providence. In other words, as the beast follows the one leading it, not [1452] concerned about where it is led, so shall I also follow when guided by your grace, not inquisitive about your providence.

(11) *You held my right hand. In your counsel you guided me and supported me with glory* (vv. 23–24). Here he refers to the events of the return: as a kind father on finding his errant child takes it by the right hand and leads it back home, so you led me back to my ancestral land, freeing me from slavery and granting me easy passage through the nations, and so you made me famous and glorious. *After all, what is there for me in heaven, and what have I wanted on earth beyond you?* (v. 25). Aquila, on the other hand, put it more clearly: "Who is in heaven for me? With you I had no wish to be on earth." He posed a question as if to say, My hope is in heaven. I expected, he is saying, and I expect you to be gracious to me in heaven and on earth: in heaven I have no other God or caretaker than you, nor in fact on earth do I rank anyone else with you—rather, both in heaven and on earth I know you are God. This is said in particular on the part of the nations believing in the Savior;[14] and he says, I eagerly accept your lordship. *My heart failed, and my flesh* (v. 26): for this reason I long for you and I thirst in soul and body, and I await your help. *God of my heart, God my portion forever:* I have you as portion and lot, and enjoyment of good things.

(12) *Because, behold, those keeping their distance from you will per-*

13. We have seen the regard Theodoret has for the version of Symmachus, frequently preferring it to his LXX.
14. A comment inserted by editor Schulze from the longer form of the text, typical in its eschatological reading of the text.

ish; you destroyed everyone who was unfaithful to you (v. 27): those, on the other hand, who place themselves far from your care and choose to serve idols will reap the destructive fruit of defection. He calls idolatry *infidelity* here; God likewise says also through Jeremiah, "She went up every high hill and under every verdant tree, and was unfaithful there; and I said after all this infidelity of hers, Return to me, and she did not return"; and again, "She committed adultery with tree and stone,"[15] meaning, Leaving me, her spouse, she served false gods. Accordingly, here too he called the worship of idols *infidelity*. He said it, however, not of the Babylonians, but of those made captive on account of impiety: though they [1453] had God as spouse, they turned adulterer, embracing the service of the demons.

(13) Learning sense through the experience, however, they cry out, *For me, on the contrary, it is good to cleave to God, to put my hope in the Lord* (v. 28): through practical experiences I shall not be separated from the God who has saved, and shall be strengthened by hope in him. *So as to sing all your praises in the gates of the daughter of Sion:* through this hope I secured return, and I shall recount your wonders in Jerusalem, which he called *daughter of Sion;* as he calls human beings "children of human beings," so he gives Sion the name *daughter of Sion.* The city had two names: it is called Sion and Jerusalem by the divine Scripture.[16]

15. Cf. Jer 3.6–7, 3.9.
16. Though we have learned not to expect Theodoret to infringe his promised conciseness with a peroration in the manner of a preacher, we might have expected some explanation of the basis of the metonymy involved in this Scriptural interchange of names.

COMMENTARY ON PSALM 74

Of understanding, for Asaph.

IN FORECASTING THE FUTURE destruction of Jerusalem, the inspired word bids those who come upon this psalm to understand[1] and grasp its sense. Some commentators in fact applied the psalm to what occurred under Antiochus Epiphanes, without taking account of the history or realizing precisely the prophecy in the psalm.[2] On the one hand, the psalm mentions the burning of the divine Temple, devastation of homes, and complete destruction of the city, whereas we have no knowledge from history of this happening under Antiochus. Nor does it actually fit the siege by the Babylonians: at that time they had many prophets—Jeremiah, Uriah son of Shemaiah,[3] Ezekiel, Daniel—whereas the psalm says, *There is no longer any prophet, and no one to know us any longer* (v. 9). If, on the other hand, the psalm relates neither to Babylonians nor to Macedonians, it is clear that it forecasts the destruction inflicted on them by Romans, after which they were granted no second chance, paying the penalty for their impiety against the Savior.[4] By contrast, the ineffable goodness of the

1. While modern commentators only hazard a guess that the term *maskil* in the title suggests a psalm genre, the LXX sees in it the roots of the verb "understand," and Theodoret proceeds on this tack, as before (cf. Ps 32).

2. The application of the psalm that Theodoret rejects is that of Diodore and Theodore; he prefers instead to see a reference to the Roman conquest, as had Eusebius, who also rejected an application to the Babylonian invasion. On scores of occasions in the *Commentary* we see Theodoret giving his reader the benefit of his acquaintance with earlier commentators, Alexandrian as well as Antiochene.

3. We have noted Theodoret's interest in marginal figures in sacred history. This prophet simply flashes before our eyes in a page of Jeremiah (Jer 26.20–21) before disappearing without trace, but he has caught Theodoret's attention.

4. In a nutshell, the theological justification for the plight of Theodoret's Jewish contemporaries.

Lord calls for admiration in foreknowing precisely their disobedience and yet trying to turn them from their impiety by the prophecy of the future evils.

(2) Now, all the same, even the very beginning of the psalm indicates that the prophecy has this theme: *Why, O God, did you reject us forever?* (v. 1). It is not like the time of the Babylonians, when you limited the time of servitude to seventy years, nor seven and a half years in the time of Antiochus, in accord with Daniel's prophecy;[5] instead, you rejected us forever, and condemned [us] to destruction. *Your anger was vented on sheep of your pasture:* you bore lasting indignation against your sheep. [1456] *Remember your congregation, which you acquired from the beginning* (v. 2): right from the beginning you were called our God and we were styled your people, Lord. *You redeemed a rod of your inheritance:* enjoying your assistance, we were freed from the servitude of Egyptians. Blessed Moses also called them *inheritance:* "Jacob became the Lord's portion, his people, Israel his allotted inheritance."[6] And he gave the name *rod* to the royal scepter, meaning, We became your portion from the beginning, we were named your inheritance, we came under your kingship. Likewise also in the forty-fourth psalm he called the royal scepter *rod,* saying, "The rod of your kingship is a rod of uprightness."[7] *This is Mount Sion, where you took up your dwelling:* having freed us from the servitude of Egyptians, you introduced the promised land to the forefathers and consecrated Mount Sion to yourself so that by living there as in some palace you might guide your people. Now, this was foretold when the Temple in Jerusalem had not yet been built: it was after the time of David and Asaph that Solomon built it.[8]

(3) *Lift your hands at their arrogance forever* (v. 3): bring them to account for pretentiousness. Now, he used the phrase *Lift your hands* by analogy with those flaying sinners with their hands. The charism of inspiration[9] uttered this with the knowl-

5. Theodoret is hazarding an interpretation of the obscure chronology and symbolism of chapter 9 of Daniel (in the mouth of Gabriel, in fact).

6. Cf. Deut 32.9.

7. Ps 45.6.

8. The tolerant Theodoret still has an open mind on the question of the psalm's authorship (cf. note 2 to Ps 73).

9. Theodoret is in no doubt of the inspiration of the psalmist—whoever he

edge of the enemies who live in impiety: it was not out of zeal for the Crucified that they embarked on the war, but to subjugate the world. God made use of them as executioners, nonetheless, so as to punish through them those practicing impiety. *All the malice that the foe practiced in your holy place.* Neither the Hebrew, nor the other translators, nor the Septuagint in the Hexapla used the plural "in the holy places"[10]—only the singular *in your holy place,* to make clear that those saying this are referring to the Temple, wailing and lamenting what had been done to it by those others.

(4) What follows also agrees with this sense. *Those who hate you boasted in the middle of your festival* (v. 4): on the festival of Passover, when all the people were assembled according to the Law, Titus had the army pitch camp and besieged [1457] their mother city. After all, since it was on the festival of Passover that they fixed the Savior to the cross, they pay the penalty for impiety at the same time. *The emblems they set up were their emblems. They were as ignorant as in the exodus previously* (vv. 4–5). The trophies, he is saying, which are the emblems and symbols of victory they raised above our entrances, rendering the victory familiar to everyone afterwards; Pilate brought the imperial emblems into the city in defiance of the Law, and the Roman emperors carved the image of a piglet on the doorposts. Through all these events they came to realize that they had become bereft of divine care. The Lord also forecast this in the divine Gospels: "When you see the abomination of desolation set up in the holy place (let the reader understand), then let those in Judea flee to the mountains."[11]

(5) *They hacked with axe heads as though in a forest of trees, togeth-*

---

be—who enjoys this *prophetike charis.* The phrase and others like it recur in commentary on this psalm, perhaps because Theodoret prefers not to be specific in reference to the author.

10. See Introduction, section 3, for the range of textual resources at Theodoret's disposal in composing his *Commentary.*

11. Mark 13.14. That ch. 9 of Daniel, of course, is the source for Mark's phrase "the abomination of desolation," a context Theodore has just referred to Antiochus; but he is either unaware of this, or unwilling to let it get in the way of his close relation of the text to Titus's destruction of Jerusalem—when in fact the profanation of the Temple previously planned by Caligula did not occur, historians point out.

er with its doors; they razed it with axe and adze (vv. 5–6): using tools of woodcutters and craftsmen, they both demolished the ramparts and hacked the doors of the dwellings, destroying the fine and beautiful workmanship like a forest. *With fire they burned your sanctuary down to the ground, they polluted the tabernacle of your name* (v. 7): the sack of the other buildings did not satisfy them; rather, they extended their frenzy even to your consecrated Temple, consigning some things to the fire, destroying others with their hands in their treatment of holy things as profane.

(6) *They said in their heart, their fellows with them, Come, let us abolish from the earth all God's festivals. We do not see our emblems, there is no longer a prophet, and no one to know us any longer* (vv. 8–9): attacking us in complete accord, they had one purpose, to wipe out the Law given by you. Through the term *festivals* he indicated the way of life in keeping with the Law. Now, they perpetrated these things, he is saying, through not beholding the wonders worked in the time of our forebears or being castigated by a charism of inspiration. They were, in fact, left bereft of all these things in a trice: they had many prophets even after the return—Haggai, Zechariah, [1460] Malachi—and the prophets older than they forecast the future to both the people and the kings, and brought the enemies' schemes to light. It is easy to learn this from history.[12]

(7) *How long, O God, will the foe reproach us? Will the adversary challenge your name forever?* (v. 10). To what point will you abandon us to their transgressions, and in your long-suffering put up with their blasphemous cries? *Why do you turn aside your hand, and forever keep your right hand in your bosom?* (v. 11). God's *bosom* is the treasury of good things, and his *right hand* is his operation. Why on earth do you not habitually provide good things instead of removing your hand from your bosom? Now, he expressed it this way by analogy with those who have a full bosom, and when requested are unwilling to give, and instead put their hand behind them.

12. As Theodoret indicated at the opening, this verse gives him clinching proof that it is not the Babylonian assaults referred to in the psalm, nor the postexilic period. He feels convinced, or wants to be, that he has the facts of history on his side—though the rest of the psalm is less supportive.

(8) *Yet God is our king from of old* (v. 12): and yet we have known you as king from the very beginning, and always enjoy gifts as from a king. *He brought about salvation in the midst of the earth:* assuredly you have made clear to everyone the care taken of us *in the midst of the earth* meaning "with everyone looking on." *You dominated the sea with your might* (v. 13): when fleeing from the Egyptians and prevented by the sea from making our way, you accorded us that remarkable opportunity by making solid what was naturally fluid, and building walls on either side through the waters. *You smashed the head of the dragons on the water, you broke the head of the dragon* (vv. 13–14). He calls the Egyptians *dragons* and their leaders, commanders, and captains *heads of dragons,* whereas by the use of the singular *dragon* he means the Pharaoh, who was over many generals. He also means the devil, however, whom the lawgiver bound and abolished by his death accepted willingly.[13] This is the reason he said he had many heads. All these you caused to drown, he is saying, and the sea that you dominated for our sakes [1461] you released on them and overwhelmed them in its billows. *You gave him as food to the Ethiopian people.* Being neighbors of the Egyptians, the Ethiopians were frequently at war with them; but when Pharaoh with his army was consigned to the sea, the Egyptians were then exposed to the Ethiopians; and just as the hungry person rapidly devours food, so they had no trouble at all in overpowering them. Therefore the prophetic word is saying, *You gave him as food to the Ethiopian people* meaning, You made them vulnerable, causing them to be rapidly devoured by the Ethiopians.

(9) *You cut openings for springs and torrents* (v. 15). The Hebrew, on the other hand, and the other translators say "spring." Even if we were to say "spring" or *springs,* we would not be wide off the mark: the inspired word calls the water flowing from the rock *spring,* but once divided it made many rivulets with the re-

---

13. Theodoret is moving briskly through these verses on what modern commentators see as mythological motifs but what is for him the exodus. As the material is not relevant to the Roman occupation, he is hurrying through with little comment and no Scriptural documentation, this intrusive reference to the devil coming from the longer form of his text.

sult that those countless hordes easily took advantage of the flood. We find this happening not on one occasion but even on two: Exodus teaches this, as does also the Book of Numbers.[14] He was right to give the term *spring* to the rock giving forth streams of water, whereas he likewise gave these the name *torrents* as not naturally flowing but giving forth for the first time on that occasion: as a torrent is not everflowing but is brought into being with rainwater, so that water gushed with the divine streams.

(10) *You dried up rivers of Etham.*[15] Symmachus, on the other hand, said, "You dried up ancient rivers": those that were not in existence or had not been created in the beginning you bade flow in the wilderness, whereas those made in olden times and following an ancient course you brought to a halt with your decision. He says this also in another psalm: "He turned rivers into desert, springs of water into thirsty ground, fruitful land into a salty waste, because of its inhabitants' wickedness. He turned desert into watery havens, a parched land into springs of water, and settled hungry people there."[16] Whereas on account of lawlessness of the inhabitants he dried up rivers of Sodom and Gomorrah and the others dwelling nearby, in the parched land he provided streams from the rock, offering rivulets to the thirsty people; it is easy for him, after all, to change the natural behavior of water as he wishes. In this, of course, the verse reveals a further truth, that he will not offer the streams of the inspired rivers to Jews on account of their lawlessness, whereas the nations, once desert places, he irrigates with springs from the rock. The rock, as the divine Apostle says, [1464] is Christ.[17] All these words from the verse, *He brought about salvation in the midst of the earth,* involve the type of the favors conferred on us: in the former case freedom from

14. Cf. Exod 17.5–6; Num 20.11.

15. The LXX is content to transliterate this Hebrew term *'eythan,* "constant," and Theodoret, obviously unaware of this but looking for light, has recourse as usual to the version of Symmachus, which has made a good fist of it.

16. Ps 107.33–36.

17. 1 Cor 10.4. This New Testament essay into typology encourages Theodoret to do the same at some length, with a characteristic sacramental bent.

slavery came through water, in our case the beginning of freedom comes through water; in the former case dragons' heads are smashed by water, in our case demons' powers are cancelled by the grace of baptism; after the sea they became vulnerable to the Ethiopians, after the holy bath our enemies were easily overcome by those who formerly had black souls; and for those prepared to pay attention it would likewise be an easy matter to discern other aspects in addition to these.[18] There a rod, here a cross; there Moses, here high priests; there a sea, here a bath; there twelve springs, here twelve apostles; there seventy codices, here seventy books.

(11) Instead, let us proceed to the rest of the commentary. *Yours is the day, and yours is the night; you brought light and sun to perfection. You made all the ends of the earth; you shaped the very summer and spring* (vv. 16–17). He shifted his attention from private benefits to common ones, teaching that the God of all is creator of everything, maker of day and night, source of light, creator of the sun, and controller of time, indicating by *spring* and *summer* the seasons. In place of *You made all the ends of the earth,* on the other hand, Aquila and Theodotion said "erected" and Symmachus, "set in place." The verse indicates that he was the one who gave it existence, and allotted some parts of it as plains, some as mountains and glens, and hollowed out some of it as a receptacle for marshes and waters of the sea.

(12) *Remember this* (v. 18). Having made all this, he is saying, creator of such wonderful things, *remember this*—that is, the assembly, which has been your possession from the outset; to that remark he supplied this as well, *A foe reproached the Lord, and a witless people challenged your name.* Have regard, he is saying, not for us but for the adversaries' blasphemies. *Do not deliver to wild beasts a soul confessing to you* (v. 19). It is not for everyone indiscriminately that the inspired word makes the prayer; instead, it requests good things for those confessing the divine name, those confessing that it was God from God, of one being with

18. Cf. Exod 15.27. With characteristic moderation, Theodoret calls a halt to the series of parallels; but the longer form of the text cannot resist gilding the lily, and adds five more.

the Father and the [1465] Spirit, who was crucified.[19] He calls *wild beasts* the ferocity not only of the enemies but also of those denying the Crucified and not confessing him to be God as has been said. *Do not forget the souls of your needy ones forever.* The *needy* would be those of humble attitude: "Blessed are the poor in spirit," as the Lord himself says in the Gospels, "because theirs is the kingdom of heaven."[20]

(13) *Have regard for the covenant of your servants, because those in the land who have fallen into darkness were filled with iniquitous dwellings* (v. 20): those not enjoying your radiance but claiming blasphemously with the Jews that you are a human being and not confessing you to be the Sun of Justice,[21] and loving the darkness of ignorance they have houses full of iniquity and the punishment ensuing from it. In other words, They were given over to evils of all kinds, and hence opted for darkness. *Let a lowly person not be turned away in shame* (v. 21): we beg that our request not be brushed aside, nor that we be sent off in shame. *Poor and needy will praise your name:* those who ask your help and gain it are accustomed to offer you hymn singing.

(14) *Rise up, O God, vindicate your cause. Remember your reproach on the part of the foolish all day long* (v. 22). It was highly appropriate for him to change the pronoun: he did not say "my cause" but *your cause.* In other words, it was fair that I should suffer this, he is saying, but they committed many blasphemies against you, those who crucified you, and those who even after the crucifixion set at naught baptism as well. *Do not forget the voice of your suppliants; the arrogance of those who hate you rose up constantly* (v. 23). Here they linked the haughtiness of the enemies with their own person, asking to be granted some leniency, not on their own account but on theirs.[22]

19. The inserts here (and in commentary on v. 22) about the Crucified, citing phrases from Constantinople's creed, are from the longer form of the text.

20. Matt 5.3.

21. A further anti-Jewish insertion from the longer text complicates the thinking and the syntax of a verse and commentary already tortuous.

22. Theodoret briskly concludes commentary on the psalm without acknowledgment that the latter half has not been susceptible of the historical interpretation involving the Roman invasion on which he was eloquent at the opening. The longer form of the text is less in tune with this interpretation.

COMMENTARY ON PSALM 75

To the end. Do not destroy.
A psalm of a song for Asaph. [1468]

YMMACHUS, ON THE OTHER HAND, "A triumphal psalm about incorruption for Asaph." Since the psalm contains a prophecy of the righteous judgment of God, and foretells also the ruin of the workers of wickedness and the just deserts of the lovers of virtue, it was right that the work urge us by means of the title not to destroy pious thoughts but to keep them healthy and inherit incorruption.[1] This psalm, then, is uttered on the part of the captives in Babylon, promising to sing God's praises if they enjoy divine grace.

(2) *We shall confess to you, O God, we shall confess to you and call upon your name* (v. 1). It is clear from this that they say this without having yet gained the return. They promise to sing God's praises, and to make his august name illustrious; the clause, *we shall call upon your name,* implies, We shall once again bear your name and be styled your people. *I shall narrate all your wonders when I take the opportunity* (vv. 1–2). Aquila and Symmachus, on the other hand, said, "when I take the assembly": when we return, he is saying, and are gathered into your holy Temple, then we shall both lawfully sing your praises and teach those ignorant your kindnesses, that opportunity allowing us to do it. As it is, in fact, we cry aloud, "How shall we sing the Lord's song in a foreign land?"[2] In this way, the inspired word, having

---

1. As with its occurrence in the title to Ps 57, Theodoret fails to see the phrase "Do not destroy" in the title as a musical cue to the conductor; so he rationalizes, looking to Symmachus—also at a loss—for some hint as to its relevance.

2. Ps 137.4. The argument here about the future prosperity of the captives rests, as often, on misconstruing Hebrew tenses. Exegetical skills are basic for sound interpretation.

taught the captives in Babylon what they should say, and instructed them through repentance to be converted to the Savior of all, gives a glimpse of God responding to the promises made, saying, *I shall deliver upright judgments.* I shall decide justly between you and the Babylonians, he is saying.

(3) *The earth was wasted, and all its inhabitants in it* (v. 3): I am judge of all the world, and shall inflict due punishments on all. *I shall strengthen its pillars:* I am master of all in being creator of all; I made the earth and established it, supporting it on my boundaries like some pillars. [1469] After all, I gave the order, and it shall not lapse. Hence, though I am also judge, I do not choose to punish, but foretell retribution so as by the threat to render the sinners more moderate; I urge and advise them to loathe every form of iniquity, on the one hand, and on the other to have a care for a righteous and balanced attitude. He taught this, in fact, by what follows.

(4) *I said to the transgressors, Do not transgress, and to the sinners, Do not raise your horn* (v. 4): this is the worst passion of all, not only sinning but even priding oneself on it. *Do not lift up your horn on high* (v. 5). Then he shows what height he is referring to: *Do not speak iniquity against God.* Horned animals, in fact, take great pride in their horns. The verse urges them not to add insolence to their iniquity, nor move their tongue against God. *Because it is not from the dawn nor from the west nor from desert mountains. Because the Lord is judge* (vv. 6–7). By *the dawn* he meant the east, as the fifth edition also said;[3] and by *desert mountains* the northern and southern parts, these parts remaining completely uninhabited owing to the extreme cold and heat. So his teaching is that it is impossible to avoid God's judgment: take east or west, try to flee to south or north, you are subject to the divine verdict.

(5) Then he teaches the vicissitudes of life which happen through God's will. *He humbles one and elevates another. Because in the Lord's hand there is a cup full of pure wine well mixed, and he*

---

3. As mentioned in Introduction, section 3, the "fifth edition" may be a fifth Greek version available in Theodoret's Hexapla. Despite the syntax in his LXX, he is in accord with Dahood in seeing reference in this verse to the four points of the compass.

moved from one to the other (vv. 7–8). The prophecy of the divinely inspired Jeremiah also teaches about this cup: he is ordered by the God of all to take it and give a drink to Jerusalem, the rulers, and the neighboring nations.[4] He calls retribution *wine* in that it undermines strength in a manner like inebriation and impairs the coordination of the limbs. So the inspired word[5] means that the righteous Judge brings retribution, at one time to us, at another time to them, and now elevates this one while humbling that one, and in turn shifts the elevation to others, transforming calamities and changing good fortune. It was not without purpose that the captives in Babylon were taught to say this; rather, [1472] they were instructed in advance about both the servitude of the Babylonians and their own freedom: not long after, Cyrus destroyed the power of the former and restored those [i.e., the Jews] to their former freedom. *But its dregs will not be emptied: all the sinners of the earth will drink.* He called the worse punishment *dregs:* I drank the milder potion, he is saying—that is, I was subjected to the lesser evils—whereas the Babylonians drink the very sediment—that is, they will suffer worse things than they committed; I gained the return after being enslaved for seventy years, whereas they will be consigned to unremitting servitude.

(6) *As for me, on the contrary, I shall rejoice forever, I shall sing to the God of Jacob* (v. 9): just as they made fun of our troubles when we drank, so we shall offer hymn singing to God on seeing their punishment, not to mock them but to prove grateful for the favors. *I shall break all the horns of sinners, and the horn of the righteous will be exalted* (v. 10). In these words they were taught in advance that they would get the better of the enemies attacking them after the return. This, of course, is the reason he said *all the horns of sinners,* since a combined force from different nations declared war on them; the prophecy of Ezekiel also mentions this, and of course that of Micah and that of Zechariah.[6] Once they were worsted, [the Jews] became famous

---

4. Cf. Jer 25.15–28.

5. Again Theodoret employs a non-committal phrase in these psalms whose authorship is a moot point.

6. As he tells us in the preface, Theodoret had completed commentaries on

and illustrious for pulling off such a victory. He called the pious mind *horn of the righteous*. If, on the other hand, one wanted to understand Zerubbabel as the one called righteous here, whom God used as his minister in achieving that victory, one would not err far from the truth.[7]

Ezekiel and The Twelve (minor prophets) before coming to the Psalms though, in fact, he makes more frequent reference to Isaiah and Jeremiah.

7. Theodoret is flexible in the positions he takes, and is prepared to allow the reader to differ, especially where the reference is debatable.

COMMENTARY ON PSALM 76

To the end. In hymns, a psalm for Asaph,
a song on the Assyrian.

 FOUND THE INSERTION of "the Assyrian" not in the Hexapla but in some copies.[1] The psalm does contain this theme, however: it forecasts events involving Sennacherib and the punishment inflicted on the army.

(2) *God is known in Judah, great is his name in Israel* (v. 1): with so many myriads struck down in one night by the death-bearing blow [1473] at the hands of an angel,[2] the God of all, who takes good care of Israel and made his own appearance in Judah, became clear to everyone. *His abode has been established in peace, and his dwelling in Sion*[3] (v. 2): at the destruction of the multitude, the survivors took to their heels, becoming messengers of the divine power; this was the reason they were not exterminated along with the others. The city enjoyed peace on that account, and everyone formed the impression that God in real fact was pleased to dwell in Sion. Then he teaches how God is known in Judah: *There he broke the force of the bows, shield, sword, and war* (v. 3). Before the city's ramparts, he is saying, he did away at the same time with shield bearers, archers, and targeteers, and rendered their weapons completely useless.

(3) *You shed light marvelously from everlasting mountains* (v. 4). Symmachus, on the other hand, put it this way, "You are conspicuous, immense from mountains of hunting": on our mountains you dispatch the adversaries to death's hunting, revealed

1. Theodoret seems to have had access to various forms of the LXX, we have noted (see Introduction, section 3).
2. Cf. 2 Kings 19.35.
3. For *Salem* the LXX reads *shalom,* and Theodoret has no difficulty rationalizing it, unaware of the solecism.

22

as conspicuous and immense to everyone; you shed light on the ignorant with the marvel, and teach [them] who you are.[4] *All the foolish of heart were confused; they slept their sleep and found nothing* (v. 5): adopting a greater arrogance in your regard, they suffered sudden confusion on account of their folly of soul, thought themselves dozing safely and were disappointed, death succeeding sleep. History also teaches this, that on arising they found everyone dead. *All the men of wealth in their hands.* Symmachus, however, is saying, "All the men, strong with regard to their hands." The strength of their hands, he is saying, was of no use to them, though they counted on it to seize everyone's wealth.

(4) To bring out what on earth it was they did not gain from it, he added, *At your rebuke, O God of Jacob, those riding the horses fell into a sleep* (v. 6). You nodded, he is saying, and immediately those priding themselves on their knowledge of equestrian skills fell down. By *fell into a sleep* he indicated the ease of death: just as the sleeper easily dozes if inclined, so they experienced a sudden end of their life. *You are fearsome, and who can withstand you?* (v. 7): who is sufficient to withstand you and flee the punishment inflicted by you? *From your rage* [1476] *at that time:* as soon as you heard the blasphemies, you were able to punish the guilty, but showed long-suffering in waiting for change.

(5) *From heaven you made judgment heard* (v. 8). From on high, he is saying, you deliver the verdicts as you wish. In place of *you made heard,* on the other hand, Symmachus said, "you will make audible." *Earth feared and was still when God arose to judgment, to save all the gentle of the earth* (vv. 8–9). All were filled with dread, he is saying, and ceased their assault on us, seeing you as a kind of judge delivering the verdict against them, and those gaining salvation who employed right reason and announced your help. *Because human pondering will confess to you, and remnant of pondering will celebrate you:* enjoying these good things, they will

4. His LXX version being less than pellucid, Theodoret turns to the different but equally obscure version of Symmachus, and does his best briefly to paraphrase each without reconciling them. His puzzlement is understandable in the light of his ignorance of the Hebrew, where homonyms *'ad,* "eternity," and *'ad,* "prey," could easily be confused by translators.

devote their thoughts to hymn singing, directing not even a small portion of them to a different concern.[5]

(6) *Make vows and perform them to the Lord, our God* (v. 11). They encourage one another both to promise gifts and keep their promises: it is shameful and completely ungrateful for neighbors, on the one hand, to do all this out of dread, and for those granted favors, on the other, to be afflicted with ingratitude. He makes this clear in what follows: *All those in his circle will bring gifts for the fearsome one, who removes breaths of rulers, fearsome before the kings of the earth* (vv. 11–12): they will provide gifts when terrified by the miracles that have happened and on learning from experience that he is truly God, who inflicts death both on the influential and on those thought to rule the earth.

---

5. Theodoret is naturally struggling to find meaning in a psalm whose text Gunkel thought "repeatedly very corrupt." Sennacherib "the Assyrian" has been left far behind.

COMMENTARY ON PSALM 77

To the end. On Jeduthun. A psalm for Asaph.

YMMACHUS, ON THE OTHER HAND, said "through Jeduthun." He was the one entrusted with the choir of
those praising God in song.[1] So Asaph either in person
or as a minister of David's inspired composition [uttered this
psalm]: making a decision on doubtful matters is not without
risk.[2] It foretells the discordant thoughts of the Israelites forced
to serve in Babylon, and the pangs stemming from this situation. He teaches also what kind of prayer they had to offer to
God when requesting freedom from the troubles. He gave the
psalm the form [of recital] by those recounting these very
things after the return and praising God in song.

(2) [1477] *I cried with my voice to the Lord, with my voice to God,
and he heard me* (v. 1). Earnestly, he is saying, I offered prayer,
and immediately I received my request. Then he teaches the
time this happened: *In a day of my tribulation I sought out God* (v.
2): buffeted by pains I diligently sought out the divine assistance; *sought out* implies the earnest prayer. Then he shows the
manner of the supplication: *With my hands at night before him,
and I was not disappointed.* Symmachus, on the other hand, put it
this way, "My hand at night was stretched out constantly": at
night I stretched out the hands to bring quiet, begging to be
granted loving-kindness, and I was not deceived in my hope.
This in fact was indicated by *I was not disappointed,* that is, It was

---

1. Cf. 1 Chron 16.37–42, a context in which both Asaph and Jeduthun are
referred to as liturgical ministers, and the opening of Ps 39 and Ps 62. If Dorival is right about references to alternative versions being later insertions, the
choirmaster Theodoret refers to is Asaph.

2. Theodoret, at least in the short form of the text, has been seen in the
preface and elsewhere to be flexible on issues such as authorship of the Psalms.
Here he formulates this admirable policy of avoiding dogmatism.

not in vain that I kept vigil, but I reaped the benefit of the prayer.

(3) *My soul refused to be consoled. I called God to mind, and was made glad* (vv. 2–3): I drove out every pretext for consolation, and had recollection of God as sole comfort. *I pondered, and my spirit fainted.* Symmachus, on the other hand, put it this way, "I talked to myself, and my spirits fell": in constant converse with myself and pondering the problems besetting me, I despaired of freedom from them and felt the bitter barbs of despondency. *My eyes anticipated watches* (v. 4). He calls *watches* the divisions of the night when the guards entrust the watch to one another, suggesting in this way staying awake all night. *I was disturbed and did not speak.* The same people said this in the forty-first psalm, "My soul was disturbed within me":[3] I could not bear to reveal my thoughts to others.

(4) *I pondered days gone by, and I recalled eternal years. I meditated* (v. 5). I renewed the memory of your former favors, he is saying, and reflected on the great number of favors our forebears were granted by you, the way they were freed from the slavery of the Egyptians, the way they passed through the Red Sea, the way they gained the land promised to the ancestors. *By night I communed with my heart, and stirred up my spirit* (v. 6). For *stirred up* Theodotion, on the other hand, said "examined" and Aquila, "poked." Considering these things within myself at night, he is saying, [1480] I asked myself why he took such care of our forebears and yet ignores our plight.

(5) In addition to these thoughts I had others: *Surely the Lord will not reject [us] forever and will not be further displeased [with us]? Will he terminate his mercy forever?* (vv. 7–8): surely he has not utterly despaired of our situation and put us beyond his particular care? *Has he put an end to his word from generation to generation?* Symmachus, on the other hand, put it this way, "He put an end to his talking on each generation." I was afraid also of this, he is saying, that foreknowing the situation of each generation from the beginning, he imposes the limits for each generation. *Surely God has not forgotten to have pity? or will not in his anger with-*

3. Ps 42.6.

hold his pity? (v. 9): but in turn I consoled myself with the thought that God, prone to pity as he is, will not bring himself to dismiss our situation as if to oblivion, and close up the fonts of mercy in anger as if by some barrier.

(6) *And I said, Now I have begun, this change of the right hand of the Most High* (v. 10). I have become, he is saying, the means of such transformation for myself; by sin I gave rise to the punishment, so I am the source of the evils. Now I have begun to be corrected by *the right hand of the Most High,* which imposes unfortunate punishments in place of the former benefits (referring to the punishment as *change of* God's *right hand* for the reason that *the right hand of the Most High* usually confers good things). But not content even with these thoughts, I reminded myself of the Lord's goodness, saying this, *I remembered the works of the Lord, because I shall remember your marvels from the beginning. I shall meditate on all your works, and muse on your exploits* (v. 11): I shall bring to the fore all marvels done by you for us from the beginning, and pondering them constantly I shall not forsake my sound hope.

(7) *O God, your way in holiness* (v. 13). Symmachus, on the other hand, put it this way, "O God, your way in sanctity." Aquila, however, has "in what is sanctified." You are holy, he is saying, and you rest in a holy place, and in them you dwell and move about. *Which god is so great as our God? You, O God, are the one who alone works wonders* (vv. 13–14): you are superior to all, Lord, alone working the wonders you wish. [1481] *You made your power known among the peoples. With your arm you redeemed your people, the children of Jacob and Joseph* (vv. 14–15): you revealed your might to all people by freeing from slavery to Egyptians the people styled your own, who had Jacob as forebear and were rendered illustrious from kinship with Joseph.

(8) *Waters saw you, O God, waters saw you and were afraid, depths were troubled, a mighty sound of waters* (v. 16): in every way, Lord, you demonstrated your power, scourging Egyptians, freeing your people, appearing in the sea, the water divided, nature flowing from either direction. *The clouds uttered a sound, with your arrows passing; sound of your thunder in the wheel* (vv. 17–18). Symmachus, on the other hand, said, "The sky gave a roar." The

sea was in fact divided, as history tells us, by a strong south wind blowing;[4] the air congealed, the clouds gathered, and a gale arose. Your punishments, however, he is saying, came like arrows against the enemy; with the crash of the thunderclap you impeded the wheels of the Egyptians' chariots. History also teaches this: "It was at the morning watch that the Lord looked upon the Egyptians' encampment, clogged their chariots' axles and did violence to them."[5] *Your lightning flashed in the world:* the light of your wonder working coursed through the whole world like a lightning flash. *The earth shook and was all of a tremble;* hearing of your power, they were all filled with dread. The prostitute Rahab also said this to the spies, "Fear and dread of you fell on us: we heard how the Lord your God divided the Red Sea before you."[6]

(9) *Your way was in the sea, and your paths in many waters, and no trace of you will be found* (v. 19): it is easy for you even to part the sea, and ride on many waters without leaving even a trace, being naturally incorporeal. He added this to what is above, meaning, You led the people without being seen, and showed us no trace of your movement. *You guided your people like sheep by the hand of Moses and Aaron* (v. 20): employing those ministers and speaking through them, you guided your people and educated them in your Law. He made mention of all this to prompt the God of all to mercy, appealing for enjoyment of the same care.

4. Cf. Exod 14.21 [LXX], an east wind in the Hebrew.
5. Exod 14.24–25. Theodoret is having trouble with the LXX reading of "wheel," which inadequately turns a Hebrew word for "jar" (from a potter's wheel?); he bravely looks beyond semantics for some light.
6. Josh 2.9–10, loosely recalled.

COMMENTARY ON PSALM 78

Of understanding, for Asaph. [1484]

HE GOD OF ALL GAVE the ancient Law to the children of Israel, and ordered them to learn it constantly, teach the children, and let their offspring see the reason for the festivals so that on learning of the divine favors they might prove grateful to the one bestowing such gifts. "You will teach them to your children, and your children's children," he is saying, "and they will keep the commandments of the Lord God so that it may be well with them."[1] The charism of inspiration has done this also in the present psalm: it reminds us of the people and their offspring, and of the ingratitude for what had been done by God and the good things provided on the part of the recipients of these.

(2) *Attend, my people, to my Law* (v. 1): I urge you to listen attentively to what is said: I offer you the present exhortation like some law. *Incline your ears to the words of my mouth:* listen with enthusiasm to what is said by me. *I shall open my mouth in parables; I shall utter riddles from the beginning* (v. 2). Since he leveled a charge at the parents for the benefit of the children, he called such an account a *parable* as an obscure saying conveying hidden benefit. He added that he offers also ancient riddles. And to teach when he got the information, he added, *The very things that we have heard and known* (v. 3). Then he gave an inkling into the teachers of these things: *and that our ancestors narrated to us. They were not hidden from their children in another generation, announcing the praises of the Lord, his powers and his marvels which he worked* (vv. 3–4). From the very beginning, he is saying, the witnesses of the marvels taught them to their own children, and they in turn transmitted the teaching to their offspring.

1. Evidently a conflation of Deuteronomic texts, such as Deut 4.9, 6.25, and 8.11.

(3) [1485] They did this, he is saying, in obedience to the divine law; he added, *He raised up testimony in Jacob, and set a Law in Israel* (v. 5). He calls *testimony* the tabernacle fixed in the wilderness, holding as it did the tables of the testimony. In fact, he calls *Law,* as we said before, the commandments, testimonies, judgments, and ordinances; we said this more clearly in the eighteenth psalm.[2] *What he commanded to our fathers for making known to their children.* This he commanded through the giving of the Law, he is saying, so that the parents might transmit to the offspring the account of the marvels like a kind of inheritance. *So that another generation might be aware, children born to them will also rise up and announce them to their children* (v. 6): Having learned this from their parents in this way, they in turn offered the same teaching to their children, and the memory of them was kept unforgettable.

(4) What is the fruit of the teaching? *That they may place their hope in God, and not forget his works but seek out his commandments* (v. 7): learning God's power and how easy it is for him to do all the good things, they will develop sound hope in him and follow the laws laid down by him. *Lest they become like their ancestors, a generation twisted and embittered* (v. 8): learning of the ungrateful attitude of their ancestors, and how they often provoked God to anger through transgression of the Law, they will be on their guard against imitating them. *A generation that did not direct its heart, and its spirit was not fixed on God:* they did not develop a firm faith in God, being unwilling to travel the straight and narrow, having instead an attitude at odds with the divine ordinances.

(5) *Children of Ephraim aiming and firing arrows were turned back on the day of battle* (v. 9). He delivers a different charge against the tribe of Ephraim, that of paying great attention to idols; the story of the Judges also teaches us this, and the third [book] of Kings. For they set up heifers and turned the nine tribes away from the worship according to the Law, thus becoming the source of apostasy.[3] It is this in particular which the

2. Cf. Ps 19.7–9.
3. Cf. 1 Kings 12.25–33. Theodoret's hermeneutics and views on the psalm's authorship are tested here, both because of the prospective viewpoint

grace of the Spirit foresees, and it accuses [them] of the sin not yet committed, offering advice suited to them while knowing they would not accept the recommendation, yet proposing the appropriate benefit all the same. He stresses their strength and archery skills, [1488] and charges them with timidity: *they were turned back on the day of battle;* conceited about their military experience, they took to flight at the outset of fighting. *They did not keep God's covenant, and refused to walk in his Law* (v. 10). It was right for him to bring out their independent decision: they refused to live in keeping with the Law, he is saying, and embrace the prescribed way of life. *They forgot his kindnesses and the marvels he had shown them* (v. 11). To show when he did this, he added, *Marvels, which he worked in the sight of their ancestors* (v. 12). Then to bring out the time and the place, *in the land of Egypt, in the field of Tanis:* all this wonder working by God that happened in Egypt, of which their ancestors became eyewitnesses, they cancelled from their memory.

(6) *He parted the sea, and led them through; he pushed waters aside like a wine bottle* (v. 13). He gives the account of the marvels concisely, giving pride of place to the chief one over the others: the marvel of the sea and their journey through it exceeded natural boundaries. The God of all made the waters, naturally prone, stand up on either side, as though by a word forcing them into a wine bottle: since the shape of wine bottles has natural ability to contain the liquid flawlessly, he was right to employ this image of the divided [water] to show the power of the divine word.[4] *He guided them with a cloud by day, and with a light of fire all through the night* (v. 14): this cloud repelled the severity of the [sun's] rays by day, and by night he provided the service of fire. *He split rock in the wilderness, and gave them to drink as if from a great depth* (v. 15): it was no little stream he made to bubble up, but a fountain fit for those many myriads. He brought this out more clearly in what follows: *He made water*

_____

he has to presume and because of the attribution to Asaph. So he falls back on oblique statements of authorship like "the grace of the Spirit," "the inspired word," or "the charism of inspiration."

4. We have noted Theodoret's sensitivity to the literary artifice of the psalmist; we can credit him with this hermeneutical skill, if not some strictly exegetical skills.

gush from rock, and brought down water like rivers (v. 16): he divided the water flowing out into many rivulets, providing ready
and generous relief to the thirsty.

(7) *They piled sin on sin against him; they provoked the Most High
in a waterless place. They tested God in their hearts to request food for
their souls* (vv. 17–18): yet this did not drive wickedness from
their mind; rather, they persisted in being beset by the affliction of ingratitude. Along with such great kindnesses they wanted to experience divine power, and being short of food they did
not seek to receive what was necessary but accused God of powerlessness. [1489] *They spoke against God and said, Will God be
unable to lay a table in the wilderness? He struck rock there, and water
flowed and torrents poured: will he not also be able to give bread or lay
a table for his people?* (vv. 19–20): the [miracle] of the waters was
simple and easy, he is saying: hidden in the hollows of the earth
it came to light. But food in the form of bread, that is sown [in
the ground] and grows over time—how could he suddenly provide that to us and satisfy our pressing hunger?

(8) *Hence the Lord heard and tarried; fire was kindled towards Jacob and anger arose against Israel* (v. 21). The Lord of all was irritated on this account, he is saying, he delayed giving them the
land promised to their fathers, and inflicted manifold punishments; yet he did not inflict sudden destruction on them, awaiting an increase in their children. The writings of blessed Moses
mentioned the punishment by fire;[5] it was a plague they suffered, he is saying. *Because they did not believe in God, nor did they
hope in his salvation* (v. 22). Nevertheless, he provided them with
food they had not grown, despite their being like this; he teaches this in what follows. *He gave directions to clouds from above, and
opened heaven's doors. He rained on them manna to eat* (vv. 23–24):
the clouds did not produce the normal outcome; instead, in
place of the rain naturally produced for watering the seed
sown, they gave birth to miraculous food. He called the supply
from above *opening of heaven's doors:* since we usually put doors
on storehouses, and open them when we want to take something out, the inspired word shows the God of all supplying the
manna as though from some storehouses.

5. Cf. Num 11.1–2.

(9) *He gave them bread of heaven; a human being ate bread of angels* (vv. 24–25). He calls it *bread of angels* on account of its being supplied by angels: angels, as we are taught by the divine Scripture, minister to the divine decisions. Likewise the divine Apostle says, "Are they not all ministering spirits, sent for service for the sake of those due to inherit salvation?" And again, "If the message spoken through angels proved reliable,"[6] and so on. He calls it *bread of heaven* for being brought down from above; the divine Scripture also refers to the birds that travel through the air as heaven's winged creatures. *He sent them provisions in abundance.* He let them share in this food and be satisfied, he is saying.

(10) Then he describes the supply of the meat. [1492] *He took the south wind from heaven, and brought on the African in his power. He rained flesh on them like dust, and winged birds like sand of the seas* (vv. 26–27): by means of the winds he drove together from all quarters the kind of those birds, and bade them fly down in the direction of the [people's] dwellings, giving them a lucky catch. *They fell in the middle of their camp around their dwellings. They ate and were completely satisfied; he met their desires, they not disappointed in their desires* (vv. 28–29). They enjoyed what they had longed for, he is saying, and satisfied their gluttony; yet they paid the penalty for their greed. *Food was still in their mouths when God's anger came upon them, and he slew some of their strongest and brought the elect of Israel up short* (vv. 30–31): though they had great experience of the divine power and yet did not believe God could supply food, he applied chastisement to teach that he was capable of doing both, providing good things and inflicting retribution.

(11) Nonetheless they persisted in sinning; [the psalmist] said as much: *In all this they still kept sinning, and did not believe in his marvels. Their days were lost in futility, and their years in frenzy* (vv. 32–33). Sinning and failing, he is saying, showing no care for what could be of benefit to them, bent on futile and useless

6. Heb 1.14; 2.2. It strikes us as a little surprising that Theodoret, who has been seen to take a sacramental interpretation of some psalm passages (especially in the longer form of his text), does not mention the eucharistic application of these phrases in liturgy and ecclesiastical music.

pursuits, they gave themselves to such things with utter frenzy and so departed this life. *When he slew them, then it was that they sought him out, they were converted and rose early to pray to God. They remembered that God is their helper, and God the Most High is their redeemer* (vv. 34–35). It was not without purpose that the loving Lord put shackles on them: they gained no little benefit from it. In fact, when enjoying the good things they had no sense of it, whereas when punished they took to imploring divine loving-kindness.

(12) *They loved him with their mouth, and were false to him with their tongue. Their heart was not straight with him, nor were they true to his covenant* (vv. 36–37): using false words they promised to love him; [1493] their thinking was at variance with their words, intending the opposite of the divine laws and reluctant to believe in the divine sayings. *But he is full of pity, and will forgive their sins and not destroy them* (v. 38): yet he practiced his characteristic goodness and could not bring himself to dispatch them to utter ruin.[7] *He will go to lengths to deflect his anger, and will not enkindle his rage altogether.* Symmachus, on the other hand, put it this way, "For the most part he deflected his rage, and did not stir up all his anger": he did not inflict on them the punishment for their sins which they deserved, he is saying. *He remembered that they are flesh, a breeze that passes and does not return* (v. 39): he knew the weakness of their nature, and the fact that they would not have a lengthy life span.

(13) *How often they provoked him in the wilderness, enraged him in waterless land. They turned about and tested God, and irritated the Holy One of Israel* (vv. 40–41). In all this he teaches the divine long-suffering, though you could gain a more precise knowledge of each event from history: on one occasion they made a god of a heifer, on another they enrolled themselves with Baal of Peor, on a different occasion they plotted rebellion against the mighty Moses, though enjoying the manna for food they were ungrateful, bidden to take possession of the promised

---

7. The psalm is proving to be a lengthy rehearsal of well-worn sacred history, and Theodoret is content with mere paraphrase as he dashes through it. Encountering verses where the LXX has rendered the Hebrew past tense as a future, he is able—perhaps with the help of Symmachus—to ignore the error.

land they pleaded fear.[8] Countless other things they committed in addition to these, which we pass over, not wishing to prolong the commentary.

(14) *They did not remember his hand on the day when he redeemed them from the hand of the persecutor* (v. 42): they were unwilling to be mindful of the former kindnesses or ponder God's strength by which they were freed from Egyptians' slavery. Then he outlines the wonder working performed there. *As he set his signs in Egypt and his prodigies in the field of Tanis* (v. 43). Tanis was the site of Pharaoh's palace; there the mighty Moses inflicted punishment on the Egyptians.[9] *He turned their rivers and their rain waters into blood so they could not drink* (v. 44): first he changed into blood not only the river water but also [the water] collected from showers, bringing the pressure of thirst on the traducers. *He sent dogflies on them, and they devoured them, and frogs, and they destroyed them. He delivered up their crops to the blight, and their labors to locusts* (vv. 45–46): [1496] employing dogflies and frogs as ministers of his rage, he inflicted harsh pains on them, and destroyed the crops of the land with blight and locusts.

(15) *He ruined their vineyards with hail, and their mulberries with frost* (v. 47): he laid waste the crops with blight and locusts, and with hail and frost he rotted the very roots of the trees. The other interpreters, however, take *mulberries* as sycamores. *He gave their cattle over to the hail, and their possessions to the fire* (v. 48). Symmachus, on the other hand, put it this way, "Giving their cattle over to hunger, and their possessions to birds of prey": coming to a sudden end, they became food for birds of prey. *He sent against them the fury of his anger—anger, fury, tribulation, a dispatch of wicked angels* (v. 49). He called the harsh punishments *anger, fury, tribulation,* and the ministers of the punishment *wicked angels,* using *wicked* not of malice of nature or of free will but of the retribution in punishment. He likewise calls the day

8. Cf. Exod 32; Num 25, 11, 14, and 16. As usual, such historical references are but mere footnotes to his text, since he has "no wish to prolong his commentary," as he insists.

9. Tanis, occurring also in v. 12, for which the Hebrew reads Zoan, has been thought by modern—and evidently ancient—geographers to have been the biblical Rameses (Exod 1) where Ramses II had his palace. Theodoret is closer to the truth in this designation than in the reference to Moses.

of punishment a "wicked day."[10] Symmachus made this clear by saying "angels who do evil" for *wicked angels*.

(16) *He made a path for his anger* (v. 50), that is, loving-kindness did not prevent punishment, but gave room for the righteous correction. He indicated this also in what follows: *He did not spare their souls from death; he confined their cattle to death. He struck every firstborn in Egypt, firstfruit of every labor of theirs, in the tents of Ham* (vv. 50–51): seeing their obstinate attitude, he inflicted punishments on them without stint—firstly inflicting ruin on the cattle, and afterwards unexpected death on the firstborn ones. He called Egypt *tents of Ham* since Mesrem was the son of Ham, and Mesrem is Egypt.[11] *He took away his people like sheep, and led them up into the wilderness like a flock* (v. 52): after chastising them in that way, he led his own people into the wilderness, after the manner of a shepherd leading the flock. *He guided them in hope, and they were not afraid* (v. 53): after giving many pledges of his peculiar might, he bade them to trust in him and not to be afraid. Now, this was done by the God of all, [1497] whereas they were unwilling to trust in the power of God. *The sea covered their foes:* the sea provided a way for them, but flooded the others with waves.

(17) *He brought them to his mountain of holiness, this mountain which his right hand acquired* (v. 54): so having freed them from there, he gave them a land he had promised; by Mount Sion [the psalmist] indicated the whole land. *He drove out nations before them, and gave them a heritage with a cord of inheritance:* having freed the land from the former occupants, he gave control of it to them in keeping with the promises. This is the meaning of *with a cord of inheritance:* owners usually measure their own land; the history of Joshua son of Nun gives more precise information on lots and divisions. *He settled the tribes of Israel in their tents:* he allotted the land according to tribes.

(18) After thus highlighting their infidelity after the wilderness, he describes the transgressions in the land of promise. *They tested and provoked God the Most High, and did not observe his testimonies* (v. 56): despite such wonderful kindnesses, they con-

10. Cf. Ps 41.1.
11. Cf. Gen 10.6.

tinued transgressing and breaking the divine commandments. *They turned away and were rebellious just as their ancestors were, too* (v. 57): they imitated the malice of their ancestors, and though perceiving their punishment, they gained nothing from it. *They were bent into a crooked bow.* A skillfully made bow shoots arrows directed in keeping with the aim, whereas one affected by a twist is unable to aim the arrows shot. So, too, those people, having lost their upright thinking, did not respond as they ought to the divine benefits either, and made an occasion of benefit into an occasion of harm. *They enraged him on their hills, and with their carvings aroused his jealousy* (v. 58): though receiving good things from the God of all, they served lifeless idols.

(19) *God heard, and was scornful* (v. 59). When they made requests, he is saying, he did not accord them his characteristic providence. The story of the Judges brings this out more clearly: he handed them over, at one time to the Ammonites, at another time to the Moabites, at a different time to Midianites and Philistines, exacting a penalty of them for impiety. *He brought Israel down altogether:* that famous people, freed against the odds from the Egyptians' slavery, which the sea beheld and took flight, and the Jordan turned backwards—that people easily defeated its neighbors in battle. [1500] *He rejected the dwelling at Shiloh, a tabernacle where he dwelt among human beings* (v. 60). The opening of the Kings teaches this in turn, mentioning Eli the high priest and the offences of his sons. *He handed over their power to captivity, and their pride into the hands of foes* (v. 61). He calls the ark *their power and pride;* when Hophni and Phinehas brought it out for assistance to their kin, they paid the penalty for their transgression, whereas the Philistines captured the ark and dedicated it like spoils of some kind to Dagon, an idol worshipped by them.[12]

(20) *He hemmed in his people with the sword, and ignored his inheritance* (v. 62): he gave them into the hands of the enemies on account of the excess of their transgression. He gave them the name *inheritance* for being always the recipients of the greatest care at his hands. The great Moses likewise gave that name to

12. Cf. 1 Sam 1–5.

them: "The Lord's portion," he is saying, "was his people Jacob, Israel cord of his inheritance."[13] He next lists the forms of punishment: *Fire consumed their young men; there was no lamentation for their maidens. Their priests were put to the sword, there was no grieving for their widows* (vv. 63–64): he surrendered them to fire, and there was no customary mourning of them, everyone preoccupied with their own troubles. The priests Hophni and Phinehas, though carrying out the ark itself, met a sticky end, learning through experience itself that those living a life of lawlessness should not expect divine care.

(21) *The Lord was awakened as if from sleep* (v. 65): still, by submitting them to the same punishments, he also taught their enemies the cause of what happened. *Like a warrior drunk with wine. He struck their foes in the rear, he gave them everlasting disgrace* (vv. 65–66): throwing off his long-suffering like some dream, he inflicted the blow on the Philistines by means of which they were disgraced in the sight of everyone. He means the condition of inactivity, as the historical account teaches; the inspired composition also indicated it,[14] saying, *He struck their foes in the rear,* solemnly referring to the place that received the blow. He called long-suffering *sleep,* and indignation [1501] *drunk with wine:* punishment justly inflicted on the guilty ones is like a novelty on God's part.

(22) *He rejected the tent of Joseph, and did not choose the tribe of Ephraim* (v. 67). Once again omitting the other tribes, he mentions only Ephraim, foreseeing the coming treachery: Jeroboam came from it, and he was the one who took the ten tribes away from the Davidic monarchy. *Joseph* and *Ephraim* refer to the same tribe, Ephraim being Joseph's son. He says it was rejected through the fact of the tabernacle's not remaining in Shiloh; instead, the gift of the divine ark was transferred to Jerusalem, where Solomon also erected the divine Temple later. *He chose the tribe of Judah, Mount Sion, which he loved* (v. 68). He chose the tribe of Judah, of course, on account of the rod of

13. Deut 32.9.

14. The distinction Theodoret seems to be making is interesting: while the Psalms are classed *propheteia,* "inspired composition," and the psalmist *prophetes,* the book of Kings is classed as *historia* or *syngraphe* and the composer *syngrapheus.*

Jesse being expected to flower. The patriarch Jacob also made a prophecy about this shoot in blessing Judah,[15] and the divinely inspired Paul also mentions it in speaking this way, "It is evident that our Lord Jesus Christ sprang from Judah."[16] So it was for this reason that he preferred the tribe of Judah to the others; but because this mystery was not known to the majority, he very wisely added, *Mount Sion, which he loved,* so as to quench the envy of the other tribes, as if to say, Take no occasion of jealousy: it was on account of Mount Sion that he chose the tribe of Judah. Furthermore, he wants to present the mountain as venerable on account of the Temple to be built on it.

(23) *He built his sanctuary like a unicorn* (v. 69). They say the unicorn is equipped with one horn, and the Law gave instructions for adoring one God; so it was right for him to liken the one Temple, dedicated to the one God, to a unicorn.[17] *He founded it on the earth forever.* Symmachus, on the other hand, put it this way, "like the earth, which he founded forever"; and the others gave the same sense. He means, then, that just as he built one earth, so he ordered the Jews to build one Temple.

(24) *He chose his servant David, and brought him from the flocks of sheep* (v. 70). In this he makes the same point, both of David's virtue, calling him God's *servant,* and of God's generosity in making the shepherd a king. [1504] *He took him from behind the young* (v. 71). Symmachus, on the other hand, put it this way, "He brought him as he was following the pregnant ones." This, too, is an extreme example of generosity: he was not an experienced shepherd nor an assistant shepherd, just following the sheep giving birth. *To be shepherd to Jacob his servant and Israel his inheritance. He shepherded them in the innocence of his heart, and guided them with the skills of his hands* (vv. 71–72). This shows the extraordinary degree of care: it was not over any people that he

15. Cf. Gen 49.10.
16. Heb 7.14.
17. A classic example of the commentator as rationalizer! By any standards the comparison he finds in his text is puzzling; and unable to check the Hebrew original, *ramim,* "high (places)," which his LXX has misread as *r'emim,* "unicorn," Theodoret—philosophically unable to admit ignorance—comes up with this ingenious piece of rationalizing. As the Italians say, *se non è vero, ben trovato.*

placed the pastor of the sheep; instead, combining skill with simplicity he guided them according to the divine laws. The Lord's lawgiving is like this: "Be wise as serpents and simple as doves":[18] eliminating vice of each kind, rejecting the evildoing of one and the folly of the other, he presented as commendable the combined virtues. We, too, should practice this virtue in our own case, called as we are like blessed David—or rather, to a higher vocation: we have been entrusted with a ministry of greater things, to walk worthily of the calling to which we are called, according to the lawgiving of the divinely inspired Paul.[19]

18. Matt 10.16. Theodoret is choosing not to advert to the relevance to authorship of this inclusion in the psalm of biographical details and encomium of David.

19. Eph 4.1. It has been a long psalm, and Theodoret has been at his most concise, but can still spare the briefest of applications of at least one verse to the life of the reader.

COMMENTARY ON PSALM 79

A psalm for Asaph.

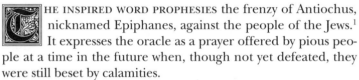HE INSPIRED WORD PROPHESIES the frenzy of Antiochus, nicknamed Epiphanes, against the people of the Jews.[1] It expresses the oracle as a prayer offered by pious people at a time in the future when, though not yet defeated, they were still beset by calamities.

(2) *O God, the nations entered your inheritance, they defiled your holy Temple* (v. 1). The grace of the Spirit wisely taught the people struggling with those difficult problems to fall to prayer: they narrated in the first place not their own suffering but the sacrilege committed against the divine Temple, the Temple having committed no fault against the divine Law. Nations given to a life of impiety and lawlessness, he is saying, gained power over your inheritance: they presumed to gain entry to the recesses of your Temple.

(3) It was not only, however, that they polluted your holy places with demons' altars and sacrifices. *They turned Jerusalem into a hut of a garden-watcher:* after totally ravaging the whole city, they made the famous Jerusalem no different from *a hut of a garden-watcher.* [1505] *They turned your servants' corpses into food for the birds of heaven, the flesh of your holy ones for the beasts of the earth* (v. 2): they directed such ferocity and frenzy against your attendants as to expose their bodies as a meal for beasts and flesh-eating birds. *They poured out their blood like water around Jerusalem, and there was no one to bury them* (v. 3): possessed of a bloodthirsty mentality, they did away with those of pious life,

1. Theodoret is aware of the association of this psalm with the Maccabean wars, while not adverting to quotation of it (v. 3 specifically, as 1 Macc 7.17) as a "word that was written" before the events described there and already enjoying canonical status. But, as usual, he sees the author (referred to obliquely in these Asaph psalms) composing with prophetic perspective before those events.

and made their blood flow in streams down onto the earth, not allowing the slaughtered to be given burial.

(4) *We have become a laughing stock to our neighbors, a mockery and taunt for those around us* (v. 4). These things rendered us an object of reproach to our neighbors; on account of them we became a source of glee to our associates. He refers to the Philistines, Idumeans, Ammonites, Moabites, and the other nearby nations as neighbors, opposed and hostile as they always were. *How long, O Lord? will you be angry forever? will your jealousy burn like fire?* (v. 5). In giving the Law God ordered [them] to serve him alone and to adore no one else as a god: "Because I am the Lord your God," he is saying, "a jealous God, a devouring fire."[2] As has often been said by us, however, no one hearing of one God should form the impression of a monarchy: he gives the name God to the being without limit and always in existence that we adore as Father, Son, and Holy Spirit; but let no one of the more scholarly be in any doubt that God the Word, who is Jesus Christ, our Savior, gives the law. The inspired word recalls this here, too: *will your jealousy burn like a fire?* Be angry with us no further, Lord, he is saying, nor inflame jealousy against us like fire on account of our failings.

(5) *Pour out your anger on the nations that do not know you, and on kingdoms that do not call on your name* (v. 6): since you require penalty for sins from human beings, I beg that you transfer your rage against those who in no way wish to learn your name, and instead are in thrall to extreme impiety. *Because they devoured Jacob and laid waste his place* (v. 7): this, too, was a clear sign of their impiety, putting us to death, ravaging the country, and devastating the cities without enduring any trouble from us. *His place,* on the other hand, Aquila rendered as "his appearance," Symmachus, "his beauty" and Theodotion, "his charm," which are better indicators of the divine [1508] house.[3] He was right to call the people *Jacob,* prompting God to mercy with mention of the ancestor.

---

2. A conflation of Exod 34.14 and Deut 4.24. The longer form of the text is now prompted to insert a theological corrective in case any nitpicking scholar argue from the mention of "jealousy" to some unitarian concept of God.

3. Theodoret's exegetical skills let him down again. Faced with alternative

(6) *Do not remember our ancient iniquities* (v. 8). Those offering this prayer were pious, displaying much zeal for piety; the Maccabees' virtue was celebrated, after all. So he was right not to require an account of the people for the former sins. They made this request, however, and in fact added nothing in second place, that God have regard for their existing piety—something which particularly reveals their great virtue, recalling former sins but hiding existing piety. *Let your pity quickly take the initiative in our regard, Lord, because we have been reduced to severe poverty. Help us, O God our savior* (vv. 8–9): extend your irresistible aid as quickly as possible: we are bereft of all providence, yet have you alone as helper and savior. *For the sake of the glory of your name, O Lord, rescue us; forgive our sins for your name's sake.* Nowhere do they mention their own virtue, asking instead to attain divine assistance on account of the divine name. We are the ones who have done evil, they say, but blasphemy comes against your name; so we beg you to overlook the sins, reverse the calamities and give a glimpse of your power to those ignorant of it.

(7) *In case the nations ever say, Where is their God?* (v. 10). The other translators, on the other hand, spoke of this as already a fact. "Why do the nations say, Where is their God?" This pains me, he is saying, this pierces me more sharply than any arrow, the nations' presumption of blaspheming against you and saying in mockery, Where is your God, who you say scourged the Egyptians, parted the sea while granting you a crossing, and performed all the other great and famous things? *Let the avenging of the shedding of the blood of your servants be known to the nations in our sight:* so we beg that some pay the penalty for blood-thirstiness, and all the others see with us your just sentence and your anger over your slain attendants. *Let the groaning of those in bondage come in before you; in keeping with the greatness of your arm preserve the children of those put to death* (v. 11): I beg you also to look upon those still surviving but lying in bondage, awaiting death, and not to condemn our race to perdition, but save the

---

versions—the LXX (correctly) reading *naweh,* "place," and the other three translators a rare form identical in the Hebrew meaning "comeliness"—without reference to the original text he decides in favor of the latter erroneous rendering by a process of rationalizing alone.

children of those put to death [1509] and establish a new beginning from them.

(8) *Repay our neighbors sevenfold into their bosom for the reproaches they leveled at you, Lord* (v. 12): inflict multiple punishment on our neighbors for the blasphemy. In these words he did not indicate a definite number, but required that the worst punishment be inflicted on them, after the manner of the saying, "A barren woman bore seven children"[4]—that is, many. He used the term *bosom* by analogy with those carrying something in their bosom and holding on to it carefully lest it fall out—in other words, Fill them with disasters constantly besetting them. *We for our part, your people, sheep of your pasture, shall freely confess to you, O God, forever, and proclaim your praise for generation after generation* (v. 13): we who are styled your people and called your little flock shall offer you hymns perpetually, and give thanks for the benefits. Having put this in writing, we shall offer the account of it to people to come. He said *freely confess* instead of *confess;* the word indicates thanksgiving.

4. 1 Sam 2.5.

COMMENTARY ON PSALM 80

*To the end. In hymns, for those
who will be changed. A testimony to Asaph.*

A psalm on the Assyrian.

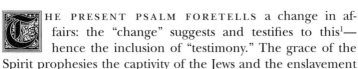HE PRESENT PSALM FORETELLS a change in af-
fairs: the "change" suggests and testifies to this[1]—
hence the inclusion of "testimony." The grace of the
Spirit prophesies the captivity of the Jews and the enslavement
in Babylon.[2] The psalm is expressed as a prayer offered to the
God of all by those same people: the charism of inspiration
teaches them what words are required to propitiate God and
prompt him to mercy. It also foretells the salvation coming to
all human beings through the Lord Christ.

(2) *You who shepherd Israel, give heed* (v. 1): I beg you, Lord,
who care for your people like a shepherd, to receive my prayer.
Who guide Joseph like a flock: when he had fallen into the clutches
of his brothers like some wolves, you freed him from their
hands, guided him to Egypt, and made him prevail over the
plotters. After describing in this way the care shown them,
[1512] [the psalmist] moved on to his power in general: *Seated
above the cherubim, shine forth.* Since the mighty Moses consecrat-

---

1. As explained in note 4 to Ps 45, Theodoret is wide off the mark here, not
simply for failing to see in this phrase in the title a cue to a melody, but for taking (with the LXX) *shoshanim,* "Lilies" (the melody cue), to be instead a form
of the verb *shanah,* "to change."

2. When the phrase "on the Assyrian" occurred in the title (in some forms
of the LXX) to Ps 76, Theodoret acknowledged it as an insertion, seeing in it a
reference to Sennacherib. Here he ignores it, continuing to see a reference to
Judah's captivity by the Babylonians, despite the psalm's accent on the northern kingdom that fell foul of the Assyrians (or he confuses Assyrian with Babylonian: see notes 3 and 8). The longer form of the text will endeavor to recover
this accent in comment on v. 2.

ed some images of these creatures alone in the Holy of Holies, placing the Mercy seat between them, and some divine appearance was granted to the high priests in that way, it was right for him to make mention of the cherubim here, too, and beg the one seated above them to make himself manifest.

(3) *Before Ephraim, Benjamin, and Manasseh* (v. 2). I beg you, he is saying, to make yourself manifest to your people; he indicated all the people by mention of the tribes. He mentioned these ones since he had referred to Joseph: Ephraim and Manasseh were sons of Joseph, and Benjamin their brother from the one mother. *Stir up your might, and come to save us.* He rouses God as one given to long-suffering and tranquillity: activate all your power, he is saying, in being concerned for our salvation. As was said by me above, this is the prayer, on the one hand, of the people held captive by the Assyrians at that time,[3] and on the other hand of the nations anxious about the salvation coming from the benefactor; the inspired mind wishes to say as much in what follows as well.

(4) *Turn us back, God of hosts* (v. 3): free [us] from slavery, and grant us return. One prays for return from Babylon, the other for conversion from idols. Then he brings out the ease of the matter. *Let your face shine forth, and we shall be saved:* for solving the problems it is sufficient if you appear. *O Lord God of hosts, how long will you be angry with your servants' prayer?* (v. 4): to what point, Lord, do you keep dismissing my entreaties in anger at my failings? He calls the people his *servant;* the other translators put "with your people's prayer" for *your servant. You will feed us bread of tears, and give us to drink tears in full measure* (v. 5). The tense has been changed here: the other translators speak of it as already happened, "You fed us bread of tears, and gave us to drink tears in full measure."[4] He means, You mixed our food and drink with tears; weeping and wailing we partake

3. In fact, as we noted above, this insertion from the longer form of the text is at odds with the shorter, making more sense of the phrase in the title and supporting a northern origin for the psalm posited by modern commentators.

4. We would like to think Theodoret has compared this further misreading of the tense by the LXX with the original; but in view of his consistent failure to detect it elsewhere, we must presume he has noticed this time that the other translators have avoided it.

of the necessary nourishment. He did this by fitting the punishment to the sins. The Lord also said this, "With the measure you measure, it will be measured to you";[5] and the prophet Zechariah also saw the measure in prophesying the destruction of Babylon:[6] [1513] he said he espied two women wearing wings of a hoopoe and carrying the measure, and ordered them to take it to Babylon. In this we are taught the justice of the divine verdict.

(5) *You placed us as a sign of contradiction to our neighbors, and our foes sneered at us* (v. 6): we were made an object of reproach to the nations nearby, who always bore us ill will. Yet we did not depart from you; he said this also in what follows. *Lord God of hosts, turn us back; let your face shine, and we shall be saved* (v. 7): so disperse with your appearance the gloomy cloud of disasters, and grant return. (The people make this request, as do the nations, meaning by "appearance" the coming in the flesh.) You are powerful, after all, and Lord of hosts, invisibly summoning the former from captivity and saving the nations by your incarnation.[7]

(6) Then he describes the ancient favors, asking to enjoy the same providence. *You moved a vine out of Egypt, you drove out nations, and planted it [in their place]. You went as guide before it, sank its roots, and filled the land* (vv. 8–9): you, O Lord, overthrew the unjust rule of the Egyptians, you consigned the nations of the Canaanites to ruin, led your people like a vine out of Egypt, and after ensuring complete comfort along the way you planted them in the land of the Canaanites. *Its shadow covered mountains, its branches the cedars of God. It extended its tendrils to the sea, its offshoots as far as rivers* (vv. 10–11). Having in figurative fashion called the people a *vine,* he persisted with the figure: he calls strength of the nearby nations *mountains,* the power of Israel set over them a *shadow* covering them, the lofty rulers, those assigned leadership by God, *cedars of God,* and the kingdom of the Israelites that proved more illustrious than they *branches* cover-

5. Matt 7.2.
6. Zech 5.9–11.
7. The longer form of the text keeps a Christological interpretation to the fore.

ing the cedars. We know this happened also in the case of blessed David and Solomon: the mighty David received tribute not only from the Philistines, Idumeans, Ammonites, and Moabites, but also from both parts of Syria, [1516] and the queen of the Ethiopians came to Solomon, so celebrated was he by all. By the vine's *tendrils* he means the multitude of the people, and by *offshoots* the proselytes that came from the nations and received knowledge of God. In all this he implies the people's former good fortune.

(7) *Why have you done away with its wall, and all who pass that way pluck its grapes?* (v. 12): why on earth have you deprived it of your providence, and rendered it vulnerable to those intent on wronging it? He called safety a *wall:* what a wall is to a vine, God's providence is to those granted it. He called the enemies *those who pass that way:* just as passersby safely pick the grapes of a vine that is unprotected and unguarded and carry off its fruit, so does the one deprived of divine care become vulnerable to those wishing to do him wrong. *A forest boar ravaged it, and a solitary animal fed off it* (v. 13). By this he indicated the different incursions of the Assyrians: Shalmaneser and Sennacherib pillaged the other cities, while Nebuchadnezzar besieged Jerusalem and took those who escaped death into captivity.[8] Since he called Israel a vine, it was right for him to give its enemy the name of a *wild boar,* this wild animal being particularly savage on vines; he called the boar *solitary animal* because it lives by itself and is fiercer than the other animals, having nothing in common with them. Since, then, Nebuchadnezzar was likewise more savage than the other kings, he was right to give him the name *solitary animal.*

(8) *O God of hosts, turn back, look down from heaven and see; and have regard for this vine. You matured that which your right hand planted* (vv. 14–15): I therefore beg you as mighty Lord to look from above on the mutilation of the vine, and grant healing to the ailment: the same providence of yours gave it the former prosperity; he called providence *right hand. And on a Son of*

8. Theodoret strangely refers both to Assyrian and to Babylonian leaders as "Assyrians," nominating the Babylonian Nebuchadnezzar as the foremost among them.

Man, whom you confirmed for yourself.[9] Here he teaches the springing up of Christ the Lord: he begs that the vine be given care on account of the temple—clearly called Son of Man—to be assumed from it. This is the way the Lord also [1517] in the sacred Gospels, though being God and man at the same time, called himself Son of Man, bestowing the name from the visible nature. Consequently the inspired Word teaches those taken captive to beseech the God of all to show some mercy to the vine on account of the saving root springing from it. The Lord, in fact, also calls himself this in the words, "I am the true vine, you [are] the branches, and my Father is the farmer":[10] as man he is the vine, as God he is also the farmer, sowing good seed in his field. You see, though he sprang from this vine, which proved useless, bearing thorns instead of grapes for the farmer,[11] he for his part became the true vine and put forth the biggest branches,[12] the multitude of those who believed in him. The shadow from these truly covered the mountains, and the limbs [covered] the cedars. The vine for its part truly extended its branches to the sea, and its offshoots as far as the rivers. There is no place, no place under heaven, in which the divine vats from this vine are not established. For its sake they beg, in narrating all its manifold sufferings, that it too enjoy mercy.

(9) *Put to the torch and dug up* (v. 16). From this in particular it is clear that the psalm prophesies events concerning the Babylonian and not Antiochus, as some thought: the Babylonian both set fire to the Temple and consigned most of the city to the flames.[13] Likewise at this place he says that they not only went off after plucking the fruit but also dug it up, pulled it out by the roots, and wasted it with fire. *They will perish at the rebuke of your countenance:* once you appear and take action, they will be utterly useless and will suffer destruction. *Let your hand be on*

9. The Hebrew at this point has inserted this half-verse from v. 17; mention of a son, which Dahood and Eissfeldt see referring to the king and Weiser to the people, and which the RSV (with the LXX) renders as "son of man" (NRSV "one"), leads Theodoret off on a Christological digression.

10. A precis of John 15.1, 5.

11. A loose recall of Isa 5.4; Matt 7.16.

12. Cf. Matt 13.32.

13. The Assyrians have now become Babylonian.

the man at your right, and on a Son of Man whom you confirmed for yourself (v. 17): we thus enjoy your care on account of your being overcome with loving-kindness in this way and taking flesh from us. He calls *Son of Man* the Lord of glory, of whom Paul said, "If they had known, they would not have crucified the very Lord of glory."[14]

(10) *May we not depart from you* (v. 18): you do not renege [1520] on your promises: once these firstfruits are received from us, the whole human race will recognize the true God and sing the praises of the loving-kindness demonstrated. *You will make us live, and we shall call on your name:* in this manner the power of death will be overcome, and we shall gain eternal life, adoring you, God the Savior. *O Lord God of hosts, turn us back; let your face shine and we shall be saved* (v. 19): so on account of all this and the salvation coming to all people through us, deliver us from this sadness and grant return: if you but appear, we shall gain salvation.

---

14. 1 Cor 2.8. The short form of the text would have passed on without further comment on this psalm verse after its appearance already as an appendage to v. 15, but not the long form with its more Christological bent.

COMMENTARY ON PSALM 81

To the end. On the winepresses. A psalm for Asaph.

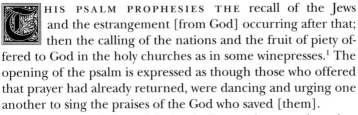HIS PSALM PROPHESIES THE recall of the Jews and the estrangement [from God] occurring after that; then the calling of the nations and the fruit of piety offered to God in the holy churches as in some winepresses.[1] The opening of the psalm is expressed as though those who offered that prayer had already returned, were dancing and urging one another to sing the praises of the God who saved [them].

(2) *Rejoice in God our help* (v. 1). Symmachus, on the other hand said "Honor" and Aquila, "Give praise." Offer the thanksgiving hymn, he is saying, to God who gives us a share in his peculiar providence. *Be glad for the God of Jacob.* Being glad is a triumphal response, as we have often said. So they urge one another to compose hymn singing to the God who bestowed the victory. *Take a psalm and beat a drum, a pleasing harp with a lute* (v. 2). They struck up the divine music with the use of different instruments; the story of the Chronicles teaches this.[2] So the theme exhorts those choirs to intermingle the harmonious sound of those instruments with one another, and to sing God's praises—some with lyres, others with drums, still others with lutes. Symmachus, on the other hand, used "lyre" for *harp.*

(3) *Blow a trumpet at the new moon, on our festival day of good omen. Because it is a command* [1521] *for Israel, a judgment of the*

---

1. The term *gittith* (which the LXX, thinking to recognize *gat*, takes as "winepresses") puzzles modern commentators. The response of the ancients was discussed above at its occurrence on Ps 8, where Theodoret also (with extended rationale) applied it to the churches, as here.

2. As a commentator on the work of the Chronicler, possibly a Levite with an interest in liturgical music, Theodoret is aware of that composer's attention to the subject, yet rarely stresses this aspect of the Psalms in Jewish or Christian worship in his commentary and fails in particular to see psalm titles as liturgically directed.

God of Jacob (vv. 3–4). God ordered the priests to use the trumpets. They reminded the people of the trumpets used on the mountain: when the God of all spoke on Mount Sinai, [Scripture] says, there was a loud noise of the trumpet.[3] So when the priests used the trumpets, they reminded the people of that appearance. Consequently, they were right to command those who had been granted return and had enjoyed the divine assistance to make use of the trumpets along with the other instruments. *He made it a testimony in Joseph when he went out from the land of Egypt* (v. 5). Here he refers to all the people as *Joseph:* since Joseph was responsible for their going to Egypt, he called the people after him. He says that he gave this law to the people after freeing them from Egypt.

(4) Then he describes the kindnesses conferred. *He heard a tongue, which he did not know:* never having had the benefit of a divine voice, he hearkened to it in the wilderness by receiving the Law. *He relieved his back of burdens, and his hands served in the basket* (v. 6). He indicated in this the labors in Egypt, the harsh slavery and the brick making: as usual, they were forced to carry the clay on their shoulders, their backs in particular feeling the effects of such labors. At this point he introduces God speaking in person: he first reminds them of the favors done, then adduces exhortation and advice, and later foretells the disobedience and the punishment of the disobedience. *In tribulation you called upon me, and I rescued you* (v. 7): suffering the hardships in Egypt you groaned, and immediately I granted you loving-kindness. History also brings this out: "The children of Israel groaned under the harsh works," [Scripture] says, "and their voice went up to God."[4]

(5) *I hearkened to you in a tempest's secret place.* Symmachus, on the other hand, put it this way, "I hearkened to you in secret places of thunder," and the others likewise spoke of thunder. He indicates through this, Though not being seen, since it is my nature to be invisible, I achieved the salvation of all people, like a kind of thunder, signaling with the plagues against the Egyptians how great the providence is which I show to all.

---

3. Cf. Exod 19.16.
4. Exod 2.23, loosely recalled.

[1524] *I tested you at the water of contradiction.* On reaching Meribah and finding the water bitter, they clamored against Moses and reviled God; so the place was named after the incident. He means, then, I convicted you of ingratitude regarding that water; I easily changed its quality and turned bitter into sweet.[5]

(6) *Listen, my people, and I shall take you to task* (v. 8): so having had experience of my power, accept with enthusiasm the laws imposed on you by me; this is what taking to task means, you see, forecasting the punishment of disobedience for you, and the benefit of compliance. *Israel, if you listen to me, there will be no novel god among you, nor will you adore a foreign god* (vv. 8–9). He manifests himself more clearly to them in saying, *I am the Lord your God, who brought you up from the land of Egypt* (v. 10). The beginning of the Law also contains this, "I am the Lord your God," it is saying, "who brought you up from the land of Egypt: you will have no other gods besides me."[6] So at this point he bids them worship not a foreign or new god but the one who had accorded them freedom. This also refutes the folly of Arius and Eunomius: if the Only-begotten were not of the same being, then he would rightly be called foreign; and if there were a time when he did not exist, [he would be called] new and not eternal. So they clearly transgressed the divine Law, especially those who taught the teaching of the impious Nestorius, in worshipping a foreign and novel god.[7] This is not the time, howev-

5. Theodoret, typically, is confusing two different incidents from the Exodus, the bitter water found at Marah and made sweet with a piece of wood (rich in hermeneutical possibilities, had he adverted to it) in Exod 15.23–25, and the shortage of water at Massah/Meribah alleviated by the striking of the rock in Exod 17.1–7. The confusion is repeated in commentary on v. 16. He does not go into linguistic details about the place name's reflecting the incident.

6. Exod 20.2–3, loosely recalled.

7. There may be room for debate as to whether Theodoret is correct in nominating polytheism (apparently the sense of "estrangement," *allotriosis* here) as the focus of the psalm on the basis of vv. 9–10; as Von Rad says, "the prohibition on serving any other divine powers is in any case *the* commandment *par excellence* for Israel." But it is surely to draw a longer bow to introduce at this point the Christological concerns of Nicea, citing its talisman *homoousios*, and Anomoeans like Eunomius—not to mention the intrusion of Nestorius (whom one doubts if Theodoret would refer to so disparagingly) from the long form of the text.

er, to refute their stupor; still, let this suffice for the censure of their lawlessness. *Open wide your mouth, and I shall fill it.* Render yourself compliant through compliance, he is saying, and receive the abundance of the good things.

(7) At this point he shifts his treatment to accusation. *My people did not listen to my voice, Israel did not heed me* (v. 11): so while I offered it advice, it could not bring itself either to listen [to me] or to heed what was said by me. [1525] *He dismissed them in keeping with the concerns of their hearts; they will travel in the way of their concerns* (v. 12). Symmachus, on the other hand, put it this way, "So I sent them off in the desire of their heart to journey by their own plans"; Aquila likewise, "He dismissed them in the crookedness of their heart, they will travel in the way of their purposes." In other words, Seeing him disobedient, I deprived him of my care; I allowed him to be carried by his own ideas, like a skiff lacking rudder or steersman. The truth of the inspired composition is available for the discernment of those ready for it:[8] the Jews, being bereft of God's help, were dispersed to every land and sea, and became enslaved instead of free; they live a life of utter impiety, adopting sorcery and demons' charms, unwilling to worship the God who saved them.

(8) *If my people listened to me, if Israel traveled in my ways, I would have brought their foes down to nothing, and laid my hand on those afflicting them* (vv. 13–14): if it had adhered to my advice and followed my commandments, I would easily have destroyed their foes; *to nothing* suggests the facility—in other words, easily and without trouble I would have been able to inflict their ruin in a trice. *The Lord's foes were false to him* (v. 15). Aquila, on the other hand, put it this way, "In their hatred they will deny the Lord": by denial of Christ the Lord they brought hatred on themselves, and by being false to him and to the covenants made they rendered themselves foes of the Lord. After the giving of the Law, [Scripture] says, the people replied, "All that

---

8. Theodoret claims that discernment, *theoria*, enables the reader of the psalm to find a fuller sense in reference to the Jews of his day, depicted in a very unflattering light.

the Lord God has said we will do and listen to."[9] While the promises were of this kind, the words were directly contrary: they crucified their own Lord on his appearance, but received a penalty for impiety, eternal ruin—not they alone, but also Arius, Eunomius, Nestorius, and the devotees of their teachings.[10]

(9) The inspired composition had also suggested this: *Their time would be forever.* Symmachus, on the other hand, said it more clearly: after saying, [1528] "Those false to him hate the Lord," he added, "but their time will be forever." He calls the calamities *time;* this is what the Syriac and Hebrew authors are accustomed to call them,[11] and many of us also give them that name. So he means that Jews will not fall foul of these things at a specified time; rather, they will continue forever to be deprived of the divine care. This resembles the beginning of the seventy-third psalm, "Why, O God, did you reject [us] forever?"[12] There, too, he foretold the complete rejection of the Jews. *He fed them with the pick of the crop, and satisfied them with honey from the rock* (v. 16). Suffering deep ingratitude, he is saying, they did not recall the good things already provided them: in the desert he brought the sweetest water out from the rock for them, which seemed to those drinking it to resemble the sweetness of honey, while in the promised land he regaled them with the fruits of the earth in abundance. He indicated the whole from the part, suggesting the abundance of the other fruits from mention of grain.

9. Exod 24.3, loosely recalled.

10. A further joust from the more polemical long form of the text.

11. As mentioned in Introduction, section 3, Theodoret is more secure in referring to Hebrew usage when he can parallel it with his native Syriac.

12. Ps 74.1.

COMMENTARY ON PSALM 82

A psalm for Asaph.

FTER MENTIONING IN THE PREVIOUS psalm the rejection of the Jews, he sets out more clearly here as well the reasons why God rejected them, teaching us at all events that, should we for our part imitate them, we shall encounter the same fate or worse.

(2) *God has taken his place in an assembly of gods, in the midst he will judge gods* (v. 1). He called the rulers of the Jews gods, entrusted as they were with judging. This is the name the Law also gives them: "You shall not revile gods, nor speak evil of your people's leader."[1] In other words, since God is truly a judge, whereas human beings are entrusted with the task of judging, those commissioned with this task were believed [to be] gods for the reason that they imitate God in this. But at this point the just Judge takes issue with those not judging justly nor adhering unswervingly to the balance of justice, and he prophesies the just judgment to be made by them in the future.

(3) *How long do you deliver unjust judgments, and take the part of sinners?* (v. 2). To what point, he asks, do you fail to deliver an unjust verdict, and instead refrain from accusing the injustice of powerful ones and sinners, and ignore those who are wronged by them and who live in penury? *Judge in favor of orphan and poor, give justice to lowly and needy* (v. 3): all of these need help. [1529] *Rescue needy and poor; deliver them from sinners' hands* (v. 4): let not the needy prove vulnerable to the wrongdoers when you preside and are entrusted with judgment.

(4) *They did not know, nor did they understand; they walk in darkness* (v. 5): they did not wish to understand this, however, nor be illuminated by the light of my words; this is the reason, to be

1. Exod 22.28 [LXX].

56

sure, why they pass a life spent in night and gloom. *All the foundations of the earth were shaken:* For reason of this truth life is full of disturbance and tempest, and the land is confused with one trouble after another.[2]

(5) *I said, You are gods, and all of you children of the Most High* (v. 6): so I gave you high status, I shared [with you] my own name, and called you my children. *But as mortals you die, and as one of the rulers you fall* (v. 7). Symmachus, on the other hand, put it this way, "But as mortals you will die, and as one of the rulers you will fall."[3] In other words, unaware of your own dignity, you suffered the same fate as the devil, who was entrusted with rule from me and was unwilling to exercise the gifts as he should, and so forfeited his dignity. You suffer the same death as other people, enjoying no reputation after death.

(6) Having in this way leveled accusation at the unjust judges, the inspired word begs the true and just Judge to pass judgment on the world. *Arise, O God, judge the earth, because you will obtain your inheritance in all the nations* (v. 8). This refers unmistakably to the judgment of Christ the Lord: to him in his humanity the Father said, "Ask of me, and I shall give you nations for your inheritance, and the ends of the earth as your possession."[4] Hence the inspired author asks him to appear promptly, judge justly, put an end to unjust judges, abandon the Jews' inheritance, and take up the nations' in their place—or rather explain it—and offer salvation to all people through his incomprehensible Incarnation.

2. The psalm is clearly not moving Theodoret to the extent it moves a modern commentator like Weiser who says of it, "The magnificent picture which the psalm unfolds before our eyes is inspired by the lofty flight of fancy of a poet and is sustained by a strong religious and moral power." Theodoret does not see the psalmist struggling with the great problem of good and evil, nor respond to similarities to Isa 3 and Ezek 28.

3. Theodoret notes the difference in tense in Symmachus—the only reason for citing him—but passes on, unable to resolve the issue.

4. Ps 2.8.

COMMENTARY ON PSALM 83

A song. A psalm for Asaph. [1532]

FTER THE RETURN from Babylon the neighboring nations noticed the rebuilding of the Temple and the Jews' splendor; they gathered together, assembled other savage nations, and declared war on the Jews. The divine Joel and Ezekiel foretold this, and the remarkable prophets Micah and Zechariah foretold it. Nevertheless, they conquered them all, with Zerubbabel in command and God lending assistance from on high and overcoming the enemies' audacity. This psalm prophesies it. The inspired composition of the divine Spirit is expressed as a prayer to teach those under attack at that time how God must be placated.

(2) *O God, who will be like you?* (v. 1). Not even all the nature of angels and mortals assembled together, he is saying, will be able to be compared to your power: you have might that is without parallel. He put *Who?* to mean "no one." *Do not keep silence or seek appeasement, God:* we beg you, Lord, not to exercise your customary long-suffering, which is what *do not seek appeasement* suggests, Symmachus rendering it "Do not be at rest." Then he brings out the reason for the appeal: *Because, behold, your enemies were sounding off, and those who hate you were lifting their head* (v. 2). They sound off and surge like a sea, he is saying, exercising arrogance and audacity against us, having declared war against us on account of opposition to you: in their hostility to you they lay siege to the people dedicated to you.

(3) *They hatch a plot against your people, and scheme the downfall of your holy ones* (v. 3). Symmachus, on the other hand, put it this way: "against your hidden one" instead of *your holy ones,* and Aquila, "against your concealed one," as did Theodotion. In other words, since Christ the Lord would spring from them according to the flesh, and the nations were anxious to pull up by

the roots the race of the Jews, the all-holy Spirit teaches them to offer this prayer: They employ malice and wiles not only against us but also against your hidden one concealed amongst us,[1] who he prophesied would blossom from the tribe of Judah. After all, if the root were cut, how would the fruit grow? Now, [1533] the God of all indicated this in Isaiah: "In the way," he is saying, "that a grape might be found in the bunch, and they were to say, Do not harm it because the blessing of the Lord is in it, so shall I act on behalf of my servant; for his sake I shall not destroy them all, but shall bring forth the seed from Jacob, and from Judah, and then," he is saying, "I shall dispatch the rest to destruction."[2] So on account of one grape the whole bunch enjoyed care, or rather the whole vineyard, whereas if it had been taken and the rest of the fruit gathered with it, the rest of the vineyard would have been given over to wild beasts, the boar from the woods damaging it, every single beast grazing [from it] and all the passersby trampling the way through it as they wish. This is what they say in their prayer at this point: They presume to rage not only against us but also against your hidden one. The cry "Away with him! Away with him! Crucify him!"[3] revealed them clearly as raging like dogs. What follows is also in harmony with this.

(4) *They said, Come, let us wipe them out from being a nation; the name of Israel will no longer be remembered* (v. 4): they want to inflict ruin on us, and consign to oblivion the celebrated Israel. Then he lists the neighbors by whom the others were summoned and gathered together. *Because they joined in concert to hatch the same plot, they entered a covenant against you* (v. 5): those who declared war in unity against you are *the tents of the Idumeans and Ishmaelites* (v. 6). Idumeans took their origin from Esau, for Edom was named Esau. The Ishmaelites, however, are descendants from Ishmael. *Moab and the Hagarites.* Moab was a

1. Theodoret prefers the reading of the alternative versions, "hidden one," for a Hebrew term of which Dahood (who opts for "your treasure") remarks, "Just what the poet intends by this term is not certain."
2. Cf. Isa 65.8–10. Theodoret is dispatching the psalm with his customary conciseness, no particular historical situation taking his fancy. But now a vague association of this verse with a passage from Isaiah comes to mind to encourage a Christological interpretation.
3. John 19.15, in a remark from the longer form of the text to gild the lily.

son of Lot, and the nation developed from him; the Hagarites were another tribe of Ishmael, named after Hagar, the mother of Ishmael. *Gebal, Ammon, and Amalek* (v. 7). Amalek was a descendant of Esau, and the nation developed from him. Ammon was Lot's son. These were also divisions of Arabia, and the Gebalenes neighbors of Idumea. *Foreigners with the inhabitants of Tyre.* The other translators give to *foreigners* the name Philistines, whom we call Palestinians: they were the sole survivors of the race of Canaan and dwelt alongside Israel, and so most of all were rightly called *foreigners*. [1536] *Assyria in fact also has joined them* (v. 8). The Assyrians were not in power at that time; the reference is therefore to the Samaritans, a colony of the Assyrians, dwelling in those cities after the captivity of the ten tribes.[4] *They became a support for the children of Lot.* The verse suggests that Moabites and Ammonites in particular were emboldened against the people and assembled the other nations.

(5) *Do to them as you did to Midian and Sisera, to Jabin in the torrent of Kishon. They were overthrown in Endor* (vv. 9–10). They gratefully recall the former favors, asking for the same assistance; Barak and the prophetess Deborah overthrew these generals.[5] *They became like dung on the ground:* they remained unburied, and disappeared, and were mixed up with the earth like some kind of dung. *Make their rulers like Oreb, Zeeb, Zebah, and Zalumna. All their rulers* (v. 11). The story of the Judges makes mention of these men: Gideon did away with them under the generalship of divine grace.[6] They beg that their own enemies be disposed of like these, and they bring out the reason: *These who said, Let us make our inheritance the sanctuary of God* (v. 12): they give free rein to youthful audacity in trying to gain possession of the Temple dedicated to you; he called the Tem-

4. Theodoret, whose interest in geography makes this gazetteer a study he relishes, has opted for a post-exilic occasion for the psalm, and so has to account for mention of Assyria. He thus illustrates Weiser's warning that no such options "are able to master the consequent difficulties and anachronisms without the help of questionable re-interpretations."

5. Cf. Judg 4. Theodoret does not pause to deal with the fact that mention of Endor "has in this context no historical or geographical propriety," according to Dahood, who finds a different meaning for the Hebrew text. *Akribeia* has its limits.

6. Cf. Judg 7.25; 8.21.

ple of God *sanctuary,* whereas Symmachus called the sanctuary "dwelling." The whole theme of the psalm is clear from this: since on their return they rebuilt the Temple, all the legitimate worship was performed in it, worshipping beyond it being contrary to the Law. On account of the way of life according to the Law, however, the neighbors were hostile to the Jews; they directed their whole assault against the Temple so as to put an end to the race and to legitimate worship along with this.

(6) *O my God, make them like a wheel* (v. 13), that is, bid them be encompassed with manifold calamities, and invest them with one trouble after another. *Like straw before wind:* scatter them like straw tossed by wind. *As fire which burns wood, as flame, which consumes mountains, in like manner pursue them in your tempest and confound them* [1537] *in your rage* (vv. 14–15). In the woods a flame is ignited of itself when the trees are moved by a violent wind and rub together, causing heat by the collision and gradually catching fire of themselves. So he begs that likewise these peoples be consumed of themselves, and become victims of their own transgressions, according to the inspired composition which says, "Walk in the light of your fire and the flame you kindled."[7] *Fill their faces with dishonor, and they will seek your name, O Lord* (v. 16): frustrated in their wishes and filled with shame, they will acknowledge your power.

(7) *Let them be ashamed and confused forever, let them feel shame and perish. Let them know that your name is Lord, that you alone [are the] Most High over all the earth* (v. 17). They seek good things for the foes, even though under attack: they beg that they be enveloped in shame rather than audacity, and by means of the shame reap the benefit of divine knowledge, be rid of the error of the idols, and learn by experience that he alone is God and Lord, dwelling in the highest, having regard for lowly things, governing and controlling all creation, whose salvation he was concerned for, God from God, the Only-begotten Son after his incomprehensible incarnation.[8]

7. Isa 50.11. There is no doubt that Theodoret is on the side of Israel and its promotion of worship according to the Law, not on the side of its enemies.
8. The long form of the text adds this codicil about salvation, citing the phrasing of the Constantinopolitan creed of 381.

COMMENTARY ON PSALM 84

On the winepresses. For the sons of Korah.

HE PSALM'S PROPHECY is twofold: it forecasts not only the Jews' recall but also the salvation of the whole world. It is the churches he calls "winepresses," as we have already said previously:[1] in them the spiritual vineyard bears its own fruit, and we prepare the saving wine which brings true joy to the hearts of the believers.

(2) *How lovable are your tabernacles, O Lord of hosts. My soul longs and faints for the courts of the Lord* (vv. 1–2). Those living in Babylon were also taught to say this so as to long for the return and hanker after worship according to the Law—like us too, of course, who have attained salvation and reap the benefit from the divine shrines.[2] To us in particular, however, is the inspired composition relevant: it forecasts that there will be many tabernacles, speaks of many winepresses, and likewise makes mention of many altars. Jews, on the other hand, had one temple and likewise one altar. [1540] Each expression of the statements inflames the mind with divine love: it speaks of God's tabernacles as *lovable* and desirable, but not simply to the extent of *longing* but even of *fainting for the courts of the Lord*. And what follows is in keeping with this: *My heart and my flesh rejoiced in the living God:* not only does the soul exult and rejoice, but also the body shared in the satisfaction of receiving the hope of resurrection; the verse, in fact, touches on this. This is the reason he also gave God the name *living,* as being the source of life: since the Babylonian gods and in fact those of our own ancestors were completely devoid of life and feeling, it was very appropriate for those rid of them to call the true God *living.* His, after

---

1. Cf. commentary on Ps 81 and note 1 there.
2. A rare application of a psalm to Christian readers.

all, is the saying, "I am the life and the resurrection," and "Whoever eats me will live in me."[3]

(3) *After all, a sparrow found a house for itself, and a turtledove a nest for itself in which to lay its nestlings* (v. 3). Aquila, on the other hand, put it this way, "Even a bird found a home for itself, and a swallow a nest for itself where it laid its nestlings." In other words, just as swallows and turtle-doves, and in fact the other birds, wander about without having an aviary, but once they settle on one they usually stay in it and nourish their own young, likewise we of old wandered about but now have received the call from your grace, have found your tabernacles, [and] we instruct our own young by your altars and with our children we attend upon you, and receive the spiritual food from you. *Your altars, Lord of hosts, my king and my God:* for us your holy altars are aviaries and nests and enjoyment of good things; from them we like gaping nestlings receive from you the divine and spiritual nourishment and salvation.[4] *Blessed are all who dwell in your house and will praise you forever* (v. 4). Each of these, while applicable in figurative fashion to those in Babylon, is in full reality relevant to us: far from the divine Temple, they declare blessed those enjoying the satisfaction of being there, whereas we, having tasted the divine sweetness, apply the term to the faithful who constantly attend upon God and are nourished on the divine goods.[5]

(4) [1541] *Blessed the man whose support is from you, steps in his heart* (v. 5). The text blesses the one always receiving the divine care, whose mind is enlightened by divine grace, and who always directs pious thoughts to it: the inspired word used the phrase *God's steps* made *into the heart* of the pious thoughts about God.[6] *He arranged for the vale of tears, for a place which he*

3. References to John 11.25 and John 6.57 supplied by the long form of the text.

4. Theodoret's interest in nature and his sensitivity to lyrical imagery allow him to bring out the force of this figure from the psalmist, and again apply it to Christian life generally.

5. While remarking on the greater degree of application of verses of this psalm to Christian life, it is also notable that sacramental possibilities in these verses are passed over—at least in the shorter form of Theodoret's text.

6. Theodoret (who quotes the verse in two forms in this edition) is definite about the puzzling reference to "steps," which has modern commentators going in various directions.

chose: the lawgiver will give blessings (v. 6): those who receive
God's steps in their heart and come to know the blessings of
the lawgiver give themselves up not to merriment and luxury
but to weeping and tears, and long for relief from it, having
heard God saying, "Blessed are those who mourn, for they will
be comforted,"[7] and, "Blessed are those who weep, for they will
laugh."[8] So after making these covenants, they look forward to
blessing from the lawgiver. At the level of figure the *vale of tears*
is the place where the angel appeared and censured the people's lawlessness, moving the multitude to weeping, the place
taking its name from that event.[9] Properly and in reality, on the
other hand, a *vale of tears* is the present life, in which Adam eats
bread in the sweat of his brow and Eve bears children in pain,[10]
and not only the sinners but also the saints groan, and one, he
says, is sorrowful unto death,[11] and another cries aloud, "Take
my soul, it is better for me to die than to live,"[12] and the great
herald of truth says, "We who have the firstfruits of the Spirit
groan within ourselves."[13] In this way it is possible to see the
saints constantly giving way to tears as they struggle and also
winning joy [in this]. In this *vale of tears,* then, those receiving
the steps and shedding the tears both embrace the life of hardship and look forward to the blessing of the lawgiver.

(5) *They will go from strength to strength* (v. 7): daily they will
grow in strength, and with the addition of virtue they obtain
great vigor. In this fashion those embracing the ascetical life
proceed from prayer to hymn singing, from hymn singing to
[1544] supplication, from there to the reading of the divine
sayings, from there to exhorting and advising the less perfect,
and by changing daily from strength to strength they will increase their own riches.[14] *The God of gods will be seen on Sion.* God
the Word, he is saying, caused this change in things by becom-

---

7. Matt 5.4.
9. Cf. Judg 2.1–5.
11. Cf. Matt 26.38.

8. Luke 6.21.
10. Cf. Gen 3.16, 19.
12. Jon 4.3.

13. Rom 8.23. Another obscure verse for which Theodoret first finds a historical reference and then develops at length a spiritual meaning.

14. Theodoret had come to know the practices of religious life from experience in his youth at Apamea, and his deposition by the Robber Synod shortly
after completion of this *Commentary* would give him a further opportunity.

ing man, appearing in flesh to human beings and making his own appearance first on Sion.

(6) *O Lord God of hosts, hearken to my prayer; give ear, O God of Jacob. See, God is our protector; gaze on the face of your Christ* (vv. 8–9). The inspired author makes this prayer, seeing from afar the salvation of human beings, and begging the God of all to receive the supplication and always to grant the people, now saved, his peculiar care, calling this *face of the Christ;* the divine Apostle likewise gave him this name, "You are the body of Christ, and individually members of it"; and again, "The eye cannot say to the hand, I have no need of you, or again the head to the feet, I have no need of you."[15]

(7) *Because a single day in your courts is better than thousands* (v. 10): your people enjoying your care always attend on your Temple, reaping much benefit therefrom; whatever benefit they gained from it on a single day they would not gather elsewhere by spending many thousands of days. This was, of course, applicable to the captives in Babylon, forced to live alongside unholy people, gaining no profit from it and pondering the former benefit from the divine Temple. *I would prefer to be cast aside in the house of my God than dwell in the tents of sinners:* the divine house is so desirable to me that I would choose to be thrown to the ground in that place and grovel in front of its doors than pass my life in the mighty and splendid houses of those living a lawless life. This is likewise a reference to those in Babylon, and relevant to us: the grace of the Spirit taught them not to overlook the desolation of the divine house, and we are instructed always to long for the buildings consecrated to God, [1545] especially when their officials are blameless and conspicuous for faith and life.[16]

(8) *Because the Lord God loves mercy and truth* (v. 11): nothing is dearer to God than almsgiving and its companion, truth. *The Lord will give grace and glory. He will not deprive of good things those who walk in innocence:* those who have this disposition to God enjoy all these good things, mercy springing up from these divine

15. 1 Cor 12.27, 21.
16. A proviso from the long form of the text, which also inserts the brief encomium of almsgiving that follows.

shrines, and from there as well a great and abundant supply of truth. From there, in fact, we receive instruction in the good teachings, and draw divine grace from the springs of the all-holy Spirit. Of course, on that basis we become the cynosure of all eyes and quite illustrious and, to put it in a nutshell, we receive complete enjoyment of good things, being free of evil and wickedness while preferring to live a life of simplicity and truth. *O Lord God of hosts, blessed the person who hopes in you* (v. 12). The ending is in keeping with the psalm as a whole: it blesses and declares enviable the one who despises all worldly good fortune while trusting only in hope in God, and reaping the benefit of salvation therefrom.[17]

17. Thanks to lack of a clear historical reference in the psalm, Theodoret atypically has been able and willing to devote much of his commentary to the spiritual life in general.

COMMENTARY ON PSALM 85

To the end. A psalm for the sons of Korah.

HE PSALM PROPHESIES both shadow and reality at one and the same time: the God of all foreshadowed salvation for all people in the fortunes of Israel, freeing them from servitude, at one time to Egyptians, at another to Babylonians. He rescued the whole human race from the devil's dominating usurpation and destruction. The psalm, then, foretells both the Jews' return from Babylon and the salvation of the whole world.

(2) *You were well-disposed, Lord, to your land* (v. 1). To be *well-disposed* is to wish some kind of good. So although on account of the lawlessness of the inhabitants he had sentenced the land of Judah to be desolate, and on Adam after the sin he had inflicted a punishment of a curse on the land, "It will bear you thorns and thistles,"[1] the inspired word indicated by the blessing the cessation of the disasters and the renewal of nature as a whole. [1548] *You cancelled the captivity of Jacob. You forgave the iniquities of your people, you covered all their sins* (vv. 1–2): undoing the harsh bonds of servitude, you also granted the captives freedom, being willing to overlook their sins; the fact that the whole human race was captive and received freedom from God our Savior he himself cries out in testimony through Isaiah, "The spirit of the Lord is upon me, and hence he anointed me, he sent me to preach good news to the poor, to heal the contrite of heart, to preach release to captives and sight to the blind."[2] The Lord in fact read this prophecy to Jews in the synagogue, "Today this Scripture has been fulfilled in your ears."[3]

(3) *You put an end to all your wrath, you turned from the wrath of*

---

1. Gen 3.18. The Fall is conceded, but a total renewal of nature follows, owing to divine benignity.
2. Isa 61.1. 3. Luke 4.21.

your anger (v. 3): you overcame your exasperation with us and showed benevolence. *Convert us, O God our salvation, and turn your anger away from us* (v. 4). It is likely that both groups had received the good news of freedom but had not yet been granted it; hence they ask to attain grace of loving-kindness completely. *Surely you will not be angry with us forever, or prolong your rage from generation to generation?* (v. 5). It is appropriate for those freed from their troubles to use these words and, instead of being confident of the forgiveness of their sins, to fear and placate the judge. Consequently, these people also beg that the same rage not be prolonged so as to last into the next generation, but be quickly dissolved.

(4) *O God, convert us and give us life, and your people will rejoice in you* (v. 6): we know you to be loving, Lord, and we believe that you will provide return and life, which for our part we shall enjoy, and we shall offer you the hymn of gladness. *Show us, O Lord, your mercy, and grant us your salvation* (v. 7). According to the prophecy of Isaiah, Cyrus, king of the Persians, gave the authority to return, and they hastened to take possession of their country. This is the reason they beg God to provide them with a prompt salvation in loving-kindness. As quickly as possible, O Lord, they say, show us your goodness, and may we gain salvation and [1549] freedom from here.

(5) Having thus offered supplication on their behalf, the inspired author receives the reply from God, and says, *I shall listen to what the Lord God will say in me; because he will speak peace to his people and to his holy ones, and to those who turn their heart to him* (v. 8). The loving Lord heard the supplication, he is saying, delivered the sentence of peace, and presented it to those who practiced repentance and had learned to direct their thinking to God. Conversion of heart to God, after all, is freedom from stumbling and the beginning of righteousness. This is also said on the part of the blessed apostles,[4] on the one hand, and on the other of those believing through them in the Savior. He

---

4. The author of the long form of the text feels an eschatological sense of this verse, calls for development, and proceeds to supply it. As usual, he is more interested in the reality than in the shadow, as Theodoret formulates his hermeneutical perspective at the psalm's opening.

says, *I shall listen to what the Lord God will say in me, because he will speak peace to his people* which he granted through the apostles to the nurslings of grace, which is in fact what he says in what follows, *and to his holy ones and to those who turn their heart to him.* How did he grant this? When from the Mount of Olives he who is everywhere and inseparable from the Father was taken up from where he also descended.[5] "My peace I give you, my peace I leave you":[6] this is the beginning of righteousness.

(6) What follows is in keeping with this. *But his salvation is near to those who fear him so that glory may dwell in our land* (v. 9): salvation comes close to those who fear God, and those who prefer to observe the divine laws enjoy it. Such a transformation also brought us the gift of return, which we shall achieve with distinction, and we shall see the former splendor of the homeland. *Mercy and truth came together, righteousness and peace kissed* (v. 10): to sinners and those practicing repentance the springs of loving-kindness supply mercy, while the streams of mercy envelop those embracing truth. Hence he said, *Mercy and truth came together:* Jews and the whole human race offered to God the acknowledgment of truth, and the one loving human beings gave mercy in return.[7] Thus once more, when they made an offering of righteousness, [1552] he accorded them peace, granted reconciliation, and dissolved the former enmity; peace came together with righteousness, mercy with truth. Consider *Mercy and truth came together:*[8] the merciful One who bears everything was born by the virgin and mother, and the righteous John leapt in the womb of Elizabeth. So the woman bearing righteousness—namely, John—kissed the woman bearing peace; "he is," as the Apostle says, "our peace, making the two one."[9]

---

5. Cf. Eph 4.9–10.   6. Cf. John 14.27.

7. In balancing the divine and human interchange here, Theodoret gives a priority to the human, which is unusual for him.

8. Theodoret moves to pass on from these vv. 10–11 quite briskly, thinking the point of divine and human interchange adequately made. The longer form of the text, however, ever concerned to give fuller attention to reality than to shadow, feels that more needs to be said, and to this end develops the role of John the Baptist, especially from Gospel infancy stories, in which Mary also figures.

9. Eph 2.14.

(7) He indicated this more clearly in what follows. *Truth sprang up from the ground* (v. 11): the Godbearer[10] is pure countless times over, yet it was from Adam, from Abraham, from David, and certainly from her that the real truth sprang. *And righteousness looked down from heaven:* the right testimony to the only-begotten Son of the Father is the one that says, "This is my Son, the beloved, in whom I am well pleased";[11] when human beings embraced the truth, the God of all took right care of them, drove out the devil's tyranny, and cancelled death's tortures, as he says in what follows. *The Lord will give goodness, after all, and our land will give its fruit* (v. 12). Once again he used the same combination, saying that while God exercised pity and loving-kindness, they would offer God suitable fruit, indicating by this not a good season but the fruitfulness of virtue.

(8) *Righteousness will go before him* (v. 13), namely, John: of him the prophet Habakkuk says, "A word will go before him, and will go forth at his feet for instruction."[12] In similar terms Zechariah [said] to his son, "And you, little child, will be called prophet of the Most High: you will go before the Lord to prepare his ways."[13] So the inspired mind (saying of John, *Righteousness will go before him and make a path for his steps,* that is, You are Lord, God the Word incarnate) nicely included the prophecy of both of them; it is the voice of John [saying], "He who comes after me is ahead of me because he existed before me," and, to summarize, "Behold, the lamb of God who takes away the sin of the world."[14] *He will make* [1553] *a path for his steps.* The end of the psalm most of all teaches us that the present inspired composition foretells the common salvation of all people: it says that the Lord exercises righteousness, and like some guide shows us the way, keeping to the way of virtue and mak-

10. Though Theodoret is commenting on the Psalms some fifteen years after the Symbol of Union of 433 in which the Antiochene bishops (reluctantly, out of respect for Nestorius) accepted the term *Theotokos* for Mary, he does not use it in the *Commentary*, unlike the longer form of the text, as in this case.

11. Matt 3.17.   12. Hab 3.5 [Greek].

13. Luke 1.76.

14. John 1.15, 30. At this point the short form of the text resumes, its author being unaware that v. 13b has already been cited, and that John the Baptist has appeared on stage. Rondeau is right, it would seem, to regard the long form as secondary—derivative even.

ing it clear to us by his own footsteps. The Lord himself confirms this statement, speaking in one case to John, "Leave it for the time being: in this way all righteousness must be fulfilled," in another to his own disciples, "Learn of me that I am gentle and humble of heart, and you will find rest for your souls."[15] Elsewhere in washing their feet he said this along with other things, "I, the Lord and teacher, wash your feet; I gave you an example for you to do as I do."[16] So he was the first to travel the way of righteousness, change the crooked places into smooth, the rough into smooth ways, and become a way for us, as the Lord himself says, "I am the way, the truth and the life; no one comes to the Father except through me."[17]

15. Matt 3.15; 11.29.   16. Cf. John 13.14–15.
17. John 14.6.

COMMENTARY ON PSALM 86

A prayer for David.

CCORDING TO THE TITLE, the blessed David offered the prayer to the Lord God, begging to enjoy some assistance. He also prophesies the assault of the Assyrians on Jerusalem, and Hezekiah's hope in God. He also forecasts the calling and salvation of all the nations.[1]

(2) *Incline your ear, O Lord, and hearken to me, because I am poor and needy* (v. 1). The prayer's beginning comes from a lowly attitude: though they both possessed the wealth of righteousness, the divinely inspired David and the remarkable Hezekiah paid no attention to that, focusing instead on natural poverty and asking God to take pity on it and the neediness going with it. The phrase *Incline your ear, O Lord* he used by analogy with a sick person unable through weakness to speak more loudly and obliging the physician to bring his ear down to his mouth. *Guard my soul, because I am holy* (v. 2). The inspired author is not inconsistent in calling himself poor and holy together: since both the one man and the other [1556] had unjust and lawless enemies who had in no way been wronged by them and yet longed for their unjustified execution. He called both himself and Hezekiah holy for giving no cause to the enemies. What he means is something like this: Judged for myself, I am poor and needy, and have no wealth of virtue, but compared with the enemies I would give the impression of being holy. After all, they are impious and lawless, whereas I enjoy knowledge of you; they pursue [me] unjustly, whereas I accept their unjust attack. The person who, contrary to any reasonable expectation, is under

---

1. So "shadow and reality" again, as Theodoret remarked of the previous psalm's reference.

assault by those intent on doing wrong would say this up to the present and throughout life.[2]

(3) In good spirits, then, he said in what follows, *Save your servant, O my God, who hopes in you:* I hoped in you, O Lord, save [me]; grant salvation in return for hope. *Have mercy on me, O Lord, because I cried to you all day long* (v. 3) provide me with your loving-kindness, O Lord: I constantly proclaim your mercy; Symmachus in fact rendered *all day long* as "every day." *Gladden the soul of your servant* (v. 4). He also says why: *Because to you I lifted up my soul:* do away with the despondency of the one embracing your service, and provide satisfaction to a soul assenting to you and waiting for your mercy. *Because you, O Lord, are good, kind, and rich in mercy to all who call upon you* (v. 5): you are by nature good and loving, and you supply the fountains of mercy to those who beg you. Aquila and Theodotion, on the other hand, said "forgiving" for *kind;* so kindness suggests long-suffering.

(4) *Give ear, O God, to my prayer; attend to the sound of my pleading* (v. 6): exercising such goodness, then, kindly accept my pleading. At the same time he indicated through what follows the time when he asked the supplication to be acceptable. *On the day of my distress I cried to you, because you hearkened to me* (v. 7): having experience of your gentleness, I offer supplication; you had already granted my request when I made it.[3]

(5) *There is no one like you among gods, O Lord, and there is nothing like your works* (v. 8). Since the impious Rabshakeh had used those arrogant words, "Surely none of the gods of the nations succeeded in rescuing [1557] their land from my hand, that the Lord would deliver Jerusalem from my hand?"[4] accordingly the inspired composition teaches Hezekiah to cry aloud, *There is no one like you among gods, O Lord, and there is nothing like your works:* while they have a name lacking substance, and even acquired it by stealth, you on the other hand bear a name corresponding to reality. It is very appropriate, in fact, that he associ-

2. The long form of the text thinks it is time to apply the psalm personally.

3. Misreading of Hebrew tenses once again affects the commentator's interpretation, a past tense not bringing out the force of the original future.

4. 2 Kings 18.35, a favorite text and character of Theodoret's.

ated the works with the divine name, *There is no one like you among gods, O Lord, and there is nothing like your works:* they are completely lifeless and incapable of assisting themselves, whereas your magnificence is beyond the tongues of human beings.

(6) *All the nations you made will come and bow down before you, O Lord* (v. 9). Now, we know this never happened in the time of blessed David, whereas in the time of Hezekiah it is likely that some were stricken by the devastation of the Assyrians and came to worship God. The time after the Incarnation of our God and Savior demonstrated the truth of the prophecy: after the saving Passion the divine choir of the apostles were sent into the whole world, the Lord saying to them, "Go, make disciples of all nations."[5] They made disciples as they were commanded, dispelling the cloud of ignorance and thus causing the believers to see the Sun of Righteousness and worship the God who saved. What follows also brings this out. *And they shall glorify your name. Because you are great, you are a worker of wonders, who alone are God* (vv. 9–10): they will offer you the hymn, knowing you alone are God; the magnitude of your wonders will furnish them with this knowledge.

(7) Note how he expressed it more clearly through what follows in saying, *Guide me in your path, O Lord, and I shall travel in your truth* (v. 11). After prophesying to the nations the coming freedom from error, [1560] he begs that he in his own person may enjoy this guidance, and make his journey in the way of truth. Note what he says in what follows. *Let my heart rejoice so as to fear your name.* The one who has reverence for God embraces the way of life in keeping with the Law, and such a life is the mother of happiness. The inspired author was therefore right to beg for his own heart to be gladdened by the divine fear; he speaks in these terms elsewhere, too, "Let the heart of those seeking the Lord rejoice"; and again, "I remembered God and rejoiced."[6]

(8) *I shall confess to you, O Lord my God, with all my heart, and I shall glorify your name forever. Because great is your mercy in my regard* (vv. 12–13). I know that you will grant my request, he is saying,

5. Matt 28.19.
6. Ps 105.3; 77.3.

dissipate my gloom, and cause me to offer grateful hymn singing for the loving-kindness shown me. *You delivered my soul from the depths of Hades.* He indicated in this the greatness of the dangers: the divine David often endured such things, under attack from Saul and pursued by Absalom, while the assault by the Assyrians was manifest disaster—hence his calling such dangers ultimate death and *depths of Hades.* But because as well the creator of everything, that is, God the Word made flesh of a virgin, choosing cross and death, descended into the deepest parts of the earth, not only to raise those in thrall to corruption for ages but also to fill them with immortality.[7]

(9) Then he says, *O God, lawless people rose up against me, an assembly of powerful ones sought my soul* (v. 14). David's enemies lived a life of lawlessness, and the Assyrians were practitioners of impiety and wickedness; to link the two he spoke of a *powerful assembly* with a view to the situation then prevailing. The one group and the other exercised might corresponding to their evil attitude; twofold was the dread arising from this in those wronged. Hence they have recourse to God, and beg assistance from that quarter. *They did not keep you before their eyes:* they did not take your providence into account. *You, O Lord my God, showing pity, merciful, long-suffering, rich in mercy, truthful, have regard for me and be merciful to me* (vv. 15–16): since you are a fount of loving-kindness, and pour forth streams of pity and mercy, and truth also belongs to you, and you judge those living a life of wickedness, [1561] allow me to share in the morsels of your goodness, and make me emerge stronger than the enemies. *Give your strength to your servant, save the son of your handmaid:* I am your servant, and son of your maidservant, that is to say, from the very outset I live life under your lordship; hence, like a servant I beg salvation from the Lord.

(10) *Give me a sign of [your] goodness* (v. 17). Some of the signs are of retribution, as in the case of the Egyptians; others [are signs] of salvation, as in the case of the Hebrews. For this reason, to be sure, the inspired author employed the distinction, seeking out not simply a sign but a good sign—that is to

---

7. Again the longer form of the text insists the reality be highlighted along with the shadow.

say, Give me a sign that brings salvation, and that through wonder working is responsible for an abundance of good things for
me. He also tells the reason why he asks this sign to be given to
him. *That those who hate me may see and be ashamed, because you, O
Lord, helped me and comforted me:* on perceiving your providence
for me, the adversaries will be filled with shame and will become an object of reproach to all. It was appropriate for the
God from God to bestow on the nations the cross as a good
sign, through which he defeated the common enemy and set
up a trophy against demons and passions. Amen.[8]

8. This final eschatological reference, citing a phrase from Constantinople's
creed and closing piously, is predictably from the long form of the text.

COMMENTARY ON PSALM 87

For the sons of Korah. A psalm. A song.

THIS PSALM ALSO PROPHESIES the salvation of the nations, and foretells the religious way of life, which Christ the Lord taught by becoming man. *Its foundations are on the holy mountains* (v. 1). The divine teachings are *foundations* of religion; *holy mountains,* on which he fixed these foundations, are our Savior's apostles: of them blessed Paul said, "Built upon the foundation of the apostles and inspired authors, with Christ Jesus himself as the cornerstone";[1] and again, "Peter and James and John, who were acknowledged to be pillars."[2] The Lord said to Peter after that true and divine confession, "You are Peter, and on this rock I shall build my church; Hades' gates will not prevail against it."[3] And again, "You are the light of the world; a city situated on a mountain cannot be hidden."[4] On these holy mountains Christ the Lord sunk the foundations of religion.

(2) *The Lord loves the gates of Sion beyond all the dwellings of Jacob* (v. 2). Let the divinely inspired Paul explain what this Sion is: "You have come to [1564] Mount Sion and the city of the living God, the heavenly Jerusalem, and to countless angels, to a festal gathering and assembly of firstborn who are enrolled in heaven";[5] and again, "The other woman corresponds to the Jerusalem above; she is free and is our mother."[6] Speaking

---

1. Eph 2.20. 2. Gal 2.9.
3. Matt 16.18.
4. Matt 5.14. Theodoret is determined to give the psalm an eschatological and Christological interpretation, as the opening rash of New Testament quotations suggests. He would therefore not be in sympathy with disparaging comments from moderns about the state of the text, to the effect that it is the most mangled and disordered of the Psalter (Beaucamp) or is devoid at first glance of a consistent sequence of thought (Weiser).
5. Heb 12.22–23. 6. Gal 4.26.

about the patriarch Abraham in the Epistle to the Hebrews, he added this as well, "He looked forward, you see, to the city that has foundations, whose architect and builder is God"; and again about the other saints, "Those who say such things make it clear that they are looking for a homeland. If they had been thinking of the one they left, they would have had the opportunity of returning; but as it is they aspire to a better one, that is, heavenly."[7] Accordingly, we learn there is a heavenly city of some kind, called Jerusalem, with no towers and ramparts nor gleaming with sparkling stones, but conspicuous for choirs of saints and adorned with an angelic way of life. You would not be wrong to call the churches on earth the gates of this city, through which it is possible to enter it: in them we are instructed and trained, and learn the way of life of that city. The inspired word said these gates were dear to the God of all, and preferred to the Jewish dwellings. *Glorious things are said of you, O city of God* (v. 3): some wonderful and remarkable things are foretold of you, surpassing all human expectation.

(3) Testimony to the fact that what is said in no way relates to the Sion below comes from what follows. *I shall remember Rahab and Babylon among those who know me. Behold, foreigners and Tyre, and people of the Ethiopians—they were there* (v. 4). These things, he is saying, O divine city, have been said of you so that those formerly living a life of ungodliness and oppressed by the gloom of ignorance may be granted residence in you and a share in your way of life. The reason, to be sure, that he recalled the above-mentioned nations [1565] as the least law-abiding and held in the power of impiety was to suggest others by mention of them. Rahab, for instance, was a Canaanite and a prostitute;[8] Babylon, ferocious and godless; the "foreigners" or Philistines (we have already indicated who they were),[9] superstitious and lawless. The prophet Ezekiel denounced both the impiety and the licentiousness of Tyre.[10] The inspired word gave the name

7. Heb 11.10, 14–16.
8. Cf. Josh 2, where in fact the Canaanite prostitute is presented favorably. The psalmist instead seems to have had in mind the Rahab of Isa 30.7, the monster that represents Egypt.
9. Cf. comment on Ps 83.7.
10. Cf. Ezek 26–28.

people of the Ethiopians not only to the Ethiopians themselves, whose souls resembled the color of their body, but to all those black in soul: in the Song of Songs the bride cries aloud, "I am black and beautiful, O daughters of Jerusalem"[11]—"black" in the sense of deceived, besmirched by the stench of wild beasts, and "beautiful" in the sense of awaiting for your arrival from heaven as Lord for the sake of my salvation; he suggested at the same time both the gloom of impiety and the charm given by divine grace. Of course, these nations in the time of the Jews did not assemble at Jerusalem or come to love the way of life in keeping with the Law, whereas after the Incarnation of our Savior they inhabit that Jerusalem, fill the churches throughout the world, move to the Sion on high, and share in that blessed way of life. From which nations, in fact, did they not come to faith in the Savior? Some of them, on the other hand, did not even take possession of the Jerusalem below with a view to bowing down before the famous and holy places where God from God was not only made flesh but also trod the ground in love.[12]

(4) So with these fine words he moved to what follows. *A person will say "mother" of Sion* (v. 5): each one will call Sion mother, and everyone will say that Sion is a mother. Blessed Paul also likewise says, "The other woman corresponds to the Jerusalem above; she is free and is mother of us all."[13] *A person was born in her.* This is connected with *A person will say:* the one calling Sion mother will admit also the origin of the person born in her. Lest anyone form the impression that this person is a nobody, he immediately added, *The Most High personally founded it:* this person born in her, being Most High, is maker, creator, God. [1568] *The Lord will describe in a record of these peoples and rulers that existed in her* (v. 6). Symmachus, on the other hand, put it this way, "The Lord will count in recording peoples, he was

11. Cant 1.5. If Theodoret's comment on the Ethiopians is less than politically correct, the following gloss from the long form of the text on the two terms from the Song of Songs, as usual, outstrips him, Theodoret's subsequent gloss being more moderate.

12. The final comment from the long form of the text suggests the contemporary practice of pilgrimage to the holy places in Jerusalem.

13. Gal 4.26, inserted here, in a somewhat different reading, by the long form of the text as though the verse had not already been cited above.

born there." That is to say, the one who granted the record on
his part to the people following their way of life in her was born
in her as far as humanity is concerned, Lord and God though
he is. Our Lord also highlighted this counting in saying to the
sacred apostles, "Even the hairs of your head are counted."[14]
And he indicated the record to his own disciples in saying, "Rejoice, not because the demons are subject to you, but because
your names are recorded in heaven."[15]

(5) *All those whose dwelling is in you are like people rejoicing* (v.
7): the way of life in heaven, removed from all despondency, is
characterized by joy and satisfaction pure and unalloyed. The
devotees of piety, far from merely sojourning there, dwell forever.

14. Matt 10.30.
15. Luke 10.20.

COMMENTARY ON PSALM 88

A song. A psalm for the sons of Korah. To the end.
On Mahalath, for responding.

Of understanding, for Heman the Israelite.

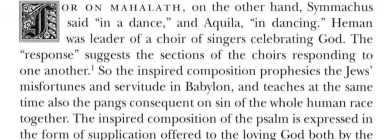OR ON MAHALATH, on the other hand, Symmachus said "in a dance," and Aquila, "in dancing." Heman was leader of a choir of singers celebrating God. The "response" suggests the sections of the choirs responding to one another.[1] So the inspired composition prophesies the Jews' misfortunes and servitude in Babylon, and teaches at the same time also the pangs consequent on sin of the whole human race together. The inspired composition of the psalm is expressed in the form of supplication offered to the loving God both by the former people and also by all in common, and the prayer is related to the more devout.

(2) *O Lord, God of my salvation, by day and night I cried in your presence. Let my prayer come in before you* (vv. 1–2): you, O Lord, I know to be Lord of my salvation; this is the reason, to be sure, I beg night and day for my appeal to be accepted. He says this in what follows: *Incline your ear to my appeal.* Why he asks he says also in what follows [1569]: *Because my soul was filled with troubles, and my life came near to Hades* (v. 3): I beg you to repel the multitude of troubles besetting me when you perceive them; I

1. Theodoret in facing up to the elements in this title can hardly have escaped the impression that directions for liturgical recital are involved. He is right about Heman's role in worship (cf. 1 Chron 16.41), though his LXX text, perhaps because of this reference, replaces Ezrahite (a term meaning native, or Canaanite) with Israelite (its opposite). Both LXX and alternative versions help him get to the roots of the puzzling Hebrew terms "On Mahalath Leannoth," possibly having to do with dance and refrain, respectively. As before, the genre of *maskil* is also taken back to its roots having to do with understanding. But Theodoret is wise enough not to delve deeper, and presses on.

am at the very doors of death, and in need of your help, bereft of it and enslaved to sin. This is what he goes on to say.

(3) *I am reckoned with those going down into the pit* (v. 4): I encountered irresistible problems and found no solution, but instead I was like those falling into a pit, unable to get out.[2] *I was like a person devoid of help:* I was deprived of all providence and care. *Free among the dead* (v. 5): though not yet enduring the end or falling under the slavery of death, I include myself among the numbers of the dead. *Like wounded people sleeping in a tomb, who are not remembered and are in fact thrust from your hand.* This is connected with *I was like: I was like a person devoid of help, free among the dead,* and not yet falling under the slavery of death. I was wounded like wounded in war, and consigned to a tomb. This, in fact, is the way Symmachus also said it: "Like the wounded lying in a tomb, who are no longer recalled, cut out of your hand": they are cut off from your providence, whereas your aid will intervene to prevent my falling foul of the same depths.

(4) *They put me in the depths of a pit, in darkness and in a shadow of death* (v. 6). These words relate to those obliged to live in Babylon, and to the whole human race:[3] the former, in thrall to wicked people, lived a painful life, and all human beings were beset with manifold calamities after the sin—death, grief, tears, weeping and wailing, widows and orphans, penury, misfortunes and countless other problems defying explanation and bringing darkness on even the living—all these came in the wake of the breaking of the commandment.[4] See what a terrible evil disobedience is, the cause not only of separation from God but also of involvement in such great evils. *Your anger against me is aggravated, and you have brought all your billows to bear against me* (v. 7). Symmachus, on the other hand, put it this way, "Your anger burst out against me, and you maltreated me with your

2. The psalm expresses in many different ways the notion of Sheol, a topic in Old Testament thought that we have noted Theodoret being unfamiliar with.

3. In a nutshell Theodoret's double perspective in interpreting a psalm. Further on he will make it even more comprehensive.

4. No doubt of Theodoret's acceptance of the effects of the Fall—not requiring the following moral comment from the long form of the text.

tempests." You continue in your punishment, he is saying, [1572] inflicting various assaults of misfortunes against me; he is speaking by analogy with shipwrecked people, victims of many assaults from waves and much buffeting of winds.

(5) *My acquaintances you kept at a distance* (v. 8): I am bereft of kith and kin. The captives in Babylon, who suffered the yoke of slavery, were scattered about and deprived of the relationship and association of loved ones, drew no consolation from the experience. On the other hand, all human beings who lived a life of impiety had no share in the care coming from the angels. *They made me an abomination to themselves,* that is, the enemies; *I was betrayed, and did not escape:* I find no freedom from the evils encroaching upon me. *My eyes grew weak from poverty* (v. 9). Symmachus, on the other hand, put it this way, "My eye filled from the abuse": I wore out my eyes with my tears, forced to weep with the pain. *I cried out to you, O Lord, all day long I stretched out my hands to you:* so give one means of relief from troubles, your providence, O Lord; I beg you with my hands always extended. This posture suggests the soul's severe pain: under pressure of need one prays more earnestly in this fashion to the person able to respond.

(6) *Surely you will not work wonders for the dead? Will physicians rise up and confess to you?* (v. 10). While I am still alive, he is saying, show me your wonder working: I shall not see it when I am dead, no physician being able to give relief from death. What kind of remedy has that power, after all? *Surely no one will recount your mercy in the tomb and your truth in corruption?* (v. 11)— that is, no one will recount or confess after the departure from here. *Surely your wonders will not be known in the darkness, and your righteousness in the land of oblivion?* (v. 12). Surely it is not possible, he is saying, for the dead gone to dust, living in death's tomb and consigned to oblivion to sense your loving-kindness and become witnesses of your marvels?

(7) *For my part, O Lord, I cried out to you, and in the morning my prayer will anticipate you* (v. 13). Symmachus, [1573] on the other hand, put it this way, "My wailing is directed to you, Lord, and at daybreak my prayer will anticipate you." [In other words,] Desiring in life to be rid of the present evils, I wail in

my pains and anticipate dawn in my praying. *Why, O Lord, do you repel my soul, turn your face from me?* (v. 14): so why on earth do you dismiss me, Lord, and do not give me a share in your benevolence? *I am poor and in difficulties from my youth* (v. 15). Israel's youth was the exodus from Egypt, whereas for humanity as a whole it was the life outside of paradise after the transgression of the commandment: both the one and the other continued to suffer hardship all the time in between. *After being lifted up I was brought down, and was at a loss.* After their eminence the Jews were involved in slavery, while human nature, after being made in the divine image and granted life in paradise, hankered after greater things and lost what it had been given.

(8) *Your wrath swept over me, your terrors alarmed me, they surrounded me like water* (vv. 16–17). You directed all your wrath against me, he is saying, you completely disturbed me with the most fearsome punishments, and submerged me in these waters, as it were. *All day long they beset me:* I am daily surrounded by them. *You kept friend and neighbor at a distance from me, and my acquaintances from hardship* (v. 18): struggling under these disasters I gain no comfort from my familiars, being deprived of association with them on account of the hardship of slavery. This applied not only to the Jews or to all human beings before the appearance of the Savior; rather, at present as well the supplication is appropriate and suited to those suffering a similar fate: "Whatever was written," according to the divine Apostle, "was written for our instruction, so that through endurance and the encouragement of the Scriptures we might have hope."[5]

5. Rom 15.4. Thanks to lack of reference in the title or the body of the psalm to either Davidic authorship or a specific historical incident, Theodoret has been able to develop his preferred threefold hermeneutical perspective for the Psalms, as emerges in commentary on vv. 15–18: the situation of the Jews in the Old Testament, the condition of the whole human race, and the circumstances affecting the reader of the Psalms today. In addition to these levels of reference, he will in some cases (not here) find a Christological meaning and an eschatological application to apostles and New Testament churches.

COMMENTARY ON PSALM 89

Of understanding, for Ethan the Israelite.

EEING THE FALSE GODS honored in shrines while the ark of God remained solitary and unrevered, blessed David [1576] promised to build the divine Temple. Accepting this resolve of his, God rewards the fine promise and guarantees to make him a rational temple from his own loins, and through it to achieve the salvation of all human beings and provide him with an unending kingdom. These promises he made to him through the prophet Nathan: the story of the Chronicles teaches it clearly,[1] and in the second book of the Kings Nathan said to him, "The Lord announces to you that he will build himself a house."[2] The story of the Acts also recalls this. Blessed Peter, when making a speech to the Jews, outlined this along with many other things: "David, being a prophet and knowing that God had sworn him an oath that the Christ according to the flesh would come from the fruit of his loins and sit on his throne, spoke with this foreknowledge of his resurrection, His soul was not abandoned to Hades, nor did his flesh see corruption."[3] Being without sin: there is no one among human beings without sin except Jesus, God the Word made flesh from David. These promises he made also to the patriarch Abraham, saying to him, "In your offspring all the nations of the earth will be blessed."[4] Commenting on this the divinely inspired Paul spoke this way, "The promises were made to Abraham and to his offspring; he does not say, And to his offspring, as in the case of many, but as in the case of one, And to his offspring, which is Christ."[5]

1. 1 Chron 17.   2. 2 Sam 7.11.
3. Acts 2.30–31 paraphrased; cf. Ps 132.11. The comment about the sinlessness of Jesus is from the long form of the text.
4. Gen 22.18.   5. Gal 3.16.

(2) Their successors, with an eye on these promises and the prospect of themselves made captive and forced to inhabit a foreign land, the royal city made desolate and the monarchy extinguished, remind the God of all of the promises. At one time they bring to the fore the patriarch Abraham, his son and descendant in reminding God of the agreements, at another time blessed David and the promises made to him. In similar fashion the blessed martyrs Hananiah, [1577] Azariah, and Mishael made mention of Abraham, Isaac, and Israel in imploring God in the furnace.[6] The charism of inspiration, therefore, composed this psalm for the benefit of those people, teaching how to appease God and gain the benefit of loving-kindness on his part. This is the reason for "Of understanding" in the title: it is particularly necessary for those under correction not to say anything out of place when voicing complaint, but await the divine mercy. Ethan was personally entrusted with a choir of singers in the Temple, who sang God's praises; in fact, it is not the psalm of Heman, as some claim—rather, as we maintain, he too was in charge of a choir of singers, receiving from the divine David the commission also of singing with the others.[7]

(3) *I shall sing of your mercies forever, O Lord, from generation to generation I shall proclaim your truth with my mouth* (v. 1). Begging the divine mercy, they sing of the mercy, and in their desire to witness the truth of the promises to David, they promise to teach each generation. *Because you said, Mercy will be built in heaven forever, your truth will be prepared* (v. 2). It is God's word spoken to David, that he would maintain his mercy to his seed forever. Accordingly, they recall this promise. You said, he means, you will increase and not lessen your mercy (the term *will be built* meaning "will be increased and receive an increment"). Symmachus said "will be set in place": you promised, he is saying, to confirm the truth of the words.

6. Dan 3.35 [Greek].

7. See note 1 to the previous psalm for Theodoret's interpretation of elements in the title. Ethan, here also described as an Israelite in defiance of the sense of the "Ezrahite" of the original, is listed in 1 Kings 4.31 along with Heman as one of the paradigmatic sages. For Mowinckel "these wise men of the past are explicitly defined with the 'guild' of temple musicians," though documentation for Heman's musical role is more explicit—hence the claim the long form of the text cites here.

(4) *I have made a covenant with my elect* (v. 3). This is said on the part of the God and Father, as well as what follows. *I swore to David my servant, I shall make arrangements for your seed forever, and build your throne for generation and generation* (vv. 3–4). This is linked also with *you said:* I made this covenant with the elect. By *elect* he refers to Abraham, Isaac, and Israel; in addition to them he swore also to David that he would keep his seed free from ruin, and his throne would flourish in every generation. After thus outlining God's promises, and not looking at their fulfillment in reality, they are forced by the disasters to say nothing untoward and rather honor in hymns the governor of all things. [1580] *The heavens will praise your wonders, O Lord, and your truth in an assembly of saints* (v. 5). Theodotion, on the other hand, said, "and your faith in an assembly of saints," that is, all who put their trust in you will keep faith with you. In other words, it is proper for your praises to be sung by all, not least by the inhabitants of heaven, who look down on your wonders more precisely and understand the reliability of your promises. Blessed Paul also mentions this heavenly assembly, saying, "You have come to Mount Sion and the city of the living God, a heavenly Jerusalem, and an assembly of firstborn ones enrolled in heaven."[8]

(5) *Because who in the clouds will be compared with the Lord, who among the sons of God will be likened to the Lord?* (v. 6). Symmachus, on the other hand, said, "After all, who in the sky will match the Lord, who among the sons of God will be like the Lord?" He calls gods *sons of God,* as he calls human beings "sons of human beings." He refers to them, however, not as true gods but as thought such by the unbelievers. So he means, You surpass the heavenly beings, you are incomparably superior to all, and nothing that exists can be compared with you: the falsity of the gods made by human beings is proven, whereas your power is everlasting and beyond corruption. He uses terms of this kind elsewhere, too, saying, "Our Lord is above all gods."[9] The inspired authors do make this comparison, however, not unaware of the extraordinary degree of difference, but proposing

8. Cf. Heb 12.22–23, loosely recalled.
9. Ps 135.5.

a teaching adapted to the limitations of the unbelieving.[10] *God is glorified in the council of saints; he is great and fearsome above all that are around him* (v. 7). Since he had made mention of those not really being gods, whereas the true God is not known by the impious, it was right for him to bring forward the saints, by whom the praises of the true God are sung, God being fearsome to them for the reason that they are close to him and recognize his ineffable power. He called the assembly of the saints *council of saints.*

(6) *O Lord God of hosts, who is like you? You are powerful, Lord, and your truth encircles you* (v. 8). They make constant mention of truth, longing to see the trustworthiness of the promises; and they say to him, [1581] Which person of the ones who exist can be compared to you, O Lord? You are Lord and God of hosts, you have power to match your will; with you everything is true and reliable. Then they outline the signs of the power. *You master the might of the sea, you subdue the surging of its waves. You humbled it like a proud [warrior] wounded, you scattered your foes with the arm of your power* (vv. 9–10). You are creator and lord of all, he is saying; it is a simple matter for you both to stir up the sea and to bring tranquillity. In mentioning the sea he calls to mind what was done in it: he uses the word *proud* of Pharaoh and the Egyptian foes, whom he consigned to the sea while preserving his own people. At the same time, however, he foretells as well the overthrow of the teachers of imposture, overcoming these with their wicked forces in all-holy baptism: as it happened on the former occasion through Moses, here it is through the priest.[11]

(7) *Yours are the heavens and yours is the earth; you laid the foundations for the world and its fullness* (v. 11): you are maker and creator not only of the sea and the whole earth but also of the skies set overhead, your work comprising not only the heaven that is visible but also that which is above it. *You created the north*

10. In many places Chrysostom can be found formulating this principle of biblical *synkatabasis* in similar terms, a principle both Antiochenes can uphold along with respect for divine transcendence (their Christology helping them achieve this balance).

11. The mention of the power of water predictably prompts a brief application to the efficacy of baptism.

wind and the sea (v. 12). Theodotion, on the other hand, put it this way, "North wind and south you created," calling *the sea* "south" since it disturbs the [sea]'s mass most of all. The winds, he is saying, and the very sections of the world are your works. It was not without purpose that he made mention of these two sections; rather, it was because the Egyptians are south of Jerusalem, whereas the Assyrians are north, and by overcoming the audacity of the Egyptians he granted them freedom: it is as easy for you, he is saying, to overcome the one as the other, and once it happens, *Tabor and Hermon will rejoice in your name.* By reference to these he indicated the whole land of promise: they are the mountains of that land. Aquila, on the other hand, said "will praise" for *will rejoice,* and Symmachus, "will celebrate." Actually, this did not mean the mountains would do it but people living on the mountains or near the mountains.

(8) [1584] *Your arm with influence* (v. 13): it belongs to you to operate everything powerfully; he used *arm* for operation, and *influence* for power. Aquila actually put "power" for *influence. Let your hand be strengthened, your right hand uplifted.* Symmachus, on the other hand, put it this way, "Your hand is invincible, your right hand uplifted." We have often remarked that he indicates operation by mention of *hand* and good operation by mention of *right hand;* so being in need of both kinds of operation they mentioned both words: they long to see the enemies overcome, and they themselves desire to attain salvation. This is the reason why they speak of the hand as invincible and the right hand as uplifted, for its ability to punish the others and liberate themselves. They indicate this also in what follows. *Righteousness and judgment* [are] *the preparation of your throne; mercy and truth will go before you* (v. 14). Begging God to pronounce judgment even on the Babylonians, they ask him to deliver a just verdict against them while showing mercy to themselves and revealing the truth of the promise. This is the reason, to be sure, why they speak of his throne as a tribunal adorned with *righteousness and judgment,* and *mercy and truth* proceeding before God, the promise having been made many years before.

(9) *Blessed the people who know jubilation* (v. 15). *Jubilation,* as we have often said, is the cry of the victors. So since they were

conquered and led off into slavery, they bless the victors; but the verse also foresees the people offering to God in the whole land and sea the mystical jubilation and singing the triumphant hymn. What follows is also in keeping with this sentiment. *Lord, they will travel in the light of your countenance. They will rejoice in your name all day long, and will be exalted in your righteousness* (vv. 15–16): they will rejoice, will sing a song of triumph against the foes and will offer the triumphal hymn to you, the author of victory, enlightened by your appearance and in receipt of light from you through the rebirth of the washing,[12] constantly enjoying satisfaction, performing prescribed duty and rendered uplifted and conspicuous therefrom.

(10) *Because you are the boast of their power* (v. 17). They glory in your power, he is saying; they got it from you, after all. *And in your righteousness our horn will be exalted.* We have this hope, he is saying, and we await your assistance, [1585] being superior to the enemies on account of it; he called strength and power *horn* by analogy with the horned animals, which are like armed warriors because of the horns and use them against the assaults of enemies. *Because support is from the Lord and our king the Holy One of Israel* (v. 18): with you as king we are nourished by hope, living under your care.

(11) *Then you spoke in a vision to your children* (v. 19). Symmachus, on the other hand, put it this way, "Then you spoke through a vision to your children": we know your promises made through the inspired authors; he called these people "seers" and "gazers."[13] *And you said, I set help on a strong one, and raised up an elect from my people. I found David my servant, I anointed him with my holy oil* (vv. 19–20). You testified to your devotee David, he is saying, and finding him strong in the works of virtue, you regaled him with your help, chose him, anointed him, and appointed him king. *My hand will always support him, in fact, and my arm strengthen him* (v. 21): you said you would provide him with strength, and give him a share in your care.

(12) *A foe will not gain an advantage over him, a child of iniquity will not proceed to abuse him* (v. 22): you promised to show up his

---

12. This brief baptismal expansion comes from the long form of the text.
13. Terms not exactly used here; perhaps Theodoret has elsewhere in mind.

foes' schemes to be idle, and render him superior to their attempts to maltreat him. *I shall crush his enemies before him, and overturn those who hate him. My truth and my mercy are with him, and his horn will be exalted in my name* (vv. 23–24): you promised to destroy all his enemies, provide him with unswerving loving-kindness, and make him the cynosure of all eyes. [1588] *I shall set his hand on sea and his right hand on rivers* (v. 25): I shall give him power over sea and over land; he indicated land by mention of *rivers. He will call upon me, You are my Father, my God, and the protector of my salvation* (v. 26) in Christ's saying, "Father, if it is possible, let this cup pass from me"; and in his saying also to the apostles, "I go to my Father and to your Father, my God and your God."[14]

(13) *I shall make him firstborn, elevated over the kings of the earth* (v. 27). This, of course, achieved its fulfillment in the time neither of David nor of the celebrated Solomon: neither Solomon nor David ruled the sea, or was called God's firstborn, or received the authority of all the kings. Aquila, in fact, rendered it this way, "most high among the kings of the earth," and Symmachus, "most elevated of the kings of the earth." But even if these words apply neither to David nor to Solomon, and since God's promise is not false, Jews are blind in refusing to adore the one who is from David according to the flesh, who has power of land and sea, and is superior to all the kings. He has worshippers who are willing, while refuting the limitation of those presuming to contradict [him]; though adopting countless wiles, they fail to get the better of the laws imposed by them. Blessed Paul also calls him *firstborn,* "So that he might be firstborn among many brethren"; and "firstborn from the dead," and "firstborn of all creation."[15] The Lord himself said to Mary after the resurrection, "Go, tell my brethren, I am going to my Father and your Father, my God and your God."[16] In other

14. In Theodoret's belief that there is no point in gilding the lily, the commentary has been reduced to brief paraphrase, interrupted here by some Scriptural documentation (Matt 26.39; John 20.17) from the long form of the text to lend a Christological flavor felt to be missing too long.

15. Rom 8.29; Col 1.18, 15.

16. John 20.17, a text that requires the theological explication Theodoret provides. The Christological implications of the verse he could not ignore.

words, just as he is only-begotten in being God (alone born of
the Father), and firstborn as a human being (in his humanity
having the believers as brethren), likewise as God he calls God
his Father, [1589] and as a human being he speaks of him as his
God. Accordingly, the prophecy reaches its fulfillment in him.
What follows also testifies to it. *Forever I shall maintain my mercy
for him, and my covenant with him will be faithful* (v. 28). He means
that the Lord would raise up the *covenant,* which God the Father
made with their ancestors, from their seed, as we said.

(14) *I shall establish his offspring forever and his throne like the
days of heaven* (v. 29). *His offspring* means the nurslings of grace
and the kingdom which he personally gave them, about which
the Lord said to those believing in him, "Come, you that are
blessed by my Father, inherit the kingdom prepared for you
from the foundation of the world."[17] Let the Jews, then, point
to the royal throne of David that lasts till this day, which God
promised to maintain forever. But let them also point to that
offspring of his adorned with the kingdom. If, however, they
are unable to demonstrate either of these, no matter how
shameless they are, one of two possibilities is left to them: either to call God's promise false or to admit the guarantee to be
true and accept the testimony of the facts. The Christ, who is
from David according to the flesh, after all, "is seated at the
right hand of the majesty on high, having become as much superior to the angels as the name he has inherited is more excellent than theirs. To which of the angels, after all, did [God]
ever say, You are my Son: this day I have begotten you?"[18] Of
him blessed David said, "Sit at my right hand until I make your
foes your footstool."[19] Actually, it is through Christ the Lord
that David's offspring lasted forever and his throne has continuity. Blessed Isaiah, in fact, prophesied to that effect. After saying, "A child has been born to us, a son has been given to us,
whose rule is on his shoulder," in case anyone should form the
impression the child was [1592] a human being and not God,
he expressed it more clearly through what follows in saying,

17. Matt 25.34, documenting an interpretation of the verse by the long
form of the text.
18. Heb 1.3–5; cf. Ps 2.7.   19. Ps 110.1.

"He has the name Angel of great counsel, wonderful, coun-
selor, mighty God, figure of authority, prince of peace, father of
the world to come." A little further on he added, "On the
throne of David and his kingdom to set it right from now and
for eternal time."[20]

(15) After thus making a prophecy about Christ the Lord,
the text treats of the kings coming in between. *If his children forsake my law and do not walk by my judgments; if they profane my ordinances and do not keep my commandments, I shall punish their iniquities with a rod and their wrongs with scourges. My mercy, however, I
shall not disperse from him nor be false to my truth* (vv. 30–33). Even
if those who take their lineage from David commit countless
transgressions, he is saying, I shall submit them to retributions
while keeping firm the promise to David. *My mercy, however, I
shall not disperse from him,* that is, from David, *nor be false to my
truth.* For *be false to* Symmachus said "break" and Aquila, "not
falsify." *I shall not be false,* that is, I shall not break or falsify my
promises.[21] *I shall not profane my covenant and nullify what proceeds
from my lips* (v. 34): I shall not falsify my pledges, I shall not
break the covenants, but show the truth of the promises when
my son, like me without beginning and end, is made flesh from
David; he says this also in what follows.

(16) *Once [and for all] I swore an oath by my holiness, not to be
false to David* (v. 35): keeping faith with my promise to him, I
shall bring it to fulfillment; he used *swore an oath* for keeping
faith, since those who make promises confirm them with an
oath. *His offspring will abide forever, and his throne like the sun in my
sight, and like the moon forever perfect, the faithful witness in heaven*
(vv. 36–37). In place of *the witness* Symmachus put "who gives
witness." In the seventy-first psalm blessed David prophesied
about Christ the Lord, "His name endures before the sun, and
[1593] will last as long as the sun, and before the moon for
generations of generations."[22] In other words, since the sun by

20. Cf. Isa 9.6–7. The paraphrase has given way to careful argumentation
(against Jewish claims) supported by Scripture, this being a key Christological
locus along with the two quoted.

21. Tautology—a vice abhorrent to Theodoret—is a weakness of the long
form of the text, as in this otiose comment.

22. Cf. Ps 72.5.

its rising and setting is responsible for the measurement of time, and is the cause of night and day, he wanted to show through the sun the permanence of the throne and promised to make his offspring eternal. All those believing in him are the *offspring* of God the Word. The one making this promise and giving this witness is in heaven and uses words that are faithful and true, as he alone does not lie.[23]

(17) Having thus mentioned the promises made to David, they lament the calamities fallen upon them. *You, however, rejected and scorned him, you repelled your anointed one, you overturned the covenant of your servant* (vv. 38–39). Symmachus, on the other hand, put it this way, "But you for your part spurned him and found him wanting; enraged against your anointed one, you delivered a curse on the covenant of your servant": but you for your part, after promising him those things, repelled David's successors, highlighted their worthlessness and gave them into slavery while also overthrowing his kingship and dissolving the covenants made with your devotee (referring to his kingship here by *anointed one*). The two successors of David, Jeconiah and Zedekiah, were taken captive, and with them the Davidic monarchy came to an end; Zerubbabel, who was in charge after the captivity, was a popular leader, not a king. *You defiled his sanctuary in the ground.* He calls *sanctuary* the Temple, which David had wished to build but Solomon erected after David; he means it was defiled by the incursion of the Babylonians, and became like a flowering plant, toppled and brought down to the dust, level with the soil.

(18) *You destroyed all his ramparts* (v. 40): you deprived him of all security. *He brought terror to his fortresses:* whoever trusted of old in the cities' walls lost confidence and became a prey to terror. *All who passed by plundered him* (v. 41): Moabites, Ammonites, Philistines, Idumeans, Syrians, Assyrians, and Babylonians. *He proved an object of reproach to his neighbors:* he became a source of ridicule and reproach to those nearby. *You exalted the right hand of those afflicting him* (v. 42): you rendered his enemies

23. These two final comments, from long and short forms of the text respectively, reveal the greater and lesser anxiety of two commentators to move to an eschatological interpretation before bringing out the literal sense of the verse.

stronger than him. [1596] *You gave joy to all his foes:* you made him a source of mockery to his adversaries. *You reversed the help given by his sword, and did not assist him in battle* (v. 43): his weapons proved useless to him, bereft as he was of your care.

(19) *You caused him to lose his cleanness* (v. 44). Symmachus, on the other hand, put it this way, "You put an end to his purity": being a captive and living far from your Temple, he was unable to purify himself with sprinkling. *You brought his throne crashing to the ground:* you completely overthrew his kingdom. *You cut short the days of his life* (v. 45): after promising to guard his kingdom forever, you limited it to a short period. *You covered him in shame.* He became an object of reproach, and was filled with shame. Zedekiah, in fact, his eyes put out, was consigned to a mill for all the rest of his life, and Jeconiah also served as a slave. This was the sum of their shame and ignominy.

(20) After thus outlining the calamities, the inspired word urges lament and supplication. *How long, O Lord? Do you turn away forever? Will your rage be inflamed like fire?* (v. 46). Symmachus, on the other hand, said, "How long, O Lord? Will you hide yourself forever? Will your anger blaze like fire?" To what point, O Lord, he is saying, do you wish to see our pangs without appearing and solving the problems, and instead enkindle your rage like fire with the recollection of our sins? *Call to mind what I am made of* (v. 47): you are maker and former, and you know the limits of my strength. *Surely it was not in vain, after all, that you created all children of human beings?* It was not idly or to no purpose that you formed human beings; rather, goodness determined creation. In other words, it was through goodness alone that you created us. So do not overlook those shackled with such great troubles. *Who is the man who will live and not see death, will rescue his soul from the hand of Hades?* (v. 48): death is everyone's fate; to survive death itself is not possible for us. So grant to the living a share in loving-kindness.

(21) Next in turn he recalls the promises. *Where are your mercies of old, Lord, which* [1597] *you swore to David in your truth?* (v. 49). He nicely offers on every occasion the testimony of truth to prompt the one making the promise to the confirmation of the pledges; he also composed his opening with mention of

mercy, and at the close recalls mercy once more, this being their particular need. *Be mindful, O Lord, of the reproach directed at your servant from many nations, which I bear in my bosom* (v. 50). Symmachus, on the other hand, put it this way, "and I carried them in my bosom from numerous nations."[24] Do not ignore the object of reproach I have become, he is saying, not in the sight of one nation but of thousands: not only Assyrians and Babylonians mock me, but as well all the neighboring peoples, who always bear a grudge against me. It is not only me they mock, but they move their tongue also against you and use blasphemous words, taking my slavery for your weakness. He indicated this, in fact, through what follows.

(22) *With which your foes reproached me, Lord, with which they reproached the exchange for your Christ* (v. 51). Symmachus and Theodotion, on the other hand, put it this way, "they reproached the footsteps of your Christ." He called the kings of that time "footsteps of Christ" since through them the word about Christ's kingdom traveled abroad. The Septuagint called them *exchange* as being his forebears according to the flesh and guiding the kingdom as though in some kind of darkness. In short, on account of your Christ whose "footsteps" and *exchange* these [kings] happen to be, bring our reproach against us to an end, Lord.[25]

(23) *Blessed be the Lord forever. So be it, so be it* (v. 52). The hymn singing arises from sound hope: having trusted that their petitions would be accepted, they offered this hymn to God. Aquila shows this sense even more clearly, rendering "Amen, Amen" by saying, "Trustworthy and reliable," that is, You are true, very true. Consequently, you are blessed forever: you confirm your promises with your works.[26]

24. Reference to Symmachus here, as often, seems a mark of deference rather than enlightenment for the reader.

25. The Septuagint and alternative versions struggle with the meaning of the Hebrew term, to determine which a modern commentator like Dahood has to have recourse to Ugaritic; and by his convenient means of rationalizing Theodoret vindicates them all to his satisfaction.

26. Theodoret shows no awareness that this verse, significant though he finds it, is a doxology forming a conclusion to the third book of Psalms, as likewise he has not noted previous divisions (ancient, if not original).

COMMENTARY ON PSALM 90

A prayer for Moses, man of God.

OME OF THE WRITERS claimed the great Moses made this prayer, others said blessed David was its composer but applied it to the divinely inspired Moses. [1600] Be that as it may, the psalm contains a twofold oracle: it not only prophesies the Jews' calamities but also teaches the corruptibility and impermanence of all human nature. It foretells, however, the change for the better in both cases. To be precise, the present psalm was also written by blessed David, like all the others.[1]

(2) *Lord, you have been our refuge in generation after generation* (v. 1). He proved a refuge for the Jews, in fact, not only in Egypt but also in the wilderness, in the time of Joshua son of Nun, Gideon, Barak and Jephthah, Samson, Samuel, and David; through the prophets he accorded them every care, and gave them every assistance when they were ruled by kings. The whole human race uses these words to remind God of the manifold favors, how he transported Enoch, how when everyone adopted the feral way of life he preserved the divinely inspired Noah as a spark for the race, how he chose the patriarch Abraham and promised the blessing for all the nations. It was not reluctantly, as some of the unbelievers presume to claim, that the Lord of all came for the betterment of the nations; rather, he always exercised his providence for all human beings as Lord of all, even before his incomprehensible Incarnation. The in-

---

1. We have previously seen Theodoret's flexibility on the question of authorship countermanded by the author of the long form of the text, who here again intervenes to show his dogmatism. Both forms of the text speak of the psalms being written, the former, unusually, even speaking of David as a *syngrapheus,* a term more applicable to a historian than to a liturgical musician.

spired composition taught us to say this, *Lord, you have been our refuge in generation after generation:* we always enjoyed your hope, O Lord. *Before the mountains were made, the earth and the world formed, and from age to age you are* (v. 2): you exist before all things came to birth—the mountains, the earth, the whole world—eternal as you are, without beginning or end, circumscribed by no boundary. The phrase *Before the mountains were made* is to be connected with *you are.*

(3) *Do not reduce a human being to lowliness* (v. 3): I therefore beg you, everlasting and eternal as you are, ever our refuge, not to ignore us completely, beset by such problems as we are. Since he had sentenced Adam to sweat and toil in the words, "In the sweat of your brow you are to eat your bread until you return to the earth from which you were taken, because you are earth and to earth you will return,"[2] it was appropriate for the inspired word to teach us to make supplication that we not be utterly reduced to a lowly state and to predestined hardship. [1601] Jews, of course, who were forced into slavery, offer this prayer, bewailing their captivity and slavery. *And you said, Turn back, sons of human beings.* Aquila, on the other hand, put it this way, "And you will say, Turn back, sons of human beings." It is not idly that we pray, he is saying, but in the clear knowledge that you receive our supplication and effect a change in our current problems, urging us to turn back and be rid of the former wickedness.

(4) *Because a thousand years in your eyes, O Lord, are like yesterday when it is past, and a watch at night* (v. 4). The expression is hyperbolic, corresponding to the former verse, *Do not reduce a human being to lowliness, because a thousand years in your eyes, O Lord, are like yesterday when it is past, and a watch at night.* But in the middle occurs the clause, *And you said, Turn back, sons of human beings.* He means, The life of human beings is a brief and extremely painful thing, whereas to you, everlasting and eternal as you are, with whom the number of a thousand years resembles one day, it is more like a brief part of the night. He referred to a quarter of the night as a night watch, as those given

2. Gen 3.19.

the charge of keeping watch divide it fourfold; the Lord also came to the apostles at the fourth watch.[3]

(5) *Their years will count for nothing* (v. 5). Over a long period, he is saying, you submitted them to this hardship. At the same time, however, he refers to the rejection of the Jews after the passion of our Savior and their deprivation of the divine care that would continue not for a short time but for a long period. *Let them disappear like grass in the morning, flowering in the morning and disappearing, falling in the evening, hardening and withering* (vv. 5–6). Simply put, in other words, Jews were beneficiaries of divine attention, they blossomed and grew, and acquired a great splendor; but they refused to provide the farmer with fruit in due season, and instead hardened their heart and were completely dried up, no longer having a share of the former irrigation. He calls *morning* the beginning of the Jews' devotion, and *evening* the cessation of the divine care, when they were deprived of it following the crucifixion because they erected the cross against the God and Savior, as he says in what follows.

(6) *Because we fainted under your rage, and were confounded by your anger* (v. 7). This relates both to the Jews and to all human beings: human nature, paying the penalty for lawlessness, was affected with [1604] disasters and beset with cataclysms of all kinds, and Jews lost their freedom on account of the wickedness of their attitude, as many people dug a pit for themselves through infidelity: "He sank a pit and dug it out, and fell into the hole he had made."[4] *You set our iniquities before you, our age as a light to your countenance* (v. 8). Symmachus, on the other hand, put it this way, "You brought our iniquities openly before you, our faults to be obvious to your face": you gave us over to these punishments, perceiving us to be neglectful of your laws and instead choosing to live a life of iniquity.

(7) *Because all our days have passed away, and we have passed away in your rage* (v. 9). Sin provoked [your] rage against us, he

3. Cf. Matt 14.25. Theodoret helps his reader to detect hyperbole in lyrical expression and other figures based on practices in biblical times.
4. Ps 7.15. The long form of the text cannot resist embellishing Theodoret's simple comparison.

is saying, rage brought retribution, and retribution inflicted pains, our short life being spent in pains. *Our years murmured like a spider.* Human nature, he is saying, has nothing firm or stable, but is torn apart easily like a spider.[5] *The days of our years amount to seventy years, and eighty years if we are at full strength, and beyond that trouble and hardship* (v. 10). This is like the saying of the patriarch Jacob, "My days are few and evil, they have not amounted to the days of my ancestors."[6] There really are some people who live longer than the period mentioned, but it happens to few; here, on the other hand, he teaches the normal experience prevailing in most cases. In other words, just as he made no mention of the death of those who die before their time, likewise he also dismissed the long life of those who live to a great age. Even this short period, he is saying, is nonetheless full of pain and troubles, just as the period of seventy years that those served who were taken captive from Jerusalem proved very harsh and painful to the captives. *Because gentleness came upon us, and we shall be chastised:* behold how many troubles beset us because of your mild rage; he called the moderate retribution befalling them *gentleness.*

(8) *Who knows the force of your rage, and your anger from fear of you?* (v. 11). Symmachus, [1605] on the other hand, put it this way, "Who knows the strength of your anger, and your rage in keeping with your fear?" If your moderate indignation imposed such chastisement, he is saying, who is capable of comprehending the retribution brought on by your rage? The verse touches on eternal punishment. *Instruct me thus in taking account of your right hand and of those whose hearts are under the constraint of wisdom* (v. 12). I beg to enjoy your kindness, he is saying, to take account of your right hand, describe the gifts, and imitate those given wisdom by your grace, who guide the others towards knowledge of you.

(9) *Turn back, O Lord! How long? Comfort your servants* (v. 13): do not ignore at length people in pain, O Lord, but receive

5. Theodoret joins the number of commentators who wonder "how the spider got into the psalm," in the title of an article by Ely Pilchik (*Science* 151 [Jan 1966]: 404–405), though Dahood sees the Hebrew meaning rather "sigh"; the sense of the verb is also puzzling.
6. Gen 47.9.

their prayer and accord your servants loving-kindness. *We were filled in the morning with your mercy, we rejoiced and were glad all our days* (v. 14). The tense has been changed by the Septuagint: Aquila and the others say this, "Fill us in the morning with your mercy, we shall praise and be glad all our days."[7] They say *in the morning* and *at dawn* to the change in the calamities: they beg there that darkness be scattered and the light [of the sun] rise for them, not on account of their own virtue but through divine mercy. Since this is to come, he is saying, in other words, we shall be filled with complete satisfaction and offer the appropriate hymn singing. *We were glad for as many days as you humbled us, as many years as we saw troubles* (v. 15). Here likewise the tense has been changed: Symmachus and the others say, "Give us joy." Provide satisfaction in place of discouragement, he is saying, and grant a change in the misfortune besetting us.

(10) *Look upon your servants and upon your works* (v. 16). From this it is clear that they spoke of this not as having happened but as yet to come: they did not say, You looked upon your servants and upon your works. We are your works, he is saying, and servants of your lordship—hence we beg to attain your providence. *And guide your children,* that is, your servants: both those in Babylon offering supplication ask God [1608] to lead back the children of his servants who have died, and the human race urges that those people who are found in the appearance of our Savior be guided to the truth.

(11) *May the splendor of the Lord our God be upon us* (v. 17). He calls the Incarnation of God the Word *splendor;* then it was that the light of the knowledge of God rendered us splendid and illustrious. Of him the Son of Thunder said, "The light shines in the darkness."[8] After the return Jews became the cynosure of all eyes again. *Direct the works of our hands upon us, direct the work of our hands.* The addition of *upon us* was nice: the benefit of righteousness is ours; and while God works in association with the lovers of virtue, and with them carries out its achievements,

---

7. It is reference to the alternative versions, not to the original, that apprises Theodoret of the misreading of tense by the LXX (in rare cases, the majority escaping notice).

8. John 1.5, the Christological comment and documentation coming from the long form of the text.

those who sow the seed reap fruit from them. God, after all, is in need of nothing, yet he rejoices in both the good fortune and success of human beings whenever they bring themselves whole and entire to him as a victim, as Paul instructs, "I urge you through the mercies of God to present your bodies as a living sacrifice, holy, pleasing to God, your rational worship."[9] Amen.

9. In commentary on v. 14 Theodoret was careful to stress the priority of divine mercy to human virtue. Here—before the long form of the text introduces a liturgical note with Pauline support—he swings the balance back, not to present an independent movement but rather a divine synergy with the behavior of the virtuous.

COMMENTARY ON PSALM 91

A song's praise, for David. No title in the Hebrew.

HILE THE PSALM HAS no title, it teaches the invincibility of hope in God. Blessed David, in fact, perceived with spiritual eyes from a distance the situation of blessed Hezekiah, and seeing how with hope in God he overthrew the army of the Assyrians, he uttered this psalm to teach all people how great an abundance of goods trusting in God yields. Everyone who is guided by this song is made secure in his life, and with his trust in the Savior makes a prayer.

(2) *The one who dwells in help of the Most High will lodge under the shelter of the God of heaven* (v. 1). Whoever is confident of the divine care, he is saying, will enjoy the protection of the God of heaven and will have this secure rampart and safe refuge. When he bears this shield and is kept safe and sound by being helped by him, then he will say, *He will say to God,*[1] *You are my protector and my refuge, my God, and I hope in* [1609] *in him* (v. 2): having a firm hope in him, he will call him leader, caretaker, and impregnable rampart. *Because he will rescue me from a hunters' snare and from a wild word* (v. 3). Here then he goes on to address his remarks to the one who trusts, saying that he renders him superior not only to obvious enemies but also to those who lie in wait, watching and hatching secret schemes, by *snare* suggesting the furtive scheme. For *a wild word* Symmachus said "a word of spite"; such people spread lies and calumnies, yet many proved superior even to them by means of hope in God. This was the way the great Joseph, subjected to the calumny of the adulteress, escaped her wiles; this the way the remarkable Susannah enjoyed assistance from on high—and not only they,

---

1. Clearly this brief insertion from the long form of the text is not original, failing to note the resultant tautology.

but even up to the present time we have heard also of vast numbers beyond counting and know them to be saved.

(3) *With his back he will overshadow you, and under his wings you
will have hope* (v. 4): he will prove your champion, and will hide
you when under attack. He used this as a figure of those posi-
tioned in the front rank, who cover those in the rear with their
back, whereas by *wings* he refers to the operation of providence, employing it by use of the image of birds, as they cover
the young with their wings. Blessed Moses likewise referred to
God's care: he guarded them as the apple of his eye, he says,
like an eagle, to cover its nest, and yearned for its young,
stretching its wings it welcomed them and took them up on its
back.[2] The Lord also said this to Jerusalem: "How often have I
desired to gather your children together in the way a bird gath-
ers together its chicks, and you refused."[3] *His truth will surround
you with a shield.* Since he mentioned above *a wild word* and
falsehood, it was appropriate here to promise his truth as his armor.

(4) *You will not fear a fear of the night, an arrow* [1612] *that flies
by day, a thing moving in darkness, a mischance and demon at noon*
(vv. 5–6): you will prevail not only over visible adversaries but
also over those of the mind, thanks to hope in God, and you
will escape the schemes working at night and the assaults made
by the enemy during the day; having confidence as one under
God's protection, you will drive out fear and, far from being in
difficulties at midday, you will escape the demons' stratagems,
sharing in the assistance from on high. He made mention of
the noonday demon in keeping with popular opinion; yet it is
not unlikely that those schemers against humankind after a
heavy meal launch an assault as though to a prey prepared for
them, and easily enslave those deprived of care from on high.[4]

(5) *A thousand will fall at your side, ten thousand at your right
hand, but to you they will not come near. You will, however, observe*

2. Cf. Deut 32.10–11.
3. Matt 23.37.
4. Weiser, who sees these verses touching on "sinister and gruesome forces
that existed in popular belief," agrees with Theodoret about the noonday devil:
"Among many peoples noonday is thought of as the hour of evil spirits just as
midnight is."

with your eyes and see retribution of sinners (vv. 7–8). For *your side* Symmachus and Aquila put "in flank." This means, Even if a vast multitude approach from the right or the left, no harm will come to you, and instead you will see them stricken with a divine blow. This happened also in the time of Hezekiah: a hundred and eighty-five thousand Assyrians were overwhelmed, not to mention military equipment;[5] likewise in the case of Gideon and Jonathan, and of course in the case also of Jehoshaphat and the prophet Elisha this same thing happened.

(6) *Because you, Lord, my hope, set the Most High as my refuge* (v. 9). You would enjoy this providence, he is saying, if you exercised hope in God and made it your refuge. There is missing from the structure of the verse the word *You said, You, Lord, are my hope;* this is a feature of Old Testament writing, especially of the Psalms.[6] Still, the sequence clarifies the ambiguity: since you hope in God, he is saying, and call him to your assistance, you will encounter care on his part. *Troubles will not come upon you, nor a scourge come near your tent* (v. 10): you will be proof against the devil's shafts and suffer no harm from them. In this way divine grace fenced round the house of Job, to which the enemy testifies in his loud cry, "Have you not put a fence round both what is inside and what is outside his house?"[7] [1613] When allowed, on the other hand, he demonstrated his characteristic wickedness, and the just Judge crowned the victorious athlete.

(7) *Because he will command his angels concerning you to guard you in all your ways* (v. 11). This he said also in the thirty-third psalm, "The angel of the Lord will encamp around those who fear him and deliver them."[8] We also heard the patriarch Jacob saying, "The angel who has delivered me from all the troubles"; and the great Abraham said by way of encouragement of his servant, "God will send his angel before you, and you will take a

5. 2 Kings 19.35, an incident Theodoret loves to cite—though would the destroying angel have busied himself with the hardware?
6. Theodoret does not pass over the ellipsis which modern commentators refer to as "a long-standing problem" (Dahood), magisterially remarking it is a common biblical phenomenon, and providing a solution of his own.
7. Job 1.10.
8. Ps 34.7.

wife for my son Isaac from there."[9] So everywhere we learn that
by means of angels the God of all guards those who trust in
him. *They will carry you in their hands lest you dash your foot against
the stone* (v. 12): you will enjoy the manifold providence on their
part lest the slightest harm come to you from there; he suggested the slight degree of harm by the kicking of the stone. The
phrase *They will carry you in their hands* means they will guide,
lead, offer all kinds of assistance.

(8) *You will tread on asp and basilisk, and tread underfoot lion
and dragon* (v. 13). He cited the most powerful and lethal animals, wishing to bring out the dominance over every form of
evil: by mention of *lion and dragon* he indicated strength, these
beasts being altogether powerful, whereas by mention of *asp
and basilisk* he hinted at the extremity of evil, the former inject-
ing deadly poison, the latter causing death on sight. Of course,
many of those who trusted in God were proof against even the
wild animals: thus the remarkable Daniel shut the lions'
mouths,[10] thus the divinely inspired Paul took no harm from
the viper,[11] and to put it in a nutshell let us revert to ancient examples; thus Noe lived among the animals and was kept free of
harm; thus countless numbers of people embracing the eremit-
ical life lived with the beasts and through hope in God were
proof against harm from them.

(9) *Because he hoped in me, and I shall deliver him; I shall overshadow him because he acknowledged my name. He will cry to me, and
I shall hearken to him* (vv. 14–15). [1616] The God of all said this
then to teach us what the fruit of hope is: *I shall deliver him,* he

9. Cf. Gen 48.16; 24.7. The amount of Scriptural documentation suggests
that in commentary on this psalm, whose lack of a title helps Theodoret play
down historical associations, he is able to plumb the true meaning at some
depth. Modern commentators, too, remark on the sense which he finds here:
"Together with Psalm 46, Psalm 91 is the most impressive testimony in the
Psalter to the strength that springs from trust in God" (Weiser).

10. The freedom Theodoret feels in commentary on this psalm to bring out
the force of imagery is enhanced here where real and fabled animals come in
for mention, natural science being an interest of his. He can also document the
psalmist's point about them from Scripture, such as Daniel's experience.

11. Cf. Acts 28.1–6. The author of the long form of the text, perhaps thinking Theodoret's procedure is retrogressive in going from Paul to Noah, and un-
mindful of the reference to Daniel, now inserts a confusing rubric.

says, from the words of visible and invisible schemers,[12] protected as he is by my hope; for this reason I shall both guard and
overshadow him, I shall listen to him when he speaks, and accept his petition. *I am with him in tribulation:* if he encounters
any trial, I shall accompany him and offer him adequate comfort. *I shall rescue him and glorify him:* not only shall I rid him of
the distress, but I shall also bring him into prominence. *I shall
fill him with length of days, and show him my salvation* (v. 16): I
shall ensure he reaches ripe old age, and shall reveal the salvation coming to him in the next life. Blessed Hezekiah also enjoyed these [benefits]: asking for an extended life, he received
a span of fifteen years,[13] and acquired great luster also from the
destruction of the Assyrians; very applicable to him, too, is the
verse, *I shall rescue him and glorify him, and I shall show him my salvation.* All those who have hoped in God, however, shall also enjoy goods of all kinds, as both the ancient accounts teach and
the events now before our eyes give witness.

12. Amidst all the troubles that beset the righteous, in the experience of
both the psalmists and Theodoret, the wiles and machinations of schemers figure prominently. Is the bishop reflecting the intrigues that marked his life?

13. 2 Kings 20.6. Fortunately, after the opening nod in this king's direction,
Theodoret has kept him at arm's length, enabling the treatment to reach an
unusual degree of general spiritual comment.

COMMENTARY ON PSALM 92

A psalm of a song, for the Sabbath day.

HE SABBATH PRESCRIBED leisure, but not complete leisure: it involved much greater spiritual activity. In fact, it required people to be concerned with prayers and hymns, and to offer to God double sacrifices. Consequently, the Law on the Sabbath prescribed abstinence from bodily exertions. So since the life to come is free of such cares, rest is properly enjoined. This is the reason, to be sure, why blessed Paul also cries out, "Let us be anxious to enter into his rest"; and again, "Sabbath rest, then, awaits [1617] the people of God."[1] So since the psalm foretells the honor for the righteous and the punishment of the wicked, and since this will happen in that rest, it is right that it takes this title.

(2) *It is good to confess to the Lord, and to sing psalms to your name, O Most High, so as to announce your mercy in the morning and your truth by night* (vv. 2–3). Useful and advantageous is it, he is saying, by night and day to sing your praises as benefactor and describe your beneficence, your loving-kindness towards us, your truth against wrongdoers: exercising truth you duly punish them while according providence to us for our acknowledgment of you. *On a ten-stringed harp with a song on a lyre* (v. 3). They normally celebrated God on such instruments; so he says, It is right for us to perform on the prescribed instruments and call into play the singing of the tongue, and thus offer you the hymn of thanksgiving. *Because you, O Lord, have made me glad with your works, and I shall rejoice in the deeds of your hands* (v. 4): observing your creations and your ineffable arrangements, I rejoice and exult, and with satisfaction of soul I move my tongue to hymn singing.

1. Heb 4.11, 9.

(3) *How your works are magnified, O Lord, your thoughts reached the very depths* (v. 5). Symmachus, on the other hand, put it this way, "Very deep are your thoughts." Aquila and Theodotion, however, [say], "[How] profound they have become." In other words, Your works, he is saying, are great and marvelous (he used *How* to indicate extension), whereas your wisdom has depths that cannot be plumbed. What mind, after all, could suffice to take account of the designs of your providence? Yet we teach it even to the ignorant, whereas those without brains and bereft of reason neither wish to understand it nor bring themselves to learn it from others. This, in fact, is what he goes on to imply: *A foolish man will not know it, and a dullard will not understand it* (v. 6). He put this in different ways: the one with brain trouble and devoid of understanding will know nothing of this, nor even wish to hear anything about it.

(4) *When sinners sprouted like hay and all workers of iniquity came to light so as to perish forever* (v. 7). Aquila said "blossomed" for *came to light,* and [1620] Symmachus likewise: the fools did not want to understand that the workers of iniquity blossomed like hay and came to light from the soil like grass, and will win themselves everlasting ruin after the present good fortune; but calling themselves enviable and blessed, they will promptly witness their own most miserable end. *You, Lord, on the contrary, are most high forever. Because, behold, your foes, O Lord, because, behold, your foes will perish, and all the workers of iniquity will be scattered* (vv. 8–9): whereas they will fade and perish like hay, you have power over all, being exalted above all and subjecting to punishments those in the grip of frenzy.

(5) *My horn will be exalted like a unicorn* (v. 10): we, on the other hand, who have knowledge of you, on seeing the overthrow of your foes shall exult in you and enjoy good cheer for being freed from the error of polytheism and adoring you as the true God, having received the horn of the cross as shield against passions and demons.[2] He introduced the unicorn again at this point to indicate through the one horn the one God: as that

2. The author of the long form of the text feels it is time for a Christological comment—whereas Theodoret is about to develop quite a different interpretation of the verse.

creature had one horn by nature, so the nurslings of religion adore one divinity. *My old age in rich oil.* Symmachus, on the other hand, put it this way, "My aging like fine oil": I shall blossom and lay aside old age, I shall be like abundant oil, and, according to the Septuagint, I shall abound in satisfaction like oil of some kind.[3]

(6) *My eye looked down on my foes, and my ear will hear of the evildoers' rising up against me* (v. 11). For *looked down* Symmachus and Theodotion and the Hebrew itself said "will look down": the words are a prophecy of the future, but the Septuagint in normal fashion rendered the future as past, by this implying the inevitability of the prophecy.[4] [1621] Just as it is impossible for what had happened not to happen, so it is impossible for the prophecy of the Spirit to remain unfulfilled; so he means, Not only shall I see the disastrous end of the wicked, but I shall also hear everyone announcing it and marveling at the justice of the retribution. This, surely, is the way it divides up: *of the evildoers' rising up against me* is here to be kept separate, then add, *my ear will hear:* I shall hear many recounting the overthrow of those living a life of lawlessness and plotting countless evils for me.

(7) *A righteous person will blossom like a palm tree and flourish like a cedar in Lebanon* (v. 12): sinners, then, having bloomed like grass, promptly withered and died, whereas the righteous person will resemble the cedar's thickness, freshness, and nourishment and the palm tree's abundance of foliage and fruit. Both last a very long time and require time for growing. The growth of virtue is like that, growing up over a long time and requiring much attention, yet reaching on high, bearing fruit in season and of pleasant taste, and providing sufficient shade for its owner, as it is planted in the divine paradise in the house of

3. Theodoret wrestles with an obscure phrase, calling first on Symmachus for enlightenment, and then doing some justice to his LXX, whereas on v. 7 he found the consensus of Aquila and Symmachus telling.

4. As with Ps 90.14, Theodoret notes that the alternative versions differ from the LXX in rendering the tense of the first verb, and sides with them, claiming support from the original. Unfortunately for him, it is the tense of the second verb that the LXX has misread, the other versions this time misreading the Hebrew of the first. "A little knowledge . . ."

God, as he says more clearly in what follows by saying, *Planted in the house of the Lord, they shall flourish in the courts of our God* (v. 13). These people, he is saying, who are compared to these trees, have God as husbandman, and the divine Temple as garden.

(8) *They will be still more productive in a rich old age, and will be well off, so as to announce that the Lord our God is upright, and there is no injustice in him* (vv. 14–15). Symmachus, on the other hand, put it this way, "As they grow old they will yield still more fruit, they will be rich and luxuriant, announcing that the God who guards me is right, and there is no injustice in him": in the future life they will receive the promised maturity, and will offer more rich fruit to God, singing of his just verdict; the Incarnation, at one time hidden, they will now see as it comes to light, and will marvel at his wisdom and celebrate his righteousness. He applied the term *old age* to maturity: [1624] we call the old person mature and the young immature; so by *old age* he indicated the future maturity in which the manifold fruit of righteousness will grow and the righteousness of God become clear to everyone.

COMMENTARY ON PSALM 93

A song of praise for David. No title in the Hebrew.

THE PHRASE "NO TITLE in the Hebrew" is not in the Hexapla, nor in Eusebius.[1] The psalm prophesies the change in people: God is immutable and unchanging,[2] always the same in manner and substance, not a king at one time and without kingship at another; rather, he is always king by nature, though this has not always been clear to people. For most of the time, in fact, the majority were ignorant of him, and offered to idols the worship due to God; but after the Incarnation of our God and Savior, the knowledge of God spanned the entire world like a light. He is, in fact, "the true light, which enlightens human beings coming into the world";[3] for this reason the inspired mind says in prospect, *The Lord reigned, he was clad in comeliness* (v. 1). Since the Passion seemed a sad event to those who understood the fruit stemming from it to the extent that the inspired author cries aloud, "We saw him, and he had no appearance of beauty, his appearance instead being dishonorable, disreputable by comparison with sons of human beings."[4] But after the birth from a Virgin, willing ac-

1. Theodoret does not indicate whether the phrase is correct in saying the Hebrew has no title (though even his minimal grasp of the language could surely have informed him), nor where he found the phrase—perhaps in some of those "copies" of the LXX he refers to at times. But he does betray that he has to hand a copy of Eusebius's *Commentary on the Psalms,* on which at least once we have seen him very dependent (cf. Ps 16.5) and which has been thought to be his principal means of accessing Alexandrian commentary.

2. Again that key term that would shortly figure in the Chalcedonian formula, ἀτρέπτως, immutable.

3. John 1.9, a text that comes to the mind of the author of the long form of the text with Theodoret's comparison.

4. Cf. Isa 53.2. The long form of the text then cites virgin birth and crucifixion to document this point, Theodoret being content to mention the ascension.

ceptance of crucifixion and ascent into heaven, he dispatched rays of light befitting God. So it was right for the inspired author to cry aloud, *The Lord reigned, he was clad in comeliness:* he did not take what was not his, but gave a glimpse of what was his. This is the way he speaks also to his own Father, "Father, glorify me with the glory I had in your presence before the world was made,"[5] not being without glory after the Incarnation, but as testimony to that text, [1625] "This is my beloved Son, in whom I am well pleased: listen to him."[6]

(2) *The Lord was clad and girded with power.* The fact that "Christ is the power of God and the wisdom of God" the divine Paul clearly taught us.[7] Consequently, he did not receive from any other source power that he did not have before; rather, it was his own power he employed against the enemies, though the inspired word presents him as a kind of king girt with royal armor, using a belt in his struggle against the enemies. He then goes on to show the achievements coming from this: *He established the world, which will not be moved.* He made the world firm and immovable, he is saying, having the stability of divine knowledge and being free of the error of falsehood: no longer do people adore some gods at one time and others at another; instead, they offer worship to the true God.

(3) *Your throne is prepared from that time, you are from eternity* (v. 2). It was not just now, he is saying, that you received election as king: you possess eternal sway and everlasting kingship. About his kingship he says also in the forty-fourth psalm, "Your throne, O God, is for ages of ages."[8] And his unchangeableness and immutability he likewise taught us in the hundred and first psalm, "You are the same," he says, "and your years will not come to an end":[9] even though you became man, you did not

5. John 17.5.

6. A conflation of texts from Gospel accounts of Jesus' baptism and transfiguration, supplied by the long form of the text to avoid the impression that Jesus was without glory after the Incarnation.

7. 1 Cor 1.24.

8. Ps 45.6.

9. Ps 102.27. The long form of the text, which has been particularly anxious in commentary on this psalm to eliminate the possibility of any theological misunderstanding by the reader, immediately inserts a further reminder.

lack divinity, nor were you separated from the Father or the all-holy Spirit, there being one substance of the undefiled Trinity, one kingship, one lordship. Both testimonies, of course, blessed Paul referred to Christ the Lord.[10]

(4) *The rivers lifted up, O Lord, the rivers lifted up their voices, the rivers will raise their pounding* (v. 3). He gives the name *rivers* to the sacred apostles and those accepting the message after them: they provided human beings with complete watering like rivers. The blessed Habakkuk also named them thus: "Earth will be split with rivers,"[11] that is, will be divided and will receive watering. The Lord also spoke in similar fashion: "As Scripture said, rivers of living water will flow from the belly of the one be-lieving in me."[12] These rivers, then, raised their voice, preach-ing the divine teachings and making their own ways. He called the paths *pounding:* since water is naturally in the habit of wear-ing down the earth under it and making a way, [1628] he was right to call the rivers' way wearing; those who were the first to be entrusted with the message prepared the way for those who came next, and rendered the teaching for them free of trouble and difficulty.[13]

(5) *Awesome the heavings of the sea beyond sounds of many waters* (v. 4): like mighty rivers pouring into the ocean and having an impact on the sand of the sea, and the waves for the most part arching under the resistance of the rivers, so too when the sweetness and taste of the apostles' teaching is brought to bear on the world's saltiness and bitterness, a storm develops and waves crash against one another. Blessed Habakkuk foresaw this as well: after saying, "Earth will be split with rivers, people will see you and be pained," to distinguish waters from the move-ment he added, "The deep uttered its voice, height of its imag-

10. Heb 1.8, 12.
11. Cf. Hab 3.9. The future tense erroneously given by the LXX to verbs in psalm and prophet encourages Theodoret to develop an eschatological sense.
12. John 7.38, which Theodoret sees dependent on Habakkuk, but which resembles also Isa 44.3 and Isa 58.11.
13. The rare Greek term, *epitripsis,* "pounding," representing a *hapax legomenon* in the Hebrew, needs explanation, and Theodoret, whom we have seen to be willing as a naturalist to unpack the psalmist's figurative language, obliges again before developing the eschatological sense.

ining."[14] Every city is filled with this kind of storm, the statement of the Lord being, "I came to bring not peace to the world but a sword, to divide a man from his neighbor, a son from his father, a daughter from her mother, a daughter-in-law from her mother-in-law."[15] The beginning of the preaching, however, was marked by a storm, whereas now the master of the sea has chastened the tempest and turned it into a breeze, its billows have fallen silent, and a great tranquillity has developed. *Awesome is the Lord in the heights.* Aquila, on the other hand, put it this way, "The Lord magnificent on high." He put it this way in keeping with the preceding to bring out the might of the achievement: the Lord is magnificent and most high, having a strength that can neither be measured in word nor grasped in mind. He calls the great patriarchs *the heights* as well as the Old Testament inspired authors and the sacred apostles, as well as all those of their kind.[16]

(6) *Your testimonies, O Lord, were made exceedingly credible* (v. 5): you prophesied all this from of old, and announced it in advance through your holy prophets, and it has been shown to be true by the testimony of the events. The addition of *exceedingly* was also good, meaning, A chance falsehood cannot be discerned in the prophecies, whereas everything now seen was prophesied precisely. *Holiness befits your house, O Lord, for length of days:* the greatest and finest of all the good things is the fact that the enjoyment of the gifts is not transitory or limited to certain times in the style of the worship of Jews;[17] rather, [1629] it is permanent, stable, and everlasting, this being suited and appropriate to your new house. The divinely inspired Paul gave the name "house of God" to the assembly of the believers, to whom the inspired author said *holiness is fitting.* Accordingly, it behooves us, in keeping with the apostolic exhortation, to "pu-

14. Cf. Hab 3.9–10.
15. Matt 10.34–35.
16. In this far-fetched codicil, the long form of the text makes the distinction between Old Testament authors *(prophetai)* and New that we have seen.
17. Though Theodoret is generally not reluctant to concede privileges of the Jews of Old Testament times, the generally eschatological sense he has given to the psalm dissuades him from allowing this verse to apply to Jews and Temple of old, unlike modern commentators.

rify ourselves of every defilement of body and spirit, and bring sanctification to completion in fear of God,"[18] so that by preparing the house of God we may welcome the eternal guest.

18. 2 Cor 7.1 (the preceding Pauline reference is not clear). No historical event having been predicated as underlying the psalm, Theodoret comes close to a rare peroration in applying the verse to general Christian living.

COMMENTARY ON PSALM 94

A psalm for David, on the fourth Sabbath day.
No title in the Hebrew.

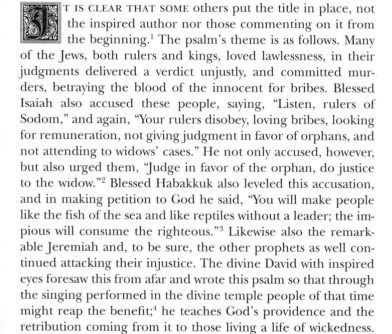T IS CLEAR THAT SOME others put the title in place, not the inspired author nor those commenting on it from the beginning.[1] The psalm's theme is as follows. Many of the Jews, both rulers and kings, loved lawlessness, in their judgments delivered a verdict unjustly, and committed murders, betraying the blood of the innocent for bribes. Blessed Isaiah also accused these people, saying, "Listen, rulers of Sodom," and again, "Your rulers disobey, loving bribes, looking for remuneration, not giving judgment in favor of orphans, and not attending to widows' cases." He not only accused, however, but also urged them, "Judge in favor of the orphan, do justice to the widow."[2] Blessed Habakkuk also leveled this accusation, and in making petition to God he said, "You will make people like the fish of the sea and like reptiles without a leader; the impious will consume the righteous."[3] Likewise also the remarkable Jeremiah and, to be sure, the other prophets as well continued attacking their injustice. The divine David with inspired eyes foresaw this from afar and wrote this psalm so that through the singing performed in the divine temple people of that time might reap the benefit;[4] he teaches God's providence and the retribution coming from it to those living a life of wickedness.

1. This represents a departure from Theodoret's position taken in the preface, where the authority of the LXX "not without divine inspiration" was invoked to defend the authenticity of the psalm titles. In the meantime he has had enough experience of titles found in Greek versions but not in the Hebrew to encourage him here to concede a different source.

2. Isa 1.10, 23, 17.

3. Cf. Hab 1.14, 13.

4. A rare acknowledgment by Theodoret of the original liturgical purpose and setting of the psalms.

He presents the psalm in the person of those nourished on piety, who were enduring these things at the hands of those people.

(2) *The Lord, God of vengeance, the God of vengeance has spoken freely* (v. 1). In place of *has spoken freely* Aquila, on the other hand, said "Appear!" and so did the other translators. I beseech you, he is saying, God and Lord of all, [1632] directing creation and inflicting due penalty on the unjust, hearken and accept my petition. *Rise up, you who judge the earth, render the haughty their just deserts* (v. 2): make clear to everyone the sublimity of your lordship, and undo the pride of the arrogant, teaching them through experience that you are the judge of the world. *How long will sinners, O Lord, how long will sinners boast? They will have their say, and will speak iniquity, all those responsible for lawlessness will speak* (vv. 3–4). His petition is not for the transgressors to suffer ruin, but for them not to have influence and enjoy authority sufficient for injustice.

(3) *They humbled your people, O Lord, and abused your inheritance. They killed widow and orphan, and murdered the stranger* (vv. 5–6): every form of injustice, O Lord, is committed by them; they swagger about in their influence, and use unjust language, while their actions are worse than their language. Women bereft of their partners and those lamenting loss of parents are their victims, like prey ripe for the taking. Those who have come from the nations in the desire to live a life in keeping with your laws suffer unmerited execution at their hands; these he called *strangers. They claimed, No one will see, nor will the God of Jacob understand* (v. 7): The height of impiety! They actually reach on this, he is saying, through not believing that you observe or take an interest in human affairs. The phrase *God of Jacob* does not occur without purpose; rather, it is to heighten the accusation: despite learning of God's great providence for the people shown through the inspired authors, through the priests,[5] in [time of] war and in [time of] peace, they have no fear of the God of all as one who observes them.

(4) Based on this consideration he introduces advice and ex-

5. Theodoret, we have seen, is not reluctant to concede the gifts God gave to the Old Testament people, such as the biblical authors and the priesthood.

hortation, not only for those affected in that way at that time but also for those ruling now and in the future. *Get some sense, you fools among the people, and finally come to your senses, you dullards* (v. 8): finally at least, O fools, you were willing to get sense and learn the way things are, that the present life is in the condition of a spider's web. [1633] *He who planted the ear, does he not hear? He who formed the eye, does he not observe?* (v. 9). He proposed the teaching very logically: the one who formed the eye from mud, he is saying, and endowed it with the faculty of sight, and likewise created the ears and granted the faculty of hearing—does he himself not see nor hear, and is he deprived of the faculty, though its creator, that he gave to the others?

(5) *Will not the one who corrects nations reprove?* (v. 10). The nations, he is saying, that neither received the Law nor enjoyed the teaching of the inspired authors—will he subject them to correction and not reprove your lawlessness? *He who teaches human beings knowledge:* it was he, in fact, who created human nature with reason, and brings about greater knowledge through the things observable in creation and happening every day. *The Lord knows that the thoughts of human beings are futile* (v. 11): he not only sees and hears, however; rather, he understands our thinking that comes up with wrong ideas about his providence. Likewise, he devises a treatment adapted to them, and offers sufficient consolation for those who are wronged; to make it more persuasive he puts it in words.

(6) *Blessed is the man whom you correct, O Lord; you will teach him from your Law* (v. 12): many are in the habit of classing as miserable those who embrace piety and resist iniquity (whereas I class them as enviable and blessed for being exercised in discipline) and those who reap the benefit of the divine Law. *To give him respite from evil days* (v. 13): receiving harsh correction in the present life, he will have a milder judgment in the future; he used *evil day* of the everlasting punishment. *Until a pit is dug for the sinner:* those embracing lawlessness will be consigned to unceasing retribution. In other words, just as it is impossible for someone falling into a deep pit to get out without someone's assistance, so it is impossible to avoid the everlasting punishment without divine loving-kindness willing it.

(7) *Because the Lord will not reject his people, and will not aban-*
don his inheritance (v. 14). It was not only Israel he called *inheri-*
tance, but also the people from the nations, and especially this
one. Of the former blessed Moses said, "His people Jacob was
the Lord's portion, Israel his rope of inheritance"; whereas of
the new people, whom the God from God acquired by his willing acceptance of death, the divine Apostle [1636] calls "co-
heirs," as he established as the new covenant and true portion
those whom he formed anew through the washing of rebirth.[6]
In the present life the divine people will enjoy the providence
that is appropriate in that they are styled *inheritance* and *his peo-*
ple.

(8) *How long is righteousness to turn to judgment?* (v. 15). They
will surely enjoy this providence until the righteousness of God
appears to give judgment on all people. The verse refers to the
Incarnation of our God and Savior and to the Jews' denial; he
used *righteousness* of Christ the Lord himself, for he is called
also Sun of Righteousness[7] and of him blessed Paul said, "There
was given to us wisdom from God, righteousness, sanctification,
and redemption."[8] So after making mention of God's providence and saying, *Because the Lord will not reject his people, and*
will not abandon his inheritance, and discerning in advance their
future denial, he was right in adding, *How long is righteousness to*
turn to judgment? In other words, as long as they do not deny the
appearance of righteousness, they will attain providence from
on high. *All the upright in heart keeping to it.* Aquila and
Theodotion, on the other hand, say, "All the upright in heart
after it": having a mind purified of unbelief and adopting upright thoughts, they will follow the savior whom he called *right-*
eousness. The Lord's words concur with these statements: on
seeing Peter and Andrew casting a net into the sea he said to
them, "Come after me, and I shall make you fishers of people";[9]

6. The long form of the text, with typically credal terminology and sacramental application, inserts a lengthy gloss on "inheritance," citing also Deut
32.9 and Eph 3.6.

7. In the liturgy, on the basis of Mal 4.2. Absence of historical reference in
the psalm title encourages Theodoret to adopt a Christological interpretation.

8. Cf. 1 Cor 1.30.

9. Matt 4.19.

and to the one who said, "Give me leave to go and bury my father," the Lord said, "Let the dead bury their own dead, but as for you, come, follow me."[10] So he will exercise providence for Jews up to the point of denial, he is saying, whereas he will have as followers *the upright in heart,* clinging and adhering to him and completely reluctant to abandon him.

(9) *Who will rise up for me against evildoers, or who will assist me against the workers of iniquity?* (v. 16). Symmachus, on the other hand, put it more clearly, "Who will rise up on my behalf against wrongdoers? Who will take my part against workers of iniquity?"[11] [1637] I am deprived of all human assistance, he is saying, but I have the mighty helper, capable of easily scattering the array of the adversaries. He indicated this, in fact, in what follows. *If the Lord had not helped me, my soul would have been close to taking up residence in Hades* (v. 17): if I had not enjoyed providence on his part, they would have utterly consigned me to death. *If I said, My foot has slipped; your mercy, O Lord, helped me* (v. 18): as soon as I called on your providence and admitted my own weakness, I enjoyed your loving-kindness. *Against the multitude of my sorrows in my heart, your consolations gave joy to my soul* (v. 19): from your goodness I received comfort corresponding to the sorrows. The blessed Paul also said in similar terms, "Just as the sufferings of Christ are abundant for us, so our consolation is abundant through Christ"; and again, "Afflicted in every way but not crushed, perplexed but not driven to despair, persecuted but not forsaken, struck down but not ruined."[12]

(10) *Surely the throne of lawlessness, giving rise to hardship by order, will not be associated with you* (v. 20). Symmachus, on the other hand, put it more clearly, "Surely the throne of contumely, giving rise to difficulty in defiance of command, will not be connected with you?" You will not bring yourself, he is saying, to share the iniquity of those judging lawlessly, who deliver the

---

10. Luke 9.59–60.

11. Once again we wonder if the reflex commendation of Symmachus as translating "more clearly" is warranted.

12. 2 Cor 1.5; 4.8–9. The degree of Scriptural documentation is, we have seen, a reliable index of Theodoret's relish for the task of commentary on a psalm that offers no historical restrictions.

verdict contrary to what was commanded by you and ensure the difficulty stemming from it. He referred, in fact, to the unjust judges as a *throne of* contumely and *lawlessness,* who reap hardship and trouble as fruit of their iniquity. *They will hunt down the soul of a righteous one, and condemn innocent blood* (v. 21): this is the role of these lawless judges, to employ every scheme against the righteous, and pass a sentence of death against the innocent and guiltless, plus other punishments, by which I mean confiscation of property, banishment, and the like.

(11) *The Lord became my refuge, and my God supporter of my hope* (v. 22): I [1640] enjoyed providence from the Lord, and had him as a strong rampart. *The Lord will repay them for their iniquity, and the Lord God will obliterate them in their wickedness* (v. 23): they will reap the fruits of their own toil, and receive the wages due to their wickedness. This was written not just for them but also for all people: the God of all is provident for all people, and brings suitable treatment to bear on all.[13]

13. With typical conciseness, Theodoret concedes that the sentiments of this psalm are applicable and salutary for readers of every age. It is about as far as he is prepared to go in applying the Psalms to their lives.

COMMENTARY ON PSALM 95

A song of praise for David. No title in the Hebrew.

ING JOSIAH WAS QUITE pious. On seeing most of the people embracing the worship of idols, he ordered all the priests of the idols to be executed, their altars turned upside down, the graves of the dead priests dug up and their bones burned on the very altars of the demons. Then he summoned all the people and urged them to have recourse to repentance, placate God, and by this means avoid the threatened destruction, the prophetess Huldah forecasting a dire fate for all the people.[1] Blessed David, then, with inspired eyes foresaw this from afar, and composed this psalm for their benefit and the instruction of all humankind. The psalm is expressed from the viewpoint of Josiah and the priests of God.

(2) *Come, let us rejoice in the Lord, let us shout to God our Savior* (v. 1). The opening is from dancers, pleased with their freedom from impiety: Let us raise the triumphal hymn to our common God, he is saying, the shout being a sound conquerors make. The band of the pious had conquered the force of the impious; so it was right for them to offer the triumphal hymn to God,[2] especially the choir of the apostles and martyrs. Beyond them, everyone of their kind would have in mind the thought, *Come, let us rejoice in the Lord, let us shout to God our Savior,* who brought about our salvation through sufferings to make us all immune

1. Cf. 2 Kings 22–23. Theodoret must get this association of the psalm with Josiah from his tradition, there being nothing in the biblical text to provide commentators with a direct connection. Despite his concerns about historicism voiced in the preface, he does not feel free to dissolve the connection.

2. The author of the long form of the text is not slow to give evidence of that concern about restricting the psalm's meaning to history, and at this point extends commentary on the verse with an eschatological and Christological interpretation.

to suffering, who chose to descend into Hades so as to raise us up to the heavens. *Let us come into his presence with confession, and raise a shout to him with psalms* (v. 2): before the time of retribution let us have recourse to repentance, and before the sentence is pronounced on us [1641] let us placate the Lord; let us offer him also appropriate hymn singing.

(3) Then he brings out God's victory and the idols' defeat. *Because the Lord is a great God and a great king over all the earth* (v. 3): beyond words is the power of our Lord; he is true God, he has power over all, and he proves the falsity of the name of the so-called gods. Next he shows, as far as is possible for human nature, the signs of the divine power. *Because in his hand are the limits of the earth, and the heights of the mountains are his. Because his is the sea, and it is he who made it; his hands shaped the dry land* (vv. 4–5): he is maker of everything, Lord of all, he personally guides all things, with his hand he encircles creation, with a word he personally created moisture and dryness; his are the tops of the mountains, even should the demons times beyond counting persuade the fools among men to build on them temples dedicated to them.

(4) *Come, let us worship and bow down before him, let us lament in the presence of the Lord who made us* (v. 6): so let us come together with enthusiasm and offer him due worship, and beg for his mercy, weeping and wailing, he being our Maker and Lord. The history of Josiah and the people instructs us about the tears they shed after the reading of Deuteronomy.[3] *Because he is our God, and we people of his pasture and sheep of his hand* (v. 7): he is our Lord by nature, and particularly is he our God: he calls us his own people, and provides care as though for his own sheep. The Lord himself also says this after his incomprehensible Incarnation: "My sheep hear my voice," and again, "I am the good shepherd, and I lay down my life for the sheep," and so on.[4]

3. Josiah certainly, less so the people and the discoverers of "the book of the law" (generally thought to be Deuteronomy on account of its own use of that term of itself at Deut 31.26) recorded in those chapters, responded to the discovery and reading with gravity, though in fact tears are not mentioned.

4. The long form of the text cannot resist relating this verse to Jesus, loosely citing John 10.3, 11, and 15.

(5) Then they go on to threaten the non-believers with retribution, terrifying them by mention of the ancestors and producing a salutary effect through that accusation. *Today if you listen to his voice, harden not your hearts as though in provocation* (vv. 7–8): since the Lord overlooked your former impiety out of his characteristic loving-kindness, now at least heed him when he exhorts and offers salutary teaching, and do not imitate your ancestors' inflexible and obstinate attitude. [1644] In fact, he often referred to the contrariness occurring in the wilderness as *provocation;* thus also in another psalm he said, "How often they provoked him in the wilderness, irked him in the desert."[5] He also revealed the independence of the attitude, saying not simply, Do not harden, but *Harden not your hearts* to teach that they are the authors of this kind of heart.

(6) Then he brings to mind more clearly the ancestors' disobedience. *Like the day of trial in the wilderness where your ancestors put me to the test, they tried me and saw my works for forty years* (vv. 8–10): since they refused to enter the promised land, defying God's bidding, feigning irrational dread and claiming fear of being themselves destroyed and their children taken captive, he caused them to spend a period of forty years in the wilderness until they wasted away. *I was angered with that generation, and said, They are always astray in their heart.* Aquila and Symmachus, on the other hand, said in place of *I was angered* "I was alienated": for this reason I detested that generation, he is saying, seeing their flippant and inconstant attitude.

(7) *They did not know my ways, as I swore in my anger, They will not enter my rest* (vv. 10–11): they refused, however, to heed the threats sworn on oath, and were not prepared to remove the threat by repentance. This was the very reason they did not enjoy the land promised to the ancestors. He called that land his *rest,* or according to the other translators "repose": since in their travels in the wilderness they made frequent changes in place under the guidance of the tabernacle in which God was believed to dwell, whereas in the land of promise they rested from their traveling and the tabernacle was set in the consecrat-

5. Cf. Ps 106.14.

ed places, he was right to call the land of promise *rest*, while calling God's arrangements *ways*.[6]

6. Theodoret, at least in the short form of the text, has resisted any attempt to give the psalm a fuller sense than the historical—whether of Josiah or the people in the wilderness. He does not make the connection other commentators have with shepherd and sheep of John 10, or allow an anagogical sense for a notion like "rest." And this despite the role of the psalm in the Christian liturgy as an invitatory. Lack of abundant Scriptural documentation, by comparison with preceding psalms, suggests a lack of relish for commentary; at least we can commend him for not exploiting possibilities for anti-Jewish rhetoric.

COMMENTARY ON PSALM 96

A psalm for David, when the house was built after the captivity.
No title in the Hebrew.

LESSED DAVID DID NOT write this title, nor indeed did the original commentators on the inspired composition; rather, it is likely that someone else gained a superficial impression of the psalm's meaning and inserted the title.[1] The literal meaning of the expression [1645] is applicable to those returning from Babylon and building the divine Temple, since in them the salvation of all people was foreshadowed. Still, the inspired composition prophesies both the first and the second appearance of our God and Savior, the judgment to come, and the salvation provided to the nations prior to that.

(2) *Sing to the Lord a new song* (v. 1): new situations require new singing. *Sing to the Lord, all the earth.* How is this applicable to Jews under assault from all people? The ones, after all, who saw their liberation, were not pleased; on the contrary, they were disappointed, and made very effort to invest them with troubles of all kinds. The inspired word, on the contrary, summons the whole world to making music. *Sing to the Lord, bless his name, announce his salvation day after day* (v. 2). Every day, he is saying, recount the favor done. Then he brings out also to whom this account must be offered. *Declare his glory among the nations, among all peoples his marvels* (v. 3): let the whole human race enjoy such teaching, and learn of the divine wonder working.

(3) *Because the Lord is great, and greatly to be praised; he is fear-*

1. Cf. note 1 to Ps 94. It is interesting that Theodoret disqualifies the title not only on the score of its not appearing in the Hebrew, but also for its failure to do justice to the universalism of the psalm, a feature modern commentators also acknowledge.

some beyond all the gods (v. 4): the Lord of all possesses ineffable greatness, and has shown his peculiar power over the so-called gods and proven their deceitfulness. He indicated this, in fact, in what follows. *Because all the gods of the nations are demons, whereas the Lord made the heavens* (v. 5). Blessed Paul also says of him, "Had they known, after all, they would not have crucified the very Lord of glory." While the so-called gods were seen as wicked demons, ours appeared as maker of the heavens. At the time of his voluntary passion not only was the sun darkened, rocks split, and the veil of the Temple was torn asunder, but also the powers of the heavens were moved and, in short, the universe threatened destruction on seeing the one who carries all things fixed to the cross.[2]

(4) *Confession and comeliness in his presence, holiness and magnificence in his sanctification* (v. 6): by assuming human nature and by means of it becoming manifest to all people, he emits flashes of his peculiar magnificence, [1648] and attracts everyone to worship; he called the temple that he assumed *his sanctification,* whereas he had previously made mention of his *comeliness* already in the forty-fourth psalm, "Comely in your charm," he says, "compared with children of human beings."[3] *Ascribe to the Lord, families of the nations, ascribe to the Lord glory and honor, ascribe to the Lord glory to his name* (vv. 7–8): so, all people, direct your steps to the Lord who wishes to save, and offering him due homage and viewing your benefactor not with the body's eyes, offer hymn singing to his name.

(5) *Bring sacrifices and enter his courts. Adore the Lord in his holy court* (vv. 8–9). He means rational sacrifices, which we see constantly offered and celebrated by the priests. By the number of *the courts* he indicates the churches. In particular, he gave no such order to Jews in case anyone form the impression of the sacrifices of the Law, but rather to *families of the nations,* who offer the sacrifices of the New Covenant in the churches. Of these

2. While Theodoret has been content to paraphrase these verses, the long form of the text—ever ready to gild the lily and to give a Christological interpretation—cites Paul (1 Cor 2.8) and the Passion narratives (Matt 27.51) for dramatic effect.

3. Ps 45.2, a verse Theodoret had also taken in reference to the humanity of Jesus.

God foretold also through another inspired author in speaking to Jews, "I have no pleasure in you, and I will not accept a sacrifice from your hands, because from the rising of the sun to its setting great is my name among the nations, and in every place incense is offered to my name, and a pure sacrifice."[4] *Let all the earth move from his presence.* Aquila, on the other hand, said, "Give birth in his presence, all the earth," and so did Symmachus. This resembles what was said by the prophet Isaiah, "On account of fear of you, Lord, we conceived, were in labor and gave birth to a spirit of your salvation, which we produced on the earth."[5] So here the inspired word bids the nations who have received the seeds of salvation to be in labor and give birth to piety, move from their former position and be established and fixed in the divine laws.

(6) *Say among the nations, The Lord reigned, he set the world in place, and it will not be moved* (v. 10): so announce the kingdom of the God of all, which transformed the world [1649] when in error, and rendered it firm when moved this way and that. Symmachus also rendered it this way, "The Lord reigned, and made the world immutable." It is obvious, of course, that God's kingdom is eternal; but at that time it was demonstrated by means of the change in circumstances. *He will judge peoples with equity.* Since he showed God to be king, it was right for him to mention judgment as well, proclaiming its equity and fairness. *Let the heavens rejoice and the earth be glad* (v. 11). Let all creation, he is saying, share joy with humankind, and things of heaven and earth be filled with satisfaction. After all, if in the case of one sinner repenting the angels rejoice,[6] they surely have greater joy at the transformation of all people. *Let the sea and its fullness be moved.* Theodotion and Symmachus, on the other hand, put it this way, "The sea with its fullness will roar": the whole life of human beings, resembling the fury of the sea, will receive the sound of the divine messages. He is forecasting at the same time as well the assaults made by the unbelievers against the

---

4. Mal 1.10–11.
5. Cf. Isa 26.18 [Greek].
6. Cf. Luke 15.10.

heralds of truth, as we have demonstrated also in other psalms.[7]

(7) *The fields will rejoice, and everything in them* (v. 12). Symmachus, on the other hand, put it this way, "The countryside will pride itself, and everything in it." The Lord also in commentary on the parable of the weeds called the world a field;[8] he says, therefore, that everything will be filled with joy and satisfaction. *Then all the trees of the forest will rejoice.* Aquila, on the other hand, said, "Then all the trees of the forest will give praise": they in particular will be responsible for the hymn to God, since from them came the saving wood on which the body of the Savior hung, from which stem good things for human beings. It should be acknowledged, of course, that the inspired word employed metonymy: neither heaven nor earth nor sea nor fields nor trees possess reason or soul; rather, it is those using them who offer hymn singing to God. Islanders dwell in the sea, people on continents dwell in the land, angels in heaven; and those who see the forests free of the worship of idols offer the hymn to God. Thus the inspired author in teaching about the passage of the children of Israel from Egypt likewise employed metonymy: "The sea saw and turned back, the Jordan [1652] reversed its course, the mountains skipped like rams, the hills like lambs of the flock." He proposes the question and receives the reply, to indicate by this the joy of those who are saved.[9]

(8) *Before the Lord, because he comes, because he comes to judge the earth* (v. 13). It was good for him to put it twice, *because he is coming, because he comes:* the first appearance gave the divine knowledge to human beings, while the second will achieve a judgment on affairs. *He will judge the world in righteousness, and peoples*

7. To be sure, in the case of this psalm, unlike some previous ones, Theodoret is insistent on taking an eschatological meaning and, as we remarked in note 1, responding to its "clear-cut universalism," in Dahood's words.

8. Cf. Matt 13.24–30.

9. Theodoret is appreciative of the literary artifice of the psalmist, we have seen, remarking on it also in commentary on that other place, Ps 114.3–4, here cited—though mention of question and answer seems to suggest he has in mind rather the following two verses, where enquiry is made of the reason for the behavior of sea and mountains: "Why is it, O sea, . . .?"

in his truth. At that time, he is saying, at that time he will achieve the fair judgment, no longer employing the former long-suffering, but scrutinizing the truth of things and delivering a right verdict on all.

COMMENTARY ON PSALM 97

*For David, when his land was established. No title
in the Hebrew.*

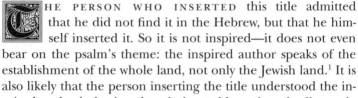HE PERSON WHO INSERTED this title admitted
that he did not find it in the Hebrew, but that he him-
self inserted it. So it is not inspired—it does not even
bear on the psalm's theme: the inspired author speaks of the
establishment of the whole land, not only the Jewish land.[1] It is
also likely that the person inserting the title understood the inspired author's *land* as the whole world, as though all people
adopted his hymn singing. Yet the psalm, on the contrary,
prophesies both the first and the second appearance of God
our Savior, the nations' knowledge of God and the judgment to
come.

(2) *The Lord has reigned, let the land rejoice, let many islands exult* (v. 1). In this way he forecasts the first appearance of the
Savior—hence his urging both mainland and island dwellers to
dance and rejoicing, both the one and the other cheered by
the comfort they gain from the hope in future things. He said,
The Lord reigned, not as if he received the kingship then, but for
revealing his particular kingship to people at that time. Lest we
repeat ourselves, we recommend to those who are interested in
learning this more clearly to read the comments we have already made.[2] *Cloud and darkness are round about him, righteousness*

1. We have seen Theodoret becoming more independent in previous
psalms on the authenticity of the psalm titles than in his preface, where he stated, "I consider it rash and foolhardy to brand them as spurious and accept
one's own judgment as more enlightened than the influence of the Spirit" (cf.
FOTC 101, p. 43). Now he is also prepared to deny their inspiration, after
claiming in the preface that they were the work of the Seventy "not without divine inspiration." Experience is teaching him to become more critical, at least
in this detail.

2. For his readers to gain some light on the problem raised by the LXX verb
tense, Theodoret has in mind his comments on v. 10 of the previous psalm.

and judgment the true role of his throne (v. 2). By *darkness* and *cloud* he brought out the invisibility of the divine nature: as it is impossible for someone enveloped in a cloud and with darkness to be descried, so is it completely impossible for the ineffable nature to be discerned. Yet he gives a reminder that he is the One [1653] who made his appearance on Mount Sinai in *cloud and darkness,* and teaches that even if it is impossible to descry the divine nature, it is still possible to discern its power through its operation: he taught human beings *righteousness,* and those performing everything without due discrimination he instructed in living with right judgment. This was the true role of his *throne* and his *reign.*

(3) *Fire will burn before him, and will burst into flame round his foes* (v. 3). This is the prophecy of the second appearance. The divine Daniel also perceived this: "His throne," he said, "a fiery flame, its wheels a burning fire; a river of fire issued forth and flowed in his presence. A thousand thousands served him, and ten thousand times ten thousand ministered to him. The court sat in judgment, and books were opened."[3] *His lightning flashes appeared in the world* (v. 4). Fire has two functions: it can not only burn but also illuminate; the choir of the holy ones, however, are affected by one and those living a lawless life by the other. The Lord also compared his coming to lightning, saying this, "As the lightning comes from the east and shines as far as the west, so will the coming of the Son of Man be."[4] *The earth saw and was moved:* who is not in dread of that fearsome court? *The mountains melt like wax before the Lord, before the Lord of all the earth* (v. 5): not only the governed but also the rulers and kings will dissolve with fear, like wax approaching fire. In fact, the more numerous the affairs entrusted to their management, the greater the liability to which they are subject; the greater the debt, the worse the dread.

(4) *The heavens proclaimed his righteousness, all peoples saw his glory* (v. 6). This both happened [in the past] and will happen [in the future]: when Christ the Lord was born, a choir of angels appeared and offered the hymn to God on the salvation of

3. Dan 3.9–10.
4. Matt 24.27.

human beings, and cried out in a hymn, "Glory to God in the highest, on earth peace and good will among human beings."[5] He used the name *heavens* of the heavenly powers, as he likewise often uses "earth" of those inhabiting the earth. [1656] The peoples throughout the world saw the power of our God and Savior in their own transformation, whereas the second coming will clearly teach all people the Lord's kingship, and then we shall all also hear the angels' hymn singing.

(5) *Let all those who adore images be put to shame, those glorying in their idols* (v. 7): so once the true light arises, let darkness yield place and let those in thrall to error sink, those worshipping the idols hide their face. *Bow down before him, all his angels.* Blessed Paul applied this inspired composition to the Savior, speaking this way in the Epistle to the Hebrews, "When further he brings the firstborn into the world, he says, Let all God's angels bow down before him."[6] It was timely for the inspired author to include this here, too: after showing those bowing down to the idols ashamed and hiding their face, he gives a glimpse of the vast numbers of angels beyond counting worshipping our God. *Sion heard and was glad, and the daughters of Judah rejoiced, on account of your judgments, O Lord* (v. 8). Here he gives the name *Sion* to the pious way of life, and *the daughters of Judah* to the churches throughout the world: the Savior's apostles, who planted and gave birth to them, took their origin from Jews. In witness the divinely inspired Paul in writing to the Corinthians said expressly, "In Christ Jesus, in fact, I gave birth to you through the good news."[7] So since the Church of the Savior is one, all the believers constituting one body, and since likewise it is also many, for the body's limbs are many, by *Sion* he referred to the common corps of the pious, and by *the daughters of Judah* to the assemblies of the believers in cities and towns, country regions and remote areas. He means that both the one group and the other were filled with joy at the righteous judgments of the judge. *Because you, Lord most high over all the earth, are exalted far above all the gods* (v. 9): all rejoice and exult, in receipt of the knowledge of the true God and King, and perceiv-

5. Cf. Luke 2.14.   6. Heb 1.6.
7. 1 Cor 4.15.

ing the censure of the false gods: their futility is censured, your [1657] exaltation demonstrated.

(6) Since we have need not only of faith but also of good actions, it is necessary that the inspired author also offers this advice. *You who love the Lord, hate wickedness* (v. 10): if the good is desired by you, abhor the opposite. "After all, what do light and darkness have in common?"[8] By *wickedness,* of course, he forbade all kinds of evil. *The Lord will guard the souls of his holy ones, from a sinner's hand he will rescue them:* rejecting wickedness and being devoted to the right and just way of life, you will have the Lord of all as caretaker and guard, and will prove superior to the adversaries attacking you.

(7) *Light dawned for the righteous, and joy for the upright in heart* (v. 11): not all people wanted to enjoy the light, nor did all receive the joy coming from faith. The Sun of Justice himself sent down the rays of salvation on everyone, but there are those who shut their eyes and were unwilling to see the light. *Rejoice, O righteous ones, in the Lord, and acknowledge the memory of his holiness* (v. 12): so all who enjoy the light and embrace their share in virtue, be glad and sing God's praises by narrating the vast number of his favors; he used *acknowledgment* here to mean giving thanks.

8. 2 Cor 6.14.

COMMENTARY ON PSALM 98

A psalm for David.

HIS PSALM HAS THE SAME sense: it prophesies both appearances of the Savior, though giving more detail of the first. *Sing to the Lord a new song* (v. 1). Since it proclaims the transformation of ancient things, and forecasts some new way of life, it is right for him to give directions also for a new song [to be offered] to God. *Because the Lord has performed marvels:* extraordinary and baffling are the things done by the God of all. *His right hand and his holy arm have brought him salvation.* We have often said that "hand" means operation and *right hand* successful operation. He means that the salvation of human beings is a function of his power; but, in an example of immeasurable loving-kindness, he considers human life to be to his own benefit.[1] This is the reason, to be sure, that he did not say, [1660] His right hand saved them, but *brought him salvation.* By freeing them from the deception of the idols, and giving a glimpse of the exaltation of his kingship, he gave them a share in salvation. He indicated this more clearly in what follows.

(2) *The Lord made known his salvation in the sight of the nations, he revealed his righteousness* (v. 2): to all people he offered the saving streams, and showed his righteous kingship to the nations. *He was mindful of his mercy to Jacob, and of his truth to the house of Israel; all the ends of the earth saw the salvation of our God* (v. 3). This bears a close resemblance to the prophecies of the prophet Isaiah: through him the God of all said to Christ the Lord, "I have given you as a covenant of a race, a light of na-

1. Commentators note the similarity of this psalm to Ps 96, and Theodoret is not disposed to spend much time on the first half of the opening verse. The LXX's version of the verb in the second half, on the other hand, which some English versions render as "brought him victory," does pose a theological problem, and he wrestles with it in his rationalizing way.

tions, for you to be salvation to the ends of the earth."[2] Since the God of all promised to the remarkable patriarchs, to Abraham, Isaac, and Jacob, and to the divinely inspired David to raise up the Christ from their seed according to the flesh, and to provide salvation to all people through him, he called the promise made to the fathers "covenant"; the other translators, in fact, said "treaty" for "covenant."[3] He called Israel his "race," since the Christ came from Jews according to the flesh,[4] as the Apostle says; so he said, "I have given you as a covenant of a race," that is to say, to fulfill the treaties made to Jews, but "as a light" no longer for Jews but for *nations,* since they shared in salvation through faith, having confessed him [in the past] and confessing God from God. [Jews], on the other hand, preferred the gloom of unbelief. Blessed David says as much here, too, *He was mindful of his mercy to Jacob, and of his truth to the house of Israel,* fulfilling the promises made to them. *All the ends of the earth,* of course, *saw the salvation of our God:* the light of truth rose not only on Jews but on all people.

(3) *Cry aloud to the Lord, all the earth, sing, be glad, and sing praise* (v. 4): so since you have all been freed from the harsh tyranny of the devil, raise the triumphal hymn to [our] saving God; *a loud cry* is a sound victors make. Hence we do as we are bid: we are in the habit of offering to God this hymn by rejoicing and crying aloud at the mystical moment, [1661] singing and playing and dancing with great cheerfulness. *Sing praise to the Lord on a lyre, with the voice of a psalm* (v. 5). You can see this law constantly fulfilled in the churches: we strike up the divine music on the spiritual lyre. We turn our bodies into rational lyres, and use our teeth for strings and our lips for an instrument, while our tongue moves more keenly than any plectrum and produces the harmonious sound of the plucking, the mind moving the tongue like a musician skillfully observing the inter-

---

2. A conflation of Isa 42.6; 49.6.

3. Do we have here a case where Theodoret uses his Hexapla to check the LXX version of Isaiah against the other versions, as though it rather than the psalm verse is the text under discussion?

4. Cf. Rom 1.3. Again Theodoret warms to the theme of universalism, prepared though he is to concede a certain priority in the historical order to "Jews" (without the article, as often).

vals. Such a lyre is more acceptable to God than a lifeless one; he himself bears testimony [to this] in crying out to Jews through the prophet, "Take away from me the sound of your songs, I shall not listen to the sound of your instruments."[5]

(4) *On beaten trumpets and sound of a horn* (v. 6). The divine Scripture often calls shouting a *trumpet;* thus the Lord says in the Gospels, "When you give alms, do not blow a trumpet before you, as the hypocrites do,"[6] in other words, Do not proclaim it or make it obvious to everyone, lest you ruin the fruit of loving-kindness with empty glory. So here he gives the name *trumpet* to the teaching, through which we learn also the favors done to us and are instructed in profitable laws. By *beaten trumpets* he means those made of bronze, and by *horns* those made from horns; it was customary for Jews to use them. Practices in use among them, however, are a shadow of ours; so just as they sacrificed the irrational lamb and we the saving one, God from God, who takes away the sin of the world,[7] likewise they used lifeless trumpets whereas we [use] those endowed with life and reason. Our trumpets, then, are the divine apostles, the divinely inspired biblical authors, and those after them who were granted the grace of teaching. *Cry aloud in the presence of the King, the Lord:* offer the triumphal hymn to the King and Lord of all.

(5) *Let the sea and its fullness be shaken, the world and all who dwell in it* (v. 7). Symmachus, on the other hand, put it this way, "Let the sea resound with its fullness, the world and its dwellers." It is particularly in the heavily populated cities that you can see the realization of this prophecy: the crowds of religiously minded peoples in the churches resemble a tossing sea; the sound of those singing psalms is also like that.[8] According

5. Amos 5.23. Whereas Theodoret generally shows no interest in details of the liturgical recital of the Psalms, here in a Homeric simile he develops the process of their being sung or at least recited in church. Could one deduce from the simile that he sees little value in instrumental accompaniment?

6. Matt 6.2.

7. John 1.29. As a teacher—and the preface and text generally bring out Theodoret's role as teacher in doing his commentary—he prides himself as successor to inspired composers of Old and New Testaments, and thus superior to "lifeless trumpets." A musician might not agree.

8. Again, as above, a (rare) indication of the fervor of religious life of the period, and in particular the practice of psalm singing in the churches.

to the [1664] Septuagint the inspired word referred to the movement and transformation of dwellers of the sea and land: what is moved is shaken, and what is transformed is moved. *Rivers will clap hands as one* (v. 8). Again he gave the name *rivers* to those sharing the charism of teaching and pouring forth the divine streams like rivers; he said they clap and sing the praises of God, clapping likewise being an action of victors.

(6) *The mountains will rejoice at the presence of the Lord because he comes, because he is coming to judge the earth* (vv. 8–9). Here he called those with an elevated and uplifted attitude *mountains,* on which the city of God is built; Scripture says, "A city situated atop a mountain cannot be hid";[9] and, "Its foundations are on the holy mountains."[10] He said these rejoice and are glad on learning of the appearance of our God and Savior: awaiting recompense for their labors, they are pleased to know the fairness of the Judge. *He will judge the world in righteousness and people in uprightness:* while the first appearance was marked by great mercy, the second will be marked by righteousness. "We shall all stand before the judgment seat of Christ," Scripture says, "so that each may receive recompense for what was done in the body, whether good or ill."[11] The inspired author also said this: "God has spoken once, twice I heard it, that power belongs to God and mercy to you, O Lord, because you repay everyone according to his works."[12]

9. Matt 5.14.
10. Ps 87.1.
11. Collation of Rom 14.10 and 2 Cor 5.10.
12. Ps 62.11–12.

COMMENTARY ON PSALM 99

A psalm for David. No title in the Hebrew.

THIS PSALM PROPHESIES the return of Jews from Babylon, and forecasts both the appearance of our Savior and the Jews' unbelief. *The Lord reigned; let peoples be enraged* (v. 1): both Jews and pagans rant and rave on hearing of the kingship of Christ the Lord. And when the Jews obtained their freedom, all their neighbors seethed with anger to behold their unexpected return, though this revealed the power of the one adored by them. *The one who is seated on the Cherubim. Let the earth be shaken.* The one proclaimed by us, he is saying, is both God and Lord of the powers above. He said *seated* as though engaged in dialogue with human beings: [1665] what kind of a seat is needed by the incorporeal nature, incomprehensible and uncircumscribed, controlling the circle of the earth and its inhabitants like locusts?[1] But he uses language to present the God of all riding upon the Cherubim in the manner of a king, terrifying and intimidating the listeners.

(2) *The Lord in Sion is great, he is exalted over all the peoples* (v. 2). When the Jews returned and built the divine Temple, the power of God was made clear to all. In particular, the one who endured the cross, in fact, emerged as Lord of the whole world, the sacred apostles offering the saving message to the nations.[2] *Let them praise your mighty name, because it is fearsome and holy* (v. 3): so everyone must sing your praises, recount your favors, and

1. Cf. Isa 40.22. In true Antiochene style, Theodoret alerts his readers to the risk of infringing divine transcendence if they do not appreciate the figurative language of the poet.
2. We feel that it is despite the obvious sense of the text that Theodoret, probably in response to his predecessors, is insisting from the outset on giving the psalm historical, eschatological, and Christological meanings.

not be inquisitive about your ineffable nature, but offer worship to your name, fearsome and all-holy as it is, sanctifying the believers, terrifying the unbelievers.

(3) *A king's honor loves judgment* (v. 4): we must dread him as king and as dealer in righteousness, the guidance of his subjects justly being proper to true kingship. *A king's honor loves judgment,* after all—that is, being fond of justice makes a king honorable. What follows also suggests as much, *You have prepared right ways, you have worked judgment and righteousness in Jacob:* as a righteous king you have delivered a right and just verdict, and freed Israel from the influence of those who enslaved it, and the nations from the devil's slavery.[3] In keeping with the other level of inspired composition, however, it should be taken this way: You showed the truth of your promise by fulfilling the pledges made to the forebears of Israel and granting salvation through the seed of Abraham. *Extol the Lord our God, and worship at his footstool, because he is holy* (v. 5): so repay the benefactor as far as you are able, and offer him due reverence. *Extol* means Proclaim his sublimity. *His footstool* is to be taken in reference to olden times as the Temple in Jerusalem, and in reference to present times as the churches throughout all land and sea, in which we offer worship to the all-holy God.

(4) *Moses and Aaron among his priests, and Samuel among those who called upon his name* (v. 6). It was not without purpose[4] that he omitted the other inspired people in mentioning only these; rather, it was to teach the Jews' innate frenzy and lust for power: in the time of Moses and Aaron they attempted to wrest the priesthood, [1668] and in the time of Samuel they scorned the divine kingship and preferred a human one. So the verse teaches that they are doing nothing new in their frenzy against the

3. This final phrase is from the long form of the text, ever anxious to supply an eschatological meaning—unaware that Theodoret is about to do just that. As often, we get the impression from that form of the text of an editor who does not always respect or even appreciate Theodoret's intent.

4. Another signature of Antiochene commentary, the phrase "not idly, not without purpose" betraying the commentator's unwillingness to allow any item of the text to pass without comment. It is the virtue of *akribeia*, precision, both in the text and in the commentator.

Savior and the rejection of his saving kingship, the madness being habitual with them from the beginning.[5] *They called upon the
Lord, and he hearkened to them; in a pillar of cloud he spoke to them*
(vv. 6–7). They had great confidence in God, he is saying: they
called upon him and he responded, granted their requests, and
engaged in converse with them in the sight of all, making a personal appearance in the cloud.[6] Then he teaches that it was not
unjust for him to share with them this grace: *Because they kept his
testimonies and his commands which he gave them:* to those conducting themselves lawfully and living in accordance with his commandments he granted this grace.

(5) *O Lord our God, you hearkened to them, you were the very merciful God to them* (v. 8). You are, O Lord, he is saying, the one
proclaimed by us, the one who shared with them such great
trust and accorded them much benevolence. *But taking
vengeance for all their doings.* Symmachus, on the other hand, put
it this way, "Avenger of their abuses": those who rebelled against
the great Moses he consigned to fire, dispatched those who fled
the flames to life in the grave, bidding the earth open, and
made the place of rebellion an improvised grave for them;
those who made their way across the sea and walked on that
depth he caused to be submerged on dry land, employing
waves of a surprising character. Those who rebelled against the
prophet Samuel, on the other hand, he handed over to the
power of Saul, and invested them with troubles of all kinds.

(6) *Extol the Lord our God, and worship at his holy mountain, because the Lord our God is holy* (v. 9): imitating the piety of these
remarkable men, therefore, offer due worship to God. While
holy mountain referred of old to Sion, it now refers to the sublimity of the knowledge of God, Isaiah and Micah prophesying
to that effect: "In the last days the mountain of the Lord will be
manifest,"[7] that is, the knowledge of God will become clear to

5. *Akribeia,* however, denotes precision, not accuracy (despite the common
mistranslation); and the commentator can be wrong, even perverse, in interpreting the textual detail, as Theodoret is here in laboring a Christological
sense to the verse despite the obvious meaning of Num 16 and 1 Sam 8 to
which reference is made.

6. Cf. Exod 13.21.

7. Cf. Isa 2.2; Mic 4.1.

all. The divine Apostle also knew that Mount Sion is to be taken spiritually: "You have come to Mount Sion and to the city of the living God, heavenly Jerusalem."[8] We are therefore bidden in keeping with the knowledge given us by God to offer him adoration, [1669] and confess him God from God and only-begotten Son of the Father, made man for our sake. Amen.[9]

8. Heb 12.22, the anagogical sense (a phrase not on the lips of Theodoret to the extent true of Chrysostom) encouraged by Pauline authority.

9. The final clause in doxology style and characteristic credal terminology comes from the long form of the text.

COMMENTARY ON PSALM 100

A psalm for David by way of confession. No title in the Hebrew.

HE INSPIRED AUTHOR HERE summons all people to hymn singing, urging them to serve God the Savior in every way. *Cry aloud to the Lord, all the earth* (v. 1): all human beings, offer the triumphal hymn to God; by *earth* he refers to the inhabitants of the earth. *Serve the Lord with gladness* (v. 2): the kingship of our God and Savior is not of the style of the harsh tyranny of the devil; rather, his lordship is mild and loving. In rejoicing in his service, then, make your approach: *Come into his presence with happiness.* Symmachus, on the other hand, said "with blessing," and Aquila, "with praise," the hymn of people who rejoice and are glad.

(2) *Know that he is our God* (v. 3): even if in his loving-kindness he chose to become man, yet he always continued to have the being of God.[1] It means, Learn from experience itself that our Lord in person is God of all. The sacred band of the apostles also proposed these teachings to the nations, as the story of the Acts teaches. *He made us, not we ourselves:* we were not appointed our own makers, but were formed by him. That is what blessed Paul taught the Athenians: "The God who made the world and everything in it, he who is Lord of heaven and earth, does not dwell in temples made by [human] hands, nor is he served by human hands as though in need of anything, having himself given to all life and breath and everything. From one bloodline he caused one nation to dwell on the whole face of the earth."[2] The inspired author also teaches this here, *He made us, not we ourselves.* Symmachus, on the other hand, put it this

1. The long form of the text is not unaccustomed to insert a theological caveat, relevant or not.
2. Acts 17.24–26.

way, "He made us when we were not." *We are his people, and sheep of his pasture.* In this he indicated not only his lordship but also his care: he is not only our Lord but also shepherd, supplying us with good pasture, whereas we also belong to him like a king's people and like a shepherd's sheep.

(3) *Enter his gates with confession, his courts with hymns* (v. 4). By *his gates* and *his courts* he refers to the churches: [1672] they provide us with approach to him, and in them it is proper to narrate his divine and saving actions, and offer the hymn of thanksgiving like a gift of some kind. *Confess to him, praise his name, because the Lord is good, his mercy forever and his truth from generation to generation* (vv. 4–5): how could it not be right to sing the praises of the one showing ineffable loving-kindness and bringing to fulfillment the good promises? After all, what he promised in the generation of our ancestors he fulfilled in ours, and the salvation he pledged he truly granted, achieving our salvation through cross and death. Amen.[3]

3. As with the previous psalm, the long form of the text supplies a phrase by way of pious conclusion, unwilling to leave the reader in any doubt of the source of the promised salvation.

COMMENTARY ON PSALM 101

A psalm for David.

OME OF THE COPIES have "On the fourth Sabbath day," but we did not find this addition in the Hebrew, in the other translators, or in the Septuagint.[1] The psalm has the following theme. King Josiah overturned all altars of the idols, cut down their priests, and guided the people to their former piety. Not only did he give thought to the soundness of the teachings, but he attended also to the practices of virtue, judging properly, respecting righteousness, assisting the wronged, punishing the wrongdoers, being solicitous for the welfare of the citizens. Blessed David perceived this from afar and composed this psalm, describing the man's virtue and proposing him to all people as a model of perfection.

(2) *Of mercy and judgment I shall sing to you, O Lord* (v. 1). Since the admirable Josiah took pity on the wronged and condemned the wrongdoers, the psalmist gave the complimentary term *mercy and judgment* to the account of it. *I shall sing, and shall understand in the way of innocence* (vv. 1–2). Symmachus, on the other hand, put it this way, "I shall make music, I shall consider the way of innocence": to the way that I perceived by the grace of the Spirit to be innocent and pleasing to God I shall now give attention in song. *When will you come to me?* This admirable man acquired such purity as to cry with confidence to God, *When will you come to me?*—that is to say, I made the palace seemly for you, I long for your presence, O Lord, I yearn for your appearance; grant my desire.

(3) *I walked in the innocence of my heart in my house:* I continued to live a life of simplicity, I did not practice [1673] duplici-

1. See Introduction, section 3, for the range of textual resources Theodoret had at his disposal in writing his *Commentary*.

ty, feigning a different appearance to outsiders while bringing myself to do the opposite at home; instead, my private face corresponded to my public one.[2] *I did not set before my eyes a lawless pursuit* (v. 3): not only did I abhor lawless practices, but I also expelled thoughts of them, controlling and guiding my mind first of all. *I hated those who commit transgressions:* I gave short shrift also to those who despise the divine ordinances. *No perverse heart stuck fast within me* (v. 4): those who honor righteousness were my familiars, while those preferring the opposite and unwilling to hold to correct thinking I kept well out of my company. *I had no relations with the wicked person of ways different from my own:* if any of my associates chose to adopt wicked habits and depart from my company, I did not regard such a loss as a loss; on this basis the one choosing evil was quite beneath contempt in my view. *I banished those who maligned their neighbor in private* (v. 5): I admitted no charges leveled in private, but drove off those attempting to do this. *I did not entertain people with haughty eye and insatiable heart:* nor did I make friends of those guilty of arrogance and greed.

(4) *My eyes are upon the faithful in the land so as to seat them in my company* (v. 6): those adorned with faith, who highly prize divine things, shared gatherings and counsel with me. *The one who treads a faultless path will minister to me:* I was very careful not only about friends and advisers but also about attendants; I employed servants devoted to virtue and guiltless of evil. *Anyone guilty of arrogance will not dwell in my house* (v. 7): I preferred to have no one given to haughtiness residing with me. *Anyone speaking false things did not prosper before my eyes:* anyone recommending or pursuing injustice left disappointed, my anxiety being to close my ears to those intent on slander.

(5) *At dawn I executed all the sinners in the land so as to rid the Lord's city of all the workers of iniquity* (v. 8). [1676] We know this clearly from history: he dispatched to death all the impious

2. Having decided, perhaps with the encouragement of tradition (the text itself not being decisive), that the psalm applies to Josiah's personal integrity, Theodoret is content to paraphrase the verses, characteristically avoiding any tendency to extend the application to the lives of his readers by any sort of moralizing. The historical reference may also explain the lack of Scriptural documentation beyond the mention of Kings and Chronicles as his sources.

priests and cleansed the holy city. By *at dawn* he refers to the rule of his kingship: like dawn he burst on the scene with seemly and illuminating righteousness.[3] Anyone wanting to gain a more precise knowledge of the man's virtue will find it in the second book of Chronicles and the fourth book of Kings.[4] Let each person, then, take pains to be an imitator of this man so as to have an equal share with him in confidence before Christ. Amen.

3. This Christological explanation of the phrase is from the long form of the text, which supplies also the closing exhortation below; execution at dawn, an established practice of autocrats, is also a possible interpretation, the NRSV's "morning by morning" suggesting inefficiency to Dahood, who prefers to take the original differently as "like cattle."

4. Cf. 2 Chron 34–35; 2 Kings 22–23 (the LXX numbering the books of Samuel as two books of Kings). Josiah clearly appeals to Theodoret as a man with priorities, which he admires and which he is credited with having emulated.

COMMENTARY ON PSALM 102

*A prayer for the poor person when feeling at a loss
and giving vent to a petition before the Lord.*

HILE THE PSALM contains a prophecy of the hardship of the people of the Jews in Babylon and the return from there, it also forecasts at the same time the calling and salvation of the nations. It is also relevant to a person struggling with calamity of any kind and begging to attain divine grace, "poor person" referring to the one in need of divine providence.[1]

(2) *Lord, hearken to my prayer, let my cry come to you* (v. 1): accept my supplication, O Lord, and extend your help to the one lamenting. For *cry* Symmachus, in fact, said "lamentation." *Do not turn your face away from me* (v. 2): Be kind to me, and dissolve your displeasure. *On the day I am distressed, incline your ear to me; on the day I call upon you, promptly hearken me.* These words of the psalm also indicate that it is a prophecy of the future and not an account of the past: since the people who found themselves in the kingdom of the divinely inspired David enjoyed great prosperity and fame, it was right for the inspired author adopting the point of view of those others, to offer the petition and to beg to attain divine care whenever occasion required it.

(3) *Because my days have passed away like smoke, and my bones are burned up like dry wood* (v. 3). Here in his characteristic manner he recounts the future calamities as though past, and says his span of life has wasted like smoke, and his body turned into burned wood from discouragement as though consumed by some bolt of fire. Aquila, in fact, also translated it this way, "My

---

1. A rare admission of a psalm's applicability to the life of ordinary readers—not really developed in the course of commentary; it is not the bishop's purpose.

bones were consumed like burning." *I was beaten down like hay, and my heart was dried up* (v. 4): I was etiolated like hay, and lost my former bloom. [1677] *Because I forgot to eat my bread. At the sound of my groaning my bones stuck to my flesh* (v. 5): I lost appetite for any food, and was completely bereft of my former good condition, my body being consumed by the wasting of discouragement; I am but skin and bones. The word of God, then, is our soul's bread: just as ordinary bread nourishes the body, so the word from heaven [nourishes] the soul's substance. In passing on the prayer, Christ said as much to the apostles, "Give us this day our daily bread."[2] So whoever forgets to eat it, that is, to be active (action, after all, constituting the eating of the spiritual bread, as is clear from the saying of the Lord to the apostles, "Be active, not for the eating which perishes, but for that which endures to life eternal"),[3] this one's heart is stricken and dried up like hay. How does hay get stricken and dry up? When rain stops falling on it. As the heart, too, when suffering from a dearth of the word, is then stricken and dries up, the flower of virtue no longer has the strength to bloom.

(4) *I became like a woodpecker in the wilderness, I resembled a night-raven in a building. I could not sleep, and became like a solitary sparrow on a rooftop* (vv. 6–7). He employs many comparisons in his wish to do justice to the calamities; through each of the birds mentioned he suggests fear and the lack of care: the *sparrow* keeps sleep at bay with its struggles, and the *night-raven* flees the inhabited parts of buildings and makes for deserted and forsaken ones, Symmachus in fact saying "ruins" for *buildings.* And the other bird likewise lives in the wilderness, too.[4] *All day long my enemies reproached me, and those praising me swore oaths against me* (v. 8): I became the laughing-stock of my adversaries, and the one who formerly was enviable and famous now became a byword to those who previously were admirers; they take oaths with my calamities in mind, saying, May I not suffer what so-and-so suffered.

2. Matt 6.11. Not content with the brief comment on v. 6, the long form of the text inserts a lengthy spiritual interpretation of bread as the word of God.
3. John 6.27.
4. We have seen Theodoret the naturalist being at an advantage in developing the psalmist's imagery for his readers.

(5) *Because I ate ashes for bread, and mingled tears with my drink in the face of your rage and your anger* (vv. 9–10). He said this also in the seventy-ninth psalm, "You will feed us bread of tears, and give us tears to drink in good measure."[5] In this he indicates the extent of the pain: if the occasion of eating were full of pain, any other time would hardly be free of it. I am beset with these troubles, he is saying, since you directed your rage against me, O Lord. *Because you lifted me up and broke me in pieces:* you made me look elevated and [1680] caused me to be the cynosure of all eyes, and all of a sudden cast me aside; he used *broke in pieces* by analogy with those lifting something up and throwing it down on the floor. *My days faded like a shadow; I am dried up like hay* (v. 11). I am at the very setting of my life, he is saying, I am like a shadow that lengthens and then fades. I have become like dried hay, inviting the hands of the reapers.

(6) *But you, O Lord, abide forever, and memory of you for generation and generation* (v. 12): But I have this kind of nature and am shackled with such calamities, whereas you, eternal and everlasting, could easily grant me some change in the present troubles. In fact, he goes on to say, *You will arise and take pity on Sion, because it is time to take pity on her, because the time has come* (v. 13). Grant the calamity a change for the better, he is saying: the time requires mercy. In this he hints at the end of the punishment determined for seventy years. Thus the remarkable Daniel, too, in numbering the period of captivity, offers also supplication.[6] The words of the spiritual singing are also in harmony with this. *Because it is time to take pity on her, because the time has come, because your servants took pleasure in her stones, and will have pity on her dust* (vv. 13–14): Sion is most dear to us, quite deserted though it is; its leveled stones are well loved, and the recollection of the piles left by its sacking instills pity in us.

(7) *The nations will fear the name of the Lord, and all the kings of the earth your glory* (v. 15): seeing our return and the building of the city, those who noticed our former calamities—kings, rulers, and ruled—will marvel at your power, and in fear will believe you alone are God. This occurred really and truly following the Incarnation of our God and Savior: after the Jews'

5. Cf. Ps 80.5.   6. Cf. Dan 9.2ff.

recall the neighboring people marveled at the event, but were so far from believing in the God of all as to declare war on them at the same time. Here, however, the verse prophesies a change in all the nations and the kings. Some of this we see happening in the past, some we hope will be in the future. The divine Apostle, in fact, says, "We do not yet see everything in subjection to him."[7] Still, he taught that every knee will bend to him, of those in heaven, on earth, and under the earth.[8]

(8) [1681] *Because the Lord will build Sion, and will be seen in his glory* (v. 16): since those ignorant of the divine purposes regarded the Jews' servitude and the desolation of Jerusalem as weakness on God's part, he was right to call the restoration of the city God's *glory,* meaning, With Sion rebuilt, everyone will recognize the God of all in the former glory. *He had regard for the prayer of the lowly, and did not scorn their petition* (v. 17): he did not despise them for being captives and slaves, but accepted the supplication and granted freedom.

(9) *Let this be recorded for another generation, and the people being created will praise the Lord* (v. 18): we shall keep this kindness in writing forever so that those to come will learn of your loving-kindness. He calls the people formed from nations *people being created,* blessed Paul saying of it, "If anyone is in Christ, he is a new creation";[9] and the divinely inspired David himself said in the twenty-first psalm, "The generation to come will be proclaimed to the Lord, and will proclaim his righteousness to the people yet to be born, whom the Lord made."[10] This people, when instructed in things both old and new, offers the due hymn to God the Savior. *That the Lord looked down from his holy eminence, he surveyed the earth from heaven, to hear the groaning of those in bondage, to release the children of the dead, to announce the name of the Lord in Sion and his praise in Jerusalem* (vv. 19–21): observing and governing all things, the God of all hearkened to those he observed and delivered the verdict of freedom so that those in bondage might return in place of the lost, build the ancestral city, and in it offer to God habitually the worship in keeping with the Law. *When peoples and kings are gathered together*

---

7. Heb 2.8.
9. 2 Cor 5.17.

8. Cf. Phil 2.10.
10. Cf. Ps 22.30–31.

to serve the Lord. He replied to him in the way of his strength, Announce to me the fewness of my days, Do not cut me off in the middle of my days (vv. 22–24). When we are granted return, he says, peoples and kings will be assembled, amazed at your power. So we will then have such great joy as to beseech your goodness to grant us additional years and not be consigned to death in the middle of our time. He calls *way of strength* the return provided on account of God's strength. *Your years in a generation of generations:* [1684] you have unlimited being, and it is easy for you to make the others also long-lived.

(10) *In the beginning, Lord, you laid the foundations of the earth, and the heavens are works of your hands. They will perish, but you abide* (vv. 25–26): what is not possible for the Creator of all? You gave being to the earth, you made the heavens from what did not exist, and whereas everything undergoes change, you have immutability.[11] From the elements constituting everything he showed him to be creator of all the other things as well. *They will all wear out like a garment, you will rotate them like clothing and they will be changed.* Symmachus, on the other hand, put it this way, "They will all wear out like a garment, you will change them like clothing and they will be changed": everything visible will grow old, and will resemble the old age of garments, whereas you will change and renew them, and will make them incorruptible instead of corruptible.[12] The divinely inspired Apostle also said this, "Because creation itself will also be freed from its subjection to corruption with a view to the freedom of the glory of the children of God."[13] *You, on the contrary, are the same, and your years will not fail* (v. 27): so you remodel creation as you wish, O Lord; you have an immutable nature, proof against change. The divine Apostle, of course, attributed these verses to the particular characteristic of the Son in the Epistle to the Hebrews;[14] yet likewise we discern the Father in the Son: for

11. The credal ἀτρέπτως, "immutable," again.

12. What the version of Symmachus contributes is debatable; if anything, it loses the sense of rotation of clothing that the LXX, and thus the NT in citing these verses, *pace* NRSV, effectively achieves.

13. Rom 8.21.

14. Heb 1.10–12, Theodoret speaking here of the Son's *idiotes;* he was unhappy about the Cyrilline term *hypostasis.* Paul has slightly muddied the waters

whatever he does the Son likewise does, and sameness of nature is recognized in each, for the operation of the Trinity is one, as we know.

(11) *The sons of your servants will settle, and their offspring will be guided forever* (v. 28). Symmachus, on the other hand, put "will abide." He indicates that those freed from slavery will inhabit Jerusalem, whereas their *offspring* will abide forever. The divine Apostle said about this offspring, "Until the offspring would come to whom the promise was made," and, "The promises were made to Abraham and to his offspring. It does not say, And to the offspring as though of many, but as of one, And to your offspring, who is Christ."[15] This offspring will abide forever: united with God the Word, he has immortal being, and grants life to the believers, according to the saying of the Lord himself, "The one who eats my flesh and drinks my blood will live forever."[16]

---

by including these verses in his series of Christological texts in that epistle, Theodoret feels, and he needs to clarify sound teaching on the Trinity.

15. Gal 3.19, 16.

16. A loose recall of John 6.54, 58. Theodoret's habitual conciseness here does not allow him to unpack his statement of the *henosis,* union, of Christ the offspring and God the Word with sufficient precision to be completely satisfying.

COMMENTARY ON PSALM 103

A psalm for David. [1685]

HIS PSALM SEEMS TO CONFORM to the previous one and to deal with the same theme: for in that one those lamenting the calamities in Babylon begged God to grant them return, while here they have gained what they asked and sing the praises of the benefactor. Yet I believe the hymn singing is relevant to all people freed from even harsher servitude and accorded greater freedom. The sense of the words will reveal that the latter theme is more relevant than the former.[1]

(2) *Bless the Lord, my soul, and all that is within me his holy name* (v. 1). Those feeling grateful for the divine graces bestir themselves to hymn singing, repaying the benefactor to the extent possible. It is always possible to sing his praises and to carry about a fresh recollection of the favors. These people also consecrate all that is within, and direct their whole thinking to the divine hymn; by *within*, in fact, he referred to thinking, pondering, and all the movements of the soul. *Bless the Lord, my soul, and do not forget all his rewards* (v. 2). Again the soul is instructed to bestir itself, expel the cloud of forgetfulness, and renew the recollection of the favors. For *the rewards* Symmachus, by contrast, said *kindnesses.*

(3) Then he outlines these individually. *Who forgives all your iniquities, who heals all your diseases* (v. 3): he has granted you the pardon for sins, he has granted you the healing of sufferings. The palsied man benefited from this: he heard at one and the same time, "Your sins are forgiven," and "Take up your bed and

---

1. It is rare (otherwise unknown?) for Theodoret formally to relegate the psalm's supposed historical associations to second place in order of relevance, despite his disclaimer in the preface. He proceeds to develop the psalm's spiritual meaning.

155

go home."[2] Likewise the sinful woman attained forgiveness,[3] likewise the brigand,[4] likewise the tax collectors,[5] likewise all who believed. *Who redeems your life from decay* (v. 4): while he freed those taken off as captives in Babylon from slavery, he did not free them from life's corruption. To us, on the contrary, he has granted the hope of resurrection, given the pledge of the Spirit, and clad us in the robe of incorruption.[6] *Who crowns you with mercy and compassion:* "by grace you have been saved," as the divine Apostle says, and, "this is not your own doing, it is the gift of God, so that no one may boast"; and again, "Jesus Christ came into the world to save sinners, of whom I am the foremost. But the reason I received mercy was that in me as the foremost Christ Jesus might give evidence of his utter long-suffering as an example to those who would believe [1688] in him for eternal life."[7] Accordingly, it is a crown of grace and loving-kindness. Likewise the divinely inspired Isaiah also cries out in the person of the bride, "Let my soul rejoice in the Lord, for he clad me in a garment of salvation, and clad me in a robe of joy; he invested me with a garland like a bridegroom, and adorned me with adornments like a bride"; and a little later, "You shall be a crown of beauty in the hand of the Lord, and a royal diadem in the hand of your God."[8] All these are the groom's [wedding] presents and gifts: the bride brought faith alone.

(4) *Who satisfies your desire with good things* (v. 5). Since desire is culpable, and the divine Law forbids it, it was good for him to add *with good things:* the Lord fulfills our good desires, saying, "Ask, and it will be given to you; seek, and you shall find; knock, and [the door] will be opened for you: whoever asks receives,

2. Matt 9.2, 6.   3. Cf. Luke 7.47–48.
4. Cf. Luke 23.43.
5. Cf. Luke 19.1–10. The degree of Scriptural documentation is an index of his relish for developing the psalm's spiritual meaning. In fact, his familiarity with the Gospels, at least in general outline, leads us to wonder why he seems not to have reached on a Gospel commentary, unless it was out of respect for his predecessors, heeding Jerome's advice to Augustine when he contemplated a commentary on the Psalms: if they had succeeded, it would be superfluous; if not, presumptuous.
6. Cf. 2 Cor 1.22; 1 Cor 15.53.
7. 1 Tim 1.15–16.
8. Isa 61.10; 62.3.

whoever seeks finds, to the one knocking [the door] will be opened . . . But seek the kingdom of God and his righteousness, and all these things as well will be given to you in abundance."[9] *Your youth will be renewed like the eagle's.* The Lord granted us this renewal in turn through all-holy baptism, and by stripping away the old age of sin he made us young instead of old. In harmony with this God says through the prophet Isaiah, "Those who wait for me will adjust their strength, they will take wings like eagles":[10] since in our creation we received a divine and regal character, and then besmirched and destroyed it with all kinds of sinful pursuits, the inspired word promises us the recovery of the regality. This bird is regal, after all, entrusted with the kingship of feathered creatures.

(5) He teaches us also the manner of the divine generosity. *The Lord does deeds of mercy and judgment in favor of all the wronged* (v. 6): "it was not through the righteous deeds we performed," as the divine Apostle says, "but according to his great mercy that he saved us by the washing of rebirth and the Holy Spirit's renewal."[11] Perceiving us to be wronged by the enemy of truth, he opened for us the founts of mercy, and delivered a just verdict against him. *He made known his ways to Moses, and his wishes to the children of Israel* (v. 7): it was not by any change of heart that he concerned himself with this salvation of ours; rather, he had announced these things through the biblical authors, and foreshadowed our salvation through the divinely inspired Moses. [1689] The sea was made a type of all-holy baptism, the rock was seen as a foreshadowing of the immortal streams, and the manna as an image of the heavenly food; and it is possible,

9. Matt 7.7–8; 6.33.
10. Isa 40.31. The spiritual meaning Theodoret is developing takes on a sacramental dimension, interesting both for mention only of baptism as a sacrament of forgiveness and for lack of any reference to an original sin as destructive of the "divine and regal character" received in creation. As well, he resonates as a naturalist with mention of the king of the birds without appearing to know anything of the fable of its rejuvenation (or that of the phoenix) implied by the psalmist.
11. Titus 3.5, a text that might have set Chrysostom weighing up the respective roles of human effort and divine grace in the process of salvation. We have seen Theodoret touch on this question; but he is not so anxious to uphold the former influence as his predecessor is (see Introduction, section 8).

without my touching on each individually, to find the other realities likewise foreshadowed in those things.[12]

(6) *The Lord is compassionate and merciful, long-suffering and rich in mercy* (v. 8). The depths of divine goodness, he is saying, the immeasurable mercy, the ocean of loving-kindness are the cause of these goods. *He will not be angered forever, nor vent his wrath endlessly. He has not dealt with us according to our sins, nor repaid us according to our iniquities* (vv. 9–10): he could not bring himself to gauge the punishment by our sins, nor extend his displeasure against us to great lengths. *Because according to the height of heaven from earth the Lord magnified his mercy towards those who fear him; as far as the east is from the west he put our sins at a distance from us* (vv. 11–12). If [the psalmist] had found distances greater than these, he definitely would have brought them to bear in his desire to bring out the unlimited quality of the divine goodness. But human reason could not find a more exalted measure than heaven, nor anything greater than the distance between west and east. *As a father has compassion on his children, so the Lord had compassion on those who fear him* (v. 13): being creator and maker, he imitated a father's goodness, and displayed the same affection for his servants as a father for his children.

(7) *Because he knew our shaping, he remembered that we are dust* (v. 14): the creator knows the limitations of our nature, he knows also what we are made of and where we shall finally go. *Man, his days like hay, like a flower of the field he will flourish* (v. 15): we are no different from hay and a flower, which blooms early, but shortly after fades and disappears. *Because a breeze passes over it, and it is no more, and it will no longer recognize its place* (v. 16). Symmachus, on the other hand, put it this way, "Because a breeze crosses over it, then it is no more." By *breeze* he means the soul: when it is present the body also lives and works, but when it takes flight it is snuffed out and destroyed, with the result that its former characteristics are not recognized and it is impossible to tell that this body belongs to such a one, that

12. In Theodoret's book, typology is an acceptable hermeneutical process if Scripture encourages it, and it even throws divine mercy into greater relief.

body to somebody else. You would notice this more precisely if you were to peep into a grave: all fall victim to the same corruption, and preserve none of their former characteristics.[13]

(8) [1692] *But the mercy of the Lord is from age to age on those who fear him, and his righteousness to children's children, to those who keep his covenant and remember his commandments so as to do them* (vv. 17–18): so while [human] nature is subject to death in that way, the divine loving-kindness grants the favor of living a long life, and continues to their successors the reward of righteousness due to the forebears. Thus for Jehu he preserved the kingship to the fourth generation, even though admittedly he did not acquire perfect piety but gave evidence of zeal at the beginning of his reign.[14] Thus for the divinely inspired David he kept the spark of his line alive, even though many impious members sprang up in the middle. He extends this mercy, however, to *those who keep his covenant,* he is saying, and not simply to *those who remember his commandments* but who add deeds to words and conduct their own life in accordance with them.

(9) *The Lord established his throne in heaven, and his kingdom rules over all* (v. 19). This resembles what is said in another psalm, "He who dwells in the heights, and looks down on what is below."[15] Here, in fact, the inspired word teaches us that while the Lord of all has his throne in heaven, he looks down and governs creation as creator of all, as king, and lord. *Bless the Lord, all his angels, his mighty ones, who carry out his word, so as to listen to the sound of his words* (v. 20). It was right for him to summon the unseen powers to share in the hymn singing: human nature is not capable of worthily singing your praises as benefactor, whereas the incorporeal and holy natures have a life free of passions and are capable of fulfilling the divine commands. *Bless the Lord, all his powers, his servants who do his will* (v. 21). The heavenly ranks are many and varied: Principalities and Powers,

13. Despite the typical conciseness, the description of complete reversal in death is effective; but the commentator allows himself none of the moralizing that a preacher like Chrysostom, who has left a commentary not on this psalm but on the similar Ps 49, cannot resist.

14. Cf. 2 Kings 10.30–31.

15. Cf. Ps 33.13.

Thrones and Dominations, Seraphim and Cherubim, and other names unknown to us, as the divine Apostle says. But the inspired word included them all in these two names: he called them *angels* as servants of the divine commands and transmitting the divine words, and *powers* as capable of doing his bidding and receiving from the Creator the power by nature.

(10) *Bless the Lord, all his works, in every place of his dominion* (v. 22). This does not [1693] apply to the Jews: when they were bidden by their captors to sing some of the songs of Sion, they replied in obedience to the Law, "How shall we sing the song of the Lord in a foreign land?"[16] It is to us, on the contrary, that the divine Apostle gives the exhortation to lift holy hands in every place.[17] Christ the Lord also said this to the Samaritan woman, "Amen, Amen, I say to you, the hour is coming, and is now here, when they will worship the Father neither in this place nor in Jerusalem. God is spirit, after all, and those who worship him must worship in spirit and truth."[18] *Bless the Lord, my soul.* The conclusion is in harmony with the opening: summoning intellectual beings to hymn singing in common, he also teaches us to reverence the Creator to the extent possible, and to offer the thanksgiving hymn in the measure of our ability.

16. Ps 137.4.
17. Cf. 1 Tim 2.8. To the end Theodoret is resisting a historical reading of the psalm.
18. John 4.21, 23–24, loosely recalled.

COMMENTARY ON PSALM 104

A psalm for David.

HE GRACE OF THE ALL-HOLY Spirit offers people not only moral and dogmatic teaching, but also gives precise instruction on the way we ought to sing the praises of the Creator.[1] This was the reason he composed this psalm, to be sure, employing as minister blessed David,[2] that we should all come to know with which hymns we should make response to the benefactor. Here he recounts the common favors, and portrays the God of all to be both maker and governor of everything.

(2) *Bless the Lord, my soul* (v. 1). He teaches each student of piety to sing the praises of God the benefactor. *O Lord my God, how extremely great you are!* Here *how* is a mark of hyperbole. *You are great* is not indicative of increase, but suggests immeasurable greatness; Symmachus translated it this way, too, "O my God, you are extremely great." In other words, it is not a case of his being small and becoming big, but of his being great by nature and this being demonstrated to devout people—not his complete greatness but to the extent human nature allows. *You have clothed yourself in confession and magnificence.* Symmachus put it this way, "You wrapped yourself in praise and glory": the beneficiaries of your good things are no longer in ignorance of you, nor do they pay reverence due to you to the idols; instead, they sing your praises and repay the debt of praise.

---

1. The Psalms are primarily meant for teaching, moral and dogmatic, Theodoret believes and says so in preface and conclusion. Yet here he concedes that they have a role in worship.

2. So for Theodoret the Spirit is author of the Psalms as of all the Scriptures, and David, like the other biblical authors, his minister, assistant, *hypourgos*—not a mere instrument, as in Platonic thinking. See my "Psalm 45: a *locus classicus* for patristic thinking on biblical inspiration."

(3) *Wrapped in light like a garment* (v. 2). The Apostle also said things in harmony with this, "It is he alone who has immortality and dwells in unapproachable light":[3] that light is such that no one dares to come near it, the intensity of the rays turning one's eyes away. After all, if the visible [light of the] sun forces those [1696] avidly trying to discern it to do this, who could manage to come to an understanding of the unapproachable light? He is, then, himself true light, and as well *he is wrapped in light like a garment*, and "dwells in unapproachable light," with cloud and gloom around him,[4] and he made darkness his canopy.[5] These things are not inconsistent with one another: the unapproachable light is the same as gloom and darkness to those unable to see it; it is impossible to discern what is in the one and in the other. The one case and the other, of course, indicate the invisible quality of the divine nature. *Stretching out heaven like canvas.* In this he taught the facility of the Creator: as it is easy for someone to stretch canvas and make a tent, so by employing but a word the God of all spread out the furthest reaches of the heavens.

(4) *Who covers his chambers with waters* (v. 3). Blessed Moses also taught this, saying God had given the order, "Let there be a firmament in the midst of the water; it will separate the water above the firmament from the water below the firmament."[6] *Who makes clouds his pavement, who walks on wings of winds.* By this he indicated his providence reaching everywhere: he takes his position on winds and clouds, he is saying, he personally controls and guides them, and at the right time confers the benefit stemming from them. He teaches at the same time that the divine nature is present everywhere and surveys all things: since the winds are the fastest of all material things, traveling in a flash from west to east and from east to west, he found no more precise image of speed among material things and so said God is carried on winds' wings, indicating by this that he is present everywhere. We also find the God of all appearing in a cloud to the children of Israel, and making his personal appearance in

3. 1 Tim 4.16.   4. Cf. Ps 97.2.
5. Cf. Ps 18.11.   6. Gen 1.6–7, loosely recalled.

the tabernacle by way of a cloud.[7] When Solomon dedicated
the house [of the Temple], of course, a cloud covered the
house.[8] And Christ the Lord on the mountain with the three
apostles gave a glimpse of a cloud shining around him;[9] and at
his ascension a shining cloud took him out of their sight.[10]

(5) *Who makes winds his angels and a flaming fire his ministers* (v.
4). He presented him as Creator not only of the visible things
but also of the invisible; he spoke of them as *winds* and *fire* to
bring out power and speed in each case: wind is naturally rapid,
while fire is strong in its action. The God of all employs angels
as assistants both to be [1697] of service to the worthy and to
punish the opposite—hence the mention of fire, suggesting
punitive action. *Who laid the foundations of the earth on its stability*
(v. 5). Aquila and Symmachus, on the other hand, said, "on its
base." *It will not be overturned forever:* after building it on itself, he
gave it immobility, and it will remain in this condition as long as
he wishes. [Scripture] says this elsewhere as well, "Hanging
earth upon nothing."[11]

(6) *The depths his covering like a garment* (v. 6). He put *his* for
"its," both Aquila and Theodotion giving as version, "You covered it with the depths like clothing." The divine Scripture
gives the name *depths* to the watery substance; blessed Moses
also spoke this way in the beginning of creation, "The earth was
invisible and formless, and darkness was upon the depths."[12] So
since the earth is encircled by waters from all sides, and the vast
unnavigable oceans are its boundary while many others divide
it, he was right to speak of *the depths* placed on the earth *like a
garment. Waters will stand on the mountains. They will flee from your
censure, they will be terrified by the sound of your thunder. They will
climb mountains and descend into plains to the place, which you have
established for them* (vv. 6–8). In this he brings out God's provi-

7. Cf. Exod 13.21; 40.34.   8. Cf. 2 Chron 5.13–14.
9. Cf. Matt 17.5.
10. Acts 1.9. The picture of God riding the clouds has intrigued commentators from the beginning up to Mowinckel and Dahood, who point to cultic and
biblical parallels such as are assembled by Theodoret, who also brings to the
task his talents as a naturalist and his theological concerns.
11. Job 26.7.
12. Gen 1.2.

dence presiding over creation: thanks to it the sea resembles the mountain peaks in its waves without inundating the dry land; rather, just as we cower down at the thunder, so does it respect the limit placed on it. *Waters will stand on the mountains* means "They stood like a mountain," and *They will climb mountains* means "like mountains."[13] *You set a limit, which they shall not pass, nor will they turn back to cover the earth* (v. 9): the sea feels revulsion at the sand, and though raging to that point, it rears up when halted by the divine limit as though by a bridle, rears up, and turns back.

(7) *Who makes springs flow from the ravines; waters will travel between the mountains* (v. 10). Then he gives a glimpse of the benefit from this: *They will give drink to all the beasts of the field; wild asses will look forward to quenching their thirst. On them the birds of heaven will dwell, they will give voice amidst the rocks* (vv. 11–12). This is the greatest index of divine providence, meeting the needs not only of human beings but also of brute beasts. [1700] That is the reason he shaped passages with the waters by cutting through the mountains, so that not only human beings but also the species of land animals and those that are airborne should have streams from springs in abundance. The phrase, *wild asses will look forward to quenching their thirst,* Symmachus rendered this way, "a wild ass will recover its thirst." *Who waters mountains from his upper chambers; the earth will be satisfied with the fruit of your works* (v. 13): he not only gushes forth from below and prepares the nature of the waters, but provides moisture from on high through clouds.

(8) Then at this point he gives a glimpse of its usefulness. *Who makes grass grow for the cattle and crops for the service of human beings so as to produce bread from the earth* (v. 14): herbs grow and nourish cattle, created for human use; fruits are also nourished by rain, become ripe, and are made available to human beings. He said this also in another psalm, "You will save human beings and cattle, O Lord."[14] Yet it is for the sake of human beings that

13. As the original of these verses is "much contested" (Dahood), so even the Greek forms puzzle ancient and modern commentators.
14. Ps 36.6. The naturalist in Theodoret is enjoying this zoological onomasticon.

the cattle also enjoy this providence. *Wine cheers the human heart for gladdening the face with oil; bread strengthens the human heart* (v. 15). Symmachus, on the other hand, said it more clearly, "Growing grass for cattle and crops for the service of human beings so that nourishment may spring from the earth and wine cheer the human heart, brighten the face with oil, and bread strengthen the human heart." This is the reason, he is saying, that the God of all constantly provides rain for the earth, to make fruits of all kinds grow, to strengthen and nourish human nature with bread, with wine to give cheer and to make life more satisfying, and with oil not only to nourish from within but also to make the bodies glisten on the outside.

(9) *The trees of the plain will be satisfied* (v. 16). The Hebrew and the other translators add "the Lord's." After listing the fruitbearing trees, it was necessary for him to mention also those that bear no fruit, providing as they also do necessary help to human beings. This was the reason for calling them "the Lord's," as being natural, not the product of human hands but growing in response to the divine word. Hence he added as well *the cedars of Lebanon, which you planted:* it was not simply that certain husbandmen were responsible for their growth; rather, the divine word caused the mountaintops to abound with them. By mentioning Lebanon for its fame as well as its cedars, of course, he thereby suggested also the other mountains and trees. [1701] *Sparrows will build their nests there; the home of the heron outranks them* (v. 17). Aquila, on the other hand, says, "Birds will build their nests there, pines provide a home for a heron," while Symmachus has, "Where sparrows will build a nest, a plane tree a dwelling for the marten": the trees themselves provide for the needs of human beings and for the different needs of the birds; some are suitable for making a home for people, others accommodate the dwellings of birds. *The high mountains are for the deer, rock a refuge for the hares* (v. 18). Your providence does not overlook even the tiniest of animals, he is saying; instead, you give the mountain peaks to the deer as a place to live, and to the smaller animals the holes in rocks.

(10) *You made the moon for seasons* (v. 19). After listing everything on earth, showing the creation of the invisible natures

and giving a glimpse of the making of the heavens, he makes mention of the lights created on the fourth day. He says the creation of the moon happened with a view to teaching the seasons: its phases are responsible for time being measured, as it achieves the measuring of the month by waxing and waning in so many days. *The sun knows its setting,* not by being endowed with life or enjoying the use of reason, but by traveling within divine limits and thus by its appearance bringing about daytime and keeping night at bay; it always has the same course and retains its dimensions.[15] *You put darkness in place, and night fell* (v. 20). The advantage of this, too, is considerable: it takes effect with the departure of the light, providing repose for human beings. *All the beasts of the forest travel about in it, lion cubs roaring for the hunt and the search for food from God for themselves* (vv. 20–21): While night brings about rest for human beings, it provides a means for the animals to fill their hungry stomachs. The phrase, *the search for food from God for themselves,* means, Divine providence meets this need for them: asking from God belongs to rational beings, whereas searching to irrational ones. Still, God supplies them, too, with the needed nourishment. *The sun rose, and they gathered and will sleep in their lairs. Man will go to his work and his business until evening* (vv. 22–23): with the rising of the sun, some creatures retire to their own holes, whereas human beings, having put behind them the labor of the previous day, eagerly pass the day again at their business.

(11) [1704] *How magnified are your works, O Lord! You made everything in wisdom* (v. 24). Pondering everything that had been said, and learning of God's great care, the inspired author uttered the hymn in the middle of the account, saying, All God's doings are marvelous, quite admirable, and full of wisdom. He found, in fact, the night misrepresented by some impious people and extremely valuable, the trees that bear no fruit providing another advantage, and the species of wild animals suited in many respects to human beings. *The earth is filled*

15. In Theodoret's cosmology the sun moved about the earth and thus produced night and day, while the moon through its phases was the basis of the (lunar) calendar in use in his time, before the adjustments made by the Gregorian calendar and Copernican cosmology.

with your possession. The other translators, on the other hand, put "creation," meaning, You have filled it with good things of many kinds. Moving from the earth, however, to the nearby sea, he says, *The sea itself, vast and wide; reptiles are there beyond number, small animals along with large* (v. 25): this is also a sign of divine care, the small species living with the large and in no way being consumed by them.

(12) *Ships sail there* (v. 26). This, too, is of the greatest utility to human beings: through the shipbuilder's art and the steersman's science, we trade with one another in necessities and in the produce we grow and supply to others, and we receive their produce. *The serpent you made to play in it.* By *serpent* he suggested the large animals which like to dwell in the great oceans. Now, *to play in it* means "in the sea itself"; it is a masculine word in the Hebrew and the Syriac.[16] [The sea] is so vast, he is saying, that it contains countless species of fish, and the largest animals safely swim in it. Some people, on the other hand, opt for taking the *serpent* allegorically, on account of the verse found also in Isaiah, "His great sword, holy and strong, moves against the serpent, the twisting snake in the sea";[17] and we do not deprecate such a meaning, since we find also in Job this creature being played with by the divine angels;[18] and the Lord gave his disciples authority to walk on snakes and scorpions and all the power of the foe.[19]

(13) *They all look to you to give them their food in due season* (v. 27). At your hands, he is saying, everything has its needs met at the right time: the brute beasts search for food without know-

16. A rare comment by Theodoret on the Hebrew text outside of psalm titles, and, as usual, only with the assistance of his native Syriac; see Introduction, section 3. His reading could be valid, and is supported by the NRSV; Dahood prefers a reading "to sport with" on the basis of the Job text Theodoret goes on to cite, "Will you sport with him?"

17. Isa 27.1. The *Isaiah* text is not such a helpful example of taking an allegorical sense (Theodoret employing the verb *allegorein*), as the prophet introduces the mythical monster as the final instance of cosmic powers falling under the Lord's triumphant control. He might rather have referred back to Ps 74.13, where he himself had interpreted the monster allegorically as Pharaoh and the devil.

18. Cf. Job 41.5, the mythical monster again, but still not allegorical.

19. Luke 10.19. Is Theodoret taking this dominical saying as allegorical?

ing the provider, yet it is from the Creator that they receive it. *When you give it to them, they will gather it* (v. 28): when you provide the abundance, each of them stands to benefit from the provisions. *When you open your hand,* [1705] *they will be filled with the totality of goodness.* He indicated in this the ease of the supply of good things: as it is a simple matter to extend clenched fingers, so it is easy for God to make a gift of all good things in abundance.

(14) *On the other hand, when you turn away your face, they will be alarmed* (v. 29): just as you fill those enjoying the good things with complete satisfaction, granting them in your benevolence, likewise when you turn away, everything is filled with alarm and dread. *When you take away their spirit, they will fade and will go back to their dust:* when you decide, a separation occurs between soul and body, after which the body is consigned to corruption and dissolves into its original dust. By *spirit* here he refers to the soul.[20] *When you send forth your spirit, they will be created, and you will renew the face of the earth* (v. 30). Here he clearly predicted the resurrection and the new life through the all-holy Spirit. Likewise the famous Elijah also breathed three times into the widow's little son, and through the spiritual grace dwelling within brought him back to life;[21] likewise Elisha also resuscitated the son of the Shunammite woman by use of the spiritual breathing and bringing about life through the life-giving breath.[22] In like manner, after bringing out this activity, he directs his speech to singing the praises of the divine power.

(15) *May the glory of the Lord be forever* (v. 31). It is always right, he is saying, for his praises to be sung. *The Lord will rejoice in his works.* In this he prophesied people's knowledge of God in the future: when people are freed from their former error

20. The rendering "*their* spirit" of LXX (and NRSV), for which Dahood proposes instead a reading of the Hebrew as "*your* spirit/breath," discourages Theodoret from explaining to his readers at this point the essential difference between Hebrew and Greek anthropology underlying their opposed eschatology, an area he himself is somewhat unclear about.

21. 1 Kings 17.21 [LXX]; in the Hebrew Elijah simply stretches himself on the child.

22. 2 Kings 4.34–35, no breathing being mentioned, simply mouth upon mouth, eyes on eyes, . . .

and accept the knowledge of God, God will rejoice, not for being worshipped, but for seeing them saved. *Who looks down on the earth, and makes it tremble; who touches the mountains, and they will smoke* (v. 32) It was right for him to add this, teaching the absence of need in the divine nature: it is not out of need that he is pleased to be adored; rather, out of a desire to save he demonstrates the truth. And though capable of punishing, he does not impose the punishment, even if admittedly shaking the earth by his mere appearance and filling the mountains with fire and smoke. He did this also on Mount Sinai: by making his characteristic appearance, he caused the whole mountain to be seen giving forth smoke.[23]

(16) *I shall sing to the Lord in my life, I shall play psalms to my God as long as I live* (v. 33). He was right to add this, too; after all, "There is no one in death to mention him: in Hades who will confess [1708] him?"[24] This was the reason the door was closed on the bridegroom's foolish virgins, who by buying oil wasted the opportunity of bearing lamps.[25] *May my converse be pleasing to him* (v. 34). For *converse* Symmachus said "conversation," Aquila, on the other hand, "association." I pray, he is saying, that my hymn singing be seen to be most sweet and pleasing.[26] *I shall rejoice in the Lord:* when this happens, he is saying, I shall gain satisfaction from it.

(17) *May sinners disappear from the earth, and the lawless be no more* (v. 35). After describing the divine beauty and the untold riches as far as human nature can, he desires that all people share the same knowledge, and begs that the company of sinners disappear completely, not demanding that they perish but asking that they be changed, and begging that their forces come to a halt once they are redeployed and come to a different mind about the divine [truths]. If, on the other hand, you wished to understand these words differently, as the author's subjecting those living a life of impiety to curses, you would

23. Cf. Exod 19.18.   24. Ps 6.5.
25. Cf. Matt 25.10.
26. A commentator bent on the spiritual direction of his readers might have found this verse a suitable basis for instruction on prayer; but that is not the focus of Theodoret's work, and at any rate the end of a long psalm is in sight.

find the inspired composition also corresponding to the apostolic teaching: in his letter to the Corinthians blessed Paul wrote this conclusion, "Let anyone be cursed who does not love the Lord Jesus"[27]—a mark of those with ardent affection. *Bless the Lord, my soul:* so let those who refuse to sing the praises of the provider of such good things suffer what I have said, whereas you, my soul, perpetually sing the praises of your Creator and Savior.

27. 1 Cor 16.22.

COMMENTARY ON PSALM 105

Alleluia.

HIS PSALM ALSO makes the recommendation to sing the praises of the God of all, as the title indicates:[1] *Alleluia* is translated, Praise the Lord. It recalls the promises made by God to the patriarchs and the good things provided by him through them to their successors. Mention of the one and the other, in fact, suffices to stir and provoke those enjoying such favors to imitation of their forebears' virtue. At the same time it also teaches the new people that it was not without just cause that he deprived that ungrateful people of his characteristic care. In other words, since they were styled God's people and plainly enjoyed the divine providence, but were later completely deprived of it, he teaches all human beings through the preceding psalms the degree and number of the benefits he gave them and how they proved ungrateful for the favors [1709] so that all might at the same time come to know the justice of the sentence passed on them, and on seeing the retributions for the ingratitude might not take the same path as theirs but tread the straight path.

(2) *Confess to the Lord, and call upon his name* (v. 1). For *call upon* Symmachus said "proclaim." The verse urges them to offer thankful hymn singing and recount the divine favors. *Announce among the nations his works.* It is clear and obvious that he has at heart the interests not only of Jews but of all the nations. *Sing to him, and play to him, recount all his marvels* (v. 2): repay

---

1. Though our present Hebrew text shifts the Alleluia to the end of the previous psalm, where it impairs the inclusion provided by vv. 1 and 35 there, the LXX is right to place it here, where it could likewise have formed an inclusion with the final Alleluia—had this not been omitted by the LXX (perhaps because of the Alleluia beginning Ps 106)! Theodoret does not seem any more aware of Hebrew prosodic patterns than his version.

him with hymns and music, and teach those unaware of them the wonders worked by him. *Take credit in his holy name* (v. 3). Aquila, on the other hand, put "Boast" for *Take credit.* The verse urges them to pride themselves not on riches or health or influence, but on the knowledge of God and on his providence. This was the exhortation also of the divine Apostle, "Let the one who boasts," he says, "boast in the Lord."[2] The most wise Anna also gives the same account, "Let the wise not boast in his wisdom, the strong not boast in his strength";[3] and, "Let the rich not boast in his riches, but let the one who boasts boast in this, in understanding and knowing the Lord, and performing judgments and righteousness on the earth."[4] *Let the heart of those seeking the Lord rejoice:* for the fruit of hope in the Lord is joy.

(3) *Seek the Lord and be strengthened* (v. 4). To teach how to do it he added, *Seek his face always:* it is necessary to seek his assistance from above not once or twice, but right throughout life, and thus reap the benefit; invincible and insuperable will the seekers be. In laying down the law the Lord also made this promise, "Ask and it will be given to you, seek and you will find, knock and [the door] will be opened to you; everyone who asks receives, everyone who seeks finds, and to everyone who knocks [the door] will be opened."[5] *Remember the marvels he has done, his prodigies, and the judgments from his mouth* (v. 5): do not consign to oblivion the ineffable wonders, which the Lord worked in ordering things by his righteous verdict. He gave the name *judgments* here to the miracles justly performed by God: when he recounts what was done in Egypt, he teaches ahead of time the justice of the punishment of the Egyptians. *Offspring of Abraham, his servants, children of Jacob, his chosen ones* (v. 6). He is referring to the same group by applying one name or another to them, [1712] styled successors and children, whereas he named them *chosen ones* as called God's people ahead of all the nations. He also indicated this in what follows.

(4) *He is the Lord our God, his judgments in all the earth* (v. 7): the one who is God and Lord of all, and in control of the whole

---

2. 2 Cor 10.17; cf. Jer 9.24. 3. Cf. 1 Sam 2.10 [LXX].
4. Cf. Jer 9.23–24. 5. Matt 5.7–8.

world, called them his own people. *He was mindful of his coven-*
ant forever, of a word he commanded for a thousand generations (v. 8).
In this he teaches the permanence and stability of the promises
made to Abraham: the verse is not hyperbolic, as some suspected, but true and divine. The God of all promised to bless all the
nations in his offspring;[6] his offspring, however, is Christ the
Lord according to the flesh, who has eternal sway and indestructible kingship. The remembrance of *a thousand generations*
indicates this: the term does not suggest a number of years;
rather, the multitude of the generations implies succession and
eternity.

(5) *Which he established by treaty with Abraham, and of his oath*
with Isaac. He confirmed it as a precept with Jacob and an eternal
covenant with Israel (vv. 9–10). The divinely inspired Moses also
made mention of these oaths: "God said to Abraham," Scripture says, "I swore by myself that I would indeed bless you and
would indeed make your offspring as numerous as the stars of
heaven; all the tribes of the earth will be blessed in your offspring."[7] He also reminds Isaac with this oath; he also confirms
the treaties with Jacob and fulfills them by freeing their successors from the slavery of Egyptians by means of Moses, and by
giving the promised land through Joshua son of Nun, though
perfecting the fulfillment of the promise through Christ the
Lord. *Saying, I shall give you the land of Canaan, a cord of your in-*
heritance (v. 11). He used *cord* of the control of the land: it belongs to those in possession to subject the land to measurement.

(6) *When they were hardly worth counting, very few in number and*
sojourners in it (v. 12). He made this promise, he is saying, to the
ancestors, few though they were and very easily numbered; by
this he makes clear the power of the one making the promise,
because even though they were so few, he could provide them
with control of so much land. *They passed from nation to nation,*
and from one kingdom to a different people (v. 13): the patriarchs

6. Cf. Gen 12.3. Theodoret asserts both his acquaintance with his predecessors and his independent critical stance.
7. Gen 22.17–18.

continued to be sojourners, settling in no one [1713] place; instead, they shifted their dwellings now to one place, now to another. *He allowed no one to wrong them* (v. 14): he made them superior to those trying to wrong them. *And rebuked kings on their account, Lay no hand on my anointed, nor abuse my prophets* (v. 15). This was the way he tested Pharaoh with great and fearsome trials over Abraham's wife Sarah;[8] this was the way he put fear into Abimelech at night by saying, "Behold, you are going to die over Abraham's wife Sarah; she is married with a husband."[9] This was the way he made Isaac venerable to the inhabitants of Palestine of the time;[10] this was the way he threatened Laban bent on murder, "Take care," he said, "not to make harsh remarks against my servant Jacob."[11] He called them *anointed,* not for being anointed with oil, but for being chosen; and it was God himself who gave the name *prophet* to Abraham, saying, "Return to the man his wife, because he is a prophet; he will pray for you, and you will be saved."[12]

(7) *He called down famine on the land* (v. 16). Sin invites correction, correction censures a life out of control, and censure effects a change in life. So he inflicted famine on account of the lawless life of the people of the time, while at the same time showing care in this way for his own servants. *He broke every support from bread,* meaning, He caused everything capable of providing nourishment to be scarce, not only corn but also barley, lentils, and everything else by which people are sustained. *He sent someone ahead of them: Joseph was sold as a slave* (v. 17). He indicated both things at the same time, the brothers' evil behavior and his wisdom, as he put their wickedness to proper effect: for he did not force them to sell their brother, but he gave way to their malice. However, he put it to good effect, turning the slave into a king, and he managed the descent into Egypt by the

8. Cf. Gen 12.17. Today we read these incidents of the risk to which Sarah is put with less sympathy for Abraham than the biblical authors—or Theodoret—perhaps intended. But at least this time she is given her name.

9. Cf. Gen 20.3.

10. Is Theodoret on the same track, with Abimelech's response in mind here when Rebekah likewise is put at risk (Gen 26.11)?

11. Cf. Gen 31.24.

12. Gen 20.7.

race. It was necessary, after all, for those due to be styled God's people to become famous and illustrious through the marvels worked on their behalf: the care shown to them proclaimed their God, and illuminated the listeners with the light of the knowledge of God.

(8) *They humbled his feet in shackles, his soul was put in irons* (v. 18): in the wake of the adulteress's calumny, he was confined to prison, and as you would expect they immediately clapped him in irons. Symmachus actually said as much, [1716] "His soul was clapped in irons,"[13] that is, he ran the risk of execution. *Until his word came to pass, the Lord's saying tested him by fire* (v. 19): he endured all this in being tested like gold, not for the God of all, who knows everything before it happens, to learn the genuineness of Joseph's virtue, but to show other people the man's sound values and to put him forward as a model of truth. *A king sent and released him, ruler of people and he let him go. He made him lord of his house and ruler of all his possessions* (vv. 20–21). And to show the benefit coming from his management, he added, *To instruct his officials to be like himself, and to teach his elders wisdom* (v. 22): distinguishing himself by the interpretation of dreams for the king and gaining authority, he guided the others to knowledge of God, not only by his use of words but also by attracting them to the same piety by his works.

(9) *Israel entered Egypt, and Jacob dwelt in the land of Ham* (v. 23). This proved the occasion, he is saying, for the patriarch's going into exile in Egypt. He calls Egypt *the land of Ham* since Mizraim was the second son of Ham.[14] "Ham," Scripture says, "fathered Cush his firstborn and Mizraim his brother." The divine Scripture calls Ethiopia Cush and *Egypt* Mizraim, and it calls the same man *Israel* and *Jacob,* who got the former name from his ancestors and was given the second by God, to indicate by the name the divine appearance which happened to him.[15]

13. What does Symmachus add to the version of the LXX, we have to ask.

14 Cf. Gen 10.6, the versions differing in the use of Mizraim and Egypt. The following citation from Scripture (if meant as such) does not seem to be documented.

15. Cf. Gen 32.28, the biblical text itself essaying a popular etymology of the name that could be refined by a stricter kind, Theodoret not quite in touch with either.

He greatly increased his people, and gave him power over his foes (v. 24). The story of the Exodus also teaches this: "The more the Egyptians abused them," he says, "the more numerous they became, and the land multiplied them."[16] *He changed their heart so that they hated his people* (v. 25): it was not that he changed the attitude of the Egyptians but he yielded to their free will; without obstructing their schemes, he made those schemed against appear stronger than the schemers. *So that they plotted against his servants:* at one time the Egyptians ordered the nurses to kill the Hebrews' infants, at another time they bade them be thrown into the river. Despite that, the race escaped the wiles of death.

(10) *He sent his servant Moses, and Aaron, whom he had chosen for himself. He proposed to them the words of his signs and* [1717] *of his portents in the land of Ham* (vv. 26–27): designating them as assistants and ministers of the freedom of the tribes, he entrusted to them the power of wonder working. *He sent darkness and darkened* [*the land*] *because they provoked his words* (v. 28): his blessed attendants were not opposed to the divine commands; instead, they performed his commands, and inflicted on them the longest night that was actually of three days' duration, or rather the darkness was even more obscure than night. The night, in fact, even if there was no moon, was tempered by the light of the stars; the divine Scripture calls that *darkness* "palpable."[17] *He turned their water into blood, and killed their fish* (v. 29): he changed not only the color of the water but even changed the kind of taste itself with the result that the species of all the fish were destroyed.

(11) *Their land swarmed with frogs, even in the private chambers of their kings* (v. 30): since they had cast the Hebrews' infants into the river, he changed the water of the river into blood to condemn the slaughter committed in it, and he caused frogs to abound there, crawling about like the slaughtered infants, getting into the houses and making their way even into the very chambers of the king. *He spoke, and there came dog-flies and gnats*

16. Cf. Exod 1.12.
17. Cf. Exod 10.21–23.

in all their territories (v. 31): the deeds followed the words; God at once gave orders, and when Moses spoke, both dog-flies and gnats filled the land, not crossing the borders of Egypt or bringing harm on other people, but inflicting correction on [God's] enemies, this being the sense of *in all their territories,* that is, Beyond the borders of Egypt nothing like this could be seen happening.

(12) *He turned their rain into hail, flaming fire in their land. He struck their vines and their figtrees, and smashed every tree in their territory* (vv. 32–33): the clouds changed their normal delivery, and gave vent to hail instead of showers; thunderbolts and hurricanes accompanied the hail, and water and fire, though naturally opposite to one another, were not in conflict with one another, the fire not melting the frozen water of the hail, nor the water extinguishing the flame. Instead, putting aside the natural resistance, they inflicted a concerted correction on the Egyptians and castigated their savagery for failing to respect their nature, human though they were, and [1720] forcing their fellows into harsh servitude. Owing to that, their vines and figtrees and all the other species of plants were completely destroyed by them.

(13) *He spoke, and there came locusts and wingless locusts beyond counting. They devoured all the vegetation in their land, and ate all the fruit of their land* (vv. 34–35): from the hail and the fire the trees failed, and from the locusts and the wingless locusts swamps, meadows, and crops [failed], as they consumed not only the fruit but also their vegetation.[18] *He struck every firstborn in their land, the firstfruit of all their labor* (v. 36): he inflicted this final plague on the Egyptians, after which he urged the Jews to leave; every house was filled with weeping and wailing once all the firstborn had suffered sudden death. After all, it was on the dearest he had inflicted the plague, striking with harsher shafts those least distressed by the former plagues.

(14) *He led them out with silver and gold* (v. 37): since the Egyptians did not allow the Hebrews to take even their own posses-

18. Theodoret has found the midrash of the story of the plagues in Exod 7–10 to his liking, and he has not been content simply to paraphrase it; the naturalist in him has helped him to further elaboration.

sions, they took in addition to their own possessions the Egyptians' wealth, carrying off gold and silver as a kind of reward for their burdensome slavery. It was not wrong, in fact, for God to order this to be done; rather, it was to correct the wrongdoers and console the wronged. *And there was no weak one among their tribes:* they experienced no effect of the plagues inflicted on the Egyptians. *Egypt was glad at their exodus, because fear of them had fallen on them* (v. 38): they were so terrified by the punishments of all kinds as to consider the Hebrews' freedom a blessing for themselves.

(15) *He spread out a cloud for their covering, and fire to light up for them during the night* (v. 39): the cloud was a shade for them by day, and prevented the harm from the [sun's] rays, while by night it took on the character of fire and met their need for light. *They made a request, and quails came, and he filled them with bread from heaven* (v. 40): since they were desperate also for meat, he provided them even with an effortless catch of birds, and met their need for bread from heaven, regaling them not with rain from the clouds but with nourishment itself. *He opened a rock, and waters gushed out, and rivers flowed in dry places* (v. 41): he also slaked [1721] their thirst with the baffling deliveries from the rock, in dry land devoid of moisture bidding rivers spring up; he gave the name *rivers* to the streams of water given out from the rock.

(16) *Because he remembered the word of his holy one, made to Abraham his servant; he led out his people in joy, and his chosen ones in rejoicing* (vv. 42–43): he gave them a share in all this to fulfill the promises made by him to Abraham. *He gave them lands of nations, and they inherited labors of peoples* (v. 44): he not only freed [them] from the slavery to Egyptians but also granted them land of the Canaanites and made them masters of others' labors, punishing the latter rightfully and confirming his own promises. The fact that it was not unjust of him to expel the original inhabitants of Palestine he brings out through the laws he imposed on Jews, bidding them to avoid imitating their way of life. Yet he also brings out in making the promises to Abraham why he did not immediately give him control of that land and instead let him have a longer sojourn, saying, "The sins of

the Amorites are not yet complete," meaning, They have not yet committed sins deserving of destruction. It would have been unjust to impose punishment on them, and to sentence them to punishment on foreknowledge of their greater sin; better to await the outcome of events. I employ a measure, in other words, and govern by law: I do nothing by whim—hence my waiting a period of four hundred years. On that basis he expelled the one and fulfilled the promises to the other.[19] *That they might keep his ordinances and seek out his law* (v. 45). He gave them, he is saying, the land he promised, giving them a law and bidding them live in accord with it.

19. It is interesting to see Theodoret responding as we might today to the ethnic cleansing of the Canaanites. He looks to Gen 15.13–16 to find a basis of rough justice in what might seem to his readers to be arbitrary behavior on God's part, whereas we look beyond the text to the author's concerns in his time.

COMMENTARY ON PSALM 106

Alleluia.

N THE HUNDRED AND FOURTH psalm the inspired word outlined divine deeds of kindness, whereas in this one it also mentions the deeds and calls in question the ingratitude of the beneficiaries, and teaches the punishments variously imposed on them. It is expressed in the person of the more observant ones, lamenting the common disasters and begging to attain pardon.

(2) *Confess to the Lord that he is good, because his mercy is forever* (v. 1): sing the praises of the Lord even for the former deeds of kindness, and look forward to brighter prospects. The Lord, in fact, is good and loving, and always continues to exercise mercy. [1724] Then he brings out the fact that description of the divine marvels exceeds the nature of human beings. *Who will tell the powers of the Lord, will make all his praises heard?* (v. 2): no word suffices for singing the praises of the God of all. *Blessed are those who respect judgment, and exercise righteousness on every occasion* (v. 3): the beatitude of virtue follows hard on the heels of the sense of sin, the person paying its toll declaring blessed those rid of it and adorned with righteousness in their life. It blesses not the one exercising righteousness on one occasion but sticking fast to its traces forever and always.

(3) *Remember us, O Lord, in favor for your people, have regard to us in your salvation* (v. 4). Here he refers to the new people, the Church from the nations, on which he bestowed salvation; the throng of the Jews, as he teaches, is presented as grasping at association with them.[1] What follows is also in keeping with this idea. *So as to see in the goodness of your elect, to rejoice in the joy of*

1. Though in the previous psalm he was content to see simply a rehearsal of the deeds of salvation history in favor of the people he styled Jewish or Hebrew,

your race, to be praised along with your inheritance (v. 5). We beg, he is saying, to share in the joy of your new people, and be made sharers in the goodness provided them.

(4) *We sinned along with our fathers, we broke the Law, we did wrong* (v. 6). From our fathers we succeeded to the breaking of your laws as if to some inheritance, he is saying, calling *fathers* not the holy patriarchs but those coming after them. He indicated this, in fact, in what follows. *Our fathers in Egypt did not understand your wonders, and did not recall the vastness of your mercy* (v. 7): despite so many marvels being worked for them in Egypt, they refused to understand your power. *They provoked [you] when they went up on the Red Sea:* perceiving the Egyptians in pursuit and the sea checking their flight, they were unwilling to await your assistance; instead, they cried out to the mighty Moses in the words, "For there not being tombs in Egypt you led us out to die in this wilderness."[2] Yet even those appearing ungrateful you regaled with salvation.

(5) He added, in fact, *He saved them for his name's sake so as to make them aware of his power. He rebuked the Red Sea and it dried up;* [1725] *he led them in deep water as though in a desert. He saved them from the hand of the one hating them, and redeemed them from the hand of the foe* (vv. 8–10): with a word he laid bare the depths of the sea, and for them he made that great deep a desert fit for horse-riding; after all, the desert is very easy to travel on, no trees in the way or ramparts hindering progress, so by comparison with *desert* he suggested ease of crossing.[3] *Water covered those harassing them; not a single one of them was left* (v. 11): he caused all the Egyptians to drown; the same sea brought salvation to the Hebrews and retribution to the Egyptians. *They believed his word, and sang his praise* (v. 12): the mighty Moses led the men in singing, and the prophetess Miriam the choir of the women, the song being recorded.[4]

---

here—perhaps because the psalm promises to reinforce this—Theodoret wishes to see the Gentile Church at the focus, and speaks of "the throng of the Jews" as the outsiders. The commentary also closes on this note.

2. Exod 14.11.

3. By comparison with commentary on the previous psalm, this one is bare except where, as here, Theodoret the naturalist feels a comment may throw some light.

4. A modern commentator like Weiser agrees with Theodoret that the verse

(6) *They lost no time in forgetting his works, they did not respond to his counsel. They developed a longing in the wilderness, and tested God in the desert* (vv. 13–14): despite receiving so many and so marvelous pledges of divine power, they did not ask to have their needs met nor did they look forward to the divine largesse; instead, they directed abuse against the divine attendants. *He granted them their request, he instilled satiety into their souls* (v. 15). He called the longing *request:* instead of requesting, they blurted it out. All the same, he gave them also meat in abundance, bread not made by hand, and water of the sweetest in abundance.

(7) *They provoked Moses in the camp, Aaron, the Lord's holy one* (v. 16): Korah and his company tried to wrest the priesthood; Dathan and Abiram contemplated further insurrection. *The earth opened and swallowed Dathan, and engulfed the faction of Abiram. Fire broke out in their faction, flames burned up sinners* (vv. 17–18): Dathan and Abiram were swallowed up with their whole family, while Korah with his henchmen were consumed by fire sent by God.[5] God inflicted these punishments to force the others to come to their senses, but they were not prepared to gain any profit from it, as the outline of their exploits reveals.

(8) *They made a calf at Horeb* (v. 19). His mention of the mountain was not without purpose, but to teach the excess of the impiety: the Lord of all made his appearance on it; he filled them with dread on it, [1728] appearing with almighty fire, using a trumpet, resounding with thunder and offering laws with such fearful effect. In this they were guilty of impiety. *They worshipped the image.* This is an accusation of further derangement: though they saw it taking shape with human skill, they offered it the divine reverence. *They exchanged his glory for the image of a hay-eating calf* (v. 20). He presented their folly in a very telling way: in preference to the one who had worked such wonders,

seems to refer to the hymn in Exod 15, styled variously the song of Moses (Exod 15.1) and of Miriam (Exod 15.21), and also the Song of the Sea.

5. According to Num 16 Korah, Dathan, and Abiram were linked in their revolt as in their being swallowed up by the earth, the fire consuming their two hundred and fifty supporters. The psalm verse perhaps accounts for Theodoret's confusion of details.

granted them that unexpected salvation, and was capable of such marvelous actions they made obeisance to an image of a calf whose original was in need of nourishment; the calf's nourishment is not bread, provided for rational beings, but grass and hay. Over the calf, whose nature is irrational and whose nourishment is hay, control has been granted to human beings, and its image is worth much less: it is not only irrational but also lifeless, powerless to act, to moo, to eat—yet they did obeisance to an impotent thing ahead of the God of all.[6]

(9) *They forgot the God who saves them, who did great things in Egypt, marvels in the land of Ham, fearsome things on the Red Sea* (vv. 21–22): they recalled neither their own salvation nor the Egyptians' punishment nor the great miracle of the sea; instead, they completely spurned it all. *He said he would destroy them, had not Moses, his chosen one, stood in the breach before him to divert his anger from destroying them* (v. 23): when the God of all said, "Let me be, and in my anger I shall annihilate them with rage and make you into a great nation," blessed Moses replied, "If you forgive them their sin, forgive; but if not, blot me out from the book you have written."[7]

(10) *They despised a land that was desirable, they did not trust his word. They grumbled in their tents, they did not hearken to the voice of the Lord* (vv. 24–25). He recalls further perfidy: when God bade them enter the promised land, under the pressure of fear they resisted openly, claiming the Canaanites were strong whereas they themselves were under strength for a maneuver against them. This was a clear sign of lack of trust: it would have been proper for them as eyewitnesses of so many and so marvelous wonders to have complete confidence in the power of the one who saved. [1729] *He lifted his hand against them to fell them in the wilderness, to fell their offspring among the nations and scatter them in their territories* (vv. 26–27): he intended to impose the punishment befitting the lack of trust, and at the same time inflict destruction on everyone, but he still exercised his habitual lovingkindness and imposed on them partial punishment.

(11) *They were initiated in the rites of Baal Peor, and ate sacrifices*

6. The irony of this incident is not lost on an Antiochene.
7. Cf. Exod 32.10, 32.

of the dead. They provoked him with their exploits (vv. 28–29): they fell headlong into intemperance once more, got involved with Moabite women, and gained a better knowledge of their impiety. *Baal Peor* is an idol honored by them, *Peor* the name of the place of the idol, *Baal* the idol, called Kronos in the Greek language.[8] He calls *sacrifices of the dead* what are known as libations among the Greeks, which they are in the habit of offering to the dead; but you would not be wrong to give the name *dead* to the so-called gods. *The plague spread among them:* once more he inflicted death on them. *Phinehas stood up and appeased him, and the trembling stopped. It has been counted as righteousness for him from generation to generation forever* (vv. 30–31). Symmachus spoke of *trembling* as "plague." History also teaches this: using a spear, he did away with Zimri, who was unashamed in brazenly associating with some Midianite woman. God welcomed his zeal and celebrated him, while checking the punishment inflicted on the others.[9]

(12) *They irked him at the water of contradiction, and Moses was distressed on their account; because they provoked his spirit, and he dissembled with his lips* (vv. 32–33): when he was mourning for his sister, they came to him and begged necessary assistance in great confusion. He for his part was affected by depression from the mourning, and perceiving their intemperance and seized with anger and grief he did not discharge the divine command with his customary responsiveness. Instead, mingling a certain ambiguity with his words, he struck the rock and drew forth the water. This is suggested by *he dissembled* [1732] *with his lips,* meaning, he did not use words unambiguously. Scripture says, "Moses said to them, Shall I not draw water for you from this rock?"[10] As a result of this the God of all was very incensed, and did not give him the reward of the land promised to the

8. A helpful footnote based on Num 25.1–5; the incident is disposed of accurately, concisely and—unusually—with some sarcasm (arising out of the phrase in Num 25.2, "sacrifices of their gods"; the text of that book must have been open before him).

9. Cf. Num 25.6–9. In recalling the incident, Theodoret places the blame on Zimri, not the Midianite woman, who for Chrysostom (in commentary on Ps 8.2) is the culprit and "a harlot."

10. Num 20.10.

ancestors, bidding him instead to accept his life's end, while fulfilling his promise by means of Joshua son of Nun. While it seems that the governor of all things imposed this on him as a punishment, it was for the sake of other arrangements that he put it into effect. Firstly, he understood the Jews' stupidity and did not allow the whole promise to reach its fulfillment through him lest they take him for a god. Having made an image of a calf into a god, what sort of reverence would they not have paid the procurer of such wonderful marvels that were performed? This is surely the reason, too, why God caused his tomb to be forgotten;[11] as well, he wanted to bring out the temporary character of the laws by what happened to the lawgiver himself: if the lawgiver did not enjoy the promised land, it was easy to understand from this that they, too, would not enjoy the providence for long.

(13) After narrating in this way what happened in the wilderness, he levels an accusation against their lawlessness in the land of promise. *They did not destroy the nations as the Lord had commanded them. They mingled with the nations and learned their practices. They served their idols, and they became a stumbling block to them* (vv. 34–36): he checked their mingling to avoid complicity in impiety, removing the end with the beginning and tearing up the fruit along with the root, and thus checking the worse by the lesser evil. Even in this, nevertheless, they broke the divine Law, not destroying the impious nations nor shunning association with them, but imitating their wicked way of life. *They sacrificed their sons and their daughters to the demons. They shed innocent blood, blood of their sons and daughters, whom they sacrificed to the idols of Canaan; the land was stained with their blood, and besmirched with their actions* (vv. 37–39): they left behind as legacy the final excess of impiety. After all, what extraordinary degree of ungodliness is the legacy of polluting the land with the blood of sons and daughters and offering them in sacrifice to the bloodsucking demons? Whereas, in fact, they offered God nothing prescribed by Law, to the idols they offered the

11. Cf. Deut 34.6. Theodoret goes to some length to rationalize these verses of the psalm, partly to justify the fate of "the mighty Moses," partly to vindicate God's later treatment of the Jews—a theme of this commentary.

slaughter of their children. *They were promiscuous in their dealings.* By *promiscuity* here he refers not only to their incontinence but also to the worship of the idols; since while attached to God they were fond of worshipping them, it was right for him to speak of the superstition as *promiscuity.*

(14) [1733] *The Lord was filled with anger with his people, and he abhorred his inheritance. He gave them into the hands of foes, and those, who hated them, lorded it over them. Their foes oppressed them, and humbled them under their hands* (vv. 40–42). The story of the Judges also teaches this, and of course the history of the Kings:[12] he handed them over at one time to the Moabites, at another time to the Ammonites, at another to the Amalekites, the Midianites, and the Philistines, reaping the benefit from the correction. *Many times he rescued them, whereas they provoked him in their willfulness, and they were humbled in their iniquities* (v. 43): by inflicting correction once again, he gave them a share in his loving-kindness, whereas they responded in contrary fashion.

(15) *The Lord saw them in their tribulation, in hearkening to their petition* (v. 44). The histories also teach this, that under the pressure of necessity they petitioned God, and that in their petition they were heard. *He remembered his covenant, and in the abundance of his mercy he repented* (v. 45): on account of the promises to the ancestors he lavished his mercy [on them]. He uses *repentance* of the stop to the correction: God does not have the feeling of repentance,[13] nor is he well-disposed now to these people, now to those; rather, in governing all things wisely he applies correction and extends loving-kindness. *He caused them to meet with compassion in the sight of all their captors* (v. 46). Thus he mollified Cyrus, inclined him to mercy, and caused him to give the captives freedom.

(16) *Save us, O Lord our God, and assemble us from the nations,*

12. Though Theodoret does not deny inspiration to the Deuteronomist, he refers to the work as *historia* or *syngraphe* rather than *propheteia*, as does Chrysostom.

13. This biblical expression, which Theodoret does not prefer or is unable to document from elsewhere in Scripture (cf. Ps 110.4; 1 Sam 15.35), he instinctively feels to be an infringement of divine transcendence, requiring some dilution for his readers.

that we may confess to your holy name, glory in your praise (v. 47). He indicates this, that the inspired word teaches them how they must placate God and be granted care from him. The divinely inspired Apostle also foretold through Elijah the Tishbite the salvation coming to the Jews, "The deliverer will come from Sion, and will turn away impiety from Jacob; and this is the covenant with them on my part, when I remove their sins."[14] It is, of course, necessary to look forward, not to the rebuilding of Jerusalem, in foolish people's fancies, or to worship by the Law, irrational sacrifices, circumcision, the Sabbath, and shadowy sprinkling after all-holy baptism (these are tipsy old wives' tales), but to vocation and knowledge of truth, faith in Christ the Lord and the way of life of the New Covenant.

(17) [1736] *Blessed be the Lord, the God of Israel, from age to age. All the people will say, So be it, so be it* (v. 48): to be praised in everything is the Lord of all, styled the God of Israel, who achieved so much for the sake of the salvation of human beings. All the people should add "Amen" to the words of the hymn singers, the Hebrew saying "Amen and Amen" for *So be it, so be it.* From this comes also the custom that has continued in the churches of the people's assenting to the doxology of the priest with the Amen, offering the sharing at that point and receiving the blessing.[15]

14. Rom 11.26–27, quoting—not Elijah the Tishbite: a slip of the tongue, surely—but Isaiah of Jerusalem (Isa 59.20–21) and possibly Jer 31.33. Theodoret rightly sees in the psalm verse something of the quandary facing Paul on the question of the salvation of Israel in the wake of rejection of the offer. Like Paul in places, he takes pains to assert that prescriptions of the Old Dispensation have lapsed in favor of new realities.

15. A rare liturgical rubric from Theodoret on the Great Amen at the conclusion of the eucharistic prayer that closes with a doxology, to which the congregation reply Amen, and shortly after engage in "sharing," *koinonia,* with a kiss of peace and also a communion rite, the celebration terminating in a rite of blessing. On the other hand, Theodoret does not recognize in this verse and its Amen the conclusion of the fourth book of Psalms, as we observed he did not recognize similar conclusion of earlier books after Ps 41, 72, and 89. With his LXX he also transposes the final "Alleluia" to the next psalm, thus impairing the inclusion it formed with the opening. His mind thinks differently.

COMMENTARY ON PSALM 107

Alleluia.

E HAVE OFTEN DEMONSTRATED that the Old Testament is a shadow of the New.[1] It is no less easy to grasp that from this psalm, too: it both prophesies the Jews' liberation and foretells the salvation of all human beings. It has a close connection with the previous ones: the hundred and fourth [psalm] contains an outline of the promises made by God to the patriarchs and the gifts provided to their offspring, while the one after that brought out in addition to the favors the Jews' ingratitude as well and the punishments inflicted on them for it. This one, on the other hand, foretells the freedom from captivity on account of the ineffable loving-kindness shown by God. And since our situation is foreshadowed in theirs, we recognize also in this psalm the prophecies of our salvation; the greater part of the inspired composition bears on us rather than on them.

(2) *Confess to the Lord that he is good, because his mercy is forever* (v. 1). Once again the inspired word urges singing the praises of God the benefactor, and it says loving-kindness is the basis of the hymn singing. *Let those redeemed by the Lord, whom he redeemed from the hand of the foe, say so* (v. 2). Jews freed from the slavery of Babylonians ought to have sung his praises, and it always behooves us to do it, freed as we are from the devil's tyranny. *He gathered them from all quarters, from east and west, from north and sea* (v. 3). We have not found this realized in the case of Jews: they live scattered throughout the whole world. The Church from

1. Shadow and reality is another way Theodoret has of formulating the hermeneutic he declared in his preface for approaching the Psalms; earlier in the series he took more seriously the "shadow" of the historical facts, especially when encouraged by psalm titles, whereas he can also find an eschatological sense in them, as he proceeds to do here in a unique way.

the nations, on the other hand, he summoned and assembled in all parts of the world, east and west, south and north, and it is possible to see such gatherings everywhere on land and sea.

(3) In the case of Jews, however, this has happened faintly, some returning from Babylon, some few assembled at that time from Egypt and nearby nations. [1737] *Some wandered in the waterless wilderness* (v. 4): Babylon was a wilderness and waterless, being bereft of God; and the throng of the Jews, in thrall to it, was deprived of spiritual watering. Those from the nations who have come to faith were living, as it were, *in a waterless wilderness,* "having no hope and being godless,"[2] the divine Apostle says. *They found no way to an inhabited city:* neither Jews had the strength to escape their captors and recover their own homeland, nor did those from the nations who have come to faith find the way leading to the divine city before the Incarnation of the Savior. *City* here is to be understood as the devout way of life.

(4) *Hungry and thirsty, their soul fainted within them* (v. 5). Hunger for the divine teaching oppressed the one and the other: Jews in servitude in Babylon were deprived of priests and could not perform worship according to the Law, while the nations in turn did not accept a divine Law nor enjoy spiritual teaching, though these are the means by which souls are normally nourished. God, to be sure, threatened Jews with this hunger: "I shall inflict famine on the land," he is saying, "not a famine of bread or a thirst for water, but a hunger for hearing the word of the Lord."[3] *They cried to the Lord in their distress, and he delivered them from their needs* (v. 6). The more devout among the Jews offered supplication to God; the inspired composition of Daniel also teaches us this: he, Hananiah, Azariah, and Mishael cried aloud for all and sought divine mercy.[4] The nations, on the other hand, groaned as they wrestled with calamities of all kinds, and had recourse to inconsolable weeping and wailing, being without hope of resurrection. While they did not seek from the God of all release from the troubles besetting them, he in his love nevertheless saw them groaning and ex-

2. Eph 2.12.   3. Amos 8.11.
4. Cf. Dan 2.17–18.

tended mercy. *He led them to a straight path for traveling to a city of habitation* (v. 7): to the Jews he granted return through Cyrus the Persian, whereas the nations he guided by the holy apostles and gave a glimpse of the city above, which has its foundations on holy mountains and whose craftsman and maker is God.[5]

(5) *Let them confess to the Lord his mercies, and his marvels to the sons of human beings* (v. 8). Symmachus, on the other hand, put it this way, "and his portents produced for the sons of human beings."[6] [1740] It is not *mercy* nor *the marvels* that offer to God the hymn of gratitude, to be sure, but those enjoying such good things: while the Jews' freedom was wonderful and admirable, more remarkable and admirable is the salvation of the world, the change for the better, the end of error, and the knowledge of truth. Divine mercy was responsible for all this. "It was not through our righteous deeds that we performed," the divine Apostle says, "but in his great mercy that he saved us through the washing of rebirth and renewal by the Holy Spirit, whom he poured out richly on us."[7]

(6) *Because he satisfied an empty soul, and filled a hungry soul with good things. Seated in darkness and a shadow of death, shackled by poverty and iron* (vv. 9–10): Jews subjected to slavery and abuse and wasting with hunger he freed from the troubles besetting them. All human nature he nourished with divine teachings, he freed from the gloom of ignorance, illuminated with the light of the knowledge of God, dissipated the shadow of death lying upon them by giving the hope of resurrection, and broke the strong bonds of sin. "Everyone is caught fast in the ropes of his own sins,"[8] Scripture says; and, "Woe to those who drag their sins as if by a long cord, and their iniquities as if by a thong of a heifer's yoke."[9]

---

5. Cf. Heb 11.10. Theodoret is keeping to his formula of Shadow and Reality to give the psalm a spiritual and at times anagogical sense.

6. In these long psalms of praise and thanksgiving, with which Theodoret has had little difficulty, citation of the alternative versions has been rare; and this one, introduced as if by a whim, contributes nothing. What would be worthwhile remarking on is the recurrence of this refrain as vv. 15, 21, and 31, which has the effect of dividing the psalm into four stanzas; but Theodoret does not advert to it.

7. Titus 3.5–6.   8. Prov 5.22.
9. Cf. Isa 5.18.

(7) *Because they provoked the sayings of God, and spurred on the counsel of the Most High. Their heart was brought low by sufferings, they were weakened and there was no one to help* (vv. 11–12). The cause of all these calamities both for the Jews and of course for all human beings was sin: to pay the penalty the former were consigned to the slavery of the Babylonians, and all human beings after the transgression of the command were subjected to the hardship of labors, Adam later heard the words, "Cursed is the ground because of your deeds: it will grown thorns and thistles for you; in sorrows you are to eat of it all the days of your life, in the sweat of your brow you are to eat your bread until you return to the ground from which you were taken, because you are dirt and to dirt you will return."[10] Beset with such calamities they found no solution to the troubles affecting them; but the one who allotted them these [evils] also personally granted [them] release from them. The text goes on, in fact, *They cried to the Lord when distressed, and he saved them from their anguish. He led them out of darkness and shadow of death, and broke their bonds* (vv. 13–14): he had compassion on both the one group and the other, [1741] and by freeing the former from the current problems and liberating the latter from the darkness of ignorance he broke the bonds of slavery.

(8) *Let them confess to the Lord his mercies and his marvels for the sons of human beings. Because he shattered bronze doors and broke iron bars* (vv. 15–16). He called the inescapable character of the evils *bronze doors* and *iron bars:* just as it is impossible for a person inside to escape from the confinement of such doors and bars, likewise no means was available for the Jews to avoid the Babylonians' servitude, and for all people [to avoid] the power of death. The divine mercy alone was capable, however, of destroying the power of the one and the other and granting release from the distress. *He lifted them up from their way of iniquity; they had been brought low because of their iniquities* (v. 17): neither the

10. Gen 3.17–19, loosely recalled. Theodoret is in no doubt of the primal sin that underlies human problems and of divine liberation from them, the summary ending on an upbeat note. He is still endeavoring, in a way we have not seen before, to relate the whole content of the psalm bearing on Jewish experience to the overall human situation, if not to apply it to his readers' lives.

Jews nor the whole of human nature fell into these troubles
without good reason: both the one and the other pay the penalty for their faults. Nonetheless, he granted both the one and
the other salvation, caught up as they were in such great evils.

(9) *Their soul loathed all food, and they were close to the gates of
death* (v. 18): Jews, oppressed by the multitude of troubles, were
even averse to food itself; the inspired author said as much also
in another psalm, as if on their part, "Because I forgot to eat my
bread."[11] Not even the nations were prepared to heed the
teachings of their own philosophers; this was the reason some
condemned Socrates to death, others committed Anaxarchos
to an alien punishment, still others harshly tortured successors
of Pythagoras and imposed an untimely death on them.[12] Yet
the God of all gave even these a share in the immortal nourishment, convinced them to hasten to it with complete enthusiasm, and freed them from the gates of death.

(10) *They cried to the Lord when distressed, and he saved them
from their anguish* (v. 19). Then he teaches the manner of the
salvation: *He sent his word, and it healed them and rescued them from
their destruction* (v. 20): God the Word became man, was sent as
man (as God, after all, uncircumscribed, he is present everywhere and encompasses all things),[13] healed the souls' wounds
of all kinds and cured corrupt ways of thought. This was the
way he healed that sinful woman and bade her be of good
cheer; this was the way he gave strength to the palsied man in
the words, [1744] "Your sins are forgiven";[14] this was the way he
opened paradise to the brigand, this was the way he made tax
collectors the world's teachers,[15] this is the way he renews and

11. Cf. Ps 102.4.
12. Theodoret's interpretation of this psalm, by which he continues to look
for a wider context than Jewish history, leads him here—uniquely—to introduce a bevy of classical Greek philosophers as transmitters of sound teaching
rejected by benighted pagans in a way similar to Jewish rejection of their spiritual guides.
13. Theodoret's acceptance of the reality of the Incarnation is, of course,
beyond question. But, as Kelly remarks, his expression of the *communicatio idiomatum* can be less than satisfying.
14. Cf. Matt 9.22, 2. In calling the menstruating woman "sinful," Theodoret
would be appalled to think he was perpetuating Jewish cultic attitudes, and
even exceeding them in transforming a social pariah into a formal sinner.
15. Cf. Luke 23.43; 5.27.

purifies those approaching all-holy baptism and frees them from the wounds of sin.

(1 1) *Let them confess to the Lord his mercies and his marvels for the sons of human beings. Let them offer to him a sacrifice of praise, and announce his works with happiness* (vv. 2 1–2 2). It is right, he is saying, to sing the praises of the loving God for all these things, since he exercises such mercy and grants us salvation beyond expectations. It behooves us not to be alone in knowing the divine wonder working, but also to teach the ignorant and prompt everyone to hymn singing. It is in fact necessary to indicate that here, too, he urged the offering of *a sacrifice of praise* to God and not the sacrifices of brute beasts. So here, too, he rejects the worship according to the Law. Aquila, on the other hand, called *a sacrifice of praise* "a sacrifice of thanksgiving."

(1 2) *Those who go down to the sea in ships, conducting business in many waters. They saw the works of the Lord, and his wonders in the deep* (vv. 2 3–2 4). The inspired author expressed this by way of a similitude; he means, Just as sailors plying the vast oceans gain a particular view of the great divine achievement as they encounter difficult seas and enjoy salvation beyond all human hope, so too Jews encountered those calamities and received freedom, and came to know the divine power. All human beings as well actually observed the surprising transformation of things, the end to the former error, the calm of the souls and the harbor of resurrection, and so they marvel at the provider of these things. *He spoke, and the wind of the storm took its place and its waves were uplifted. They mount to the heavens and descend to the deeps* (vv. 2 5–2 6). In this he brought out that, when he wills it, distress occurs and satisfaction takes its place. *Their soul fainted in the troubles. They were alarmed and shaken like a drunken person, and all their wisdom was swallowed up* (vv. 2 6–2 7). He continues the figure: while seeming to speak of sailors, he is referring in this to nature's manifold calamities, with which no one relying on human wisdom is capable of dealing. Steersmen are borne this way and that like drunken men when the tempest strikes and, though applying all their skill, they do not succeed in prevailing over the troubles.

(1 3) *They cried to the Lord when distressed* [1745] *and he led them out of their problems. He commanded the storm and it turned into a breeze, and its billows fell silent. They were glad because they were quiet* (vv. 28–30): he extends his particular influence also to these navigators who call on him, he gives his direction, and at once the storm is turned into a gentle breeze, the ocean is rid of tempest, and those struggling with difficulties discover a transformation of the problems by his grace. In this way Jews were liberated from that harsh slavery. *He guided them to the haven of his will:* as soon as he willed it, a solution to their evils occurred, and in place of the storm the haven appeared. This is even more applicable to us than to them: he gave us a berth in the haven of his will by according us the divine knowledge.

(14) *Let them confess to the Lord his mercies and his marvels for the sons of human beings. Let them exalt him in the congregation of the people, and praise him on the seat of the elders* (vv. 31–32). You can see this happening constantly with the nations who have come to faith: in all the churches throughout the world, with the sacred assembly leading the way, all the people sing the praises of the benefactor, recounting the wonder working of the divine loving-kindness.[16] *He turned rivers into a desert and channels of water into thirst, fertile land into salinity from the evil of those who dwell in it* (vv. 33–34). Those attaining salvation sing his praises on seeing the surprising transformation: those who of old were bedewed with many rivers of inspiration and offered to God fruit in season now enjoy not even the slightest moisture, but are completely deprived of the previous irrigation owing to their own wickedness. *He turned a desert into streams of water, and dry land into channels of water* (v. 35). The nations that were formerly dry and contained not even the slightest spring are surrounded with the waters of teaching, receiving the rational flow beyond need.[17]

(15) *He settled hungry people there, and established cities for habitation* (v. 36): those formerly wasting with hunger and in need of the spiritual nourishment he settled on those rivers, and established the religious way of life. *They sowed fields and planted*

16. A brief glance at Christian liturgical practice, of which the Psalms might have been expected to elicit more in a commentator (and bishop).

17. Natural imagery is not lost on Theodoret, no mean poet himself.

vines, and produced fruit of growth (v. 37). All this the inspired author uttered in figurative fashion. The Lord used parables like that: sometimes he called the apostles reapers,[18] sometimes [1748] himself sower and farmer, and those who received the seeds of the word obediently good earth.[19] The Apostle also says, "I planted, Apollos watered, but God gave the increase"; and again, "You are God's field, you are God's building."[20] So the apostles sowed the saving message and planted the rational gardens for God, and conveyed the fruit of righteousness in due season for God; all who are entrusted with the role of teaching after them continue to do the very same thing.[21] *He blessed them, and they were greatly multiplied, and their cattle did not decrease* (v. 38). The one who sows with blessings will also reap with blessings,[22] according to the divine Apostle. He calls *cattle* those tended by them, whom he increased by granting the power of wonder working. Blessed Luke is witness in the Acts in the words, "The Lord himself added to the Church each day those who were being saved."[23] And the Lord in person calls the believers sheep, "My sheep," he says, "hear my voice. I know them, and they follow me, and I give them eternal life."[24]

(16) At this point once more he prophesies the evils that will befall Jews. *They became few in number, and suffered distress from tribulations of evils and pain* (v. 39). He means this: Those who dwelt of old in desolate and waterless [places] enjoyed such great blessing and prosperity on coming to faith, whereas those who of old enjoyed the irrigation coming from inspired streams were then deprived of it owing to the wickedness of their attitude, remained completely bereft and fruitless, fell foul of calamities of all kinds and were dispersed throughout the whole world with the result that their populous mother city was inhabited by few.[25] *Contempt was poured out on their rulers* (v. 40).

---

18. Cf. John 4.35–38.   19. Cf. Mark 4.14–20; John 15.1.
20. 1 Cor 3.6, 9.
21. We have seen before the importance Theodoret gives to the role of teaching in the community, as to this aspect of the *Psalms Commentary*.
22. 2 Cor 9.6.   23. Acts 2.47.
24. John 10.27–28.
25. The hermeneutical procedure followed in this psalm also has the effect of bringing Theodoret to develop his thinking on the respective fates of Jews

The facts bear witness to the prophecy: those who seemed to be their rulers and teachers were rendered worthy of no regard; instead, those once famous and illustrious are completely insignificant and despised by their own. *He made them roam in trackless wastes.* Symmachus, on the other hand, put it this way, "He will make them roam in futility of thinking." Far from bringing on error, God forbids error, yet he allows the disobedient to go leaderless, and the misguided roam around, carried this way and that. Jews also suffer that fate: deserting the divine way, they follow their own thoughts.

(17) [1749] *He helped the needy escape poverty* (v. 41): the nations that once were beggars enjoyed divine assistance and acquired spiritual wealth. *And made their families like sheep.* Aquila, on the other hand, put it this way, "He will lift up the poor from neediness, and make their kin like a flock": he tends them like his own sheep, and shows them providence and care as though [they were] his kin according to the flesh. *Upright people will see and be glad, and every iniquity will stop its mouth* (v. 42): on seeing this, those who practice uprightness in thinking are filled with satisfaction, while those choosing to live a life of impiety and lawlessness are forced to hang their heads to the ground and stay silent, held in check by the righteous sentence.

(18) *Who is the wise person who will respect this and understand the mercies of the Lord?* (v. 43): it is not for everyone to understand and recognize the loving designs of the Savior, nor to respect the divine laws; it is rather for the one who exercises wisdom and understanding, and cries aloud to the Lord, "Open my eyes, and I shall consider the marvels coming from your Law."[26]

---

and convert pagans, and the basis for the divine rejection of the former—briefly, as often before, "they brought it on themselves."

26. Ps 119.18.

COMMENTARY ON PSALM 108

A song of a psalm for David.

HIS PSALM LIKEWISE both prophesies the Jews' return and forecasts the salvation of the nations. It has a close relationship with both the fifty-sixth psalm and the fifty-ninth psalm.[1]

(2) *My heart is ready, O God, my heart is ready. I shall sing and play in my glory* (v. 1). We said already that the inspired author calls the charism of inspiration his own *glory.*[2] Employing the singing of inspired composition, he is saying, I tell you, Lord, that the heart I have is ample and ready to receive your divine grace. *Awake, my glory, awake, harp and lyre, I shall awake at dawn. I shall confess to you among peoples, O Lord, I shall play to you among nations* (vv. 2–3). The inspired author calls himself *harp and lyre:* as though on a musical instrument, the grace of the Spirit would strike up the inspired singing in him.[3] Having bestirred himself to singing the Lord's praises, therefore, he responds once more and promises to do so at dawn for the reason that at

---

1. Like modern commentators, Theodoret observes the similarity of Ps 108 to these earlier psalms. He perhaps demonstrates a sager critical sense, speaking simply of a "relationship" without defining it, unlike Weiser, who sees it as a relationship of dependence and thus is disqualifying the psalm from particular comment. For Dahood, prepared only to admit a common source, this "goes beyond the available evidence"; and Theodoret feels he owes it to his readers to say something, albeit concisely, on this member of the Psalter as well.

2. Cf. his comment on Ps 57.8. The reading of the original has invited emendation by commentators.

3. The analogy of a musician playing a musical instrument was employed by the Fathers, and the philosophers before them, for divine influence exerted on authors in the process of composition. As it did not do complete justice to the role of the human author—an important component of Antioch's thinking on Jesus, the Scriptures, and the process of salvation—we find Theodoret and Chrysostom choosing other analogies. See my "Psalm 45: a *locus classicus* for patristic thinking on biblical inspiration."

that time he will not be alone in offering the hymn; rather, he already composed the divine song along with countless nations and peoples. [1752] By *dawn* he refers to the Incarnation of our God and Savior: from him sprang forth the light of truth; from him throughout the whole world the blessed David sings in the mouths of all people and sounds the praises of the divine favors.

(3) *Because your mercy is great above the heavens, and your truth to the clouds* (v. 4): the greatness of your mercy surpasses the vaults of the heavens, the rays of your truth sped in all directions. As we have already mentioned, by *clouds* he refers to the inspired authors of the Old Testament, the apostles, and those granted the charism of teaching:[4] through them, as through clouds of some kind, he offers people the spiritual irrigation; through them we have come to learn the true teachings. *Be exalted above the heavens, O God, and your glory above all the earth* (v. 5). This is what blessed Habakkuk also said, "His virtue covered heavens, and the earth is full of his praise."[5] Blessed David also said as much in the eighth psalm, "O Lord our Lord, how marvelous [is] your name in all the earth! Because your magnificence is raised above the heavens."[6] *Be exalted* means, then, Be seen to be elevated and superior to all, and let all the earth learn your glory. *So that your beloved may be rescued, save me with your right hand and hearken to me* (v. 6): the salvation of those accorded familiarity with you shows your power to all people; so accept my petition and extend your right hand. By *right hand* he is referring to good action.

(4) *God has spoken in his holy one*—that is, through the grace of the all-holy Spirit—*I shall be exalted, and shall divide Shechem and distribute portions of the valley of the tabernacles* (v. 7). What the inspired author requested he attained: since he said, *Be exalted above the heavens, O God*, the Lord replied in the words, *I shall be exalted.* Then he shows the way as well: *I shall divide Shechem* (this city was given to Joseph as a privilege), but *the valley* that was

4. Bishop Theodoret sees himself in this line, and accentuates this aspect of the Psalms.
5. Hab 3.3.
6. Ps 8.1.

rendered desolate and occupied by shepherds' *tabernacles* I shall fill with inhabitants again and cause to be distributed to those returning. *Gilead is mine, Manasseh is mine, Ephraim protector of my head, and Judah my king* (v. 8): I shall make my own not only *Manasseh* but also his land (*Gilead* being a place name, *Manasseh* a tribe's title), but I shall also return to *Ephraim* its former power and make *Judah* king of all the tribes. [1753] After the return the tribes had remained undivided, and Zerubbabel was in charge of one group and the other. Christ the Lord, who sprang from Judah according to the flesh, in an appropriate and real sense is king of all creation.[7] *Moab is a basin of my hope; on Idumea I shall hurl my sandal; Philistines were subjected to me* (v. 9): I shall provide my people with such strength that they will dominate the Philistines and make subjects of Moabites and Idumeans. We made more precise comment on this in the sixtieth psalm.

(5) *Who will bring me to a fortified city? or who will guide me to Idumea? Is it not you, O God, who has rejected us?* (vv. 10–11). The inspired author was filled with satisfaction at the prophecy of the good things, and longs to see both the city once destroyed rebuilt and the Idumeans enslaved by the Jews. No one else is capable of providing this, he is saying, than you alone, who have now rejected us and bidden us be enslaved. *You will not sally forth, O God, with our forces.* Symmachus, on the other hand, put it this way, "Not going at the head of our armies, God": we were never overcome when you led and guided the column. *Grant us help out of tribulation: human salvation is futile* (v. 12): so put an end to the troubles, and extend your aid; it is impossible to attain it from any other source. All human assistance is futile and useless without your cooperation.[8] *With God we shall do powerfully, and he will make naught of our foes* (v. 13): this is the reason, to be sure, that we call upon your providence, being able to prevail over the adversaries through it alone.

7. Theodoret is trying rather desperately to get beyond the historical references in the psalm.

8. This statement of the gratuity and necessity of divine grace does not elicit, as sometimes elsewhere, any qualifying accent on the validity of human effort. See note 3 above and Introduction, section 8.

COMMENTARY ON PSALM 109

To the end. A psalm for David.

HIS PSALM PROPHESIES the saving Passion, the Jews' madness and the betrayal of Judas. It leads us to this meaning, and the great Peter was speaking publicly [about it], both in charging Judas with betrayal and in giving a demonstration of the prophecy from it.[1] Let no one who hears the Lord imposing the obligation to bless our persecutors[2] consider the prophecy to be in opposition to the obligation: the inspired word in this case does not proceed by way of cursing but by foretelling the punishments coming both to Jews and to Judas. This prophecy is expressed as a prayer, as is very much the custom everywhere in the divine Scripture.

(2) [1756] *O God, do not keep my praise quiet, because a sinner's mouth and a traitor's mouth was opened against me* (vv. 1–2). Christ the Lord says this in human fashion: as a human being prays out of respect for the limits of human nature, so God accepts the prayers of those who pray sincerely. He calls the Passion a *hymn:* in the divine Gospels he gives it the name "glory." "The hour has come," he says, "for the Son of Man to be glorified."[3] He called Judas *a sinner's mouth and a traitor's mouth:* he acted deceitfully in forging with Jews the pacts of betrayal. *They spoke against me with deceitful tongue, and hateful ones beset me with their words* (vv. 2–3). He shifted the focus from Judas to the whole Sanhedrin of the Jews: in thrall to envy, they plotted the unjust death.

(3) *They warred against me without cause. In return for my love,*

---

1. Cf. Acts 1.20 in reference to v. 8. Theodoret can thus claim at least some Scriptural support for seeing reference in this psalm to Judas and the Passion of Jesus.
2. Actually, the obligation is to pray for them (Matt 5.44).
3. John 12.23. In fact, the psalm verse spoke of "praise" rather than "hymn."

they slandered me (vv. 3–4): not only were they not provoked by any evil on my part, but they even enjoyed so many countless good things; obliged to love me on that account, they acted the part of adversaries. *Whereas I prayed.* The story of the sacred Gospels is witness to this: fixed to the plank of the cross he cried out, "Father, forgive them: they do not know what they are doing."[4] *They set evil against me in return for good, and hate in return for my love* (v. 5): so while I swamped them with kindnesses, they rewarded me with the opposite.

(4) *Appoint a sinner over him, and let a devil stand at his right hand* (v. 6). *Appoint* means You will appoint, and *let him stand* He will stand, as the divine evangelist clearly taught us: the divinely inspired John asked who was the traitor, and the Lord replied, "The one to whom I give the morsel on dipping it, he it is"; he dipped it, the text says, and gave it to Judas, and after the morsel the Satan entered into him, finding easy entry.[5] Setting off of his own accord to the Jews, he made a pact of betrayal, and though swamped with many kindnesses after that he remained ungrateful. So willingly he accepted the enemy as an associate. *At his trial, let him be found*—that is, he will emerge—*guilty; and let his prayer be taken*—that is, will be taken—*as sin* (v. 7): the traitor is devoid of any excuse. Hence at his trial he is found guilty, and the prayer offered by him will add to his guilt: far from being ignorant of the benefactor, he even had the advantage of the divine words, [1757] and was not only a witness but also an agent of greatest miracles, receiving authority from him.

(5) *Let his days be few, and another take his position* (v. 8). This prophecy had its fulfillment: he immediately suffered death by hanging, and instead of him Matthias took his place in the number of the apostles. *Let his children be orphans, and his wife a widow* (v. 9). This applied not only to Judas but also to all the unbelieving Jews: with the passing of a few years after the cruci-

---

4. Luke 23.34.
5. Cf. John 13.26–27. By Theodoret's time, clearly, the Satan and the devil have become identified, this psalm verse with its parallelism being one of the Old Testament items that promote the identification, not to mention New Testament usage.

fixion, the whole race was driven from their homes, some being done away with, while the wives of others were taken into slavery along with the children. The inspired word even prayed for this.[6] *Let his children be tossed around and moved out, let them beg and be driven from their buildings* (v. 10), or according to the others "from their ruins": the houses and buildings were burned or left in ruins, and some inhabitants were done away with and others taken captive. *Let a creditor take possession of all that belongs to him* (v. 11). Symmachus, on the other hand, put it this way, "Let a bailiff strike all his possessions," bailiffs and Roman emperors exacting the tribute levied. They seized all the Jews' possessions, searching it out precisely so as both to find what was hidden and to appropriate it.

(6) *Let strangers plunder his labors. Let there be no protector for him, nor any one to pity his orphans* (vv. 11–12): when this happens and enemies divide up what belongs to them, there will be no helper for them nor will their children be thought worth sparing. *Let his children meet with destruction, his name be wiped out in one generation* (v. 13): forty years had not elapsed when the people of the Jews suffered annihilation; they no longer conduct their own affairs, have their own kings and rulers or that celebrated mother city, or perform the worship according to the Law. Instead, all that is gone—ark, tablets, figures of the Cherubim, mercy seat, candelabra, altar, high priest's robe, and all the other famous gifts of God in their possession.[7] *Let the iniquity of his fathers be remembered in the sight of the Lord, and the sin of his mother not be wiped out* (v. 14). Fathers' virtue was often of benefit [1760] even for sinful children, like Abraham's faith for the Jews, like David's piety for Solomon. On the other hand, fathers' wickedness will add to the retribution of likeminded children: no excuse on any score will be found for sparing

6. Theodoret, whom we have seen ready to concede the privileges of the Jews of Old Testament times, takes the following verses—less easily applicable to Judas—of the Jewish people of the time after Jesus, and quite trenchantly develops the theme of their merited punishment. Even Chrysostom, more prone to anti-Jewish polemic, did not see this theme touched on here.

7. While not exhibiting relish in this litany or departing from his habitual conciseness, Theodoret's depiction of the Jews' misery in the wake of the crucifixion is at least powerful and ironical.

them. So the inspired word said as much, that Jews suffer annihilation and will emerge as abhorrent for the memory of their
fathers' evils in addition to their own impieties. By *fathers* he
refers to those practicing godlessness in the wilderness, in the
time of the Judges, in the time of the Kings, and those addicted
to lawlessness after the return from Babylon, whereas he spoke
of Jerusalem as *mother* because in her was committed the abomination of murder against Christ the Lord. In fact, the Lord in
the Gospels said as much, "So that upon this generation may
come all the innocent blood shed on the earth, from the blood
of the righteous Abel to the blood of Zechariah, whom you
murdered between the sanctuary and the altar."[8] They will pay
the penalty for all at the same time.

(7) *Let them be ever before the Lord, and their memory be blotted out
from the earth* (v. 15). Always perceiving all the crimes committed by them, he is saying, God will consider them unworthy of
any sparing, and instead will consign them to annihilation.
From this, of course, it is clear that he recounted this in reference not to Judas alone but to all the unbelievers, changing the
viewpoint from a single person to a multiple reference, saying
no longer "his" but *theirs.*[9] *For this he did not remember to show mercy. He persecuted the needy, poor, and contrite of heart to kill him* (v.
16). They will suffer this, he is saying, for having practiced murder harshly and fiercely, and hunted to death the one who practiced every moderation and gentleness. The Apostle also testifies to these words, as does the Lord himself, the Apostle crying
aloud, "Though rich, for our sake he became poor so that we
might become rich by his poverty," and again, "Though he was
in the form of God, he did not consider being equal to God as
something to be exploited, instead emptying himself by taking
the form of a slave."[10] The Lord says in one place, "Learn of me
because I am gentle and humble in heart, and you will find rest
for your souls," and in another, "The foxes have lairs, and birds

8. Cf. Matt 23.35.

9. Theodoret is looking for some justification for applying these verses to
the Jews' misfortune. The morphological excuse he finds, unfortunately, immediately expires; but he is not to be deterred.

10. 2 Cor 8.9; Phil 2.6–7.

of heaven nests, whereas the Son of Man has nowhere to lay his head."[11]

(8) *He loved a curse, and it will fall upon him; he refused blessing, and it will keep its distance from* [1761] *him* (v. 17). Here he clearly shifted from the optative mood, and made both statements in prophetic form, that they will bear the curse they loved, and they will be deprived of the blessing they refused to accept. *He clothed himself with a curse as with a garment* (v. 18), that is, they will be enveloped in it from all sides. *It will enter his innards like water:* evils will come to bear not only from outside but also from within, and they will be surrounded by them as if by water. Then, since water bedews and moistens the body but does not have a lasting moisture, he added, *and in his bones like oil,* oil namely remains longer on the body. He means something like this, The force of evils will be brought to bear, more severe than water and resembling oil in its permanence. *Let it be to him like a garment which he wears, and like a belt with which he always girds himself* (v. 19). Let him be like covered on all sides by the aforementioned evils, he is saying, and let him be constrained as if by a cincture.

(9) *This is the work of my calumniators from the Lord* (v. 20). The others, on the contrary, rendered it "adversaries." *And of those speaking evil against my soul:* they will pluck these fruits, both those who display hatred for me and the betrayer assisting them. Since in fact they call him enemy of God and lawbreaker, he was right to say *my calumniators from the Lord. You, Lord, O Lord, behave towards me for your name's sake, because your mercy is good* (v. 21). Christ the Lord spoke this in human fashion; after all, he discharged all human functions except sin, being born according to the law of nature and beyond the law of nature: [to be born] of a woman belongs to human nature, but [to be born] of a virgin is beyond it.[12] He accepted swaddling clothes,

11. Matt 11.29; 8.20.

12 Theodoret now adopts a Christological hermeneutic, and in Antiochene fashion moves from the humanity of the expression (*synkatabasis* in Chrysostom's term) to the humanity of Jesus, listing the details of Jesus' life by way of proof. Unusually, he makes a point of bringing out as well the virgin birth (as an index of Jesus' freedom from inherited sin?), without expanding on Mary's dignity. See Introduction, section 6.

circumcision, and nourishment from milk. He offered sacrifices, fasted, went hungry and thirsty, and felt weariness. He is likewise also constantly recorded in the sacred Gospels as praying. Consequently, at this point, too, in human fashion he invokes divine help.

(10) *Rescue me, because I am poor and needy, and my heart is disturbed within me* (v. 22). We find this said by him also in the sacred Gospels: about to enter his Passion, he said, "Now my soul is troubled: what shall I say? Father, save me from this hour? But this is the reason I have come to this hour."[13] [1764] *Like a shadow when it declines I am swept away, shaken off like locusts* (v. 23). In this he referred to his death: like a shadow, he says, declining and disappearing I have reached the end of life; but like locusts blown about by winds and carried this way and that I lived my life, with no city or town or house, but shifting at one time to this, at another to that, at another to the hills, and hastening into the wilderness.

(11) *My knees are weak from fasting, and my flesh altered on account of oil* (v. 24): I did not live a loose and delicate life, but an ordinary, rigorous, and rough one. Witnesses to this are those given the privilege of the sacred discipleship, the barley loaves they brought, and the ears of corn they plucked and rubbed in their hands out of hunger.[14] The clause, *my flesh is altered on account of oil,* Symmachus rendered this way, "my flesh is altered from lack of anointing."[15] *I have become an object of scorn to them; they saw me and shook their heads* (v. 25). This had its fulfillment: seeing him on the cross, they shook their heads, saying, "Aha, you who destroy this temple and in three days raise it up, come down from the cross," whereas others said, "He saved others, he cannot save himself."[16]

(12) *Help me, O Lord my God, and save me according to your mercy. Let them know that this is your hand, and you, O Lord, did it* (vv. 26–27). Let them learn, he is saying, that it was not against my will that they gave me over to the cross, but it was a work of your

13. John 12.27.
14. Cf. John 6.9; Luke 6.1.
15. One particularly difficult phrase in a psalm Dahood classes as "a perplexing Hebrew text."
16. Cf. Matt 27.40, 42.

disposition: through my Passion you wanted to grant human beings impassibility. By *hand* he refers to God's operation. *They will curse, and you will bless* (v. 28): to this day Jews persisted in using blasphemies against the Savior, but despite their blaspheming the preaching became daily more illustrious. *Let those who rose up against me be put to shame, while your servant will rejoice:* This verse does not force us, either, to take the psalm in a different sense: we hear the divinely inspired Paul also saying, "He emptied himself taking the form of a slave."[17] And he himself speaks this way crying out in the words of Isaiah, "Who from the womb formed me to be a servant for him," and a little later, "I set you as a covenant for the races, a light of nations, to be for salvation to the end of the earth."[18] And in the sacred Gospels he spoke this way, "As the Son of Man came [1765] not to be served but to serve and to give his life as a redemption for many."[19] So *servant* is a term for the nature assumed, not because he serves it—how could he, linked as it is to God the Word, and in receipt of lordship over all things?—but for a demonstration of the particular characteristics of the nature itself. The term *servant,* then, is here indicative not of dignity but of nature.

(13) *Let my calumniators be clothed in shame and clad in their disgrace like a double cloak* (v. 29). Once again the other translators render *calumniators* as "adversaries." The facts witness to the prophecy: they continue in shame and wear it like a covering. *I shall confess strongly to the Lord with my mouth, and praise him in the midst of many people* (v. 30). Christ the Lord is called head of the Church, and the assembly of the Church is styled his body;[20] [the psalmist] calls its hymn of praise his hymn of praise.

(14) *Because he is present at the right hand of the needy to save me*

17. Phil 2.7. Theodoret feels there could be some resistance to his pressing his text to suit the theme of his choice. He has already quoted Paul above in support from Philippians, the phrase "form of a slave" occurring frequently in his earlier commentaries in reference to Jesus.

18. A collation of Isa 42.6, 49.6, and 49.8.

19. Matt 20.28. The distinction of natures in Jesus that follows (it is the period of Monophysite debate, after all) shows how precise he can be about the *communicatio idiomatum* that was less exactly expressed in commentary on Ps 107.

20. Cf. Col 1.18.

from those persecuting my soul (v. 31). He said this also in the fifteenth psalm, "I saw the Lord always before me, because he is at my right hand lest I be moved."[21] In other words, the divine nature, by making the union indivisible,[22] was present to the human nature, but permits it to suffer for securing the salvation of human beings. It was easy for him, after all, to render the nature which he assumed immortal; but since the Passion was the salvation of the world, he allowed the Passion to happen, and after the Passion he gave a share in immortality and incorruptibility. While he received no harm from its sufferings, he filled it with his own glory, and with it he reigns and has dominion over all. When he had the nature,[23] which is itself corruptible, he allowed it to suffer and to say everything in human fashion, with the exception of sin.[24]

21. Ps 16.8.

22. The sufferings of Jesus prompt Theodoret to insist again on the reality of the union, *henosis,* of natures in Jesus as indivisible, *achoristos*—one of the key terms in the Chalcedonian definition against the Monophysites some years later.

23. Despite Theodoret's insistence on the unity of natures, is there a sense in these words of the human nature in Jesus being an appendage, especially in this clause, "At the time when he had the nature"—as though now sloughed off?

24. Cf. Heb 4.15—a phrase (cited also on v. 21) also incorporated into the Chalcedonian definition.

COMMENTARY ON PSALM 110

A psalm for David.

AVING IN THE PRECEDING psalm made the prophecy about the saving Passion, he predicts the Savior's ascension after the Passion. The most divine Peter in the
Acts cites the opening of the psalm, speaking this way, "David
did not ascend into the heavens, but he himself says, The Lord
said to my Lord, Sit at my right hand until I make your foes
your footstool."[1] The Lord himself, seeing the Pharisees having
other opinions about Christ, put this question to them, [1768]
"What do you think about Christ: whose son is he?" When they
said, "David's," he replied, "How then does David by the Spirit
call him Lord, saying, The Lord said to my Lord, Sit at my right
hand?" Then he reasons, "If then David by the Spirit calls him
Lord, how is he his son?"[2] He said this, not to reject the idea of
the Lord's being son of David, but to add the unknown to what
was acknowledged: the Pharisees acknowledged that the Christ
is son of David, but that the Lord was also from David they had
no idea. So, without canceling what they acknowledged, he
adds the missing link, teaching that he himself is both his son
according to the flesh and his Lord as God and creator.

(2) Accordingly, blessed David clearly proclaims the divinity
of Christ the Lord, saying, *The Lord said to my Lord, Sit at my right
hand* (v. 1). If David, king and pious king, who vouchsafed also
the charism of inspiration, calls Christ the Lord his Lord, surely
he is not merely a human being, according to the Jews' folly,
but also God, in so far as he is both creator and Lord of David.
The sharing of the names indicates the identity of being: Lord

1. Acts 2.34–35.
2. Cf. Matt 22.41–45. And frequently elsewhere in the New Testament this
psalm is cited as a favorite Christological text.

says to Lord, and not Lord to creature nor Lord to artifact, *Sit at my right hand.* This, too, is marvelous, and not only surpasses human nature but also surpasses the whole of creation. But it is still expressed in human fashion: as God, the Son has an everlasting throne, Scripture saying, "Your throne, O God, is forever."[3] In other words, it was not after the cross and the Passion that as God he was accorded this dignity; rather, as a human being he received what he had as God: it was not that being lowly he was exalted, but that being exalted and in the form of God he humbled himself to take the form of a slave.[4] Hence the evangelist also cries aloud, "The only-begotten Son, who is in the Father's bosom, has told this." And the Lord himself says, "I am in the Father, and the Father is in me"; and elsewhere, "Glorify me yourself, Father, with the glory I had in your presence before the world existed."[5] As a human being, therefore, he hears, *Sit at my right hand,* having as God eternal power.

(3) *Until I make your foes your footstool.* The *foes* are in particular the devil, the demons ministering to him, and in addition to them also those resisting his divine teachings, Jews and pagans. The word *until* is not suggestive of time, but is a peculiar expression of the divine Scripture: God also speaks this way through the prophet, "I am, and until you grow old, I am."[6] It is clear that he does not confine God's being to the old age of human beings: [1769] if the inspired author says in connection with heaven and earth, "They will perish, but you will abide," and again, "You are the same, and your years will not fail,"[7] how much more is it the case that the Lord of all abides when human beings grow old and die. This resembles that apostolic saying, "He must reign until he has put all his enemies under his feet";[8] *until* is not suggestive of time here, either: what sense would there be for him to reign while there are still some oppo-

---

3. Ps 45.6. This Antiochene is constantly advising his readers to appreciate properly the anthropomorphisms of the text.

4. Cf. Phil 2.6–7. Adoptionism is not an option for Antiochene Christology.

5. John 1,18; 14.11; 17.5. Theodoret and his readers are clearly living in an age of intense Trinitarian and Christological debate. He credits them with the ability to appreciate the subtle theological distinctions he is making.

6. Cf. Isa 46.4.   7. Ps 102.26–27.

8. 1 Cor 15.25.

nents, but lose his reign after the subjection of all? The prophet Daniel, after the killing of the wild beasts, said he reigns forever and his kingdom would have no end;[9] but how will the saints reign with him, or with whom will they reign, if the one who promised the reign lays aside the reign? *Until,* therefore, is not suggestive of time, but occurs as a peculiar usage of the divine Scripture.

(4) *The Lord will send out to you a rod of power from Sion* (v. 2). The *rod* of Jesse is from Bethlehem: "A rod will emerge from the root of Jesse," Scripture says, "and a flower will spring up from the root, and the spirit of God will rest upon him."[10] The sequel to the saving cross makes clear the power of the *rod:* through it he subjected the whole troop of the antagonists; and it was fixed in Sion. *Rule in the midst of your foes:* the heralds of the divine Gospels were not carried on fair winds; rather, though beset by pagans and barbarians and ringed around by currents of impiety, they dominated their adversaries, converted the majority, led them like captives to the king, and ensured their embracing his service.

(5) *With you the rule in the day of your power, in the splendors of your holy ones* (v. 3): you have indestructible power; you show this particularly in the day of judgment, on which you render the holy ones resplendent and conspicuous. He called *day of power* the second coming of the Savior, when he will come with the angels in the glory of the Father;[11] then the holy ones will also shine like the sun,[12] according to the saying of the Lord himself. *From a womb before the morning star I begot you.* [1772] Here, too, he revealed the magnificence of his divinity. The Lord, who had already said to him, *Sit at my right hand,* confesses the oneness in being and proclaims the identity of nature, the phrase *before the morning star* indicating his being before

9. Cf. Dan 7.27. The psalm is clearly a classic and well-worn theological locus, and Theodoret is responding by a tight—and probably also well-worn—theological argument that exceeds his normal conciseness.

10. Isa 11.1–2. The argument presumes the readers know that Jesse is, as 1 Sam 16.1 declares, "the Bethlehemite." The next step is to associate the cross, as rod, with Jerusalem.

11. Matt 16.27.

12 Cf. Matt 13.43.

times and before ages. The phrase *from a womb* teaches the identity in being: you are born of no other source, he is saying, than my nature, *womb* to be taken in figurative fashion, obviously. That is to say, just as human beings give birth from a womb, and what is born has the same nature as the bearers, so you are born of me, and give evidence in yourself of the being of the bearer.

(6) *The Lord has sworn and will not repent. You are a priest forever according to the order of Melchizedek* (v. 4). The divine Apostle gave a precise commentary on this in the Epistle to the Hebrews, and showed the unlimited extent of this priesthood by the fact that, while the levitical priesthood did not accept the promises on oath, this one was confirmed on oath.[13] This is surely the reason he added *will not repent*, since the God of all often made many arrangements and allowed them to be subject to changes. Thus he both instituted the Jews' priesthood and terminated it; thus he both established that monarchy and dissolved it; thus he both gave permission for the kingdom of Assyrians, Babylonians, and Macedonians, and bade them come to an end. Wishing this priesthood to be eternal, however, he says he swore that he *will not repent*. He said this in human fashion: the divine is proof against passion, and repentance is a passion. Melchize-dek was a priest not of Jews, but of nations.[14] In like manner, Christ the Lord offered himself to God not only for Jews but also for all people. He begins his priesthood on the night after he endured the Passion, when he took bread, gave thanks, and said, "Take, eat of this; this is my body." In like manner he mixed the cup and gave it to his disciples, saying, "Drink of this, all; this is my blood, of the new covenant, shed for many for the forgiveness of sins."[15] We find Melchizedek to be priest and king (he was, in fact, a type of the true priest and king), offering to God not irrational sacrifices but bread and wine. He also offered these to Abraham, foreseeing in spiritual fashion

13. Cf. Heb 7.20–21.
14. Theodoret is right to read this into Melchizedek's allegiance to God under a Canaanite title as cited in Gen 14.18.
15. Matt 26.26–28. Melchizedek is accepted as a type on the basis of sound New Testament support, not to mention patristic tradition.

the archetype of his own highpriesthood in the patriarch's loins. So, if Christ is from David according to the flesh, and David from Judah, Christ, however, took the high priesthood according to the order of Melchizedek, the levitical priesthood came to an end, while the blessing of the greater priesthood shifted to the tribe of Judah. [1773] Christ, sprung from Judah according to the flesh, now serves as priest, not himself offering anything but acting as head of the offerers: he calls the Church his body, and in it he as man serves as priest, and as God receives the offerings. The Church offers the symbols of his body and blood, sanctifying all the dough through the firstfruits.[16]

(7) *The Lord at your right hand shattered kings on the day of his wrath* (v. 5): he will consign to punishment on the Day of Judgment those rulers and kings who now show resistance and audacity. The phrase *The Lord at your right hand* resembles what is said in the fifteenth psalm, "I foresaw the Lord ever before me in everything, because he is at my right hand lest I be moved."[17] In that place, in fact, he said this in human fashion, and indicated the indivisible character of the unified nature, and here he says both divine and human things at the same time: *Sit at my right hand* applies to human nature, while *From a womb before the morning star I begot you* implies the divinity, and *You are a priest forever* is likewise spoken in reference to a human being. Likewise, too, *The Lord at your right hand,* meaning, the unified divinity you have is indivisible.[18] *He will judge among the nations, he will fill them with corpses, he will smite heads on a land of many* (v. 6). Here he indicated more clearly the judgment, and the fact that on that day he will consign to manifold punishments those living a life of impiety. In the present life, of course, he often subjected them to many corrections, teaching the ignorant his peculiar force.

(8) *From a torrent in the way he will drink; hence he will raise his head* (v. 7). On becoming man, he is saying, he will exercise

16. Cf. Rom 11.16. The argumentation for the superiority of Christ's priesthood to levitical priesthood—something of a digression—is unusually lengthy and articulated; the bishop in him affects Theodoret most obviously here.

17. Ps 16.8.

18. The terms for unity, *henosis,* and indivisible, *achoristos,* are basic to the Chalcedonian statement, even if the expression here is generally less felicitous.

great humility so as to slake thirst even with water found on the way. The prophecy seems to me to contain another and more profound sense. It is usual for him to call the Passion a cup: "Father," he said, "if it is possible, let this cup pass me by."[19] He calls the Jews *torrent* because though they attained divine grace, they did not enjoy it always: as the torrent does not have the constant flow of water, and instead it is formed by the rain produced from the clouds, so Jews possessed the grace of the Law for a time, provided by the inspired authors as by some clouds. After this, however, with the coming of summer, according to the Lord's statement, "Lift up your eyes, and behold the fields, white for harvest,"[20] the torrent necessarily [1776] has remained bereft of the former abundance, and is seen to be dry, deprived of all moisture. Since, then, Jews devised the cross, and the Lord calls the Passion a cup, it was right for the inspired author, on perceiving this in advance, to say, *From a torrent in the way he will drink,* calling life *way.* What follows also testifies to this meaning: *hence he will raise his head.* The Apostle Paul also said something like this, "He humbled himself to the point of death, death on a cross; hence God also highly exalted him."[21] It is clear that he expressed this, too, in human fashion: it was not that as God he was lowly and then exalted, but as Most High he humbled himself, while as man he received what he did not have.[22]

19. Matt 26.39. Theodoret is desperate to vindicate the Christological sense of each verse of the psalm, but is really laboring to achieve this.

20. John 4.35.

21. Phil 2.8–9.

22. With this caveat, already made earlier in the *Commentary,* Theodoret completes his treatment of a psalm that elicited from the Fathers a synopsis of Christological thinking, sometimes in polemical fashion: Chrysostom begins his commentary by lining up his adversaries—"Jews, Paul of Samosata, the followers of Arius, of Marcion, the Manicheans, and those professing unbelief in the resurrection"—and picks them off one by one in "a battle line" (PG 55.264–65). Characteristically, Theodoret is more interested in theological issues than in personalities.

COMMENTARY ON PSALM 111

Alleluia.

MMONITES, MOABITES, and Idumeans, having assembled a very numerous force, at some former time waged war on the tribe of Judah. At that time Jehoshaphat was king of that [tribe], a man celebrated for piety, of the family of David. Thus on learning of the enemies' great numbers, with all the people he made an approach to God, asking for his invincible support, and in fact obtained his request: the God of all urged them to take heart against the enemies because he was their leader. At break of day, then, the enemies advanced on one another and slew one another as though [they were in] opposition, with the result that not a single one escaped the destruction. When the army of the Jews perceived this from a kind of lookout, they gave chase as though after prey at hand, despoiled the enemies and returned with great booty. As the story of the Chronicles teaches,[1] they entered the divine Temple with musical instruments, singing the praises of the provider of the victory. Foreseeing this, the inspired author composed this psalm as a hymn offered by the pious Jehoshaphat. There is also a title to the hymn: *Alleluia,* as we have already remarked, means "Praise the Lord" in the Greek language, *Allelu* "Praise," and *ia* "Lord," or "the one who is."[2]

(2) *I shall confess to you, O Lord, with all my heart* (v. 1): with all my mind, O Lord, I offer the hymn of thanksgiving. *In a council and congregation of upright people:* I am not alone; rather, the assembly of the pious is also with me. At that time, in fact, the people were freed from the error of the idols, the king instruct-

---

1. 2 Chron 20 tells of the campaign and the celebration; their relation to this psalm seems a matter of whim.

2. The term has occurred many times previously; only now does Theodoret give its etymology (a late discovery for him, too? See note 2 on Ps 113).

ing everyone in piety. Consequently, he calls the body of the pious *a council of upright people. Great are the works of the Lord* (v. 2): really marvelous and remarkable what was worked by his power. *Exquisite in all* [1777] *his wishes:* he does whatever he wishes, and everything that happens is marked by wisdom and invites praise by all. *Confession and magnificence his work* (v. 3): all things done by him—creation and its management—are great by nature and surpass nature, and deserve hymn singing by all people. By *confession* here he means thanksgiving. *His righteousness endures forever:* nothing of what is done is unjust; everything is marked by justice, as he ever employs it in governing all things.

(3) *He achieved remembrance of his marvels* (v. 4) since he obviously effected the destruction of the enemies. He did the same thing in the case of the forebears, at one time removing the Egyptians from sight, at another time cutting down the Amalekites with the extending of Moses' hands, and overcoming Canaanites, Hittites, and the other nations through Joshua son of Nun. He called the punishment of the enemies *memory of the marvels,* that is to say, your celebrated wonder workings, classed as false by the unbelieving, you showed to be true by the new wonder working, and you reminded us of what you performed in the case of our forebears.

(4) *The Lord is merciful and compassionate. He gave food to those who fear him* (vv. 4–5). The other translators render *food* as "prey." Both are correct: they made haste for the enemies' wealth like prey at hand, and procured adequate food from that source. *He will ever be mindful of his covenant.* Symmachus, on the other hand, put it this way, "He gave prey to those who fear him, remembering his eternal covenant": he has an indelible remembrance of the promises made to the fathers, and on its account he gives us a share in the good things. *He announced the force of his works to his people so as to give them an inheritance of nations* (v. 6): in a quite manifest way he showed us his characteristic power in granting us the wealth of the foes; he not only freed us from dishonor at their hands but also transferred their affluence into our houses.

(5) *Truth and judgment* [are] *works of his hands* (v. 7): far from his being unjust, he even acted very justly in this; though they

had no fault to find with us, they tried to overthrow [us] completely. So he delivered a right and just verdict against them. *All his commandments are reliable, confirmed forever, performed with truth and uprightness* (vv. 7–8): in giving the Law God promised his benevolence to those keeping the Law. At this point he also says that the promises about the keeping of the commandments are reliable and those [1780] who choose to fulfill them enjoy his providence constantly: we who made sincere supplication to him emerged superior to the adversaries. He suggested this, in fact, in what follows.

(6) *The Lord sent redemption to his people, he gave orders for his covenant forever* (v. 9): God's promises are not only reliable but retain permanence. *Holy and awesome his name:* to the believers it is holy and desirable, gushing forth with the abundance of good things, whereas those who do not believe and live a lawless life he punishes and chastises. *Fear of the Lord is the beginning of wisdom* (v. 10): so it is necessary to fear and dread him, the first requirement in the divine teaching. By *wisdom,* in fact, he refers not to fancy talk but to knowledge of divine things. So *fear* is for neophytes, whereas the possession of love belongs to the perfect. *All who practice it have a good understanding:* knowledge is not sufficient for perfection: discernment of behavior is required, and the one granted divine understanding through works ought to add luster to knowledge, and through [knowledge] serve the provider of understanding.[3] *His praise endures forever.* It was logical for him to add this, teaching that it is the lover of virtue who procures benefit here. God, after all, even if no one wishes to sing his praises, enjoys the hymn that is eternal and everlasting.

(7) They say this psalm was written alphabetically in Hebrew, being composed according to the order of the alphabet; and the one after it was composed in like manner.[4]

3. Theodoret has moved through this psalm rapidly, with no Scriptural documentation. Here he offers a brief listing of intellectual virtues. Not a devotee of the Bible's Wisdom literature, he makes no reference to similar statements in those books about the nature of wisdom. He sees the limitations of mere knowledge, asserting the need for practice as well, and for *theoria,* discernment of practice.

4. For this datum Theodoret is indebted to others, slight though the grasp of Hebrew required to enable him to recognize it for himself.

COMMENTARY ON PSALM 112

Alleluia.

HE TITLE ALSO CALLS this psalm a hymn, and offers those willing instruction in piety.

(2) *Blessed the man who fears the Lord; he will greatly delight in his commandments* (v. 1): the one furnished with this reverence and invested with divine awe directs all his counsel to the performance of the divine sayings, and hastens to discharge them with complete enthusiasm.[1] Then [the psalmist] shows the fruit of such seeds. *His seed will be mighty on the earth* (v. 2). Since this seemed desirable to the people of that time, he promises to give the gift to those keeping the commandments. And he actually gave it, to Israel for Abraham's sake, to his successors for David's sake, to his offspring for Israel's sake, even though this was to those turned lawbreakers. *Generation of the upright will be blessed:* those with a care for equity and righteousness will harvest the fruits of the divine blessing.

(3) [1781] *Glory and wealth in his house* (v. 3). He makes these promises as if to those still imperfect, not capable of giving ear to perfect things; Christ the Lord teaches the perfect the opposite in the words, "Possess no gold or silver or copper in your belts, nor wallet for the way, or sandals or staff," and again, "Unless someone renounces all his possessions, he cannot be my disciple," and, "If you wish to be perfect, sell your possessions, and give to the poor."[2] Yet in giving these laws, he makes the other promises and gifts to the imperfect: thus he increased Solomon's wealth and glory; thus he regaled the chil-

---

1. Though the psalm opens like Ps 1 by beatifying males, it does not prompt Theodoret to give a nuance to its exclusive address as happened in that case. He is content to have made his point, and in practice to ignore it afterwards, as is pointed out in Introduction, section 4.

2. Matt 10.9–10; Luke 14.35; Matt 19.21.

dren of Israel with the wealth of the Egyptians. *His righteousness abides forever:* the God of all enjoys unending remembrance, and retains his fame eternally.

(4) *He rose in darkness as a light for the nations* (v. 4). He gives the name *darkness* at one time to ignorance, at another to calamities, and likewise calls *light* knowledge in one case and freedom from evils in another. So he means that he both gives [a glimpse of] the truth to the ignorant, and extends his peculiar assistance at the onset of troubles. This was the way he snatched Joseph from the brothers' murderous intent, this the way he rendered him superior to slander, this the way he offered peculiar aid to Abraham when Sarah was snatched away,[3] this the way he terrified Laban and revealed the pursued to be more powerful than the pursuer. This too, then, is a sign of divine power, allowing troubles to be inflicted on the righteous for the sake of exercising [virtue], then dissipating a cloud of them and bringing about fine weather. *Merciful, compassionate, and righteous:* he governs these things by employing righteousness, mercy, and goodness: while he shows care out of loving-kindness, in his wish to crown the righteous he allows the struggles but concludes them as soon as possible out of immeasurable goodness.

(5) *A good man is the one who is compassionate and obliging; he will control his words in judgment* (v. 5). Symmachus, on the other hand, put it this way, "Good, generous, and obliging, managing his affairs with judgment": the man imitating his own lord attends generously to his fellow servants—compassionate as sharing in their nature, obliging as expecting repayment from the common master. Such a man does nothing thoughtlessly, instead rightly using his reason and adding luster to his words and deeds. [1784] *Because he will never be moved* (v. 6): such a man has a steady attitude that undergoes no change in the difficulties of the moment. *He will be righteous as long as people remember:* such a man will be celebrated, his praises sung by all, and he will leave behind an indelible reputation. *He will not fear a*

---

3. As before, and in keeping with note 1 above, Sarah's fate in Theodoret's eyes merits assistance being given to the patriarch who put her at risk ("snatched away" a euphemism), not to the woman herself at risk.

bad report (v. 7): he will be afraid neither of threats nor of stories capable of inducing fear. *His heart is ready to hope in the Lord.* Symmachus, on the other hand, rendered *ready* as "firm": he has a firm and steady hope in God, he is saying, and hence despises such alarms. *His heart is strengthened, he will not be afraid until he observes his foes:* not only does he not dread the adversaries, but he even expects their discomfiture on account of hope in God.

(6) *He has distributed, given to the needy; his righteousness lasts forever* (v. 9): each of those things offers instruction in virtue to those willing. He means that the man equipped with reverence and fear of God does not simply extend mercy to those in need, but does so with great generosity, imitating the sowers unsparing of their seeds, scattering them in expectation of sheaves; in similar fashion he awaits the reward of righteousness. *His horn will be exalted in glory.* He uses *horn* for strength by analogy with the animals equipped with horns and defending themselves with them against those attacking them. So he means that the one possessed of the wealth of virtue will be powerful and illustrious. *A sinner will see and be enraged, will gnash his teeth and waste away; a sinner's desire comes to nothing* (v. 10): those choosing to live a life of evil, on seeing the fame of the righteous, will waste away with envy and hatch schemes of murder; but they will fail in their plottings, and not enjoy their desire, unjust and utterly hateful to God as it is.

COMMENTARY ON PSALM 113

Alleluia.

HIS IS ALSO A FURTHER hymn composed for [our] benefit and to stir up human beings to singing the praises of the benefactor.[1]

(2) *Praise the Lord, his servants* (v. 1). He uses *servants* here, not of young people, as some suspected, but of the slaves; Aquila, Symmachus, and Theodotion also rendered it thus, and the Hebrew says *abde,* as does the Syriac. For *Praise* the Hebrew said Alleluia, so that it is clear *Alleluia* is translated as *Praise the Lord.*[2] [1785] *Praise the name of the Lord. May the name of the Lord be blessed, from now and until forever* (vv. 1–2). It behooves you, he is saying, slaves as you are, and receiving your being from God, to sing praises to his name, even if you are ignorant of his nature: he possesses the blessing and the glory that are without beginning and without end; the phrase *from now and until forever* indicates this. Nonetheless, we too must offer the thanksgiving hymn as to the creator.

(3) *From the rising of the sun to its setting is the name of the Lord*

---

1. With Theodoret's slight interest in the liturgical use of the Psalms, Jewish or Christian, we are not surprised there is no mention of this psalm beginning the Hallel (Ps 113–118) for use in Passover celebration.

2. Theodoret is chancing his arm here, linguistically speaking. He is right to cite the sense "servants" for the *paides* (which can also mean "young people") of his LXX version, though the fact that the other translators employ the same word hardly advances the argument. More to the point is the Hebrew term being translated, *'abde,* which even without the help of his native Syriac he could surely transliterate and turn into Greek. For the verb "Praise" the Hebrew in fact does not read *Alleluia* but *Allelu*—which makes us wonder further (see note 2 to Ps 111) if he really understands the elements of *Alleluia.* It would not be the first time he has come to grief when making a show of false erudition. Ironically, Dahood maintains the Hebrew clause does not parse, and he repoints *'abde* to read *'abade,* and thus "Praise the works of the Lord"—a problem and solution which would only bewilder Theodoret.

to be praised (v. 3). The psalm prophesied the knowledge of God provided to the nations after the Incarnation of the Only-begotten: of old the praises of the God of all were not sung even by all Jews but by a few living a life of piety, whereas after the birth from a virgin and the saving Passion, the sound of the heralds of truth went out into all the land, "and their words to the ends of the earth,"[3] and the whole earth was filled with the knowledge of the Lord, like volumes of water to cover seas.[4] The God of all said this also through another prophet, "I have no pleasure in you, and I shall accept no sacrifice from your hands, because from the rising of the sun to its setting my name is great among the nations, and in every place incense is offered to my name, and a pure offering."[5] The spiritual hymn singing also prophesies things in keeping with this.

(4) *Exalted over all the nations is the Lord, above the heavens his glory* (v. 4): all the nations have come to know that he is Most High, and God, and Creator of all things, and celebrated by the angels of the heavens. *Who is like the Lord our God?* (v. 5). The divine Scripture often says as much: blessed Moses says it, "Who is like you among the gods, O Lord? Who is like you, glorified among holy ones?"[6] and blessed David, "Who in the clouds will be compared with the Lord? or who will be likened to the Lord among children of God?" and again, "Who is God except the Lord, or who is God besides our God?"[7] From all these statements we learn the incomparability of the God of all, and the fact that nothing in existence can be likened to God's nature, power, or operation.

(5) *Who dwells in the heights, and on the lowly he looks down in heaven and on earth* (vv. 5–6): though seeming to dwell in the heavens he surveys all things, and allows nothing in existence to escape his care. *Who raises up a poor person from the ground, and lifts up a needy one from a dunghill, to seat him with* [1788] *princes, with princes of his people* (vv. 7–8). Blessed Hannah had also said this in composing the thanksgiving hymn to God.[8] We see this being done constantly by the God of all: thus he turned blessed

3. Ps 19.4.   4. Cf. Hab 2.14.
5. Mal 1.10–11.   6. Exod 15.11.
7. Ps 88.6; 19.31.   8. Cf. 1 Sam 2.8.

David from a shepherd into a king; thus he put Joseph on the royal throne after he had fallen into slavery; thus he made the shepherd Moses into a spokesman for the people, and appointed him Pharaoh's God; thus he accorded the nations, who were in thrall to the poverty of godlessness and seated in the dung of sin, the good things given to Israel; thus he raised up the human race, fallen into the very depths of death, lifted them on high, and seated them above every rule, authority, domination, lordship, and every name that is named, not only in this age but also in the age to come.[9]

(6) *Who gives the barren woman a home, a mother rejoicing in children* (v. 9). It is possible to see this likewise happening with human beings: Sarah, Rebekah, Rachel, Hannah, the mother of Samson, and Elizabeth, who had been barren, he made mothers of children.[10] You can see this more properly and truly, however, in the case of the Church: from being once sterile and childless, he made her a mother, rejoicing in children beyond number, according to the prophecy which says, "Rejoice, sterile one who does not bear, burst into song and shout, you who have not been in labor! Because the children of the barren woman are many, more than the woman with a husband."[11]

9. Cf. Eph 1.21.

10. Theodoret knows the women of the Bible, and this time is not shy about their names (see Introduction, section 4).

11. Isa 54.1.

COMMENTARY ON PSALM 114

Alleluia.[1] *[1789]*

HIS IS ALSO A HYMN for narrating the favors accorded the Jews by God, describing God's power and mocking the powerlessness of the idols. This hymn is also relevant, however, to those from the nations who have come to faith and been freed from the error of the idols: they learn the degree of difference between the false gods and the true God.

(2) *In the exodus of Israel from Egypt, house of Jacob from a savage people, Judah became his sanctuary, Israel his dominion* (v. 1). The Lord liberated Israel from Egypt, he is saying, freed them from the slavery of those foreign and savage ones, and made them his own people, while building in Judah his own Temple. The psalmist called this *sanctuary. The sea saw and fled, the Jordan turned backwards. The mountains skipped like rams, and the hills like lambs of flocks* (vv. 3–4). He uses metonymy in the expressions, using words to imply sense of lifeless things so as to proclaim God's power: with you as leader of the people, he is saying, the sea in fear moved from one point and another, and provided an unimpeded passage. The river, on the other hand, reared up and checked the flow of its currents, like some rational being imagining your power in the ark; and the hills and the mountains moved and seemed to dance, as though welcoming the Lord of heaven, meaning Mount Sion and Horeb, for God made his own appearance on them.

(3) Then he proposes a question to the things mentioned before. *Why is it, O sea, that you fled? and you, Jordan, that you turned backwards? Mountains, that you skipped like rams, and the*

1. The LXX has transposed the final Alleluia of the previous psalm, thus negating the author's intended inclusion. Theodoret is unaware of this; and he proceeds to give a summary of the psalm we know as two (see note 1 on the following psalm).

hills like lambs of flocks? (vv. 5–6). Since those things were irrational and lifeless, he himself supplies the response for them. *The earth was shaken at the presence of the Lord, at the presence of the God of Jacob, who turned the rock into streams of water, and the flint into fountains of water* (vv. 7–8). Each of them, he is saying, [1792] happens on account of the Lord's appearing. The shaking of the earth has this cause, and the parting of the sea: the barren rock, devoid of all moisture and resistant to splitting owing to its hardness, he personally made to gush with water by bidding fountains to flow from it in abundance. So there is nothing to be amazed at, he is saying: the maker gave orders, and the sea parted, the flinty rock gushed water, heaven provided manna, the winds gathered the quail, and all the other things happened at his direction.

COMMENTARY ON PSALM 115[1]

Not to us, o lord, *not us, but to your name give glory, because of your mercy and your truth, lest at any time the nations say, Where is their God?* (vv. 1–2). It was appropriate for those of the circumcision in olden times to say this in asking for divine help and recalling the former gifts: Do not turn away from us, O Lord, nor ignore us for our many failings; those who are ignorant of the justice of the retribution will take our servitude for your weakness, and say, Where is their God? *Our God in heaven and on earth did everything he wished* (v. 3): they say, Where is their God? But we know that you are God, maker of everything, with heaven as your dwelling, possessing power to match your will. Then by way of comparison he conducts a refutation of the idols.

(2) *The nations' idols are silver and gold, works of human hands* (v. 4): whereas you do what you will, the idols worshipped by the nations do not create but are created; the respect they have comes from the materials, being prepared from gold and silver and colors, and they take their shape from artistry, being prepared by silversmiths and goldsmiths and painters. So they acquire their substance from the material and from artistry. Then he further mocks their powerlessness in the words, [1793] *They have mouths, but will not speak; they have eyes, but will not see; they have ears, but will not hear; they have noses, but will not smell; they have hands, but will not feel; they have feet, but will not walk* (vv. 5–7):[2] they invest the images with appeals to the senses, he is

---

1. The LXX and some Hebrew manuscripts combine what appears in our Hebrew Bible and modern versions as Ps 114 and Ps 115. Theodoret seems unaware of the alternative, though noting the reverse process affecting the next psalm; so presumably the Hebrew text in his Hexapla did not separate the two psalms, either. Hence, he proceeds briskly without interruption to his commentary.

2. The LXX often does not read the tense of Hebrew verbs correctly; Theodoret rarely comments on the solecism.

saying, but they are deprived of operation; so they are of less value than not only their makers, but even the most insignificant living things. After all, flies and mosquitoes and things smaller than these possess the use of the senses: they see, they hear, they fly, they walk, whereas the gods adored [by them] do not possess the operation of the fewest and smallest animals.

(3) *They will make no sound in their throat:* since the demons operating through them and employing false oracles did not make these offerings through the lifeless idols but through people of reason, or made certain denunciations through symbols of some sort, he was right to say, *They will make no sound in their throat,* idols being completely immobile and inanimate. *Let those who make them be like them, and all who trust in them* (v. 8): but let their devotees and their makers be like them; it is right and proper that people endowed with reason and fallen victim to such stupidity should incur the same lack of sense as those things worshipped by them.

(4) *House of Israel hoped in the Lord: he is their help and protector. House of Aaron hoped in the Lord: he is their help and protector* (vv. 9–10): they incurred loss and no gain from the worship of these things, whereas the house of Israel by exercising hope in the true God enjoyed providence from him unceasingly. He made separate mention in this way to show regard for the priesthood and teach people at that time the extent of the difference between the priests and the others. *Those who fear the Lord trusted in the Lord: he is their help and protector* (v. 11). This ranking is at variance with the former ones. The word teaches that even if someone does not possess the status of priesthood or does not have the advantage of Israelite kinship, but is furnished with fear of God and practices virtue, he will personally attain the same providence from the God of all. There were many such people among the Jews of old, not sprung from the Abrahamic root but coming from different nations, who were called proselytes and held divine things in high esteem. Today, on the contrary, the nations have no kinship according to the flesh with Abraham, but they have the faith of Abraham [and thus] are styled children of Abraham.[3]

3. The universalism of Bishop Theodoret's soteriology is impressive. He

(5) [1796] *The Lord remembered us and blessed us; he blessed the house of Israel, he blessed the house of Aaron, he blessed those who fear the Lord* (vv. 12–13). He made the same distinction here, too, and gave a glimpse of the fruit of hope: he linked blessing to hope, and said a share in it would be [granted] not only to *the house of Israel* and *the house of Aaron* but also to *those who fear him.* Then in turn he makes the distinction of ages and positions, *the small with the great:* not only the young but also the elderly, not only those bedecked with wealth but also those living a life of need, not only those furnished with liberty but also those forced to carry the yoke of slavery. *May the Lord give you increase, you and your children* (v. 14). For those possessing hope in God the inspired word[4] prays for increase and abundance. *May you be blessed by the Lord, who made heaven and earth* (v. 15). You will attain this above all, he is saying, to the extent that you receive the blessing from the maker of all things.

(6) *The heaven of heaven is the Lord's, but the earth he has given to sons of human beings* (v. 16): he has the heaven as a dwelling, not the visible one but the one above it, which the former has as a roof, as we have the lower one as ours. The Lord of all, however, dwells in heaven, not with his nature circumscribed but rejoicing in the choirs of the holy angels living there. The earth, of course, he has assigned to the human race. So he takes care not only of Jews but of all human beings, to whom he has given the earth as a dwelling. *The dead will not praise you, O Lord, nor all who go down into Hades. But we the living will bless the Lord, from now and forever* (vv. 17–18). By *dead* he referred to those in thrall to the lifeless idols. What could be more insensitive than they? And by *living,* to those adoring the living God, to whom he has assigned the divine hymn. He teaches in addition to this, however, that it behooves those worshipping God with com-

---

notes separate mention of Aaronic priesthood and Israelite descent, suggesting perhaps pride of place for the clerical order. But at once he observes that the following verse amends any such prior claims to divine benevolence, finding in faith ahead of blood line or clerical status a claim to both divine providence and lineage from Abraham. It would be nice to see him relate this overview to the Christian economy.

4. Theodoret has long since given up the habit of referring to the author as David, especially in psalms that bear no such title.

plete zeal to celebrate him while they are alive insofar as death will prevent their doing it. Hence he says also in another psalm, "I shall sing to the Lord in my life, I shall play to my God while I live."[5]

5. Ps 146.2.

COMMENTARY ON PSALM 116

Alleluia. [1]

NTIOCHUS, STYLED EPIPHANES, son of Seleucus,[2] invested Jews with many and varied calamities. He caused some, [1797] who were living a life of ease, to transgress the divine Law; others, lovers of piety, willingly accepted the struggles it involved, and enjoyed the triumphal crowns. The present hymn foretells their bravery, but at the same time it recounts both the onset of distress and the aid provided them by the God of all.

(2) *I loved that the Lord will hearken to the sound of my supplication, because he inclined his ear to me* (vv. 1–2).[3] The inspired composition teaches them to say this: Things of God are more satisfying to me than anything else, and serving God is more desirable to me than all other things: he accepts my supplications and grants his peculiar aid. *And in my days I shall call upon him:* for this reason, to be sure, all my life I shall sing his praises and beg assistance from him. Then he outlined the multitude of troubles.

(3) *Pangs of death surrounded me, dangers of Hades lit upon me* (v. 3). The pregnant woman's pangs before childbirth are appropriately referred to as *pangs;* so by this analogy the calami-

---

1. This Alleluia, too, the LXX has transposed from the conclusion of the preceding psalm.

2. The phrase "son of Seleucus" is missing from the long form of the text, probably on the score of accuracy. Antiochus IV, whose father had the same name, did belong to the Seleucid dynasty founded by one of Alexander the Great's successors, Seleucus I Nicator; brother of Cleopatra, he succeeded his brother Seleucus IV in 175, his assault on Jewish religion provoking the revolt of the Maccabees.

3. Even in the original the syntax has caused v. 1 to be classed (by Ehrlich) as "one of the most difficult passages in the Psalms"—though the LXX's trouble with verb tenses does not help.

ties causing him to come near to death are called *pangs of Hades.* He means, then, that he is beset with many and varied disasters to the point of being near to death itself and laying hold of the very gates of Hades. *I experienced tribulation and pain, and I called upon the name of the Lord* (vv. 3–4): yet I did not surrender myself to rest and ease when I fell foul of those things, nor surrender myself to the other comforts of life; instead, I had recourse to weeping and wailing, and in constant lamentation I sought divine assistance. You would gain a more precise knowledge of this from the history of the Maccabees: the devotees of piety made their escape to the wilderness, and oppressed by hunger and thirst they appealed to God and enjoyed help from him.[4] *O Lord, rescue my soul.* With this lament, he is saying, I said, Come to our aid, O Lord, and free our souls from the evils pressing upon them. In my prayer I had known, of course, that I would obtain my request, having learned from experience his great loving-kindness. In fact, he added as much.

(4) *The Lord is merciful and just, and God has mercy on us* (v. 5): he pours out the fountains of mercy on human beings, and yet also exercises justice, punishing the wrongdoers unwilling to practice repentance. He mentioned *mercy* twice, however, and mentioned *justice* once: God's loving-kindness surpasses the verdict of justice. *The Lord guarding the infants* (v. 6): he takes such [1800] care of all human beings as to regale even infants with complete providence. He is not only interested in newborn children, but also preserves, saves, and matures those concealed in the very womb of their mothers, swimming in evil-smelling fluids and confined to a dark and narrow space, brings them out to the light, offers the fountains of milk, frees them of the scheming demons, and, to put it in a nutshell, gives them a share in fatherly providence.[5] It was not without purpose that the inspired word mentioned these things; rather, it was to teach that the God of all does not only repay the fruits of the

4. Cf. 1 Macc 2.28–30. The psalm's arbitrary and tenuous connection with the Maccabees, however, allows Theodoret to apply its thoughts more generally.

5. The womb is not a friendly environment for Theodoret, nor birth without its perils. Perhaps he knows more about the natural sciences than gynecology.

righteous but also takes the initiative in beneficence, creates what does not exist, takes an interest in it after forming it, on maturity awaits the fruits of righteousness, and then in turn surrounds the good with favors.

(5) *I was brought low, and he saved me.* Symmachus, on the other hand, put it this way, "I was exhausted, and he saved me": if infants, who are not yet endowed with knowledge of him, meet with such care from him, much more does he give a share in salvation to those who call upon him in sincerity. So as soon as he observes us being brought low by calamities, he regales [us] with his peculiar assistance. *Return, my soul, to your rest, because the Lord has done you kindness* (v. 7). They encourage and stimulate themselves to bravery, giving a glimpse of the multitude of divine favors, and teach themselves that even if they meet with death for the sake of piety, they will be transferred to a life that is satisfying and free of grief; he referred to it as *rest.* What follows also suggests as much.

(6) *Because he delivered my soul from death, my eyes from tears, my feet from stumbling. I shall be pleasing in the sight of the Lord in the land of the living* (vv. 8–9). By *land of the living* he refers not to the present life, in which there is weeping and wailing, disease, death, sins, and troubles, but to the life rid of all these things, in which the possession of virtue is effortless and the wealth of righteousness is acquired without hardship: those prepared to acquire it here with hardship will multiply it without hardship. Accordingly, they offer the hymn of thanksgiving for their eyes are rid of weeping, their feet escape the perilous life, their soul succeeds in escaping the death of sin; and they teach themselves to bear nobly the onset of grief and despise death for the reason that a painless life follows death.

Alleluia. [1801] The Hebrew, the other translators, and of course the Syriac combine this with the preceding verses; it has the same sense, after all. Having divided the ninth into two, by the combination of these psalms they keep the number of the psalms equal.[6] Still, it contains the same theme: those who

6. It is hardly a challenging conclusion for Theodoret, with the Hexapla before him, to realize that the LXX is dividing a psalm left as one in the original

there referred to the land of the living to achieve a conclusion in the previous one here begin by saying, *I believed; hence I spoke* (v. 10): not with the eyes of the body did I perceive that land; instead, it was faith that made it obvious to me.[7]

(8) *I was brought very low. I said in my astonishment, Every human being is false* (vv. 10–11). Aquila, on the other hand, put it this way, "I said in my amazement, 'Every human being is a cheat,'" Theodotion, "Every human being fails," and Symmachus, "I said when sorely troubled, 'Every human being will be deceived.'" I cited all the versions, not without purpose but in my wish to show that he calls human prosperity a lie, disappearing as quickly as possible, and lacking anything permanent.[8] In other words, perceiving this sudden change, he is saying, mindful of the former good fortune and observing the calamities coming in rapid succession, I said when sorely troubled, Nothing is firm, nothing stable; instead, trusting in present realities as permanent, he will be deceived and disappointed in his expectation. He said this also in the thirty-eighth psalm, "But everything is futility, every living person";[9] and the wise Solomon, having learned this lesson, though admittedly having had experience of every happiness, was ardent in his analysis of human affairs and put down this introduction, "Completely futile, everything is futile."[10]

(9) *What shall I return to the Lord for all his repayment to me?* (v.

---

and in those other ancient versions (including the Syriac—"of course," whether because it too is a version, or because it is Theodoret's habitual means of checking the Hebrew). He is aware of the opposite process happening with Ps 9 (and 10), but unaware of what happens with Ps 114 and Ps 115, on the one hand, and Ps 147 on the other; so his acceptance of the adjustment in numbering is somewhat premature. In short, his credentials as a "textual critic" (Guinot's term for him) are imperfect.

7. This verse, that Paul found so pregnant (2 Cor 4.13), and that for Chrysostom in his commentary developed into a rich essay on faith and reason, is hardly deserving of notice in Theodoret's view. It yields to the Maccabean theme.

8. Probably not even Dorival, who has questioned Theodoret's responsibility for at least some of the citations of the alternative versions in the text, would contest this instance—though one wonders if what is achieved by this multiple citation is significant, or if the occurrence arises simply from Theodoret's opening glance at all versions.

9. Cf. Ps 39.6.
10. Eccl 1.2.

12): surrounded with many and varied kindnesses, I do not know with what I shall repay the benefactor. It was not without purpose that he connected this verse with the preceding one; rather, he teaches that even in the varied changes in life the God of all extends to human beings his peculiar assistance, and offers the downhearted manifold encouragement. Blessed Paul also said this, "Blessed be the God and Father of our Lord Jesus Christ, who consoles us in any affliction of ours so that we may be able to console those in any affliction through the consolation with which we ourselves are consoled by God. Because just as [1804] the sufferings of Christ are abundant for us, so too is our consolation abundant through Christ."[11] And blessed David said as much, "Corresponding to the great number of my pains your consolations gave joy to my soul."[12]

(10) *A cup of salvation I shall take, and I shall call upon the name of the Lord* (v. 13): so it is fitting to accept death for his sake with good cheer, and make this repayment for the manifold benefi-cence; by *cup of salvation* he referred to death for the sake of godliness, this being the name Christ also gave it, saying, "Fa-ther, if it is possible, let this cup pass from me," and to the pair of apostles asking for a share in his kingdom, he said, "Are you able to drink the cup I am about to drink?"[13] So here, too, the noble and excellent champions of religion are urged to do this in their own case, he is saying; and they fulfill the promise in the sight of their clansmen so as to enkindle in them also a like zeal. Then they show the fruit of this death: *My vows I shall pay to the Lord in the sight of all his people. Honorable in the Lord's sight is the death of his holy ones* (vv. 14–15): if it is honorable to God, to which of the holy ones is it not venerable?

(11) *O Lord, I am your servant, I am your servant, and the child of your serving girl* (v. 16): if, then, we undergo that death worthy of admiration, we shall enjoy honor and glory from God, and gain everlasting reputation. If, on the other hand, we prove su-perior to the enemies and scatter their force, we shall offer the

11. Cf. 2 Cor 1.3–5.
12. Ps 94.19.
13. Matt 26.39; 20.22. We might have expected a bishop to resonate to the eucharistic overtones and usage of this verse.

hymn of thanksgiving to the Lord, acknowledging our servant role and boasting of succeeding to it from our ancestors. Those forced to serve human beings sometimes glory in having children who are free, whereas those who are content to serve God confess to receiving their servant role from their forebears in the justified belief that such service is their highest distinction. *You have burst my bonds:* you have freed me from my many and varied calamities.

(12) *I shall offer you a sacrifice of thanksgiving, and call upon the name of the Lord. My vows to the Lord I shall fulfill in the sight of all his people, in the courts of the house of the Lord, in your midst, O Jerusalem* (vv. 17–19): freed from the calamities, I shall not be ungrateful for the favors, but shall give back to you the sacrifice of praise and make the repayment of the thanksgiving hymn in the sight all the clansmen, and [1805] reap the benefit from it. I shall offer this rational liturgy in the Temple consecrated to your name. We can therefore learn also from this that even when the Law was in force those who took a more spiritual approach to the Law prized rational sacrifices ahead of irrational offerings, thus foreshadowing the New Testament. We should recognize, of course, that both psalms relate also to all the triumphant martyrs; the purpose is the same for the one group and the other: the former endured the praiseworthy death for the Law and the lawgiver, and the latter preferred to the present life an end for the sake of the one who saved them and overthrew death.[14]

14. By bringing these ten verses (known as Ps 115 to the LXX) back to the Maccabean theme, Theodoret has passed up the opportunity of a disquisition on faith like Chrysostom's, and also almost perversely has suppressed their eucharistic connotations for Christian liturgy, seeing instead a reference to martyrdom.

COMMENTARY ON PSALM 117

Alleluia.[1]

HIS, TOO, IS A HYMN RELATING to all people: the grace of the Spirit urges those who have attained salvation to sing the praises of the benefactor.

(2) *Praise the Lord, all the nations* (v. 1). He summons all to a dance at the same time: he provided the occasions of salvation for all the nations, not Greeks only and Romans, but for all savages, employing the sacred apostles as ministers of benefaction. "Go, make disciples of all the nations," he said, "baptizing them in the name of the Father and of the Son and of the Holy Spirit, teaching them to observe all I commanded you."[2] In obedience to this law they traversed all land and sea, one bringing Indians to Christ, one Egyptians, one Ethiopians. Blessed Paul teaches concisely to how many nations he offered the divine message, "so that from Jerusalem as far round as Illyricum I have fully proclaimed the Gospel of Christ." It was not, in fact, by following the direct route but by encompassing the nations situated in the middle that he offered the saving teachings: "Thus I make it my ambition not to preach the Gospel where the name of Christ has already been heard, lest I build on someone else's foundation; rather, as it is written, Those who have never been told of him shall see, and those who have never heard shall understand."[3] Later, of course, he set foot on Italy and reached Spain, and brought benefit to the islands situated in the ocean. In fact, in his letter to the Romans he said, "I hope to visit you on my travels to Spain, and to be sent on to there by you if first I have enjoyed your company for a little

---

1. Transposed by the LXX from the end of the previous psalm.
2. Matt 28.19–20.
3. Rom 15.19–21; cf. Isa 52.15.

while"; and writing to the remarkable Titus he says, "I left you behind in Crete for the reason that you should appoint elders town by town, as I directed you."[4] Thus the excellent John rid Asia of its former godlessness; thus the divinely inspired Andrew illuminated Greece with the [1808] rays of the knowledge of God; thus the divine Philip rebutted the error of both Phrygias; thus the mighty Peter traveled from Jerusalem as far as the city of Rome, offering the rays of truth to all; thus they all traversed the whole world, dispersed the gloom of ignorance, and gave a glimpse of the Sun of Righteousness. The inspired word was, therefore, right to urge all the nations to offer the hymn to God, since they all enjoyed salvation.

(3) *Praise him, all the peoples.* In former times Jews were scattered to the ends of the whole world, taught to worship the one God. So since they no longer occupied only Palestine, and did not continue to form one people under one king, but were scattered among the nations and obeyed their rulers while maintaining their own lifestyle and observing the direction of the Law, he was right to speak of them not as a people but as *peoples.* In fact, most of them accepted the divine message: in Jerusalem three thousand and five thousand were caught by the fishermen on a single occasion; and later there were large numbers beyond counting, the divine James said; and in Syria, Cilicia, Lycaonia, Pisidia, Asia [Minor], and Pamphylia,[5] and in all the other nations the apostles offered the divine message to Jews first. Some believed and enjoyed the truth, while others contradicted the beneficial teachings. The inspired word, then, is right to urge even them to sing the praises of the benefactor, calling them *peoples.*

(4) *Because his mercy to us has been deepened* (v. 2): it was by applying mercy alone that he achieved our salvation. Thus blessed Paul also says, "When the goodness and the loving-kindness of God our Savior appeared, he saved us, not through the righteous deeds we had done but in his great mercy, through wash-

---

4. Cf. Rom 15.24; Titus 1.5.

5. Cf. Acts 2.8–10, 41. Theodoret, in referring to converts to the apostolic preaching, seems to be confusing their number with the five thousand needing to be fed during Jesus' ministry.

ing of regeneration and renewal of the Holy Spirit, which he poured out on us in rich measure"; and again, "By grace you have been saved through faith: and this is not from you, but a gift of God"; and elsewhere, "The saying is sure, and worthy of complete acceptance, that Christ Jesus came into the world to save sinners, of whom I am the first but I received mercy." God proved his love for us in that while we were still sinners Christ died for us.[6] So the inspired word was right to say *his mercy to us has been deepened.*

(5) *And the truth of the Lord abides forever:* for he bestowed the salvation, which he promised through the holy authors. Blessed Paul also says as much in beginning his letter to the Romans, "Paul, a servant of Jesus Christ called to be an apostle, set apart [1809] for God's Gospel, which he promised beforehand through his inspired authors in the holy Scriptures"; and again, "I say that Jesus Christ became a minister of the circumcision on behalf of God's truth for the confirmation of the promises to the ancestors and for the nations to glorify God for his mercy."[7] Since, therefore, the God of all fulfilled the promises, bestowed the salvation he promised, and opened the fountains of mercy to all, we who have come forward from the Jews and you who have come to faith from the nations, blend together in harmonious singing and thus repay the benefactor.[8]

6. Titus 3.4–6; Eph 2.8; 1 Tim 1.15–16; Rom 5.8. Theodoret is insisting on taking this psalm in an eschatological sense so as to focus on the Christian Church's mission to the Gentiles, thus excluding attention to those great divine attributes of *hesed* and *emeth* in salvation history that are the true focus of the psalm. Thus he does not do justice to this shortest of the psalms but "theologically one of the grandest," in the view of Dahood, who says of it, "Its invitation to all nations and their gods to join in praising Yahweh for his goodness to Israel virtually recognizes that Israel's vocation was the salvation of the world."

7. Rom 1.1–2; 15.8–9.

8. The imperative is, as it were, addressed by the psalmist speaking as a Jew, Theodoret normally placing himself among the latter group.

COMMENTARY ON PSALM 118

Alleluia.

HIS, TOO, IS A HYMN offered to God by those who have attained salvation. Jews, on the one hand, offer this hymn in thanksgiving to God after the return, with all the neighboring people gathered together at the one time, envying their former prosperity and assembling other nations and savage peoples, and then consumed by plagues sent by God according to the prophecy of Joel, Ezekiel, Micah, and Zechariah. On the other hand, since our situation is prefigured in theirs, the hymn singing applies rather to those who have come to faith from the nations, who though persecuted, tortured and abused at the hands of great numbers of both rulers and ruled, mobs and mobsters, kings and generals, and though subjected to countless forms of death, emerged superior to the enemies. To the one group and the other, of course, the grace of the Spirit proposed the teaching of the hymn singing.

(2) *Confess to the Lord that he is good, because his mercy is forever* (v. 1): sing the praises of the one who is good and provider of good things; he has sufficient mercy and always offers it to those in need. *Let the house of Israel say that he is good, because his mercy is forever. Let the house of Aaron say that he is good, because his mercy is forever* (vv. 2–3). After mentioning these individually, he makes general mention of those who have come to faith from the nations: *Let all who fear the Lord say that he is good, because his mercy is forever* (v. 4). All of you, he is saying, sing the praises of God's loving-kindness, both you who take your origin from Israel, glory in the piety of your ancestors, and have been accorded the priesthood in them, as well as you who, though from different nations, have been freed from the godlessness of [your] ancestors. [1812] There is one God of all, in fact, who offers different favors to all, and extends mercy to those who ask.

(3) Then he teaches the providence of God more clearly. *Out of [my] distress I called upon the Lord, and he hearkened to my request for space* (v. 5): he did not obstruct the onset of evils, but revealed the perils and immediately scattered them. He said this also in the fourth psalm, "In [my] distress you gave me space,"[1] that is, You offered me consolation in excess of the pain. *The Lord is my helper, I shall not fear what man will do to me. The Lord is my helper, I shall look down upon my foes* (vv. 6–7): having the Lord of all to assist me, I do not fear the enemies' attacks; enjoying aid from him, I hope to see their overthrow as quickly as possible.

(4) Then he confirms the pious attitude with good thoughts. *It is better to trust in the Lord than to trust in man. It is better to hope in the Lord than to hope in rulers* (vv. 8–9): he is good, loving, intent on good things, able to do what he intends, and enjoying irresistible authority, whereas human beings, corruptible by nature and unstable in outlook, often do not intend the good and sometimes are powerless to assist the wronged when intent on it; even if they are rulers, they hold that rule [only] for a time; kingship with human beings is impermanent, in force for a short time. Hence it is better to forsake the assistance of human beings and beg divine help.

(5) *All the nations surrounded me, and I took vengeance on them in the name of the Lord* (v. 10). The Church sustained the assaults of all the nations, but Jerusalem of some, not of all; so in regard to the latter the language is expressed in hyperbolic fashion, but literally in the case of the Church:[2] those in each nation who came to faith endured the alarms and dangers at the hands of non-believers, yet likewise they and the others overcame their adversaries by trusting in God. *They surrounded me in a circle, and I took vengeance on them in the name of the Lord* (v. 11). Symmachus, on the other hand, put it this way, "They surrounded me, and in turn besieged me," that is, They applied one assault after another and all kinds of sieges, whereas I was protected by appeal to God, and scattered their forces.

1. Ps 4.1.
2. That is another criterion for adopting an eschatological rather than historical approach to the psalm, that the facts square better; by perverse logic Theodoret can claim to be choosing a literal reading over hyperbole.

(6) *They surrounded me like bees around a honeycomb* (v. 12). As bees on finding a honeycomb, he is saying, suck the sugary liquid, so they [1813] endeavored to wrest the sweetness of piety innate within me. *They were enkindled like a fire among thorns:* they also hoped to overcome me more easily, as the fire readily consumes the thorns. *I took vengeance on them in the name of the Lord:* though looking forward to this, they were disappointed in their hope, overcome by my hope; I set the Lord against them all, and through him I won the victory. *I was pushed back and set to fall, and the Lord supported me* (v. 13). This applies to both groups: the former would have met with utter ruin had they not enjoyed divine grace, while the latter would have fallen victim to godlessness had not the divine virtue sustained them. *The Lord is my strength and my celebration, and he has become my salvation* (v. 14): so we have him as power, victory, and source of hymn singing: enjoying good things from him, we offer the hymn in good spirits.

(7) *Sounds of joy and salvation in the tents of the righteous* (v. 15): after the victory, freed from the former laments, they gave vent to satisfaction and praise in celebrating God. *The Lord's right hand exercised power, the Lord's right hand exalted me* (vv. 15–16). *Right hand,* as we have often said, means successful operation. Behaving properly, they do not ascribe the victory to themselves nor trust in their own enthusiasm and power, but cry aloud that they have attained it by the divine grace. *The Lord's right hand exercised power. I shall not die, but live and recount the works of the Lord* (vv. 16–17): so enjoying assistance from on high, and proving superior to death, I shall teach even the ignorant the divine favors, remind those who know them, and enkindle love for him by mention of them. *The Lord corrected me with correction, and did not give me over to death* (v. 18): he allowed troubles to assail me, correcting me in fatherly fashion; but he dissipated their gloomy cloud, and rid me completely of harm from there.

(8) *Open to me gates of righteousness; I shall enter by them and confess to the Lord* (v. 19). By *gates of righteousness* he means not the gates of the Temple but the different forms of virtue: through them it is possible worthily to sing the praises of the God of all.

He indicated this more clearly through what follows, giving as if by way of reply the words, *This is the gate of the Lord; righteous people will enter by it* (v. 20). This was the reply the Lord gave to the young man [1816] wanting to learn the way of eternal life, "You know the commandments: You shall not commit adultery, you shall not steal, honor your father and your mother, you shall love your neighbor as yourself."[3] By this, to be sure, the Lord nominated himself as a door in so far as he is guide and teacher of virtue; "I am the door for the sheep," he says, "if anyone enters through me, he will come and go out, and will find pasture."[4] The inspired word also says this here, *This is the gate of the Lord; righteous people will enter by it.*

(9) *I shall confess to you, because you have hearkened to me, and have become salvation for me* (v. 21): so I sing your praises for receiving my petition and giving salvation. *The stone that the builders rejected was turned into head of the corner* (v. 22). No matter how many times Jews are shameless about it, this cannot be applied to anyone else: even if Zerubbabel was formerly in charge of the divided tribes, he did not continue for long. Christ the Lord, on the other hand, brought together into one and linked the opposites, the two walls standing opposite to each other, namely, those who came to faith from the Jews and those from the nations, I say, one group in thrall to godlessness, the other dragging the yoke of the Law; he combined them from both to form one Church, like a corner stone linking together two walls and binding them to one another. This was the stone, of course, that the builders of old, Pharisees and Sadducees, priests and scribes, rejected and crucified;[5] but *he became head of the corner* or, according to Symmachus, "cornerstone." Of this stone God also prophesied through Isaiah the prophet, "Behold, I am laying in Sion a precious stone, chosen, a cornerstone, respected as foundation for her; everyone believing in it will not be confounded." Blessed Paul also says as much, "Built

3. Matt 19.18–19, loosely recalled.
4. John 10.7, 9, loosely recalled.
5. Cf. Acts 4.10–11, where Peter speaks in similar terms. 1 Peter 2.6–7 does likewise, proceeding to the quotation of Isa 28.16 which Theodoret adduces.

upon the foundation of the apostles and Old Testament authors, with Jesus Christ himself as the cornerstone."[6] Blessed
Daniel also saw this stone cut without the use of [human]
hands by way of instruction in the Virgin's giving birth without
participation by anyone else: he saw the smashing of the statue—that is, the futility of life—and a great mountain formed
that covered the world.[7]

(10) *This was done by the Lord, and it is marvelous in our eyes* (v.
23): God is provider of this grace, and we marvel at his ineffable loving-kindness. *This is the day the Lord made; let us be glad
and rejoice in it* (v. 24). He gives the name the day [1817] made
by God to the day when this stone rose after the Passion: immediately after the resurrection he bade the sacred apostles go
and make disciples of all the nations.[8] In a particular sense,
however, he said this day was made by God, since God in the beginning made the light on it, and it also received the resurrection of our Savior and dispatched the rays of the Sun of Righteousness to the whole world. Having created the light, he called
the light day, and made nothing else on that day.[9] So this day
alone, like the first day, received the creation of the light: on
the second he made the firmament, on the third the plants and
seeds, and likewise on the other [days] the other [things],
whereas on the first day the light, and he called the light *day*. So
[the psalmist] is right to say, *This is the day the Lord made; let us be
glad and rejoice in it*, in so far as on it we received the sources of
good things. *O Lord, please save* [*us*], *please make* [*us*] *prosper* (v.
25): in the future, O Lord, provide salvation, and make our way
leading to you easy and trouble-free.

---

6. Eph 2.20. Theodoret had this chapter in mind in speaking of walls above;
but the Pauline passage has Jesus breaking down a dividing wall between the
two communities, not fitting two walls together on a cornerstone as representing two communities.

7. Cf. Dan 2.34–35, 45. Jesus in applying this verse of the psalm to himself
(Matt 21.44; Luke 20.18) also refers to the stone in *Daniel;* the interpretation
of its being uncut by human hands as a reference to the virginal conception
and birth must come from later sources.

8. Matt 28.19.

9. Cf. Gen 1.3–4. By his relative expansiveness of commentary, Theodoret is
reflecting the significance the New Testament and Christian liturgy find in
these verses of the psalm.

(11) *Blessed is the one who comes in the name of the Lord* (v. 26). The children also offered this cry to the Lord as an accusation against those who professed to teach the divine sayings but were unwilling to understand their true meaning. Since the Scribes and Pharisees called the Lord a Samaritan,[10] the children called him the one who is coming and blessed; and the term Hosanna likewise occurs in the prophecy, as we find the phrase *Please save* occurring as Hosanna in the Hebrew.[11] Hence blessed John the Baptist, to guide his own disciples to the truth, asked the Lord through them, "Are you the one who is to come, or should we wait for someone else?"[12] Being Lord, he has come in the name of the Lord; thus he said to Jews, "I have come in my Father's name, and you did not receive me; another comes in his own name, and him you will receive."[13] And being blessed, he is son of the Blessed One; thus the high priest also asked, "Are you the son of the Blessed One?"[14] *We blessed you from the house of the Lord.* The victors say this to their friends, We offer you the blessing of this stone, which became a house for God the Word [living] in it: "The Word was made flesh," Scripture says, "and dwelt among us"; and the Lord said to Jews, "Destroy this temple, and in three days I shall raise it up."[15]

(12) *The Lord is God, and he has appeared to us* (v. 27). Here he has clearly declared the divinity of Christ the Lord: the one he called *stone* above and later *blessed* [1820] and *coming in the name of the Lord* he named *Lord* and *God,* who made his particular appearance and regaled the believers with salvation. *Observe a festival with the garlands as far as the horns of the altar:* assemble,

10. In the Gospel of John, it is "the Jews" (a Johannine term for those not responding in faith to Jesus, not really equivalent to the Scribes and Pharisees) who say to Jesus, "You are a Samaritan and have a demon" (John 8.48), while the children on quite another occasion (John 12.13) greet Jesus with this verse from the psalm, prefacing it with "Hosanna!"

11. Theodoret is half-right in this erudite and unnecessary footnote. The children do employ Hosanna in their cry, probably not as a petition but as a cry of praise, Raymond Brown tells us (*The Gospel of John,* AB 29, Garden City, NY: Doubleday, 1966, 457). The Hebrew of "Please save" in the preceding verse of the psalm is rather *hosi'a-nna,* not the Aramaic form Hosanna more familiar to the Syriac-speaking Theodoret.

12. Matt 11.3.   13. John 5.43.
14. Mark 14.61.   15. John 1.14; 2.19.

therefore, all, and conduct a very great festal assembly in celebration of your own salvation so that a massed gathering arrives
at the very altar. He used *with the garlands* for "crowded" and
"massed in a crowd"; even those of an idiom different from
ours say "crowded" for "packed."

(13) *You are my God, and I shall confess to you; you are my God,
and I shall extol you* (v. 28): I know you are God, I know you are
Lord, through life I shall sing your praises as benefactor. *I shall
confess to you because you hearkened to me, and came to be salvation
for me. Confess to the Lord because he is good, because his mercy is forever* (vv. 28–29). After first prompting themselves to songs of
praise as ranked ahead of the others, they thus urge the others
as well to sing the praises of the good Lord as the one who without envy makes available to everyone the springs of mercy. It is
important to acknowledge, of course, that it was appropriate
also for those besieged by those nations to recognize the one
coming from them according to the flesh and providing salvation to everyone. In this way, after all, they become bolder
against the attackers, encouraged by faith in the blessing hidden in them.[16]

16. Though this comment of Theodoret's may not be the obvious implica-
tion of the closing verse, Martin Luther (as quoted by Weiser), for whom this
psalm was his favorite, could resonate with the sentiments: "This is my psalm
which I love—for truly it has deserved well of me many a time and has delivered me from many a sore affliction when neither the Emperor nor kings nor
the wise nor the cunning nor the saints were able or willing to help me."

COMMENTARY ON PSALM 119

Alleluia.

HE DIVINE DAVID EXPERIENCED many and varied
changes in circumstances: he both fled enemies and
pursued enemies, fell into despondency and in turn
experienced a more satisfying life, traveled the divine path and
stumbled in his travel, and again followed the divine laws. So he
gathered all these experiences together into one in this psalm,
and by putting together with one another the prayers offered
to God by him on each occasion,[1] he proposed a single instruction of value to people, and teaches in what he says how it is
possible to exercise [1821] virtue in practice. He is not without
concern, either, for precision in the teachings; rather, he associates the instruction about them with the moral norms.[2] So this
psalm has the capacity to bring those longing for perfection in
virtue to perfection in it, arouse to zeal those living a life of
ease, encourage the downhearted, correct the indifferent,[3]

1. So Theodoret's judgment on the genre of this unique composition,
which he is happy to associate with David after long being non-committal about
authorship, is that it is a miscellany of prayers recited over a long period. He
seems unaware of the tightly alphabetic structure of the psalm in the original,
which would disallow this view, just as we have seen him relying on information
from others about other alphabetic psalms (cf. Ps 111 and 112). So he is not
likely to have agreed with the view of a modern commentator like Weiser that
"this formal external character of the psalm stifles its subject matter," but rather
would have aligned himself with Dahood's appreciation of "a freshness of
thought and a felicity of expression." Theodoret's own grasp of ascetical lore is
limited, and he is accustomed to recycling a limited range of spiritual maxims.

2. The psalm, then, is not merely moral in theme, but also contains teachings, the focus of Theodoret's interest in the Psalter, as we have seen.

3. For Chrysostom, who possibly for reasons of length omitted this psalm
from commentary (as he omitted Ps 117, for similar reasons of brevity—length
being critical for a preacher with an audience), morality and in particular treatment of the capital sin of indifference and the cardinal virtue of zeal/enthusi-
asm were at the focus of attention.

and, in a word, apply a manifold treatment to people's diverse ailments.

(2) *Blessed the blameless in the way* (v. 1). He declares *blessed* those traveling the royal way without deflection and not transgressing the norms of the Law either to the right or to the left. He brings out who these are, *who walk in the Law of the Lord:* those who live like these have a blameless character. He calls life a *way:* we all traverse it from womb to tomb. *Blessed are those who examine his testimonies, and seek him out with their whole heart* (v. 2). In commenting on the eighteenth psalm we explained what is the difference between Law, testimonies, ordinances, judgments, and commandments;[4] but in summary form we shall recall what we said. He gives the name Law to what was given by the God of all through the divinely inspired Moses; [he also calls] it in turn commandments and orders as commanded and ordered in royal fashion; ordinances in so far as they can render the one performing [them] righteous; judgments in that they give a glimpse of the divine verdicts and the appropriate rewards both for those living lawfully and for those living lawlessly; testimonies in that it testifies and reveals to what punishments the transgressors will be liable. So here, too, he blesses those who constantly *examine God's testimonies and seek out God with their whole heart.* This does not belong to everyone, however, but to the one laying hold of the very pinnacle of virtue: such a one does not divide his attention between God and worldly concerns, but devotes himself wholly to God.

(3) *Who commit no iniquity, but walk in his ways* (v. 3). He made this distinction also in the first psalm: there he declared blessed the person meditating on the Law of the Lord day and night, he demonstrated the fruit of meditation, and added, "Not so are the godless, not so."[5] So at this place, too, after declaring blessed the blameless, he teaches that the workers of iniquity developed a different way for themselves, and abandoned that determined by God. *You commanded that your commandments be strictly observed* (v. 4). The Lord gives this bidding in the Law, in the Old Testament authors, and in the sa-

4. Cf. Ps 19.7–9.
5. Ps 1.5.

cred Gospels; all of the divine [1824] Scripture is full of such obligation.[6] He urges them not simply to observe, but strictly observe—that is, with utter precision.

(4) *Would that my steps were guided to keep your ordinances* (v. 5). This is the reason, he is saying, that I ask for my way to be directed by your Law as if by some norm, that I may observe your ordinances. And to show the fruit of this he adds, *May I not then be ashamed in fixing my eyes on all your commandments* (v. 6): shame is the fruit of lawlessness. The divine Apostle also said as much, "So what fruit did you reap from what you are now ashamed of?"[7] Those who fulfill all of God's commandments have confidence in that knowledge. *I shall confess to you in uprightness of heart, when I learn the judgments of your righteousness* (v. 7). By *confession* he means thanksgiving: I shall then be able to offer a pure hymn, he is saying, when I learn all your judgments, and I shall live by them.

(5) *I shall keep your ordinances; do not forsake me altogether* (v. 8). Divine grace often leaves some people for a little while to ensure benefit for them from the experience here. Thus the mighty Elijah was abandoned and experienced the feeling of fear, and he learned the limitations of human nature; but straightway he enjoyed divine grace once more.[8] Thus the divine Peter made his denial and stumbled, but straightway the Lord supported him. When he was completely bereft of divine providence, Judas was a ready prey for the adversary. Blessed David was abandoned after that sin, and fell foul of those extreme troubles; but again he gained confidence in God, and enjoyed care from that source, whereas Saul was completely deprived of it, and bereft of the grace of the Spirit while being in the clutches of an evil spirit. It was therefore right for the inspired author to beg *not to be forsaken altogether,* that is, not to be deprived completely of the providential grace.

(6) *By what means will the young hold his course? By observing your words* (v. 9): a young one is unstable and inclined to evil; he

6. The Lord speaks in both Old and New Testament Scriptures—the Law (through Moses), the other OT authors *(prophetai),* the Gospels—or, in another way of phrasing it, *prophetai* and apostles.

7. Rom 6.21.

8. Cf. 1 Kings 19.

is beset by various billows of passions. So he needs a guide towards the haven of uprightness. This is characteristic of the divine sayings: they are capable of turning one away from contrary ways, supplying correction, and leading to the divine way; what rein and horsebreaker are to a foal, that is the function of the divine word to the young.[9] [1825] *With my whole heart I sought you; do not cast me away from your commandments* (v. 10). Many seek God, but not with their whole heart: they divide it, not only in the direction of worldly concerns but even to unseemly longings, envy, plottings, and schemes against the neighbors. The devotee of divine things, on the other hand, consecrates all his attention to God, and depends on providence from that source.

(7) *I hid your sayings in my heart lest I sin against you* (v. 11). Whoever possesses gold or silver or precious stones does not display them; instead, he conceals them inside within storerooms and chambers so as to escape the hands of burglars. Likewise, the one in possession of the wealth of virtue hides it in the soul lest by idle display the thieves of souls carry it off. The verse teaches something else as well, urging [us] not to offer the divine sayings to everyone: "Do not give the holy things to the dogs," he is saying, "nor cast your pearls before swine."[10]

(8) *Blessed are you, O Lord; teach me your ordinances* (v. 12), that is, you are gentle and loving, and worthy to be praised by all. For this reason I beg to learn from you what can make me righteous. *With my lips I announced all the judgments of your mouth* (v. 13): whatever I learn from your goodness I shall teach to the ignorant.

(9) *I took delight in the way of your testimonies as in riches of all kinds* (v. 14). While the way of virtue is troublesome, it is nevertheless very desirable to the perfect. This is the reason, to be sure, that Christ the Lord said, "Take my yoke upon you, because my yoke is mild and my burden light."[11] The inspired

9. Theodoret, who shows no awareness that the original has now moved to the second letter of the alphabet, is thus far not finding the repetition of the synonyms for Law deadening.

10. Matt 7.6.

11. Cf. Matt 11.29–30. Had he been aware of the practice, it would have been apposite for Theodoret to mention the rabbinic practice of speaking of

word also means, The possession of your testimonies is more satisfying to me than every kind of wealth. The phrase *in riches of all kinds* he does not add idly; rather, it indicates multifarious wealth, for there are many forms of wealth: one person who is called wealthy possesses gold, another silver, another a great amount of land, in one case with crops growing, in another case with seed sown, another possesses herds of cattle. The inspired author, however, included all these, compared them to the divine testimonies and said the divine testimonies are desirable to him as all the forms of wealth are to lovers of wealth.

(10) *I shall meditate on your commandments, and ponder your ways* (v. 15). For this reason, he is saying, I shall constantly boast of the meditation on your words, and pursue [my] journey in your ways. *I shall keep your ordinances in mind, I shall not* [1828] *forget your words* (v. 16): the memory of your sayings I shall keep permanently with me.

(11) *Reward your servant* (v. 17). It is not for everyone to make this appeal: no one carrying about a bad conscience prompts the judge to reward, whereas the person exercising pure reasoning makes this appeal with confidence. *Give me life, and I shall keep your words:* enjoying your assistance, I shall flee the death of sin, and gain life from your words. *Open my eyes, and I shall ponder the marvels of your Law* (v. 18). Not everyone reading the divine sayings ponders the marvels in them, but those enjoying radiance from above. Blessed Paul also said just that: "When one turns to the Lord, the veil is removed. Now, the Spirit is the Lord." He himself, illuminated by the divine light, was right to cry aloud, "All of us with unveiled face behold the glory of the Lord as though reflected in a mirror and are being changed into the same image from glory to glory, as though from the Lord, the Spirit."[12] We, however, should beg the Lord to remove the veil from the eyes of our mind and show the power of the divine sayings.

(12) *I am a sojourner in the land; do not hide your commandments*

---

the Law as a yoke, and reinforce Jesus' claim to a teaching that is "quantitatively easier because shorter and centred on the essential," as Benedict Viviano says (*NJBC*, 653).

12. 2 Cor 3.16–18.

from me (v. 19): we do not dwell but sojourn in the land, living a short time and changing to another life. Not all, however, want to acknowledge this; instead, they take great satisfaction in the good things of this life as though lasting and permanent, whereas the person instructed in the divine [truths] recognizes the transitoriness of life. Hence [the psalmist] calls himself *a sojourner,* and asks never to ignore the divine commandments. *My soul desired to have a longing for your judgments at every moment* (v. 20). Many people long for the divine judgments, and hanker after the kingdom of heaven, but not always: at one time they are satisfied with divine things, at another they follow the body's passions, whereas the inspired author yearns to have this longing constantly.

(13) *You rebuked the haughty* (v. 21): those who despise the divine laws contract the disease of haughtiness, but become liable to retribution from the righteous Judge. This was the experience of Absalom, of Saul, of Pharaoh, of Sennacherib, of Nebuchadnezzar, and of countless others. Aware of this, the inspired author, being inspired, added, *Accursed those who turn away from your* [1829] *commandments.* The Law imposes this curse on the transgressors: "Cursed be anyone," Scripture says, "who does not adhere to the contents of the book of the Law so as to practice them."[13]

(14) *Take from me insult and scorn, because I sought out your testimonies* (v. 22). Nabal insulted the inspired author, calling him a runaway slave; the Gathites insulted him.[14] Distressed at them, therefore, he prays for the insults to be deleted on the grounds that he sought out the divine testimonies. So the present words do not apply to the insults by Shimei:[15] they happened after the sin, whereas those of Nabal and the others before the sin. *Rulers in fact took their seat and maligned me* (v. 23). Saul, Abner, Ahithophel, and Absalom abused David. *Whereas your servant meditated on your ordinances:* acknowledging your lordship, I kept your ordinances in mind. *Your testimonies, in fact, are my constant*

13. Cf. Deut 27.26.
14 Cf. 1 Sam 25.10–11; 21.10–15.
15. Cf. 2 Sam 16. Theodoret is here taking the historical reference of the psalm so closely as to provide evidence for dating.

meditation, and your ordinances my deliberations (v. 24): rejecting all human explanation, I follow your norms.

(15) *My soul adhered to the foundation* (v. 25). In this he indicated the extraordinary degree of humiliation. He spoke this way also in the forty-third psalm, "Because our soul is brought down to the dust, our stomach adhered to the ground."[16] *Enliven me with your word.* He asks for life, not indiscriminately but for life in keeping with the Law. *I recounted my ways, and you hearkened to me; teach me your ordinances* (v. 26): I have indicated to you, Lord, all my actions, and did not allow any of my doings to remain hidden. For that reason accede to my requests: I ask to gain a precise knowledge of your ordinances. *Make me understand the way of your ordinances, and I shall meditate on your marvels* (v. 27). We need divine understanding to practice virtue according to the divine Law, by exercising loving-kindness not to have regard for vainglory, through spiritual exercises not to cast about for human commendation, and through the continence that arises not from the shame of intemperance but from the desire for virtue to practice continence. Thus the inspired author is right to ask for a share in divine understanding so as to discern the way of righteousness.

(16) *My soul dozed from weariness; strengthen me with your words* (v. 28). The constant assault of sin often impairs the quality of thinking, causes the athlete to fail, [1832] and produces the so-called *weariness*,[17] while the soul that is puffed up invites sleep; sleep, however, brings on death. Hence the inspired author asks to be strengthened and confirmed. He said this also in another psalm, "Give light to my eyes lest I should ever fall into the sleep of death,"[18] referring to sin as death. *Remove the way of iniquity from me, and with your Law have mercy on me. I have chosen the way of truth, I have not forgotten your judgments* (vv. 29–30). This request is necessary: it behooves us to ask help from the God of all so that we may be deflected from the way of iniquity,

16. Cf. Ps 44.25.
17. The psalmist uses a term, *akedia* in the LXX, which rings a bell with Theodoret as a well-known item in lists of hazards of the spiritual life, familiar to later Byzantine spiritual directors like John Climacus, and known in the West as *accidie.* Chrysostom would speak of *rhathumia.*
18. Ps 13.3.

choose the path of truth, and retain an indelible memory of God's testimonies.

(17) *I adhered to your testimonies, O Lord; do not put* [*me*] *to shame* (v. 31). He did not say simply "followed," but *adhered to,* that is, I did not exclude even the slightest of them from my thinking. He seeks to gain the fruit of such an attitude, namely, having no experience of shame. *I ran the way of your commandments when you gave me largeness of heart* (v. 32). There is need of both, our enthusiasm and God's providence: divine grace is not given to those who lack a lively enthusiasm, nor can human nature practice virtue without help from above.[19] The inspired author also teaches this: I ran the way of your commandments without hindrance on receiving from you facility in running. He calls facility *largeness.* He says in another place, "In my distress you gave me space," and again, "You gave my steps room under me, and my footprints were not weakened."[20]

(18) *Make the way of your ordinances a law for me, Lord, and I shall ever seek it out* (v. 33). For *Make a law* Symmachus said, "Give a glimpse," and Aquila and Theodotion, "Give light." I always need, he is saying, your illuminating guidance and legislation so as to know the way of your ordinances and to travel it without hindrance.[21] *Make me understand, and I shall search your Law and observe it with all my heart* (v. 34). The Lord bade us search the Scriptures,[22] but there is need of light from above for those searching if they are to find what they are looking for and keep what they have run to ground.

(19) *Guide me in the path of your commandments because I have chosen it* (v. 35). He does not simply ask the God of all to be-

19. This balanced statement of the respective roles of human effort and divine grace in salvation, typically Antiochene, could even be a well-rehearsed dictum, with even a jingle to the formula of both necessary ingredients, "our enthusiasm *(prothumia)* and God's providence *(prometheia).*"

20. Ps 4.1; 18.36.

21. Theodoret tries to preserve the force of the differing translations of both LXX and alternative versions—a deliberateness that offsets Dorival's reference to the latter in this particular psalm as evidence of insertion by a later copyist.

22. Cf. John 5.39; again that balance between human effort and divine grace.

come his guide, but shows his desire for the journey. *Turn my heart to your testimonies and not to avarice* (v. 36). Water naturally flows downhill, and if it happens upon any outlet, [1833] it all goes in that direction. Likewise, when the devil opened the way to sin, human nature took a turn for the worse.[23] So it is very appropriate for the inspired author to ask that his heart be turned to the divine testimonies, and avoid having the other experience.

(20) *Turn my eyes from looking at futility* (v. 37). *Futile* is worthless and stupid; what are seen as life's pleasures are like that. Solomon the sage spoke in that vein about them, "Utter futility, everything is futility"; and after describing how he built houses, planted gardens, and dug pools, he added, "Behold, it was all futility, an option for the wind."[24] So the inspired author asks to incline the eyes of his mind towards a different vision, and not to be taken in by the futility of realities of the present life. *Give me life in your way:* let me live my life in accordance with your laws. *Set fast your direction for your servant to develop fear of you* (v. 38): make me steadfast in observing your sayings, keeping them unswervingly in fear of you, that is to say, May fear of you rest upon me, terrifying me and not letting me stray from your sayings.

(21) *Remove the reproach against me which I have detected, because your judgments are good* (v. 39). Aquila, on the other hand, said "dreaded" for *detected,* and Theodotion likewise, whereas Symmachus said, "which I reverence." By *reproach* here he means what was done by sin: he dreaded it, feared it, and lived a suspect life. Hence he did not add in his usual manner, Because I sought out or observed your judgments, but *Because your judgments are good:* not only did you threaten sinners with retribution, but you also promised salvation to those who repent; he gave the name *judgments* to God's just verdicts. *Behold, I longed for your commandments; in your righteousness give me life* (v. 40):

23. Theodoret acknowledges the Fall, but does not dwell on it.
24. Cf. Eccl 1.2; 2.11. If his readers include people living a life in the world, Theodoret is in danger of encouraging in them an unhelpfully simplistic rejection of this life and "what are seen as its pleasures."

provide for the one hankering after it the life in righteousness.

(22) *May your mercy come upon me, Lord* (v. 41): all are in need of divine loving-kindness, and the one who has attained to the very pinnacle of virtue needs it constantly. *Your salvation according to your word. I shall reply to those casting words of reproach against me* (vv. 41–42): make available the salvation you promised in your sacred words, O Lord, so that I may speak confidently with those who mock me; the person in the midst of calamities bears the reproaches in silence, whereas the one living the pleasant way converses with those engaging in insults. *Because I hoped* [1836] *in your words:* I depend on your promise, and go forward in this hope.

(23) *Do not take a word of truth utterly from my mouth, because I was buoyed up with hope in your judgments* (v. 43). The inspired author teaches us to love truth and request it from the God of all with great confidence. *I shall observe your Law always, forever and ever* (v. 44): thus I shall become more zealous in regard to observance of your laws. By the phrase *forever and ever,* to be sure, he indicated the future life, in which the observance of the divine laws, pure and undefiled, will be granted to everyone.

(24) *I walked in open space because I sought out your commandments. I spoke in the presence of kings, using your testimonies, and was not ashamed* (vv. 45–46):[25] traveling with great ease, and living according to your commandments, he is saying, far from dreading kings' influence I engaged them in conversation with great confidence; the life in keeping with the Law is productive of confidence. The mighty David is witness to this: before the sin he spoke with Saul with great confidence, whereas after the sin in flight from his parricide son he went about with eyes on the ground and head covered. With the confidence of righteousness the great Elijah charged Achab with impiety;[26] likewise the divinely inspired Daniel said to Nebuchadnezzar, "Now, O King, let my advice be acceptable to you, wash away your iniquities with almsgiving and your sins with compassion for the needy";[27]

---

25. The oscillation in tenses in these verses owing to the LXX's difficulty with the original forms goes without comment by Theodoret.

26. 1 Kings 18.

27. Dan 4.27.

likewise the divinely inspired Paul addressed Agrippa, Festus, and Felix;[28] likewise the triumphant martyrs scorned the impious kings.

(25) *I meditated on your commandments, which I loved exceedingly. I raised my hands to your commandments, which I loved* (vv. 47–48). God's kingship [operates] not through word but through power;[29] the one who does and who teaches will be called great in the kingdom of heaven.[30] This is surely the reason the divinely inspired author combined meditation with action: after saying, *I meditated on your commandments, which I loved exceedingly,* and giving evidence of his ardent desire, he added, *I raised my hands to your commandments, which I loved,* that is, what I learned in the divine sayings I put into action. After all, it is not listeners to the Law who are righteous before God, says the divine Apostle, but doers of the Law who will be justified.[31] *I pondered your ordinances:* I engaged in constant meditation on them.

(26) [1837] *Remember your words to your servant, with which you buoyed me up in hope* (v. 49). In giving the Law God promised both his particular benevolence to those keeping the Law and retribution to the transgressors. So [the psalmist] asks God to remember his own promises: you taught me to hope in them, he says. And to show the benefit of the hope, he added, *It consoled me in my humiliation, because your word gave me life* (v. 50): I had this consolation in the calamities, and borne up by it I negotiated the billows.

(27) *Haughty people acted with extreme lawlessness, but I did not turn from your Law* (v. 51). He calls *haughty* Saul, Absalom, and the king of the Ammonites, who committed those atrocities against the people sent by him:[32] but they embraced a lawless life, he is saying, whereas I followed your laws. The triumphant martyrs, suffering harsh and cruel things from the inhumane and godless tyrants, would also say this. *I remembered your judgments from of old, Lord, and was consoled* (v. 52): I gave thought to the story of Abel, of Abraham, of Isaac, of Jacob, of Joseph, of Job, of Moses, how they were allowed to fall foul of various tri-

---

28. Acts 24–26.
29. 1 Cor 4.20.
30. Matt 5.19.
31. Rom 2.13.
32. Cf. 2 Sam 10.1–4.

als, and you later rendered them famous and illustrious, from which I drew fitting comfort.[33] *Despondency gripped me at sinners' abandonment of your Law* (v. 53): suffering badly I was heartened by the memory of your judgments; yet likewise I grieved and continued to be distressed on seeing many people transgressing your laws without fear.

(28) *Your ordinances were themes for my singing in my place of sojourn* (v. 54). Blessed David sojourned with the Philistines when pursued by Saul;[34] but in my view he refers in *sojourn* not to that period but to the whole of life: he passed it not as a dweller but as a sojourner, and spent his life singing of God's ordinances. The other translators, in fact, rendered it thus, "All your orders were songs for me in my place of sojourn." *I remembered your name at night, O Lord, and I kept your Law* (v. 55). While the choir of the saints always rises at night for praying and celebrating the God of all,[35] I am of the view here that he calls the time of temptations *night,* as it brings gloom and falls upon people like night. [1840] In this situation the recollection of the God of all is particularly necessary, encouraging, heartening, and driving out contrary thoughts. *This has happened to me because I sought out your ordinances* (v. 56). Thus I managed to survive, he is saying, and opt for the possession of your ordinances.

(29) *You are my portion, O Lord, I said I would keep your Law* (v. 57). God is the portion not of everyone but of those embracing perfection. That is why he also became the portion and inheritance of the priests and Levites: "For the sons of Levi," Scripture says, "there will be no portion in the midst of their brethren, because I the Lord am their portion."[36] Likewise in the fifteenth psalm he said, "The Lord is the portion of my inheritance and of my cup."[37] So here, too, he means, Despising

33. The repetition of a narrow range of sentiments on the Law, which some commentators find "stifling," has not wearied Theodoret, who can still document them with a series of biblical figures which we might find undiscriminating.

34. Cf. 1 Sam 27.5–7.

35. Theodoret referred in the preface and occasionally elsewhere throughout the *Commentary* to this practice of religious communities, which he himself had experienced and would again at the time of his approaching deposition.

36. Cf. Josh 13.33; Num 18.20.

37. Ps 16.5.

everything else I have you as portion, affluence, and wealth; hence I hasten also to keep your laws.

(30) *I made supplication to your countenance with all my heart* (v. 58). Everywhere he inserts the phrase *with all my heart,* obeying the Law even in this: for this the God of all also commanded, "You will love the Lord your God with all your heart, with all your soul, with all your strength, and with all your might."[38] *Have mercy on me in keeping with your saying.* He begs, not to have mercy shown to him indiscriminately, but to attain the mercy in keeping with the divine saying. This is also what a sensible patient would say to the physician, Attend to me as you know how, as [medical] science prescribes. It is also what a sensible merchant would say to the steersman, Guide the vessel according to the norms of sailing, [steer it] as also knowledge dictates. It is also the way we should announce the divine mercy; after all, the one making the petition knows the way of mercy: often it achieves salvation through correction, and retribution turns out to be loving-kindness. This is also the way the surgeon cuts and burns to achieve health for the sufferer. It is also the way we should request mercy: there are times when he regales us with mercy even through penury, proffers loving-kindness through sickness, and in keeping with surgical practice heals by the application of opposites.[39]

(31) *I pondered your ways, and directed my feet towards your testimonies* (v. 59). The Hebrew, on the other hand, has "my ways," and the other translators rendered it likewise, as well as the Septuagint in the Hexapla.[40] He means, Considering my ways, I guided my steps towards your testimonies, not allowing them to be diverted from the path leading to you. *I was prepared and was not alarmed in keeping your commandments* (v. 60): since I made

38. Mark 12.30; cf. Deut 6.5.

39. The analogies of the physician and the surgeon in spiritual lore, and even the navigator, are not novel, of course; Chrysostom, too, employed them frequently. See my "The spirituality of Chrysostom's *Commentary on the Psalms.*"

40. Theodoret as "textual critic" has a choice to make here. The array of Greek textual resources available to him (see Introduction, section 3), and perhaps the Peshitta, alert him to the fact that the (Masoretic) Hebrew text is pointed to mean "my ways," which his own (Antiochene) LXX has corrected, along with modern versions; so he goes with the flow, and despite the incongruity offers a paraphrase.

myself ready for the onslaught of troubles, [1841] I did not panic at their sudden onset. Thus the divine Daniel, thus the blessed children, thus the remarkable Maccabees, thus all the Savior's martyrs overcame the onslaughts of adversaries. The Lord also gives this exhortation in the sacred Gospels, "Keep awake because you do not know at what hour the thief is coming."[41]

(32) *Cords of sinners encircled me, and I did not forget your Law* (v. 61). He called the schemes either of demons or of human beings *cords,* taking the basis of the figure from the encircling. Likewise Isaiah, [saying,] "Aha, those who drag their sins along as though by a long cord."[42] Although these cords wrapped around me, he is saying, I did not expunge the memory of the divine Law. Then he teaches also the reasons for the memory. *At midnight I rose to confess to you for the judgments of your righteousness* (v. 62): not only by day, but also by night at the very midpoint of the night, when sleep comes upon human beings with the greatest pleasure, I continued singing your praises, giving full voice to your righteous verdicts. This was the experience also of the divine Apostle [Paul] along with Silas, for he was in prison with Silas:[43] imprisoned in the stocks after abuse and scourging, he mingled hymn singing with prayer and reaped the fruit of his excellent vigil, enjoying divine generosity.

(33) *I am a partner of all who fear you and keep your commandments* (v. 63). Symmachus, on the other hand, said "associate" instead of *partner,* and the Syriac, "friend": turning away from those who choose what is opposed to your laws, I kept close company with those who put great store by fear of you and choose to live in lawful fashion. He said as much also in another psalm, "To me your friends are extremely honorable, O God."[44] *The earth is full of your mercy, O Lord; teach me your ordinances* (v. 64). You pour out the fountains of mercy richly on

41. A loose reference to Matt 24.42–43.
42. Isa 5.18.
43. The long form of the text inserts this note in reference to Acts 16.19–25.
44. Ps 139.17 [Greek].

all, he says, make your sun rise on bad and good, send the rain on righteous and unrighteous,[45] and instead of giving vent to anger every day, you show long-suffering to those who break up others' marriages, those who are stained with innocent blood, others who appropriate what is not rightly theirs, those who besmirch their tongue with blasphemies, and others who commit other kinds of lawlessness. Exercising such loving-kindness, then, regale me with it, too, Lord, by providing me with the knowledge of your ordinances.

(34) *You have shown kindness to your servant,* [1844] *Lord, in keeping with your word* (v. 65): I had experience of your goodness; hence I beg to enjoy it once more, and ask to live in accordance with your laws. *Teach me goodness and discipline and knowledge, because I had faith in your commandments* (v. 66). The inspired author knows the usefulness of discipline, and the fact that the Lord is exercising loving-kindness in applying it to human beings. This is the reason he asks to have a share in it: God exercises goodness in applying correction, and correction produces knowledge. Likewise the prophet Jeremiah begs, "Correct us, O Lord, but in just measure, not in anger, lest you make us few."[46] Likewise a sick person who longs for health goes in search of cutting by steel and burning.

(35) Then he brings out the source of his knowledge of the usefulness of correction. *Before my humiliation I failed; hence I observed your saying* (v. 67). I brought correction on myself, he is saying: the verdict of punishment was free of any injustice, correction following upon sin, and observance of the laws upon correction. I fell ill, I had surgery, I got better. *You are good, O Lord* (v. 68): in reality you are good and loving. *In your goodness teach me your ordinances:* being confident for that reason, I beg to receive from you the knowledge of your ordinances.

(36) *Iniquity of haughty people in my regard was multiplied, whereas I shall study your commandments with my whole heart* (v. 69):

45. Matt 5.45. At this point Bishop Theodoret launches into a catalogue of capital vices that probably occurs to him from experience.

46. Jer 10.24. The generally moral nature of this psalm, without close historical association, allows Theodoret to give it a similarly general moral and ascetical application that is not true of commentary on other psalms. It is also noteworthy that he finds almost no Christological sense in this long psalm.

those practicing arrogance [towards me] hatch every type of scheme against me, yet I am not provoked to respond to their lawlessness, being restrained by your commandments. *Their heart was curdled like milk, whereas I meditated on your law* (v. 70). This resembles the inspired remark, "The heart of this people became crass, they were dull in listening with their ears, and shut their eyes."[47] It also resembles what is said in Exodus about Pharaoh, "Pharaoh's heart was hardened."[48] So he is saying, While these latter people had a stubborn heart, the others made their soft one hard, firming it and curdling it like milk, but I adhered to the meditation of your Law.

(37) *It was good for me that I was humbled so that I might learn your ordinances* (v. 71). The inspired author gives thanks for the harsh remedies of the surgeon, having learned the health that comes from them. [1845] *The Law of your mouth is good for me beyond thousands of gold and silver pieces* (v. 72): even if I was driven out of the kingdom by my child, nevertheless, through correction I recovered your Law, which I consider of greater esteem than all riches.

(38) *Your hands made me and shaped me; give me understanding, and I shall learn your commandments* (v. 73). He reminds the Creator of his love for human nature: having devised everything by a word, he is said to have formed humankind, not by use of hands, being incorporeal, but by giving evidence of greater affection towards this creature. So he begs the one who formed it to furnish the creature with understanding. *Those who fear you will see me and rejoice, because I am buoyed up with hope in your words* (v. 74). I shall prove to be a basis of joy for the pious, he is saying, by hoping in you and finding the fitting outcome of hope.

(39) *I know, O Lord, that your judgments are righteousness, and it was in truth that you humbled me* (v. 75). He says this in particular to show [God's] characteristic benevolence. I know precisely, he is saying, that you are right and just in condemning me and investing me with manifold troubles. *Let your mercy, O Lord, have the effect of consoling me* (v. 76). But now is the time for loving-kindness and comfort. *According to your saying to your servant:* to

47. Isa 6.10; cf. Matt 13.15.
48. Exod 7.13.

those practicing penance you promised your benevolence. He said this also through Isaiah, "When you turn back and groan, then you will be saved";[49] and through Jeremiah he cries aloud, "Turn towards me, and I shall turn towards you."[50] *Let your compassion come to me, and I shall live, because your Law is my meditation* (v. 77). He considers himself a corpse devoid of divine benevolence; for this reason he begs to return to life through divine loving-kindness.

(40) *Let arrogant people be put to shame because they did me wrong, whereas I shall meditate on your commandments* (v. 78): instead of cursing the foes, I pray for them: shame effects salvation. So the healing he enjoyed he asks they, too, may attain. *Let those who fear you and know your testimonies turn to me* (v. 79). As one who is far from the band of the righteous on account of his sin, and with all of them alienated [from him] as from God, he begs to be united once more with them and reestablish the communion with them. Symmachus, in fact, indicated this more clearly, "Let those who fear you bring me back." [1848] *May my heart be blameless in your ordinances so as not to be ashamed* (v. 80). He longs to have his heart free of all blame: such [a heart] is proof against shame. This is the reason, to be sure, that at the very beginning of the psalm he declared the blameless blessed.

(41) *My soul languishes for your salvation because I was buoyed up with hope in your words* (v. 81). Those who long for a thing and are deprived of what they long for are said to *languish;* it is the case with those very thirsty and short of water; it is the case with those waiting for one of their friends from abroad, always waiting, worn out by being disappointed in their longing. It is also the case with those wrestling with some problems and awaiting divine benevolence, *languishing* at the sight of this being delayed. *My eyes languished for your saying, asking, When will you console me?* (v. 82). Both the divine promise and the divinely inspired Scripture are also called a *saying.* So not only the one awaiting the divine promise and expecting the solution of the current problems *languishes,* but also the one reading the di-

49. Isa 30.15.
50. Jer 3.22.

vine sayings and longing to gain a precise knowledge of their meaning interprets the discovery as comfort and consolation.[51]

(42) *Because I have become like a wineskin in frost; I have not forgotten your ordinances* (v. 83). When a wineskin is heated it becomes puffed up, and swelling up it gets bigger, whereas in the frost it hardens and freezes. Thus also the body naturally gets puffed up with luxury, swells and revolts against the soul, whereas by the roughness of exercise it is brought low and repressed. Paul is witness to this when he cries aloud, "But I punish my body and enslave it lest after preaching to others I should fail the test."[52] So the inspired author, too, when pursued by Saul, was stronger than the passions; but when he enjoyed peace, he fell foul of the impulses stemming from luxury, and when brought low in his body he renewed the memory of the divine laws. *How many are the days of your servant? When will you deliver judgment on those who persecute me?* (v. 84). Human nature's time is limited, he is saying: "the days of our years amount to seventy years."[53] So when will you do me justice and rid me of the adversaries?

(43) *Lawless people told me idle tales, not at all like your Law, O Lord* (v. 85). They advised the inspired author to do away with the foes, but he obeyed the divine Law and awaited the divine verdict. [1849] Yet the teaching of these sayings is very useful to us as well: we ought to shun not only the fairy stories of pagans and the unbelief of Jews but also the blasphemous teachings of the heretics. *All your commandments are truth* (v. 86): this is the reason I choose your Law, because I see all your commandments adorned with truth.

(44) *They unjustly persecuted me, help me. They came close to bringing me to the grave, but I did not abandon your commandments* (vv. 86–87). The adversaries' injustice and influence are consid-

---

51. An eloquent statement not only of the inspiration *(theopneustos)* of the Scriptures but also of the salutary effects that come from their proper interpretation.

52. 1 Cor 9.27. Theodoret does his best to respond to the psalmist's imagery, and makes a good fist of the figure of the wineskin for which, Dahood observes, "in the long history of psalms interpretation no commentator has proposed an acceptable interpretation."

53. Ps 90.10.

erable, he is saying; they were not far from depriving me of life itself. *In your mercy give me life, and I shall observe the testimonies of your mouth* (v. 88). He embellished the remark with humility: he did not ask for life as a reward for righteousness, but begged to receive it as a gift of mercy, promising to observe God's testimonies.

(45) *Forever, O Lord, your word abides in heaven* (v. 89): everything, he says, is easy and possible for you the Lord; your command keeps the vaults of the heavens immovable. He said this also in the hundred and forty-eighth psalm, "He established it forever and ever; he issued a command, and it will not pass away."[54] At the same time he hints that the ranks of angels that dwell in heaven observe the divine Law and are free of any violation. *For generation and generation is your truth* (v. 90): you kept it both for the generation of the Jews and for the other one that came after it, meaning the people from the nations, who have attained salvation through Jesus Christ our Savior. *You established the earth, and it continues. By your arrangement the day continues* (vv. 90–91): you gave to the earth permanence for a long period, and it has abided as you commanded; you distinguished the day from the night, and it advances according to your laws. *Because all things are your servants:* everything serves you, and yields to your wishes, for you are the Creator of all things.

(46) *If your Law had not been my meditation, then I would have perished in my lowliness* (v. 92). Each of the pious could say this on encountering troubles: Joseph fleeing slavery, adultery, and calumny; Daniel prevented from praying; those three [children] obliged to worship the statue; the triumphant martyrs enduring all kinds of punishment. Blessed David was right to say this after being driven out by Saul and forced to live with Philistines and godless people; after all, he would have been a participant in their impiety had he not made the divine laws his meditation. [1852] *May I never forget your ordinances, because through them you gave me life* (v. 93): learning by experience that your ordinances lead to life, I shall preserve the memory of them indelibly. *I am yours, save me, because I sought out your ordi-*

54. Ps 148.6.

nances (v. 94). We cannot all employ this appeal: a slave to sin is lying when naming himself [servant] of God; one is a slave of the person by whom one is vanquished. So if we are free of sin and have chosen the divine laws, we can employ that appeal.

(47) *Sinners waited for me so as to ruin me; I understood your testimonies* (v. 95). For *waited for* Symmachus and Theodotion said, "looked forward to": while they hoped to dispatch me to death, I heeded your testimonies, and from that I reaped the fruit of life. *I saw the outcome of the whole process; your commandment is all-embracing* (v. 96). Symmachus, on the other hand, put it this way, "I saw the outcome of every scheme; your commandment is very comprehensive." All human things, he is saying—wealth, affluence, influence, offices, commands, empires, and kingdoms—come to an end, and a rapid end, whereas your commandment is extensive and indestructible, and it procures for those who observe it that unending and eternal life, and good things subject to no change.

(48) *How I loved your Law, O Lord, it is my meditation all day long* (v. 97). Not everyone who fulfills the divine Law does so with love: some are moved by dread and fear of punishment, others are intent on glory from human beings. Sincere lovers of virtue, on the other hand, hasten to fulfill the divine commands through the disposition to good. *Beyond my foes did you instruct me in your commandment, because it is forever of interest to me* (v. 98). After admitting his ardent love for the divine Law, the inspired author attributes everything to divine grace. Receiving wisdom and knowledge from you, he is saying, I was content with your Law: you gave me a greater insight than the foes. Hence some are anxious to do away with me, whereas I cannot bring myself even to take vengeance on the wrongdoers, keeping before my eyes the everlasting gain of virtue.

(49) *You gave me understanding above all my teachers, because your testimonies are my meditation. You gave me understanding above [my] elders because I sought out your commandments* (vv. 99–100). To kings it belongs to teach, to the ruled to be taught. Saul ruled as king, and in age he was an elder, yet likewise neither the authority of kingship nor his age in years [1853] brought him sense; instead, he longed to do away with his benefactor.

The mighty David, on the other hand, while still ranked among his subjects and of green years, had a love for good sense, and could not bring himself to be involved in wrongdoing or take vengeance on wrongdoers.

(50) *I kept my feet from every evil way so as to keep your words* (v. 101). It is not possible to travel two ways at once, intemperance and moderation, righteousness and iniquity; instead, you must avoid opposites and travel the straight. This, in other words, is like you becoming guardian of the divine words. *I did not stray from your judgments, because you gave me your Law* (v. 102): knowing you to be the lawgiver of these, I embraced them with complete willingness.

(51) *How sweet your sayings in my throat, beyond honey in my mouth* (v. 103): the sweetness of honey does not leave so pleasant a taste in my mouth as the joy brought to my spirit by meditation on your sayings. He used *throat* as the organ of speech; meditation is through speech. By using those [sayings] the soul reaps benefit here. *I gained understanding from your commandments; for that reason I hated every way of iniquity* (v. 104): understanding what is pleasing to you, I shunned all forms of evil.

(52) *Your Law is a lamp to my feet and a light to my paths* (v. 105): I do not walk in darkness, enlightened as I am by your Law as by some lamp. We should realize, of course, that while the Law is called a *lamp,* our Savior and Lord is the Sun of Justice: it hardly illuminated one people like a lamp, whereas he shed light on the whole world. Thus Christ the Lord called the divinely inspired John a lamp, appearing to the Jews while it was still night; but then the true light dawned, which enlightens everyone coming into the world.[55] He called the sacred apostles *light* as sharing in that light and enlightening all people through their teaching.[56] *I swore an oath, and determined to observe*

55. Theodoret has been dispatching these verses with a simple paraphrase, not surprisingly considering the material; Scriptural documentation has been missing. But with this verse he cannot resist a Christological reading, naturally resonating with the Johannine prologue—though one wonders if he respects the evangelist's meaning there in speaking of John as a light ("he himself was not the light": John 1.8) and as "divinely inspired": does he take the John of the prologue to be the evangelist?

56. Cf. Matt 5.14–16.

the judgments of your righteousness (v. 106). He called the firm decision of the soul an *oath* since most [human] affairs are confirmed by an oath.

(53) *I was brought exceedingly low, O Lord; give me life according to your word* (v. 107). He did not say simply that he was brought low, but *was brought exceedingly low,* and this despite being king and inspired author, with the confidence of virtue, the splendor of wealth, and power over the enemies. Yet he could never bring himself to trust in wisdom, or bravery, or righteousness: these he guessed to be gifts of divine grace. [1856] And the life he requests from the one able to give it is not requested indiscriminately: it is [the life] that is rational, lawful, made splendid by the divine Law.

(54) *Be pleased with the willing sentiments of my mouth, O Lord, and teach me your judgments* (v. 108). The divine laws make plain the majority of the works of virtue, but free will also adds a few. So some sacrifices [are prescribed] by law, some come from free will. The Law commanded the offering of some things in regard to sin and failure and in regard to involuntary faults, and payment of these was made to God like a debt of some kind, whereas the offerings coming from the generosity of free will he called gifts. Likewise in our time, too, the evangelical sayings prescribe temperance and righteousness, whereas virginity, continence after marriage, poverty, solitary life, and living in the desert are works of free will, transcending law.[57] Accordingly, the inspired author called them *willing:* what does not fall under the necessity of laws, but is the fruit of a free will in love with God, he rightly called *willing. My soul is ever in your hands, and I did not forget your Law* (v. 109): protected by your providence, I banished forgetfulness of your laws.

(55) *Sinners laid a trap for me, and I did not forget your commandments* (v. 110): both human beings and demons hatch many and varied plots against me, whereas I chose to travel the direct path of your commandments. *I received your testimonies as*

57. As one versed in religious life, Theodoret is able to distinguish the living of the evangelical counsels from the prescriptions of evangelical law. He sees the *gnome,* free will, as critical factor, operating in both Old and New dispensations.

an inheritance forever, because they are my heart's joy (v. 111): believing your testimonies to be an eternal and inviolate inheritance, I am glad and rejoice in their possession. *I inclined my heart to perform your ordinances forever by way of recompense* (v. 112). The soul's counsel is like a balance, but it is the mind, which has been given the function of taking the initiative, that holds the balance; so if it applies itself to pious thoughts, it is necessary to bend the beam in the direction of better things. The inspired author claims to have done this, *I inclined my heart to perform your ordinances forever by way of recompense:* perceiving the advantage stemming from them, I gladly welcomed the labors involved in them.[58]

(56) To bring out how he chose the divine things, he added, *I hated lawless people, but loved your Law* (v. 113): rejecting thoughts proposing transgression, I preferred your Law. *You are my help and my support;* [1857] *I am buoyed up with hope in your words* (v. 114): I did not do this without your help, but I enjoyed your aid and was nourished on your hope. *Part company with me, evildoers, and I shall study the commandments of my God* (v. 115). I addressed this, he is saying, to improper thoughts and to those endeavoring to give me worthless advice: Propose no such advice to me; life in accord with the divine commandments is preferable to me. I shall not simply follow them, but shall investigate them with utter precision so that no detail of them shall escape my notice; instead, I shall discharge everything the Lord of all ordained.

(57) *Support me according to your saying, and give me life; do not shame me in my expectation* (v. 116): so, as I have this purpose, grant me your providence lest I be disappointed in my hope and be filled with shame. Here *saying* means promise, that is, Provide me with the promised salvation. *Help me, and I shall be saved and shall meditate on your ordinances continually* (v. 117): I

58. After dealing with the figure he sees underlying the verb "incline," Theodoret briefly touches on the sense of "recompense," which is in fact a mistranslation of the Hebrew *'ereb,* occurring also in v. 33 where the LXX correctly rendered it "to the end," but is dissuaded from repeating that sense here by the presence of "forever" immediately preceding. The niceties are beyond Theodoret, of course.

shall not be negligent in attaining the salvation of your ordinances; rather, I shall make them my constant meditation. He means *meditation* not only in words but also in deed. *You spurned all who departed from your ordinances, because their reasoning is unjust* (v. 118): I shall exercise this zeal regarding your commandments in the knowledge that their transgressors have become figures of ridicule and obloquy.

(58) *I regarded all the sinners of the earth as transgressors; hence I loved your testimonies* (v. 119). For *transgressors* Theodotion said "worthless" and Symmachus, "dross." The inspired author suggested that, like God, he personally scorned the transgressors, and devoted all his enthusiasm to fulfillment of the divine sayings for the reason that he knew the loss involved in transgression. *Pierce my flesh with your fear: I was in fear of your judgments* (v. 120). My soul, he is saying, is enveloped in fear of you; but since the body and its limbs rebel against it, I beg you pierce them with this fear so that they become dead to sin and follow the guidance of the soul. This resembles that apostolic saying, "Put to death your earthly limbs—fornication, impurity, passion, evil desire, and avarice, which is idolatry";[59] [1860] and again, "I have been crucified with Christ; it is no longer I who live but Christ lives in me."[60]

(59) *I performed judgment and righteousness; do not hand me over to those who wrong me* (v. 121). Having chosen to follow your laws, he is saying, let me not become an easy prey to the adversaries. But who today has purity of soul like this so as to use such words with confidence? The divine Apostle, to be sure, said things resembling it: "This, in fact, is our boast, the testimony of our conscience."[61] *Welcome your servant to good things* (v. 122). Symmachus, on the other hand, said, "Receive me as your good servant," and Aquila and Theodotion, "Accept as a pledge"—that is, I speak the truth, I am not lying; believe your servant's promise, let it become a surety for my promise, because I shall be zealous to fulfill your laws. *Let arrogant people not calumniate me.* Calumny is distressing, even if it brings great reward; even the remarkable Joseph fell foul of it, and countless

59. Col 3.5.
61. 2 Cor 1.12.

60. Gal 2.19–20.

others. The Lord also bids us pray not to enter a period of trial.[62] So it was nothing inappropriate that the inspired author did in making this request: the calumny of the haughty and powerful is especially harmful, injustice combined with influence wreaking greater damage.

(60) *My eyes failed in [expectation of] your salvation and of the saying of your righteousness* (v. 123). Here again he calls the promise a *saying*. I constantly look forward to salvation from you, he is saying, and await the fulfillment of the promise. He put *failed* to bring out the intensity of the longing. *Deal with your servant according to your mercy, and teach me your ordinances* (v. 124). The practitioner of such a great virtue asks to attain mercy, and begs to enjoy salvation through it. Far from requiring reward, he begs loving-kindness.

(61) *I am your servant, give me understanding and I shall know your testimonies* (v. 125). While all people are servants of God by nature, it is by disposition that some choose God's lordship. As one of this company, the inspired author calls himself *servant,* and asks to be granted understanding so as to know God's testimonies. *Time for the Lord to act: they have scattered your Law to the winds* (v. 126). Being the one who governs everything with measure and rule, God puts up with people's sins for a long time; but when he sees evil on the increase through long-suffering, then he brings retribution to bear. So [the psalmist] says this here, too: It is time to rise up to assist the wronged, O Lord; the enemies absolutely trampled on your Law.

(62) [1861] *Hence I loved your commandments above gold and topaz* (v. 127): so while they scorned your Law, I consider your commandments more valuable than gold and precious stones. *Topaz* is one of the precious stones, and by [mention of] one he implied them all, though it is likely that at that time it was esteemed ahead of the others. *Hence I took all your commandments as my rule; I hated every unjust way* (v. 128): desire produces enthusiasm, and enthusiasm led him to recommend the straight path, and he loathed the way of iniquity.

(63) *Wonderful are your testimonies; hence my soul studied them* (v.

62. Matt 6.13.

129). He showed that it was not without reason that he loved them: they are estimable, he is saying, capable of enchanting and prompting love in those able to discern them. And whence did you come to learn their virtue? *The explanation of your words sheds light and imparts understanding to infants* (v. 130). Illuminated by your light, he is saying, I received this knowledge; your Law imparts understanding to all held in the grip of ignorance, resembling babies.

(64) *I opened my mouth and sucked in breath, because I panted after your commandments* (v. 131). By *mouth* here he refers to the mind's enthusiasm: it draws in the grace of the Spirit. He says elsewhere, "Open wide your mouth, and I shall fill it";[63] and the divine Apostle prayed that a word be given in the opening of the mouth;[64] and the inspired author himself said in another psalm, "The Lord will give a word to those bringing the good news with great power."[65] He said this here, too, *I opened my mouth, and sucked in breath, because I panted after your commandments:* since you saw me longing for your commandments, you accorded [me] your grace. *Gaze upon me and have mercy on me in the judgment of those loving your name* (v. 132). He asks to attain the divine benevolence, not simply but, he says, as you are in the habit of providing mercy to those who love you; this is the meaning of *in the judgment of those loving your name,* that is, I beg to enjoy the same verdict as they do.

(65) *Guide my steps by your saying; may no iniquity gain control over me* (v. 133): with our prior movement of enthusiasm, and God's provision of help and guidance in the journey, there is no room for the influence of sin.[66] *Redeem me from people's calumny, and I shall keep your commandments* (v. 134). Christ the Lord declared enviable and blessed those who are mocked and calumniated, [1864] but also bade them pray not to enter into temptation.[67] So the prayer of the inspired author accords with the evangelical laws.

---

63. Ps 81.10.   64. Eph 6.19.
65. Ps 68.11.

66. Though we have seen Theodoret elsewhere carefully balancing the role of human and divine in the spiritual life (cf. notes 19 and 22 above, e.g.), here he concedes a priority to the former.

67. Cf. Matt 5.11; 6.13.

(66) *Make your face shine on your servant, and teach me your ordinances* (v. 135). The divine is incorporeal, simple, and without composition. Sacred Scripture, however, speaks about it in a rather corporeal and concrete fashion, adjusting its language to human nature.[68] So the shining of the divine face is to be taken as the end to sorrows and the provision of good things. *My eyes shed streams of water since I did not keep your Law* (v. 136). This is also the apostolic law, "If one member suffers," it says, "all members suffer with it."[69] So the inspired author aims at the evangelical perfection, lamenting the others' transgressions. By *streams of water* he referred to the abundance of tears, meaning, I shed tears like a spring on perceiving people's transgressions.

(67) *You are righteous, O Lord, and your judgments upright. The testimonies you enjoined are righteousness and truth pure and simple* (vv. 137–38): you manage all things justly, O Lord, out of care for people and in your wish to make them doers of righteousness. You gave a Law, you leave transgressors in no doubt what penalties they will pay, you promise good rewards to the observant, and you confirm your promises by actions. The phrase *truth pure and simple* indicates this. *Zeal for you consumed me, because my foes forgot your words* (v. 139). The inspired author laments those living a life of lawlessness, and on seeing the lawgiver despised he is rightly angered. This zeal made Phinehas celebrated; this [zeal] rendered the great Elijah famous; burning with this [zeal] the triumphant Stephen accused the Jews of unbelief; exemplifying this [zeal] in himself, the divinely inspired Paul cried aloud, "Who is weak and I am not weak? who is scandalized and I am not on fire?"[70] And blessed Luke says of him that in Athens his spirit was afflicted within him seeing the city given over to idolatry.[71]

(68) *Your saying is tested exceedingly, and your servant loved it* (v.

68. Chrysostom, whose term *synkatabasis* does not occur here, could not have expressed the principle better himself: God communicates himself in (Jesus and) the language of the Scriptures in human fashion. Antiochenes, with their wholehearted acceptance of the Incarnation, understand this better than most; Theodoret, for instance, exemplifies it in his earnest efforts to unpack the psalmist's imagery.
69. 1 Cor 12.26.   70. 2 Cor 11.29.
71. Cf. Acts 17.16.

140). Your word is tried and true, he is saying, and free of all blame; I have an ardent affection for it. *I am too young and despised; I have not forgotten your ordinances* (v. 141). When God commanded the divine Samuel to entrust kingship to one of the sons of Jesse, [1865] he rejected all the others, boasting though they did of good health, strength, and beauty of form; he asked Jesse if there were no children left, and on his saying there was a tiny stripling remaining, who tended flocks and was therefore unsuitable for kingship, the prophet bade him be brought and immediately on his arrival anointed him.[72] The inspired author recalls this gift here, saying, Though I was young and considered insignificant by my parents, you granted me such great grace, and made me both prophet and king, in gratitude for which I long with complete enthusiasm to observe your ordinances.

(69) *Your righteousness is righteousness forever, and your Law [is] truth* (v. 142). The one who obeys human laws does not enjoy esteem in the present life from the lawgivers, whereas those following the divine commandments have eternal life as a reward for their labors. As well, human laws do not all have what is right on their side in every case, whereas the Law of God is conspicuous for truth. So he is right to say, *Your righteousness is righteousness forever, and your Law [is] truth. Tribulations and trials have come upon me* (v. 143). The lovers of virtue are saddled with these things. *Your commandments are my concern:* from their teaching I learn fortitude, and bear distress nobly. *Your testimonies are righteousness forever* (v. 144), that is, They are the source of eternal goods. *Give me understanding, and I shall live:* enlightened by you I shall enjoy the true life.

(70) *I cried out with my whole heart; hearken to me, O Lord, I shall seek out your ordinances* (v. 145). Again he calls the soul's enthusiasm a *cry;* hence he added *with all my heart.* Thus Moses also cried aloud while saying nothing, and God replied to him as he prayed in his mind, "Why are you crying aloud to me?"[73] *I cried*

72. Cf. 1 Sam 16.
73. Exod 14.15.

out to you; save me, and I shall observe your testimonies (v. 146): receiving salvation from you, I shall become a guardian of your laws.

(71) *I rose at an early hour and cried out, I was buoyed up by hope in your words* (v. 147). Though the inspired author was king, enveloped in countless concerns, and in addition to them committed to contests in war, he offered supplications to God not only in daylight but also in the middle of the night, not waiting for cockcrow. This was the extent of his longing for God, the Creator, this was the enthusiasm with which he requested help there. *My eyes anticipated dawn to meditate on your sayings* (v. 148). He did his meditating on the divine laws not only at the time of sweet sleep but also at dawn. [1868] We, on the other hand, though living a life of poverty and free of any worry, spend the night wallowing in our bed, not even after daybreak offering the hymn to the giver of good things.

(72) *Hear my voice, O Lord, in your mercy; in your judgment give me life* (v. 149). The man abounding in so many good things begs to attain mercy; he asks for mercy not indiscriminately but according to an advantageous verdict. *Those persecuting me unlawfully made their approach; they were far from your Law* (v. 150). Those bent on attacking the righteous person are far from the divine laws; Scripture says, "Whoever rejects you rejects not you but the one who sent you,"[74] and, "I shall be a foe to your foes, and an adversary to your adversaries."[75]

(73) *You are near, O Lord, and all your ways are truth* (v. 151). You see everything, Lord, he is saying; instead of keeping your distance, you fill the world, and you govern creation by exercising truth. God himself also says this through the prophet, "I am a God who is nearby, and not a God far away";[76] and blessed Paul says, "In him we live and move and have our being."[77] *From the beginning I knew from your testimonies that you established them forever* (v. 152). He calls heaven and earth *testimonies:* "Go

74. Luke 10.16, loosely recalled.
75. Exod 23.22.
76. Jer 23.23 [LXX].
77. The words of Epimenides, in fact, quoted by Paul in Acts 17.28.

down," he says, "and call heaven and earth to testify to them."[78] Hence the mighty Moses in beginning the song said, "Take heed, heaven, and I shall speak; and let earth hear words of my mouth."[79] In them God's providence is constantly visible: everything travels with great speed. From this I have precise knowledge, he is saying, that you are near, you are part of what happens, and no development escapes your notice.

(74) *Behold my lowliness and deliver me, because I have not forgotten your Law* (v. 153). "The one who humbles himself will be exalted," according to the Lord's saying; and "Blessed are the poor in spirit, because theirs is the kingdom of heaven."[80] The divine author arrayed the other virtues along with this, and with it as an enticement he appeals for divine help. *Deliver judgment in my favor, and redeem me; for the sake of your word give me life* (v. 154). He reminds the Lord of his promises, asks for salvation from him, and begs him to judge himself and his adversaries.

(75) *Salvation is far from sinners, because* [1869] *they have not sought out your ordinances* (v. 155). Those living a life of lawlessness, he is saying, deprived themselves of the very salvation from you, unwilling as they were to learn what your law required them to do. *Your mercies are many, O Lord; according to your judgment give me life* (v. 156): the wealth of your loving-kindness is great, your verdict [is] just. On that basis I beg salvation.

(76) *Many are those who persecute me and trouble me; I have not turned away from your testimonies* (v. 157). Despite being beset with numerous calamities, he is saying, I could not bring myself to transgress any of the laws laid down by you. In stating the theme of the psalm, we claimed that the divine David assembled in this psalm all that had happened to him, and that some [verses] relate to the troubles that originally happened to him under Saul, and others at the hands of Absalom.[81] It is clear, of

78. One wonders why Theodoret feels it necessary to come to this far-fetched interpretation of "testimonies." The text he quotes in support from Exod 19.21 says nothing of the sort, unless he has to hand a rogue form of the LXX, and the quotation from the Song of Moses is hardly relevant. We have seen him insecure in his recall of Scripture before, of course.

79. Deut 32.1.   80. Matt 23.12; 5.3.

81. This is indeed the judgment Theodoret made on the psalm's origins at

course, that he spoke this verse when pursued by Saul: at that time he was not experienced in sin. *I saw heedless people, and I was aghast, because they did not observe your sayings* (v. 158). Thus blessed Paul mourned for Jews, thus the Lord mourned for Jerusalem, thus the divine Jeremiah lamented the people's lawlessness.

(77) *See that I loved your commandments, O Lord; in your mercy give me life* (v. 159). He constantly makes mention of commandments, laws, ordinances, and testimonies, revealing his longing in their regard. *The beginning of your words is truth, and all the judgments of your righteousness are forever* (v. 160): you have promises that are unfailing; you adorn your pledges with truth, you confirm [your] words in action. By *beginning of [your] words* he refers to the promises to Abraham: from him sprang the race of Jews. But he fulfilled the promises and made the people grow like the stars of heaven in number, and in his seed he blessed all the nations in keeping with the promises.[82] He indicated this, in fact, in saying, *all the judgments of your righteousness are forever:* being a prophet he saw Christ's everlasting sway. Hence he also said the beginning of the divine sayings was *adorned with truth.*

(78) *Rulers persecuted me without cause, and my heart was in dread of your words* (v. 161). I was not afraid of those attacking and pursuing me, he is saying, but I was in dread of your laws. Hence even on finding the enemy asleep, I did not dare to kill [him]; and in pity for that loathsome, parricidal son, I said, "Spare me my little son."[83] [1872] *I rejoice at your sayings like someone discovering many spoils* (v. 162). Since he had mentioned enemies in pursuit, it was right for him to make mention also of spoils. He means, If I had slain them all and had taken as much booty as I collected, I would not have been so happy as in rejoicing at your laws.[84]

---

the beginning. Fortunately, he has not been specific about the provenance of most verses, and we have had from him an unusual amount of general spiritual teaching—if repetitious and platitudinous like the psalm itself.

82. Cf. Gen 12.2–3.   83. 2 Sam 18.5.

84. No one can say Theodoret has not done his best to find something original—if not Dahood's "freshness of thought and felicity of expression"—in each of the psalm's many verses on a limited theme.

(79) *I hated and loathed iniquity, but I loved your Law* (v. 163). This verse is true, too: the person ardently in favor of divine things abhors the opposite. *Seven times a day I praised you for the judgments of your righteousness* (v. 164). Some rendered *seven times* as "many times." Both imply the ardent love of the inspired author: he did not experience a surfeit of divine hymn singing.

(80) *Great peace for those who love your Law, and they suffer no stumbling* (v. 165): those on fire with love of God and in possession of peace with him through observance of the commandments, even if attacked by all human beings, live a satisfying life. The divinely inspired Paul testifies to this in his cry, "Afflicted in every way but not crushed, perplexed but not driven to despair, persecuted but not forsaken, cast down but not ruined."[85] And the Lord sent the sacred apostles, like sheep among wolves, into the whole world, saying to them, "My peace I give to you, my peace I leave to you."[86]

(81) *I looked forward to your salvation, O Lord, and loved your commandments* (v. 166): not even when beset with calamities did I abandon sound hope; instead, I continued to await your salvation and follow your commandments. *My soul observed your testimonies, and loved them exceedingly. I kept your commandments and your testimonies, because all my ways are before you, O Lord* (vv. 167–68): knowing that you have sight of everything, as one living under your gaze I not only discharged your commandments but even did so with ardent affection.

(82) *Let my prayer come near in your presence, O Lord; give me understanding according to your saying* (v. 169). Offering every supplication, he begs that his prayer be accepted and not rejected; and he asks to receive understanding, not of the human kind, but the knowledge of the divine sayings. *Let my request come in before you, O Lord; according to your saying rescue me* (v. 170). He calls supplication *request;* I found it also in the other [1873] translators. By using different expressions, of course, he appeases the Lord.[87]

---

85. 2 Cor 4.8–9.
86. Cf. Matt 10.16; John 14.27.
87. Theodoret has no problem with the psalmist's ringing the changes on a

(83) *May my lips belch forth a hymn when you teach me your ordinances* (v. 171). The *belch* corresponds to the food: on learning your ordinances, he is saying, I shall offer hymn singing to you, the teacher of such things.[88] *Let my tongue utter your sayings, because all your commandments are righteousness* (v. 172): I shall dedicate my tongue to meditation on your sayings, knowing your commandments are adorned with complete righteousness.

(84) *Let your hand be active to save me, because I chose your commandments* (v. 173). While Symmachus said "preferred," Aquila and Theodotion said, "made a choice." By *hand* he refers to the divine action, by which he begs to attain the divine salvation. *I longed for your salvation, O Lord, and your Law is my concern* (v. 174). I long to attain salvation from you, he is saying, having your Law as my constant concern. *My soul will live and praise you, and your judgments will help me* (v. 175): I know that I will not be disappointed in my hope, but will attain the true life from you, and will praise you, the giver of goods.

(85) *I went astray like a lost sheep* (v. 176). To say this was appropriate both for the inspired author after the sin and for the whole human race. *Seek your servant, because I did not forget your commandments.* Even if he transgressed some of them, he did not resign himself to complete forgetfulness of them. Nevertheless, the inspired author offered this prayer, while the whole human race attained salvation. The good shepherd went in haste after the straying sheep, and after going around mountains and hills—going astray in those times meant worshipping the demons—he found it and took it back on his shoulders, and he was happier with it than with the ninety-nine that did not go astray.[89]

(86) After making our commentary on the psalm in summa-

---

few simple ideas on observance of the Law, as he says on v. 159: if it is not sufficient to entertain the thought of David suffering a range of difficulties, he sees imprecatory value in his dressing up the few ideas differently. Fortunately, ignorance kept him from having to account for the psalm's alphabetic structure.

88. This figure, perhaps for reasons of delicacy shown also at Ps 145.7, Theodoret does not develop, as he did not do so at the opening of Ps 45.1 unlike Chrysostom's exploitation of it to explore the notion of biblical inspiration. See my "Psalm 45: a *locus classicus* for patristic thinking on biblical inspiration."

89. Cf. Matt 18.12–13.

ry fashion, we urge the readers not to be satisfied with what is written, nor to consider that this applies only to the inspired author. Instead, let each one draw fitting benefit from these [writings], and ensure that the remedy wards off one's own passions.[90]

90. It has been a lengthy work of commentary, and Theodoret is doing himself less than justice in admitting to his readers—a rare address—that he was unusually concise in its performance. Unlike his opening remarks, he sees the commentary being more moral than expository (cf. note 2); and—also a rarity—he concedes that the psalm has a general applicability.

COMMENTARY ON PSALM 120

A Song of the Steps.

HEODOTION HAS "MELODY of the Ascents," while Symmachus and Aquila have "for [1876] the Ascents." Of course, "the ascents" or "the steps" indicate the return of the captured people from Babylon.[1] The grace of the Spirit, foreknowing both the captivity and the coming liberation, foretold both the one and the other, both devising their benefit and offering us an advantage from it. Not every [psalm] of the Steps, however, prophesies the same things; instead, one treats of the troubles in Babylon, another the good tidings of the return, another the joy en route, still another the wars breaking out after the return, a different one the building of the Temple. The variety of the inspired discourse dispels the [sense of] surfeit from the singing. Each of these psalms is drawn up with a view to the chorus of holy people then living: the inspired word brings them forward to utter the contents.

(2) The first [psalm] of the Steps, of course, explains both the troubles and the divine benevolence. *I cried to the Lord in my tribulation, and he hearkened to me* (v. 1). The opening taught both the magnitude of the distress and the remarkable degree of divine loving-kindness: in my distress, he is saying, I pleaded with the Lord, and enjoyed benevolence. Then he mentions also what words he used in his pleading: *Lord, rescue my soul from unjust lips and from a deceitful tongue* (v. 2). I beg to be delivered,

---

1. This psalm begins a series of fifteen Songs of the Steps (so-called possibly for structural reasons), also known as Pilgrim Songs for their traditional association with the captivity and return. As in Chrysostom's case, this historical interpretation may be the reason why direct reference to David as author is shelved by Theodoret in favor of alternative phrases we noted also in the case of psalms bearing Asaph's name, like "the grace of the Spirit," and "the inspired word."

he is saying, from those plotting unjust schemes and employing treacherous stratagems. Of this kind were those who set snares for Daniel in connection with his vow,[2] the harsh accusers of those of Hananiah's company.

(3) *What should be given to you, and what further supplied to you for a deceitful tongue? The warrior's sharpened arrows together with the coals from the wilderness* (vv. 3–4). The grace of the Spirit here gives heart to those depressed, and gives a glimpse of the just sentence delivered against those employing guile. He calls the God of all *warrior,* and the sharpness of punishments the *warrior's arrows* by analogy with the arrows fired and easily cleaving the air; *coals from the wilderness* means the severity, devastating and desolate effect of the punishment; fire is naturally like this. The meaning is, Do not be discouraged when stricken by the unjust tongue: the punishments sent by the just Judge are fitting, resembling as they do the swiftness of arrows and the action of desolating coals.

(4) *Alas, my sojourn is prolonged* (v. 5). This is what I uttered in my prayer, he is saying, and on hearing it the loving [God] took pity. He calls life in a foreign land *sojourn.* A period of seventy [years] is rightly called long: the inspired author said such a life of human beings is complete, "The days of our years," he says, "amount to [1877] seventy years."[3] *I dwelt with the tents of Kedar.* Kedar was the second son of Ishmael, and his progeny have dwelt not far from Babylon to this day. So since from the beginning they were in opposition with one another—"Cast out the slave girl and her son; the son of the slave girl shall not inherit along with my son Isaac,"[4] Scripture says,—they were right to deplore their own fate of losing their former freedom, living like half-slaves and obliged to serve.

(5) *My soul sojourned a long time* (v. 6). My period of sojourn was long, he is saying. *With those who hate peace I was peaceable; when I spoke to them, they warred against me without reason* (vv. 6–7). Here he teaches [us] the depravity of the Babylonians: having

2. Cf. Dan 1.
3. Ps 90.10.
4. Gen 21.10.

no charge to level they kept hatching plots, and treated those embracing peace like enemies.[5]

5. Though Albright has suggested that the tight "step" structure of these psalms in the original restricted the composer's inspiration, this cannot be the reason why Theodoret (and Chrysostom) dispatches them so curtly. Perhaps he sees them as simply stanzas of the one work, rather like the divisions of Ps 119 just completed, and to be disposed of with equal brevity. The strength of the traditional association with return from captivity may also preclude his adopting an eschatological interpretation.

COMMENTARY ON PSALM 121

A Song of the Steps.

HIS PSALM ALSO BEARS on those living in Babylon. *I lifted up my eyes to the mountains, from where will come my help* (v. 1): beset by many and varied sorrows, I cast my eyes in all directions in my desire to enjoy some assistance. *My help is from the Lord, the maker of heaven and earth* (v. 2): but I know that, while I shall enjoy no human help, God's benevolence alone is sufficient for me. To bring out the efficacy of the help, he went on, *The maker of heaven and earth:* he who formed these things by a word is capable of meeting my needs, too. At this point the inspired author explains what needs to be done for them: *May he not let your foot slip, nor the one guarding you slumber* (v. 3). If you continue to have firm hope in him, he is saying, you will receive complete care from him. He employed the phrase *nor the one guarding you slumber* in human fashion by analogy with those keeping careful guard over flocks and armies and cities. For he indicated the fact that the divine nature is free from passion by what follows.

(2) *Behold, he will not slumber, nor will the one guarding Israel go to sleep* (v. 4): the guard is naturally wakeful, whereas you totter, and for his part he will treat neglect like a kind of slumber; he will no longer take care of you, giving free rein instead to those choosing to devise schemes.[1] *The Lord will guard you, the Lord your protection at your right hand* (v. 5). This he said also in the fifteenth psalm, "I foresaw the Lord ever before me, because he is at my right hand lest I totter."[2] So at this place, too, [1880] he is saying that he is at your right hand and will protect and guard you and accord you complete providence.

---

1. The comment does not seem to bear on the drift of the verse, or the psalm as a whole.
2. Ps 16.8.

(3) *By day the sun will not burn you, nor the moon by night* (v. 6). They say the moon is not only wet but also hot, and burns bodies like the sun. [The psalmist] means instead, By night and by day you will enjoy providence from him and be kept clear of harm. He reminds them also of past history: when they were freed from the slavery of the Egyptians, they were covered by the cloud and suffered no effects of the sun's rays.[3] *The Lord will guard you from all evil, the Lord will guard your soul. The Lord will guard your coming in and your going out, from now and forever* (vv. 7–8). In these words he indicated the manifold providence of God: when it is present we prove stronger than the hostile enemy and avoid the snares of people seen and unseen.[4]

---

3. Not quite the function of the cloud spoken of in *Exodus* and *Numbers.* Theodoret seems aware of ancient ideas of the moon's harmful potency, though (*pace* Dahood) taking the verse in a more benign fashion.

4. Again the psalm is dispatched curtly, despite the spiritually fertile sentiments of the psalmist, which could—had Theodoret been inclined—have been applied at some little length to the lives of his readers. He hardly shares Weiser's response: "This psalm produces by the simplicity of its language and piety a deep impression that continues until this day."

COMMENTARY ON PSALM 122

A Song of the Steps.

HEREAS THE INSPIRED AUTHOR applied the previous psalms to those who were discouraged, the one to hand [he applied] to those already in receipt of the good news of return and engaged in the longed-for journey. Rejoicing and dancing, in fact, they say to one another, *I was pleased with those who said to me, We shall go to the Lord's house* (v. 1). This is the voice of piety: they exult and are glad at the prospect, not of recovering their houses but of seeing the divine house. *Our feet are standing in your halls, O Jerusalem* (v. 2). Already, he is saying, we seem to be standing in those sacred halls and performing the divine rituals.[1]

(2) *Jerusalem built as a city, to be part of it at the same time* (v. 3). Symmachus, on the other hand, put it this way, "Jerusalem built as an interconnected city": now deserted and with scattered houses, it will flourish again and be populated, and will recover its former ramparts. *There it was, in fact, that the tribes went up, tribes of the Lord, Israel's testimony to confess to the name of the Lord* (v. 4). The tribes were divided in the time of Rehoboam, and ten were separated from the Davidic kingdom; but after the return a single rule prevailed, everyone trekking to Jerusalem in keeping with the divine Law to offer to God [1881] the customary worship.[2] So at this point the inspired author prophesies this, that the tribes will recover their former unity and converge

1. This might seem an appropriate place to make some remark about the Christian liturgy; but Theodoret is in no mood to expand on the text. Any eschatological sense would be a luxury at this time.

2. The picture of national unity after the return from (Judah's) exile in commentary on these verses does not take account of the annihilation of Israel in the eighth century; north and south were no longer on equal terms to reconstitute a confederacy.

on Jerusalem, singing God's praises in customary fashion. He used the term *testimony* of the divine Law, which explicitly bade Israel come together at the place chosen by the Lord God. *Because there thrones were set up for judgment, thrones for David's house* (v. 5). After prophesying divine things, he prophesies also human things: since in Jerusalem not only the divine Temple had been built but also the palace, and to there also all flocked to settle the matters of dispute, necessarily the inspired author forecast this as well, that the ten tribes would not make their way to Samaria. Instead, just as in David's time they had that permanent tribunal, so too after the return all would gather there.

(3) *Pray for what is for the peace of Jerusalem, prosperity for those who love you* (v. 6). Symmachus, on the other hand, put it this way, "Embrace Jerusalem, those who love you will have tranquillity," that is, enjoying profound peace, embrace the occupation of Jerusalem: those loving her will pass their lives in complete satisfaction. *May peace be in your might, and prosperity in your towers* (v. 7). Symmachus, on the other hand, put it this way, "May peace be in your rampart, tranquillity in your palaces." The divine David prays for good things for it so that its ramparts, its palaces and the houses in it will enjoy complete peace.

(4) *For the sake of my brethren and my neighbors I spoke peace of you. For the sake of the house of the Lord our God I sought good things for you* (v. 9). This is my prayer for you, he is saying, not myself as one living in you—for how could he, after all, having long before reached the end of his life?[3]—but in my longing that related tribes should attain peace, and in my desire that the house of my God should recover its former glory.

---

3. On this and the former verse Theodoret, willy-nilly, has had to make some passing reference to David as the putative author.

COMMENTARY ON PSALM 123

A Song of the Steps.

THIS PSALM, TOO, REVEALS the piety of the righteous people of that time.[1] *I lifted up my eyes to you, who
dwell in heaven* (v. 1): despising all human help, I await
your aid, O Lord, and depend on your providence, knowing
you to be Lord of the heavens. He said he dwells in heaven, not
as though confined to a place, but as rejoicing in the unseen
powers that inhabit heaven. [1884] *Behold, as servants' eyes are
on the hands of their masters, as a servant girl's eyes are on the hands
of her mistress, so are our eyes on the Lord our God* (v. 2). Just as attendants watch their lords' hands, he is saying, for the reason
that they receive the basis of life from that source, so too we, O
Lord, expect to receive from you the enjoyment of good things.
It was not an example of tautology, of course, for him to mention the servant girl,[2] but to show the intensity of feeling: servant girls are more important than servants in so far as they
share the company of their mistresses in their chambers, and
usually pay them constant attention and long for a kindly attitude from them. *Until he has pity on us:* far from placing a time
limit on our hope, we wait until we are accorded leniency.

(2) *Have mercy on us, O Lord, have mercy on us* (v. 3). The repetition reveals the ardor of the request.[3] *Because we have had more*

1. Again a curt understatement compared with Weiser's discovery in the
psalm of "moving tenderness," "a disposition of heartfelt and profound piety,"
"one of the finest examples of piety, expressed in prayer—simple, truthful, natural and sincere."

2. The pace may be breakneck, but the *akribeia* of the biblical author—and
the commentator—has to be vindicated.

3. If Theodoret earns our commendation for moderation, this paucity of
comment, even if respecting a principle enunciated in the preface, is an im-
moderate example of it. He could well heed the saying, "All things, including
moderation, should not be taken to excess."

than enough of contempt. Our soul has had more than its fill (vv. 3–4). We beg your mercy, he is saying, not as worthy to attain it, but for having become objects of deep ignominy. *The reproach of the affluent and the scorn of the arrogant.* Symmachus, on the other hand, put it this way, "Our soul is fed up with the mockery of the affluent and the disparagement of the arrogant": we are distressed with the haughty Babylonians mocking and jeering at us. According to the Septuagint, however, it should be understood this way,[4] *The reproach of the affluent and the scorn of the arrogant:* reverse the situation, Lord, he is saying, and inflict our troubles on those now boasting of the good fortune in which they find themselves.

4. As is his frequent practice, Theodoret entertains the alternative rendering from Symmachus, but returns to the LXX—without a clear distinction emerging between them. Perhaps in an equal contest the "inspired" Seventy have to be awarded a decision on points.

COMMENTARY ON PSALM 124

A Song of the Steps.

FTER THE RETURN from Babylon, all the neighboring peoples were disappointed at the Jews' liberation and together declared war on them. Assembling savage nations, they deployed forces at one time against them in the hope of wiping out even their very memory. But in response the God of all came to the assistance of his own and cut down all their enemies. Most of the prophets say this—Joel, Ezekiel, Micah, Zechariah, and many others in addition to them. Here blessed David also prophesies it.

(2) *Had not the Lord been with us, let Israel say, had not the Lord been with us when people rose up against us, then they would have swallowed us alive* (vv. 1–3). Do not attribute the victory to your own power, he is saying: God was responsible for it. [1885] So dance for joy and tell one another, If we had not been granted divine assistance with so many adversaries besetting us in concert, we would not even have been granted burial, and instead would have been consumed alive as though by wild beasts. *When his anger was raging against us.* By this he indicated the envy and hostility of the neighboring nations: they were mortified to see the Jews' freedom.

(3) *Then the water would have overwhelmed us, the torrent passed over our soul; then our soul would have passed over the irresistible water* (vv. 4–5). He said it all in figurative fashion. Since he said, *then they would have swallowed us alive,* he shows the extraordinary dimensions of the forces, hurtling against them like a torrent and calculated to cover them all over. The image of the torrent was an appropriate one for him to employ:[1] as the tor-

---

1. Though not disposed to dwell on these psalms, as we have seen, Theodoret does not forgo the opportunity to highlight the psalmist's literary artistry.

rent is built up from much rainwater and becomes very powerful, so those attacking Jerusalem at the time were built up from many and varied nations. They were wiped out, however, by a just decree, as the inspired author teaches.

(4) *Blessed be the Lord, who did not give us as a prey to their teeth* (v. 6). He indicated together both the enemies' ferocity and God's assistance, mentioning *teeth* to show their ferocity. *Our soul like a sparrow was rescued from the snare of the hunters* (v. 7). In gratitude they admit also their own weakness, comparing themselves to a sparrow, proclaiming God's power, and revealing the strength of the enemies: they call them hunters. He also teaches the manner of salvation,[2] *The snare was broken and we were freed:* we not only enjoyed salvation but also saw the ruin of the foes. *Our help is in the name of the Lord, maker of heaven and earth* (v. 8): for this reason we despise all human power, having the Maker of heaven and earth as our helper, whose mere name is sufficient for salvation for us.

2. Theodoret must feel there is an embargo on giving such verses an eschatological, even Christological, interpretation, possibly because of the traditional association of the Songs of the Steps with historical events. Even the use of v. 8 in Christian liturgy does not prompt a comment.

COMMENTARY ON PSALM 125

A Song of the Steps.

HOSE WHO WON that victory sing the triumphal hymn and proclaim the force of hope in God. *Those who trust in the Lord are like Mount Sion* (v. 1): whoever is fortified with hope in God will remain unmoved like Mount Sion, undisturbed, illustrious, the cynosure of all eyes. *The one who dwells in Jerusalem will not be moved forever:* the one who dwells in [1888] Jerusalem must live according to the laws of Jerusalem; to those dwelling in [it] this way and trusting in the effect of the Law the inspired author promised stability. *Mountains surround it, and the Lord surrounds his people* (v. 2): just as the mountains surround the city, so divine care is a guard around the godly people. *From now and forever:* God's power is not temporary but eternal, and he bestows it on those who give importance to his service.

(2) *Because the Lord will not allow the rod of the sinners [to rest] on the inheritance of the righteous* (v. 3). Through the prophet Isaiah God used "rod of anger" of the Assyrians: "Alas, rod of my anger and my wrath," he said to the Assyrians, "in their hands. I shall send my wrath against a lawless nation, and bid it make spoils and booty of my people."[1] In other words, I chastise the worthy as I used a rod on the Assyrians. So the inspired author means here, too, that the Lord of all will exercise a just verdict and not allow the rod of lawless people to be inflicted on the company of the righteous. Then he teaches [us] also the reason: *Lest the righteous reach out their hands to wrongdoing.* In case those who attend to duty, he is saying, think that everything is

1. Cf. Isa 10.5–6. Theodoret seems uncertain here as to whether the Assyrians were the means or the object of divine wrath.

without order or governance, turn to what is worse, and experience harm from it.

(3) *Do good, O Lord, to the good and to the upright of heart* (v. 4). Having shown God's righteousness, he makes a righteous request: he begs that the good meet with their just deserts. The Lord also said as much: "The measure you apply will be applied to you," and, "Blessed are the merciful because they will have mercy shown them."[2] *Those who turn aside to devious ways the Lord will lead away with the evildoers* (v. 5). For *devious ways* Aquila translated, "complicated ways," Symmachus, "twisted ways," and Theodotion, "perverted ways."[3] Of course, the inspired author asked for nothing unfair—simply that the good enjoy good things, and those who have forsaken the divine path and adopted devious and complicated ways meet with the opposite fate. *Peace upon Israel.* While those experience ruin, they enjoyed peace. You should know, to be sure, that Jacob was given this name after being accorded a divine vision.[4] He therefore shares his name with those whose behavior is of that kind, possessing a pure faith and soul: not all from Israel are Israelites—only those embracing the piety of Israel.

---

2. Matt 7.2; 5.7.

3. Reference here to the other translators for light on this rare word (Dahood coming up with a similar meaning by reference to Ugaritic) reminds us that Theodoret's perfunctory treatment of the Pilgrim Songs has not involved his customary recourse even to them.

4. Theodoret seems to be relating the granting of the name Israel to Jacob, narrated in Gen 32.28–30, not to the struggle with God preceding (as the name suggests etymologically) but to the vision of God mentioned later and incorporated in the place name Peniel. Close acquaintance with the text, let alone Semitic science, should have preserved him from that misunderstanding.

COMMENTARY ON PSALM 126

A Song of the Steps. [1889]

HEN CYRUS BECAME KING he bade all Jews to return, but most of them had a poor attitude and in
every respect were opposed to the divine laws, and they
were unwilling to return. All who had a concern for their ancestral piety, however, and hankered after worship in keeping with
the Law made the return [journey] gladly. Accordingly, in this
psalm these people recognize their own freedom and exult;
and they pray for their kin to attain it.

(2) *When the Lord reversed the captivity of Sion, we were like people
enjoying consolation* (v. 1). The word *like* here conveys intensity:
we enjoyed great satisfaction when God put an end to punishment and granted freedom to the captives. *Then our mouth was
filled with joy, and our tongue with rejoicing* (v. 2): immediately suf-
fused with satisfaction we gave our tongues to hymn singing,
Aquila rendering *rejoicing* as "praise" and Symmachus as "blessing." *Then they will say among the nations, The Lord has been mag-
nanimous in dealing with them:* this made us well-known to all,
everyone amazed at God's magnificence in freeing us from that
harsh slavery; and of course we cry aloud, *The Lord has been mag-
nanimous in dealing with us, we have been gladdened* (v. 3): it is ab-
surd [for us], who were deprived of the knowledge of God, to
marvel at his loving-kindness in our regard, when having been
recipients of his beneficence we were afflicted with ingratitude.

(3) *Reverse our captivity, O Lord, like torrents in the south* (v. 4).
Their desire is that the others of their kin enjoy the good things
they attained, and they beseech the common Lord to give them
a share in freedom as well, so that the great number of people
returning may resemble torrents. In calling Jerusalem *south* he
took the term from its position; both Ezekiel and Habakkuk

call it that, too.[1] The word suggests something else as well: since the south is a humid wind, it fills the air with clouds and brings on severe rainstorms; and of course since it has the capacity to melt snow, it builds up the torrents with water. Accordingly, he is saying, bid our kin, who are scattered in all directions, come together in this way and make their way like a torrent.[2]

(4) *Those who sow in tears will reap with rejoicing* (v. 5): instead of making our petitions to no purpose, however, it is with the knowledge of the fruit of the tears; those casting seed with them rejoice to see the generous harvest. [1892] *They wended their way, and they wailed as they scattered their seed; on return they will return in joy, carrying their sheaves* (v. 6). He uttered the one thought in different ways, producing greater benefit from the diversity of teaching.

1. Cf. Ezek 40–42; Hab 3.3, in a reading of Theodotion.
2. Theodoret here is trying to get the most out of the psalmist's figurative language.

COMMENTARY ON PSALM 127

A Song of the Steps of Solomon.

N FORMER TIMES SOLOMON built the divine Temple, but after it was razed by the Babylonians Zerubbabel restored it. I think this psalm is called Solomonic both because it takes its genre from Solomon and because it was a work of Solomon that was being restored. The inspired word, in fact, applies it not to the building of Solomon but to the one built by Zerubbabel after the return.[1] Although they themselves tried to build it at that time, the neighboring peoples prevented them both by waging incessant war themselves and by provoking the kingdom of the Persians against them. The writing of Ezra teaches this more clearly. The company of Zerubbabel, therefore, and Jeshua son of Shealtiel and those along with them who were endowed with piety provide the explanation of this psalm.[2]

(2) *Unless the Lord built a house, it was in vain that the builders labored. Unless the Lord guarded a city, it was in vain that the guard kept watch* (v. 1): let no one, either builders or guards, trust in their own power; let them instead invoke divine aid; with its cooperation, each [task] is easier, whereas if God delays his assistance, vain is people's effort. *It is futile for you to rise early, get up after sitting down, you who eat bread of pain* (v. 2). The form *get up*

1. Theodoret is aware of different approaches to the psalm's drift. Mention of "house" in v. 1 had led some to see the Temple, original or rebuilt, referred to, and the rabbis wanted to see Solomon's building there; modern commentators see the piece as a Wisdom psalm, and so traditionally attributed to Solomon. Theodoret avoids the rabbinic application, preferring to accept both the Wisdom character and yet—if only because of the relationship of these Pilgrim Songs to the return from captivity—allowing reference to the rebuilding of the Temple.

2. Theodoret is thinking of Ezra 2, though he has confused details of "Zerubbabel son of Shealtiel and Jeshua son of Jozadak" (Ezra 2.8).

is not imperative but infinitive.[3] He means that everything is futile if the God of all does not cooperate, both rising early and getting up, either for guarding the city or for the building in hand. Hence he urges those who eat their bread with pain on account of the assaults of the enemies to have hope in God.

(3) *When he gives sleep to his beloved ones. Behold, the Lord's heritage is sons, a reward of the fruit of the womb* (vv. 2–3). Here in figurative fashion he called rest *sleep;* sleep gives people repose. So with God granting his peculiar care, he is saying, we shall manage to prevail over the enemies, build without difficulty, live a secure life, sleep without care, and become parents of very many children according to the divine promise; he promised to make our race like sand on the sea shore.[4] [1893] He said it here, too: *Behold, the Lord's heritage is sons, the reward of the fruit of the womb*—that is, the divine promise and the blessing of children is given like a kind of reward to us for hoping in him.

(4) *Like arrows in the hand of a warrior, so are the sons of those shaken* (v. 4). Theodotion, on the other hand, said, "As arrows in the hand of a warrior, so are sons of youth," and Aquila and Symmachus rendered it the same way. He means, By trusting in God we shall be not only numerous but also powerful, like some arrows shot by a warrior; and those who are now weak and suffering extreme hardship—this being the meaning of *shaken off*[5]—will be very strong through enjoying aid from on high. *Blessed is the one who satisfies his desire with them* (v. 5)—that is, with the enemies: not only shall we not be beaten, but we shall even overcome them and be the object of everyone's envy. *They will not be ashamed when they speak with their foes in the gates,* that is, when we hold discussions in front of the gates with the

3. Certainly an infinitive would make more sense, but Theodoret's text seems not to have one.

4. Cf. Gen 22.17. Theodoret is capable of giving commentary on a verse from a Jewish perspective.

5. Theodoret makes an unconvincing effort to rationalize the version of the Hebrew *n'r* he finds in the LXX (citing, in fact, two forms of it), which has confused it with a similar form. Obviously puzzled, he consults the alternative versions, which avoided such confusion. Unable to deal with the resulting dilemma by recourse to the original, and not even seeking help from the Syriac, he is left with a commentator's last ploy, rationalizing.

legates from the enemies. He said this in keeping with the ancient custom: it was not inside the gates that they received the legates that were sent, but gave their response outside. He showed the invincibility of hope in God in every circumstance.[6]

6. The LXX is further astray with its rendering "desire" for the original "quiver," leading Theodoret further off the track laid by the psalmist. A commentator's limited exegetical skills are a liability for a reader.

COMMENTARY ON PSALM 128

A Song of the Steps.

FTER SHOWING IN THE PRECEDING psalm for how many good things trusting in God is responsible, here he pronounces blessed those having along with hope divine fear, through which the acquisition of virtue is secured. Necessary for those believing in God is a way of life in keeping with God's will, this being the perfect culmination of piety.

(2) *Blessed are all who fear the Lord* (v. 1). The inspired word declared blessed not the one from Abraham's stock nor from Israel's seed but the person adorned with the divine fear. Blessed Peter also says this in the Acts: "In truth I grasp the fact that God shows no partiality, but in every nation the person fearing him and performing righteousness is acceptable to him."[1] The inspired word also gave a glimpse of the character of the divine fear, adding, *those walking in his ways:* "Not everyone saying to me, Lord, Lord, will enter the kingdom of heaven, but the one doing the will of my Father who is in heaven."[2] So it is typical of those fearing the Lord not to stray from the divine ways but to travel in them without fail.

(3) [1896] *You will eat the labors of your palms* (v. 2). Symmachus, on the other hand, says, "eating toil of your hands," suggesting that the Septuagint called *palms* not the profit but the part of the hands.[3] He means, You will gather the fruits of

1. Acts 10.34–35.
2. Matt 7.21.
3. Raised on a paraphrase of the Hebrew, "You shall eat (the fruit of) the labor of your hands," we have even more difficulty with the challenge facing the LXX, which employs a Homeric term *karpos*, "palm," of identical form with *karpos*, "fruit"; and Theodoret has to remind the reader not to confuse the two. The credit, of course, goes not to him but to the LXX and to Symmachus for avoiding the confusing paraphrase.

the good things sown by you. This is what the divine Apostle also said, "The one who sows sparingly will also reap sparingly, and the one who sows bountifully will also reap bountifully."[4] *Blessed are you, and it will be well with you:* not by word alone will you be the object of envy and admiration; instead, by deed also will you have good fortune.

(4) *Your wife like a vine flourishing in the recesses of your house* (v. 3). Since they thought this well-being was a seasonal thing, the text promises them also fertility of wives comparable with blooming vines and heavily laden bunches. *Your children like olive shoots around your table.* In the fifty-first psalm, too, he compared the righteous person to an olive tree, "I am like a fruitful olive tree bearing fruit in the house of God."[5] Here he likened the children of the person fearing the Lord to *olive shoots* for providing the watering from piety and fruit in season, not losing its leaves, like the man declared blessed in the first psalm.[6]

(5) *Behold, this is the way the person who fears the Lord will be blessed* (v. 4): God is a judge of behavior, not race. This is the way he awarded the crown to Job, who descended from Esau; this is the way he led Abimelech to the truth,[7] this way the eunuch, this way Cornelius, this way all the nations. *May the Lord bless you from Sion* (v. 5), according to the view then current: it was thought God dwelt in that place. *May you see the good things of Jerusalem all the days of your life.* Those returning from Babylon, seeing the desolation of the city, longed to see this. *May you see your children's children* (v. 6). It was thought a great blessing to reach extreme old age and see children; so he defines blessings suited to attitudes. Blessed Isaiah, however, taught that it was not in these things that he saw attainment of good: "Let not the eunuch say, I am a dry tree, because the Lord says, To the eunuchs preserving my sabbaths and choosing what I

4. 2 Cor 9.6.
5. Ps 52.8.
6. Cf. Ps 1.3. That psalm does in fact speak of the blessed man, though there (alone) Theodoret makes a point of claiming women are not excluded.
7. If Theodoret has the name right this time, perhaps he is referring to the king of Gerar who had dealings with Abraham and Isaac, and came to a better frame of mind therefrom (Gen 21–22, 26). The eunuch and Cornelius appear in Acts 8,10–11.

wish I shall give within my house and within my wall a famous place and a good name, something better than sons and daughters."[8]

(6) *Peace upon Israel.* Again he prays for the peace of Israel. True peace is peace with God, but the Israel of the flesh lost the one and was deprived of the other.

8. Cf. Isa 56.3–5.

COMMENTARY ON PSALM 129

A Song of the Steps. [1897]

THIS PSALM, TOO, CONTAINS a prophecy of the gentiles' assaults on Jews after the return. They are taught to say, *Often have they attacked me from my youth, let Israel say, often have they attacked me from my youth: they have not prevailed against me* (vv. 1–2). He calls the life in Egypt and the liberation from there *youth.* Singing the praises of the benefactor he lists the divine favors: From the very beginning many adversaries rose up against me, and attempted to surround me with manifold evils, but through the divine assistance I eluded those wiles. More exactly, however, he relates this to the new people, the victim of many assaults from enemies but prevailing over them all and turning enemies into suppliants.

(2) *The sinners did their worst on my back* (v. 3). Aquila and Theodotion, on the other hand, translated it "plowed."[1] The verse refers to the scourges and the abuses inflicted on the victorious martyrs by the adversaries. These things were also endured by those in the company of blessed Daniel, the remarkable Hananiah, Azariah, and Mishael, and in the time of Antiochus by the Maccabees. *They prolonged their lawlessness.* Aquila, on the other hand, has "extended," and Symmachus, "they persisted in doing evil," meaning, They continued at length warring against me and adding to their own iniquity.

(3) *The righteous Lord cut the throats of sinners* (v. 4). Aquila and Symmachus translated *throats* as "snares," and Theodotion

---

1. Dahood observes that the evidently original sense preserved in the Masoretic text, "The plowers ploughed on my back," moves to a form found at Qumran and in some of the Greek versions, "The sinners ploughed," and then, as the sense of the metaphor was further lost, to Theodoret's LXX form. He would not be in a position to do any fruitful cross-checking, of course, beyond noting differences in versions.

as "collars"; each is correct: the God of these cut in pieces the snares which they made for the holy ones, broke the collars encircling them, and cut the very throats of the sinners.[2] *Let all who hate Sion be ashamed and turned backwards.* Let those warring against Sion fall short of their wicked endeavors, he is saying, and be put to flight.

(4) *Let them become like grass on housetops, which withered before being plucked out. The reaper did not fill his hand with it, nor the binder of sheaves his bosom* (vv. 6–7). Some copies do not have *being withered* but "being plucked,"[3] which is what we invariably see happening with crops: no one brings himself to reap the ear while still green, but waits until it is matured and dried, and then applies the sickle. The growth springing up on housetops, by contrast, dries up with the effect of the sun before producing fruit; he prays that the enemies' forays be like that, and come to an untimely end in a similar way to that.

(5) [1900] *Those who passed by did not say, Blessing of the Lord upon you, we have blessed in the name of the Lord* (v. 8). Those who observe the flourishing crops usually admire the farmers' diligence, and on passing by they congratulate them as they reap harvests of this kind;[4] but no one ever gave voice to such sentiments to those collecting the grass on housetops.

2. Again the limitations of Theodoret's exegetical skills appear. Either because he finds the meaning of the LXX rather raw, or just for the sake of it, he assembles the alternative versions of one word, notes the different sense each lends to the verse, but simply (and helplessly) in relativist fashion declares all valid. There is no attempt to look at the original behind the three different versions, or relate them to the metaphor in the previous verse—which, in any case, the LXX has lost.

3. As mentioned in Introduction, section 3, a further resource available to Theodoret in his task as exegete and commentator were other forms of the LXX beyond his local form and the one in the Hexapla; he refers to them as "copies," as here. In this case one wonders if he is confused in comparing readings, as his text does not correspond to the readings he now cites. He is on firmer ground respecting agricultural lore.

4. Had Theodoret been in a mood to relate these Pilgrim Songs to other parts of Scripture or been aware of such connection, he might have cited—in addition to agricultural lore—a greeting such as that of Boaz to the reapers in Ruth 2.4.

COMMENTARY ON PSALM 130

A Song of the Steps.

 CHORUS OF THE RIGHTEOUS offers this supplication to God; the psalm's opening testifies to this: *Out of the depths I have cried to you, O Lord* (v. 1), that is to say, From the very bottom of my heart I pour out the supplication. The divine Scripture condemns those who employ only their lips: at one place the prophet Jeremiah says to the God of all, "You are near to their mouth, but far from their innards";[1] at another place God himself through the prophet Isaiah condemns Jews in the words, "This people honors me with their lips, but the heart is far from me."[2] In this case those making supplication from the bottom of the heart pour out the prayer. *Lord, hearken to my voice; let your ears be attentive to the sound of my request* (v. 2). He knows God is bodiless, despite using human expressions: he uses terms for the sense of hearing and sight.[3] Our eyes, of course, have the power of sight, and our ears have been equipped with the sense of hearing. What God hears with, on the contrary, he also sees with, and what he sees with he also hears with.

(2) *If you took note of iniquities, O Lord* (v. 3). The choir of the righteous beseeches the Lord not to measure punishments against sins. In this way those of the company of blessed Hananiah attributed the transgressions of the people to their own

1. Jer 12.2.
2. Isa 29.13.
3. Despite his extremely concise treatment of this much-loved psalm, which was Luther's favorite and which Weiser sees combining "tender sentiments, simple and sincere language, and a most profound understanding of the nature of sin and grace" (themes not, in fact, developed here), Theodoret does remind the reader characteristically not to fail to appreciate the anthropomorphism at this point. Concise commentary cannot run the risk of having divine transcendence infringed.

person. *Lord, who would stand it?* In other words, If you were to impose the yoke of judgment as justice requires, who would be in a position to sustain the sentence laid down by it? Everyone, in fact, would have to face ruin. *Because with you is forgiveness* (v. 4): you have loving-kindness joined with righteousness, and you are in the habit of employing the former rather than the latter.

(3) *For your name's sake I waited for you, O Lord, my soul waited for your word* (v. 5). For *name* Aquila and Theodotion gave the translation "fear," and Symmachus, "law." Nevertheless, the sense of the expression is the same; he means, Aware of this your goodness (you employed mercy like some law), I do not renounce firm hope as I await [1901] the promise of good things. He called the good promise here *word;* loving-kindness, however, he promised to the repentant.[4] *My soul hoped in the Lord, from morning watch until night* (v. 6), that is, all day; *morning watch* is, in fact, the last hour of the night: the last watchers keep watch until that time. *From morning watch let Israel hope in the Lord* (v. 7). The righteous are not satisfied only to have the wealth of hope in God; instead, they urge all others to a like possession, and declare the advantage stemming from it.

(4) *Because with the Lord there is mercy, and with him copious re-demption:* full of pity and loving-kindness is the Lord, who furnishes salvation to the repentant. *He it is who will redeem Israel from all its iniquities* (v. 8). The verse directs its prophecy to the Lord: he is the Lamb of God in person, who takes away the sin of the world.[5] This was also the way the divine Gabriel spoke to the holy Virgin: "You will have a son, and you will give him the name Jesus, because he is the one who will save his people from their sins."[6]

4. We have seen Theodoret previously acknowledging the penitential psalms of the early Church, of which this is the sixth and one of the most powerful—little though his reader would grasp this from the commentary.

5. John 1.29.

6. A collation of Luke 1.31 and Matt 1.21, involving a rare reference to Mary.

COMMENTARY ON PSALM 131

A Song of the Steps.

 HE INSPIRED WORD GIVES instruction in humility, and presents the person of its devotees as those praying and importuning God. *Lord, my heart is not elevated* (v. 1). Elevation of the heart is harmful not only to the ungodly but also to the holy. The story of the Chronicles teaches this in connection with the pious king Hezekiah, saying, "Because he was brought down from the elevation of his heart."[1] Hence the Lord also exhorts his sacred disciples, saying, "Everyone who humbles himself will be elevated, and he who elevates himself will be humbled."[2] *Nor my eyes lifted up.* Raising the eyebrows, puffing up the cheeks, and looking askance at everyone is typical of the haughty. Those free of this failing do not teach the judge this fact as though he were ignorant [of it], but call him to witness as though aware [of it]. *I did not spend my time with mighty matters.* Symmachus, on the other hand, said "majestic," and Aquila, "magnificent." *Nor with matters too marvelous for me.* Symmachus, on the other hand, said, "Nor with matters beyond me," that is, I kept myself in check, and did not attempt what was beyond my state.[3]

(2) [1904] *Unless I remained humble instead of elevating my soul, like a weaned child with its mother, you would have repaid my soul in due fashion* (v. 2). Symmachus, on the other hand, [says,] "Unless I had made my soul similar and comparable to a weaned child towards its mother, response would have been made to

---

1. 2 Chron 32.26.
2. Luke 18.14, loosely recalled.
3. With the accent so much on conciseness, one acknowledgment of the alternative versions seems pointless (as Dorival suggests of some on Ps 119, perhaps the work of a copyist), while the other from Symmachus is not a distinct improvement but at least evokes explication.

my soul in like fashion." If I had not feared you, he is saying, and subjected myself to you like an infant recently taken from the teat and fearful of the mother, and instead had had an elevated mind, I would have deserved to meet the same response.[4] *Let Israel hope in the Lord, from now and forever* (v. 3). The inspired word showed the reason for giving the outline of virtuous behavior—not to rehearse their own virtue by magnifying themselves, but to stir up the others to the same zeal. Hence they exhorted all Israel to cling to the same hope, have it always, and gain the fruits stemming from it.

4. The bishop is not about wringing our withers in commenting on this affecting picture from a very personal psalm, which Weiser rightly calls "a wonderfully tender and intimate little song." Teaching, yes, and even some New Testament reinforcement—but sentiment, no.

COMMENTARY ON PSALM 132

A Song of the Steps.

HIS PSALM HAS A CLOSE relationship with the eighty-eighth: in both cases the captives in Babylon petition the God of all, offering in place of petitions the promises made by him to the mighty David and asking to attain pardon. It also contains prophecy of the Savior of the world sprung according to the flesh from the race of David.[1]

(2) *Remember David, O Lord, and all his gentleness* (v. 1): since in our great sinfulness we are bereft of all confidence, we beseech you, O Lord, to remember David, and his gentleness and piety. The previous psalm also made mention of this, and taught clearly his moderation in attitude. *How he swore to the Lord, made a vow to the God of Jacob: If I enter into my tent, if I climb on my bed, if I give sleep to my eyes, slumber to my eyelids, and rest to my temples before I find a place for the Lord, a tabernacle for the God of Jacob* (vv. 2–5). The story of the Chronicles teaches this more clearly: he first asked to build the divine Temple, but when God through the prophet Nathan prevented it and foretold the future building by Solomon, he postponed the building without falling into indolence; instead, he gathered gold, silver, iron, bronze, wood and precious stones. All this, as I said, that book teaches those prepared to read it.[2]

(3) [1905] *Behold, we heard it in Ephrathah, we found it in the plains of the forest* (v. 6). His petition was to build a temple to God, whereas the only-begotten Word of God from the fruit of

1. Mention of the Temple in the body of this Song of the Steps proves too pregnant with New Testament associations for Theodoret to avoid finding a Christological sense and being more expansive in commentary. He also admits to finding historical associations unconvincing.
2. Cf. 1 Chron 17, 22. Theodoret would do a brief study of the work of the Chronicler.

his loins promised to build for himself a temple endowed both with soul and with reason.[3] Hence the inspired text says, *Behold, we heard it in Ephrathah, we found it in the plains of the forest.* The now called Bethlehem is named Ephrathah: Christ the Lord was born there, and in giving the Jews a glimpse of his own body he said, "Destroy this temple." And he calls the place of the Temple in Jerusalem *plains of forest* for being desolate and having no building: there it was that the mighty David, in checking the destroying angel by prayers to God, set up an altar, offered sacrifice, and devoted [the place] to the building of the Temple. Since, however, there were two tabernacles, one of stones and timbers and the other of body and soul, and one was made by Solomon in Jerusalem whereas the grace of the all-holy Spirit composed the other in Bethlehem, and the pious people of that time saw the one but looked forward to the other, the inspired word was right to say, *Behold, we heard it in Ephrathah*—that is, what would be made by the Holy Spirit—*we found it in the plains of the forest,* the one built by Solomon according to the promise of the Spirit.

(4) *Let us enter his tabernacles, let us worship in the place where his feet stood* (v. 7). He changed the time. He means, We go in there and adore, believing the Temple has been accorded a divine apparition; this is the sense of *where his feet stood.* We believe, after all, that the divinity is not only incorporeal but also uncircumscribed. The divine Scripture speaks in more corporeal terms about it, however, accommodating the language to human ears.[4]

(5) *Rise up, O Lord, to your rest* (v. 8). They call worship according to the Law God's *rising up*—not that he is in need of it or finds satisfaction in it, but he welcomes the piety of the offerers. They also beg that his grace be manifested again, and the former glory be given to the Temple. *You and the ark of your*

3. In citing John 2.19, Theodoret is implicitly refuting, as he had done explicitly in commentary on Ps 16.11 (see note 22 there), the denial by Arius of a rational soul in Jesus and by Apollinaris of Laodicea of a rational mind and will. The Johannine reference is also sufficient for Theodoret to conduct his typological argument here of the two temples.

4. Chrysostom himself could not have stated better the principle of Scriptural *synkatabasis.*

sanctification. Since in the Holy of Holies the ark stood with the tables of the Law inside, and the mercy seat was situated alongside, and through the latter some indications of the divine manifestation were given to the high priest, he was right to make mention of the ark: the God who made heaven and earth, according to the saying of blessed Paul,[5] does not dwell in temples made by [human] hands. The wise Solomon also prayed this way, "If the [1908] heaven and the heaven of heavens are not sufficient for you."[6] The very God of all also said this, "The Heaven is my throne and the earth my footstool: what sort of house will you build for me? or what is my resting place?"[7]

(6) *Your priests will be clothed in righteousness, and your holy ones will rejoice* (v. 9). Once this happens, he is saying, both that the house is built and the ark is placed again in the innermost sanctuary, the priests will perform worship according to the Law and be made righteous, whereas those not worthy of participation in priesthood and yet attentive to piety will be filled with every happiness. *For the sake of David your servant do not turn your face away from your anointed* (v. 10). He calls the king *anointed* here. Since the kings at that time were impious, they pray on David's account that they be not eliminated from the kingly race.[8]

(7) Then he recalls the promises made: *The Lord swore truth to David, and he will not set it aside* (v. 11). The one promising is free of falsehood, he is saying, he is a fountain of truth, and it is impossible that his promise should not take effect. *I shall set on your throne someone of the fruit of your body.* This promise was singular, and took effect: not only Solomon but also Solomon's successors were granted the royal thrones. Christ the Lord, however, made good the realization of the promise, reinforcing

5. Acts 17.24.
6. Cf. 2 Chron 6.18.
7. Isa 66.1. The Christological color to this Song of the Steps is eliciting a relish for commentary in Theodoret that is shown also by the relative amount of Scriptural documentation.
8. As indicated in his opening remark, Theodoret sees this psalm sung by the community in Babylon—a rare acknowledgment of the liturgical use of a psalm—while he employs oblique expressions about its author, as (we noted) with other Pilgrim Songs.

David's kingship. For the blessed Isaiah prophesied this, [saying,] "A child has been born to us, a son was given to us; his rule is on his shoulder, and his name is Angel of great counsel, Wonderful Adviser, Mighty God, powerful, Prince of peace, Father of the world to come, Amen"; and a little later, "On the throne of David and his kingdom, so as to set it right from now and for eternal time."[9] Christ the Lord, as I said, made good this promise, whereas God gave another one that is not unconditional. He spoke this way, *If your sons keep my covenant and these testimonies of mine which I shall teach them, their sons also will sit on your throne forever* (v. 12). Such, then, was the Lord's promise, whereas their lawlessness interrupted the course of the kingship: once Solomon was involved in impiety, he attracted the divine wrath. For this reason the throne became despotic, and the ten tribes accepted [allegiance to] another king; later even the two [remaining] tribes lost the Davidic kingship.

(8) *Because the Lord elected Sion, chose it as his habitation* (v. 13). From the beginning, he is saying O Lord, you preferred it to the other cities, and made it your dwelling. [1909] *This is my repose forever* (v. 14). You said this, O Lord, he is saying, and promised to take your rest on Sion forever. And this came to pass at the end: even if the former Temple was made desolate owing to Jews' frenzy, yet through divine grace again that spot was thought worthy of being the place of the cross, the resurrection, and the ascension, and from every land and sea all converged there to draw the blessing gushing up. *I shall dwell here, because I have chosen it.* This also came to pass at the end, and a kind of change happened to the buildings. The inspired word made mention of Sion; on it was the place of the cross and the resurrection.

(9) *With blessings I shall bless its wild game* (v. 15). Symmachus, on the other hand, [says,] "With blessings I shall bless its feeding," that is, I shall provide them with an abundance of all good things. *I shall feed its poor with bread:* and to the needy I shall make necessities available. *I shall clothe its priests with salvation* (v. 16). Here he gave the name *salvation* to what he called above

9. Cf. Isa 9.6–7.

righteousness, salvation being the fruit of righteousness. *And its holy ones shall rejoice with rejoicing:* the lovers of piety will be made full of all satisfaction.

(10) *There I shall cause a horn of David to spring up* (v. 17). The obvious sense, then, suggests Zerubbabel; but since he transmitted his rule neither to his successors nor even to his children, you would not be justified to call him *horn,* ruling for a short time as he did.[10] The *horn* in fact implies something strong and stable; but since the prophecy does not fit Zerubbabel, the verse prophesies the coming of Christ in the flesh. Blessed Peter also said as much in the Acts: "Since David was a prophet and knew that God had sworn an oath to him to raise up from the fruit of his loins the Christ according to the flesh and seat him on his throne, he spoke with foreknowledge of his resurrection."[11] *I prepared a lamp for my anointed one.* Once more the inspired word calls David's temple *lamp* for receiving into it the light of divinity.

(11) *His enemies I shall clothe with disgrace, but on him my sanctification will flourish* (v. 18). Jews, then, are witnesses of the shame, adopting hostility as they did and reaping the shame [as a result]. *Sanctification,* on the other hand, means the churches in all land and sea, styled the body of Christ the Lord, conveying from him the founts of holiness.

---

10. Theodoret implies that he would like to have retained the historical or obvious sense, but that the facts oblige him to move to a Christological sense.

11. Cf. Acts 2.30–31.

COMMENTARY ON PSALM 133

A Song of the Steps.

NDER REHOBOAM [1912] the tribes were split up, ten following Jeroboam and two holding fast to the Davidic monarchy. After the return from Babylon, however, they came together again and loved the harmony, they had the one government and performed in common the worship according to the Law.[1] This psalm, then, prophesies these developments.

(2) *Behold, what a beautiful and charming thing it is for brethren to dwell together* (v. 1). Through experience itself, he is saying, we have learned that nothing gives more satisfaction than brotherly harmony. He calls the tribes *brethren* since the tribal leaders who gave them their names were sons of one father. *Like balm on the head, flowing down on a beard, the beard of Aaron* (v. 2). The high priestly oil was composed of different aromas; none of them of itself emitted such a wonderful fragrance, whereas the combination and mixture of all of them produced as great a fragrance as possible. To this he rightly compared brotherly harmony: the combination of the best deeds produces the aroma of perfect virtue. *Flowing down on the edge of his robe.* The gift of love, he is saying, resembles that balm which covered the head of Aaron, reaching not just the chin but going as far as the part of his tunic around his breast; he called *edge* what we call collar, and Aquila said "garments' mouth" for it. So just as the sacred balm ran on from the head past the chin as far as the clothing and enveloped the priest in fragrance, so the benefit

1. Theodoret does not see this as simply a Wisdom psalm, but insists on finding historical reference for it. And as in comment on Ps 122 (see note 2 there), he has an idealized account of national unity after the return from (Judah's) exile, unaware of the different fates suffered by northern and southern kingdoms.

coming from harmony reaches from the leadership to the subjects.

(3) *Like dew of Hermon falling on Mount Sion* (v. 3). Again he
changed to another image, teaching the advantage of harmony;
he said it is like the dew carried down from Hermon to Sion.
There is so much of it that the jars release drops. Hermon is a
mountain—in Palestine, in fact—and some distance from the
land of Israel.[2] *Because there it was that the Lord ordained his blessing, life forever*—not on Hermon, but on Sion, where the life-giving dew of the all-holy Spirit was sent down on the sacred apostles, through which all the believers reap the everlasting
blessing.

2. Geography is one area where Theodoret feels he has some competence,
as we have seen. Perhaps he could have adverted to passages like Deut 4.48 that
put Mount Hermon on Israel's northern border. An observation on geography
is felt pertinent by him—but nothing of a general nature on the value of harmony in the Christian community from the psalm, which has much to offer on
the theme.

COMMENTARY ON PSALM 134

A Song of the Steps.

LSO THIS [PSALM] RELATES to those returned from Babylon. It also offers advice to all the pious to sing God's praises not only by day but also by night. *Behold, bless the Lord, all you servants of the Lord* (v. 1): [1913] it is not for everyone to sing, but for those who have embraced the divine service and place much store by the worship of the Lord. In other words, to those who have been affected by the wounds of sin it is appropriate to weep, to lament, and to request the divine loving-kindness. *Those who stand in the house of the Lord, in courts of our God's house.* In urging [them] to sing, he taught also the style of hymn singing. While the divine Paul prescribed the lifting up of holy hands everywhere, it is not least necessary to offer due adoration to God in the consecrated places.[1]

(2) *At night lift up your hands to the holy places, and bless the Lord* (v. 2). Having taught [them] the place, he teaches also the time: the night is suitable for hymn singing, providing great tranquillity and being free from many disturbances. He gives instructions about both the raising of the hands and the prevailing custom. *May the Lord bless you from Sion, Maker of heaven and earth* (v. 3). Lest anyone get the idea that the God of all is confined to Sion, he is right to present him as creator of everything, including all creation in *heaven and earth:* in heaven are angels, on earth human beings and the things made for their sake.[2]

---

1. We regret that the bishop passes up the opportunity, as we noted of the previous psalm on a key Christian virtue, to speak of the liturgy of Old or New Testaments, for which this psalm provides an obvious occasion.

2. Thus closes the group of fifteen Songs of the Steps, or Pilgrim Songs (though Theodoret's LXX text of Ps 135 may also bear such a title). With the

exception of Ps 132, which he could not allow to pass without a Christological interpretation, if only because of its citation in Acts, these psalms have consistently failed to move him, commentary being concise, if not curt, and Scriptural documentation conspicuously lacking. This lack of enthusiasm is probably not due to stylistic or structural features in the original pointed out by Albright; to blame may rather be the close traditional association of them with one historical situation, return from exile, as well as the difficulty of tracing them back to David.

COMMENTARY ON PSALM 135

Alleluia. A Song of the Steps.

HIS IS ANOTHER HYMN of praise, offered to God in fact by those who had attained freedom. We have already made a comment on "Alleluia."[1] *Praise the name of the Lord, praise the Lord, you his servants* (v. 1). Since the divine nature is invisible and yet he bids [them] sing its praises, he was right to say, *Praise the name of the Lord.* Be content with God's title, he is saying, and do not seek to see what it is not proper to see. *You who stand in the house of the Lord, in the courts of the house of our God* (v. 2). Freed from slavery of Babylonians, he is saying, and enjoying the splendor of the divine halls, sing the praises of the provider of these good things. *Praise the Lord, because the Lord is good* (v. 3): make the goodness of the one you praise the occasion for hymn singing. *Sing to his name, because it is good:* much benefit also comes to you from that.

(2) Then he makes mention of the favors conferred on them. *Because the Lord has chosen Jacob for himself, Israel for his own possession* (v. 4). Symmachus, on the other hand, put it this way, "and Israel as his chosen." He accorded them greater attention, he is saying, styled them his own people, and though having care of all people, [1916] he was mindful of them in a different way. Blessed Moses also said this: "When the Most High apportioned nations, as he separated Adam's sons, he established nations' boundaries according to the number of God's messengers; Jacob became the Lord's portion, his people, Israel his

1. Cf. opening of commentary on Ps 111. This opening comment also suggests that Theodoret's text does in fact have a title reading "A Song of the Steps" like the others, unlike the Hebrew and other forms of the LXX. This would have encouraged in the commentator a like conciseness, and so the liturgical character of the hymn is not developed in commentary.

allotted inheritance."[2] *Because I know the Lord is great, and our Lord is above all the gods* (v. 5). We have learned from experience itself, he is saying, the strength of our God, and the fact that in no way the gods adored by the other nations will be able to be compared with him: nothing, anything which really does not exist is comparable with the one who is and always has been.

(3) Then he gives a glimpse of the power of God from creation. *Whatever the Lord wished he did in heaven and on earth, in the seas and in all the depths* (v. 6). What has been made is a measure not of his power but of his will: he was capable of creating more and much greater things than these, but his will was for this number and kind. Yet all are of his making, heaven and heavenly beings, earth and earthly beings, sea and what is in it. He calls *depths* the boundless mass of water, and spoke of *seas* in the plural since one sea is divided into many oceans—Atlantic gulf, Ocean, Tyrrhenian, Ionian, Aegean, Arabian, Indian, Euxine sea, Propontis, Hellespont, and the other seas more numerous than the aforementioned.[3] *Bringing down clouds from the end of the earth* (v. 7). The waters that naturally fall, in fact, are drawn up by the divine Word to become elevated, watering the whole continent; but he said they are *brought down from the end of the earth* since they are composed of sea water, the ocean gulfs being the boundaries of the earth. *He made lightning flashes for rain.* He gives prior mention to the provision of rain through lightning flashes, and shows the most baffling of all marvels: a fire of lightning flashes coursing through water neither heats it nor is itself extinguished by it. *Bringing out winds from his storehouses.* By winds' *storehouses* he does not mean some kind of deposits; rather, since the air is free of wind and the divine will without difficulty frequently moves it merely by willing to, he spoke of a *storehouse of winds:* once he wishes it, they come from all directions.

(4) After giving a glimpse in this way of the creation and

2. Deut 32.8–9. Theodoret has no qualms about outlining the privileges of Israel as chosen people, though upholding the principle of divine care for all peoples.

3. Again Theodoret shows his propensity to lecture on geography, as also on natural science.

providence affecting all, he then outlines the Jews' favors. *He struck the firstborn of Egypt, from human being to beast* (v. 8). He put the final plague first since they were affected by it after the liberation. [1917] *He sent out signs and wonders in your midst, O Egypt* (v. 9). He indicated the manifold wonder workings and chastisements in this way. *On Pharaoh and on all his servants.* The kingship was not sufficient to spare him from the divinely imposed scourges: ruler and ruled were both affected by the same evils. The God of all said as much to the mighty Moses: "Behold, I shall strike every firstborn of Egypt, from the firstborn of Pharaoh seated on his throne to the firstborn of the female slave by the millstone."[4]

(5) *He struck many nations* (v. 10), inhabiting Palestine in olden times. *And slew mighty kings, Sihon king of the Amorites and Og king of Bashan* (vv. 10–11). The divine Moses destroyed their kingdom. *And all the kingdoms of Canaan.* Blessed Joshua subdued them, and divided up among the people the regions and cities occupied by them. The inspired author says so here, too. *He gave their land as an inheritance, an inheritance to Israel his people* (v. 12): like a kind of ancestral bequest, their God gave to Israel the land formerly occupied by those godless kings. *Lord, your name is forever and your memory from generation to generation* (v. 13): the greatness of the marvels done by you taught everyone your name, and of course the recollection of your favors will be preserved for generations to come. *Because the Lord will judge his people, and will console his servants* (v. 14): you will not ignore us when you see us attacked by the godless, nor inflict punishments our sins deserve; instead, you will be merciful and kind.

(6) Having in this way shown the power of the true God, he mocks the weakness of those so-called [gods], who are not really gods; since he named them gods, he made clear that they were void [of being god] according to deed and name. *The idols of the nations are silver and gold, works of human hands* (v. 15). Whereas our God is maker of all things, he is saying, they not only have no creative power, but even their very form they get from human skill, as their substance depends on matter and

4. Cf. Exod 11.5.

skill. *They have a mouth, but do not speak; they have eyes, but do not see; they have ears, but do not hear* (vv. 16–17). They give the impression of having senses, he is saying, but lack their operation. *Nor, in fact, is there breath in their mouths:* even brute beasts naturally share in this, as every living thing breathes, whereas the idols do not even share in it in similar fashion. [1920] *May their makers be like them, and all who believe in them* (v. 18): both those making them and those worshipping them deserve to share this insensibility; though having the gift of reason, they take as gods [things] which are bereft of life and reason, and so it is fair that they share their irrationality.

(7) *House of Israel, bless the Lord* (v. 19). While they accord the lifeless idols such worship, you sing the praises of the Maker of all things. *House of Aaron, bless the Lord.* He distinguished the priests from the people, and urged them to sing on their own, showing the difference by this. *House of Levi, bless the Lord* (v. 20). Here again another difference: while the Levites were more important than the others, they were inferior to the priests. In case, then, they should arrogate to themselves the priestly dignity (they attempted this in the past, when the divine Moses was alive),[5] it was necessary for him to distinguish them also from the priests. *Those who fear the Lord, bless the Lord.* This was a still further group, not taking their race from Jacob, but embracing his piety; and so they called the pious ones proselytes. This was sufficient to teach Jews that the God of all ranks kinship in manners ahead of bodily kinship.

(8) *Blessed be the Lord from Sion, who dwells in Jerusalem* (v. 21). In being blessed the Lord blesses; but whereas he blesses in deed, it is in word that he is blessed. Those singing his praises offer words, whereas it is in action that he repays the blessing. He said he dwells in Jerusalem, not to confine the divine nature to that place, but in the knowledge of the divine manifestation there at that time.[6]

---

5. To what occasion is Theodoret referring? Cf. Moses' commendation of the Levites, Exod 32.25–29.

6. The closing Alleluia of this psalm, forming an inclusion with the opening, has been transposed by the LXX to the beginning of the next.

COMMENTARY ON PSALM 136

Alleluia.[1]

HE CHARISM OF INSPIRATION composed also this psalm for the same [people], showing concern for their benefit through further lessons given them. *Confess to the Lord that he is good, because his mercy is forever* (v. 1). Offer to God, he is saying, the thanksgiving hymn, mindful of the good things supplied by him, and marveling at his immeasurable mercy. *Confess to the God of gods, because his mercy is forever* (v. 2). By *gods* here he does not mean idols: he would not have called him God of what does not exist; after all, God is God not of the dead but of the living.[2] Accordingly, he calls *gods* those given the status of priesthood, styled sons of God, as it says also in the Law, "You shall not revile gods, nor speak evil of a leader of your people";[3] and, "Israel my firstborn son";[4] and in Isaiah, [1921] "I had children and reared them";[5] and in the Psalms, "I said, 'You are gods, and all children of the Most High.'"[6] He called them gods in being styled children of God.

(2) *Confess to the Lord of lords, because his mercy is forever* (v. 3). Both kings and rulers, receiving authority from God, rule over their subjects. Thus the Lord also said, "The kings of the nations lord it over them, and the rulers dominate them."[7] There are also certain angels called Dominations. Hence the divine Apostle also said, "I mean, even if there are so-called gods (many so-called but not real, sharing the name, not the reality), whether in heaven or on earth, there being many gods, yet for us there is one God, the Father, from whom all things are and

---

1. Cf. closing note to the previous psalm. Theodoret obviously knows nothing of this psalm's name in Judaism, the "Great Hallel."
2. Cf. Matt 22.32.   3. Cf. Exod 22.28.
4. Exod 4.22.   5. Isa 1.2.
6. Ps 82.6.   7. Matt 20.25.

for whom we exist, and one Lord Jesus Christ, through whom all things are and through whom we exist."[8] The psalm called him Lord of the true lords.

(3) *Who alone worked great wonders, because his mercy is forever* (v. 4). Wonder working belongs also to his well-disposed servants; but we give the name divine also to the miracles of Moses, of Joshua, and of Elijah, as likewise to the signs worked by the sacred apostles. So the inspired author was right to say that he alone is worker of the great wonders. Then he highlights also his great works of creation: *Who by understanding made the heavens, because his mercy is forever* (v. 5): heaven also, once it is merely seen, proclaims God's wisdom; great is its extent, its beauty, and its long duration. *Who secured the earth on the waters, because his mercy is forever* (v. 6). This, too, is admirable and surpassing human conception, that the earth is everywhere encircled by waters and yet abides, thanks to its own nature. The recorder of these marvels was right to relate the everlasting mercy to all these verses since the loving Creator made them all not out of any need of his but solely out of loving-kindness.[9]

(4) *Who alone made great lights, because his mercy is forever* (v. 7). Sharing in the divine providence, human beings are in the habit of lighting lamps; but all the fire on earth is no match for the brightness of a single star. The sun is the brightest among all stars and the moon itself: once it shines it obscures even [the stars] and dulls the [moon's] rays. *The sun to rule over the day, because his mercy is forever; the moon and the stars to rule over the night, because his mercy is* [1924] *forever* (vv. 8–9): he apportioned, he said, time to the lights, making the day with the sun's rays while lighting up the night with moon and stars. Through the creation of these things he shows his peculiar goodness.

(5) *Who struck Egypt with its firstborn ones, because his mercy is forever* (v. 10). Perhaps, however, you might be at a loss to ex-

8. Cf. 1 Cor 8.5–6, loosely recalled. With the Songs of the Steps behind him, with all their constricting features, Theodoret is becoming more expansive, as the degree of Scriptural documentation suggests.

9. Finally Theodoret adverts to a distinguishing feature of the psalm, its refrain, but says nothing of liturgical usage with this refrain as a *responsorium*. As he says in the conclusion to the *Commentary* as a whole, his interest is in teaching, not liturgy.

plain how the provision for death is due to mercy. Consider, then, the solution offered by the present words: he has pity on the wronged and punishes the wrongdoers, which is in fact what the inspired author added at this point, *And brought Israel out from their midst, because his mercy is forever* (v. 11): mercy in their regard inflicted punishment on the others, though even former and latter are linked to righteousness; it was righteous of him to have mercy on the ones, and just of him to punish the others. *With a strong hand and an upraised arm, because his mercy is forever* (v. 12). He called his operation *hand* and his strength *arm;* through both, however, he indicated that by the salvation worked for the people he revealed his peculiar power.

(6) *Who divided the Red Sea into parts, because his mercy is forever* (v. 13). Some people, following the Jewish fairytales, have claimed that divisions were made to the Red Sea equal in number to the twelve tribes since the inspired author did not say "division" but *divisions.* They ought to understand, on the contrary, that the mass of water was divided in half, becoming two instead of one: the water turned into a wall for them on the right and a wall on the left[10]—hence his speaking of the division of the water mass into two as *divisions. And led Israel through its midst, because his mercy is forever; and shook off Pharaoh and his might into the Red Sea, because his mercy is forever* (vv. 14–15): both were works of his power, their crossing the water mass trouble-free, and the others' being drowned in the water. *Who led his people in the wilderness, because his mercy is forever* (v. 16). This, too, was a demonstration of the divine might, nourishing such a large populace over such a lengthy period in the wilderness and supplying them with an abundance of necessities.

(7) *Who struck mighty kings, because his mercy is forever; and killed powerful kings, because his mercy is forever* (vv. 17–18). We have already given a brief comment on these.[11] [1925] *Sihon*

10. Though the pace is on to dispatch this lengthy psalm, despite its liturgical significance as the "Great Hallel," Theodoret takes a moment to deal with a Jewish midrash, disposing of it not by any profound exegetical examination of the text, but by a simple reference to the text of Exod 14.22. He is probably unaware of the various forms of the narrative of the crossing of the Sea that have come together in chapters 14 and 15 of that book.

11. It is high time for Theodoret to advert to the close resemblance of this

king of the Amorites, because his mercy is forever; and Og king of Bashan, because his mercy is forever (vv. 19–20). It was not without purpose that he omitted the other kings and made mention of these in particular; rather, it was to recall the victory that came to the people as a divine gift; those [kings] gloried in their strength, might and bodily greatness, after all. Og used an iron bed, which on account of the size of his body was nine cubits long and five cubits wide.[12] *And gave their land as a heritage, because his mercy is forever; a heritage to his servant Israel, because his mercy is forever* (vv. 21–22): after consuming all those people in death, he made Israel lord of their land.[13]

(8) *Because our Lord remembered our lowly estate, because his mercy is forever; and he redeemed us from our foes, because his mercy is forever* (vv. 23–24). Blessed Moses also makes mention of these things: "The children of Israel groaned under the labors," he says, "and their cry went up to God."[14] [God] in turn had pity on their being made captive again, and led [them] back to their ancestral land. *He gives food to all flesh, because his mercy is forever* (v. 25). He switches in turn from the particular providence to the universal, proclaiming the care of God for everyone: not only to human beings but also to the brute beasts he offers appropriate nourishment. The Lord also said as much in the sacred Gospels, "Look at the birds of heaven that neither sow nor gather into barns, and your heavenly Father feeds them."[15] *Confess to the God of heaven, because his mercy is forever* (v. 26). God is God of everything, for he is maker of everything; but it is appropriate that he is styled God of heaven in that he is attended by the angels whose existence is in heaven, that being the place free from sin.

---

whole section to the preceding psalm. He does not proceed, however, to account for the resemblance, whether due to a dependence of one psalm on the other or arising from access to common traditions; this he would leave to "the scholars," doubtless.

12. In keeping with his interest in quaint items marginal to the import of sacred history, Theodoret is taken by this comment in Deuteronomy 3.11 on Og's bed (or sarcophagus, in Von Rad's view) of larger-than-life dimensions, which not atypically he has extended from four to five cubits in length in recalling the intriguing text.

13. We might expect of a commentator today some observation on this example of ethnic cleansing. The bishop, however, as we note in Introduction, section 8, does not make much moral comment on the Psalms, let alone moralize.

14. Exod 2.23.   15. Matt 6.26.

COMMENTARY ON PSALM 137

HIS PSALM IS WITHOUT TITLE in the Hebrew; but some have had the audacity to write a title, "For David through Jeremiah," and add, "Without a title in the Hebrew."[1] The very concoction of the inscription declares the inscribers' folly: Jeremiah, namely, was not taken off to Babylon with the captives; instead, he passed a short time in Jerusalem, and under pressure from the lawless Jews he shared their journey into Egypt. So how does it fit Jeremiah to say, *On the rivers of Babylon there we sat* [1928] *and wept?* It is clear from what has been said that it relates in no way to that inspired author. In any case, the psalm's theme is clear: those taken captive and granted the return describe the happenings in Babylon.

(2) *On the rivers of Babylon there we sat and wept in our remembering Sion* (v. 1). Depressed people usually take up the more deserted spots and there lament their own misfortunes; so these people also took up their position on the banks of the rivers, pondering the deprivation of their mother city, and wept many tears like currents of rivers. *On the willows in its midst we hung up our instruments* (v. 2). They were completely useless to them, since the Law prescribed performance of worship in one place.

(3) *Because there our captors asked us words of songs, and those who led us away, Sing for us a hymn from the songs of Sion* (v. 3): mocking us and harping on our misfortunes they bade us to sing and charm them with our songs, not to get any benefit there but to make fun of our situation. *How are we to sing the song of the Lord in a foreign land?* (v. 4): aware of the illegality of the order, we will not give in to those bidding us. This was proof

---

1. For an Antiochene this is utter hybris, to presume to insert details into an inspired text: *akribeia* forbids it, and Theodoret had to make the point about the first psalm.

323

of Jews' transgressions, careful to observe the Law but performing the prescribed rites away from prescribed places.

(4) *If I forget you, Jerusalem, may my right hand go for nothing. May my tongue stick to my throat if I do not remember you* (vv. 5–6). They are instructed by the inspired author to say this so as to keep the recollection of the sacred city clear and, buoyed up by the hope of return, not to pick up the impiety of their captors. So they say, Even though happening to be distant from you, O Jerusalem, I did not consign your memory to oblivion; should I do so, however, may I suffer this and not attain help from above, which he calls *right hand. If I do not set Jerusalem at the zenith of my happiness.* Sight of you, your restoration, and the celebrations performed in you, he is saying, I hold to be the acme of happiness, these being the source of my true satisfaction.

(5) *Remember, O Lord, the children of Edom that day in Jerusalem, when they said, Raze it! Raze it down to its foundations!* (v. 7). The Idumeans, descended from Esau, persisted in their ancestral hostility. When Jerusalem was put to the torch and destroyed, they exulted and said, [1929] *Raze it! Raze it down to its foundations!*—that is, root it up from its base so that not even traces remain of its foundations. *O wretched daughter of Babylon* (v. 8). Passing over to God the judgment of the Jews in this way, he foretells the future destruction of Babylon as well, calling her *wretched* for facing future distress; Aquila, on the other hand, for *wretched* said "crushed."[2]

(6) *Blessed is the one who gives you your just deserts for the treatment you meted out to us.* What is the meaning of this? *Blessed is the one who will take up and dash your infants against the rock* (v. 9). In other words, since they for their part treated their infants cruelly, the inspired author prophesied the like punishment for them. Consequently Cyrus is declared blessed for punishing them and freeing these [i.e., the Jews],[3] not because he was

2. Instead of remarking, as do modern commentators, on "the contrast between the tender poignancy of the first six verses and the bitter imprecations of the last three" (Dahood), Theodoret simply supplies the background to the reference to Edom, and passes on to note an insignificant alternative version from Aquila. At least the following curse has him asking, as his readers must have asked, the reason for the curse.

3. Cyrus, in fact, was lenient with Babylon when he took it in 539.

reared on sincere piety but because he accorded the pious people liberty and gave directions for the building of the divine
Temple. God receives few fruits and provides generous rewards—hence his hailing the widow's two coins.[4]

4. Mark 12.42, coins which in fact were not the *oboloi* mentioned here but
the even less valuable *lepta;* but we are still intrigued to see Theodoret making
some attempt—however trifling—to draw a general moral lesson from this
psalm for his reader.

COMMENTARY ON PSALM 138

For David.

FTER THE RETURN from Babylon, the Jews, having through divine aid put down the nations attacking them, offer a thanksgiving hymn to God. The divine David therefore foretells this: *I shall confess to you, Lord, with all my heart* (v. 1). They were not ungrateful to their benefactor; instead, after offering supplication and gaining help, they repay the favors to the best of their ability and offer hymns in return for the assistance.[1] *And in the sight of angels I shall sing to you.* We shall imitate the troops of angels, he is saying, and just as in the heavens they dance and sing the praises of the God of all, so shall we also on earth offer you spiritual music.

(2) *I shall bow down towards your holy temple, and confess to your name for your mercy and your truth* (v. 2): the temple consecrated to your name will take for me the place of heaven; in it I shall worship you and render a grateful act of praise on seeing the loving-kindness towards me and righteousness against the enemies. On these, in fact, you in your truth delivered a sentence of destruction for their wrongdoing, whereas me you saved in your mercy. *Because you magnified your holy name over all:* in every way your name is venerable and will be celebrated by all who recognize your strength. *On whatever day I called upon you, you quickly hearkened to me* (v. 3): I ask to enjoy this happiness constantly. *In your might you will take good care of me in my soul,* [1932] that is to say, In your might you will take good care of my soul and fill it with consolation and confidence. Symmachus, on the other hand, put it this way, "You established my soul in power."

1. Theodoret's form of the LXX does not contain the clause "because you heard the words of my mouth" that modern versions like the Jerusalem Bible take from other LXX forms, and that Dahood, on prosodic grounds and with the support of the Dead Sea remains, rejects.

You accorded me, he is saying, much assistance and providence.

(3) *All the kings of the earth will confess to you, O Lord, because they heard all the words of my mouth* (v. 4). At that time all learned of that very great victory and marveled at the power of the God of all. In particular, however, after the incarnation of our God and Savior both kings and rulers sing the praises of the Creator of all. In the case of the former victory, of course, they did not hear words but had a vision of a remarkable event, whereas in this case they both heard words and enjoy the evangelical preachings. *Let them sing in the ways of the Lord because great is the Lord's glory* (v. 5). He speaks of coming events by way of a wish, and foretells the change in things, that all will marvel at God's providence and planning, calling [his] plans *ways*.[2] *Because the Lord is exalted, and he has regard for lowly things* (v. 6). This he also said in another psalm: "He dwells on the heights and looks down on the lowly."[3] He means, Though being by nature elevated and ineffable, he is not inattentive to small things; instead, he accords them, too, his peculiar providence. *And lofty things he knows from afar:* he knows everything before their coming to be; seeing from afar those in positions of influence, he offers to each appropriate remedies.

(4) *If I walk in the midst of tribulation, you will give me life* (v. 7). This is the voice of unalloyed faith. I am confident, he is saying, that even if I am beset with disasters from all directions, I shall be stronger than my adversaries, and gain life from your assistance. *You stretched out your hands against foes' wrath, and your right hand saved me:* enraged against my enemies, you consigned them to punishment while according me salvation. From this it is clear that he calls his operation *hand* and his kind operation *right hand:* he involved his hand in the punishment of the foes, but his right hand in beneficence towards [the psalmist]. *The Lord will deliver just deserts for my sake* (v. 8). Human being that I am, he is saying, and implicated in sins, I am not able to repay

2. With the historical connection of the psalm being flimsy, Theodoret is able to give it an eschatological sense, with the Incarnation in mind, the particular feature of God's "planning," *oikonomia.*
3. Cf. Ps 113.5–6.

his kindnesses; whereas he is Lord, who proved to be a patron for me in these things, and by becoming incarnate, taking my nature, he pays my debt. The divine Apostle agrees with this in saying that Christ the Lord erased [1933] the record that stood against us.[4] *Lord, your mercy is forever; do not neglect the works of your hands:* since, then, your mercy is beyond measure and extends forever, provide your creatures with prompt salvation. The inspired author offered this prayer under instruction from the grace of the all-holy Spirit,[5] that the Creator of nature would discharge nature's debt.

4. Col 2.14.
5. Again a clear statement of the inspiration of the biblical author.

COMMENTARY ON PSALM 139

To the end. A psalm for David.

N SOME COPIES THERE OCCURS [the phrase], "Of Zechariah for the diaspora." I did not find it in the Hebrew, nor the Septuagint nor the other translators; rather someone has inserted the title on taking the psalm in a way preferred.[1] The psalm, however, contains a prophecy of King Josiah: sprung from a godless father and offspring of such a grandfather, he detested their impiety, took the path of complete virtue, and, consumed with divine zeal, he disposed of all the priests of the idols, whereas on those embracing piety he lavished all attention. The psalm foretells this.

(2) The inspired word introduces him at prayer, marveling at the foreknowledge of him: *Lord, you examined me and know me.* Not only penury and discouragement are a trial of virtue, but also royal status and success: just as we are tested in sorrows to see if we bear nobly the distress besetting us, so too we are exercised in prosperous ventures, and we show whether we are carried away by good fortune or understand its nature. Accordingly, on attaining kingship and conducting it with piety, blessed Josiah had grounds for saying, *Lord, you examined me and you know me. You know my sitting down and my rising up* (vv. 1–2). You have a precise knowledge of everything, he is saying, what I achieved while seated and what I did on standing up; by *sitting down* and *rising up* he indicated the whole of life. The words come from a pure soul and sound conscience.

(3) After he said, *You examined me and you know me,* he very appropriately added, lest anyone form the idea that God learns

---

1. As was mentioned in Introduction, section 3, Theodoret could easily check any different forms of the LXX against his Hexapla, which contained the Hebrew text and versions by the LXX and the other three translators.

what happens after the conclusion of events, *You understand my thoughts from afar:* from of old, from the very beginning and many generations before my making you not only foresaw my doings but foresaw my future thoughts. *You investigated my path and my cord* (v. 3). Theodotion, on the other hand, put it this way, "You investigated my path and my way." He calls his doings way and path, and their directness *cord* by analogy [1936] with builders leveling the walls with a thin cord. You have a precise knowledge of my doings, he is saying, and nothing about me escapes your knowledge. *You foresaw all my ways, that there is no deceit on my tongue* (v. 4). Not only did the God of all foresee but he also foretold through the prophets, and prophesied to Jeroboam as he sacrificed and offered the divine worship with young steers that a son would be raised up to David, Josiah by name, and he would consign to death the priests of the idols and would burn their bones on that altar.[2]

(4) *Behold, Lord, you know everything, the latest and the earliest* (v. 5): I have learned through experience itself that you have complete knowledge both of what happened long ago and what has not yet happened. *You formed me, and you placed your hand on me:* how could anything of mine escape my maker, who formed me in my mother's womb and accorded me complete providence? The phrase, *You placed your hand on me,* resembles, "Your hands made me and shaped me."[3] It indicates in the same fashion the providence taken after shaping. *Your knowledge is too wonderful for me, too overwhelming for me to be able to take it in* (v. 6): from what has happened to me I know your power; wishing to sing the praises of your wisdom, then falling short of your dignity, I admit defeat.

(5) After thus marveling at the knowledge and the foreknowledge of the God of all, that nothing escaped him either of the past or of the future, he moves to a different point in this explanation. *Where am I to go from your Spirit? and where am I to flee from your face?* (v. 7): how is it possible for anyone running

2. The incident is recorded in 1 Kings 13.1–2, though its citation here is puzzling. The prophet bears no name—"a man out of Judah"—but the grisly incident has caught Theodoret's fancy.
3. Job 10.8.

away [to escape] the attention of the one who understands everything so clearly? It should be noted that he taught that both God and the all-holy Spirit have the same operation:[4] *Where am I to go from your Spirit?* he says, *and where am I to flee from your face?* The operation is one, altogether one also the power; their power is one, one the nature; one, then, the nature of God and the Spirit. *If I ascend to heaven, you are there; if I descend to Hades, you are present* (v. 8). You fill every [place], he is saying, both those above and those below; one is the limit of height, the other of depth. It was good for him to link the phrase *you are there* with heaven, and *you are present* with Hades: with the angels whose existence is in heaven he is at rest, whereas he is present everywhere and is ready to assist everyone. "In him we live," according to the divine Apostle, "we move and have our being."[5]

(6) [1937] *If I were to take my wings at dawn, and dwell at the farthest limits of the sea, even there your hand would guide me and your right hand hold me* (vv. 9–10). He called the east *dawn,* and the west *the farthest limits of the sea,* adding the length and the breadth to the height and the depth to teach the absence of limits to the divine nature. The prophet Jonah also experienced this power: attempting to flee the God of all, he was caught, bound by the waves, consigned to the sea monster like to some prison, and brought to the city to which he had been sent. So the words of the inspired composition are seen to be true in this case, too, *If I were to dwell at the farthest limits of the sea, there your hand would guide me and your right hand hold me. I said, Darkness will trample me underfoot, then, and night be illumination in my delight* (vv. 9–11). Symmachus, on the other hand, put it this way, "If I were to say, Perhaps darkness will cover me, yet

4. As he had done in commentary on Ps 36.9, Theodoret finds traces of Trinitarian thinking in this text (choosing not to entertain the obvious interpretation of the word *pneuma*), and takes occasion to oppose any thinking of the inferiority of the Spirit in either operation or nature. His phrasing "God and the all-holy Spirit" (repeated), however, could have been improved to achieve the theological precision regarding the Spirit that he achieves in his Christology. In commentary on Ps 148 he will refer to a work of his on the Holy Spirit.
5. Acts 17.28.

even night will be bright around me": even if I flee to the rising sun, he is saying, to the setting sun, I shall not escape your power; even if I try to be hidden by the darkness of night, not even this way shall I escape detection. To you, in other words, darkness is light. *Because darkness will not be dark for you, and night will be made as bright as day* (v. 12). Symmachus, on the other hand, put it this way, "Nor will darkness be dark in your case; rather, even night will become as bright as day." The darkness, he is saying, is darkness as far as I am concerned—for me, after all, there is a difference between light and darkness—whereas for you with the light of the intellect even night is most bright, more light-filled than high noon. *As is its darkness, so also is its light:* just as night is dark to me, so is it light to you.

(7) *Because you took possession of my vitals* (v. 13). It is not idly, he is saying, that I mention this, but enlightened by your grace and benefiting in my thoughts from your brightness. He called thoughts *vitals* here: since the passion of desire is situated in the vitals, and the thoughts are affected by its impulse, he used the term *vitals* of the thoughts. *You took hold of me from my mother's womb:* you became my coach, caretaker and teacher, and I enjoyed your providence immediately on leaving the womb. *I confess to you because you worked wonders in a fearful manner; wonderful are your works, and my soul is well aware of it* (v. 14): for this reason I continue singing your praises, illumined by your magnificence, and stirred to do it.

(8) [1940] *My bone was no secret to you, for you made it in secret along with my substance in the bowels of the earth* (v. 15). All there is to me, he is saying, you know precisely: you formed me when I was still hidden in my mother's womb, and you brought me to light as if I were in the furthest part of the earth. This, in fact, is the way Aquila also rendered it, "My bones were not hidden from you, with which I was made in hiding, I was crafted as though in the depth of the earth." Nothing can escape your notice, he is saying, since you shape the human race in nature's hidden workshop. *Your eyes saw my incompleteness, and all will be written in your book; days will be formed, and no one in them* (v. 16). Symmachus, on the other hand, put it this way, "Your eyes fore-

saw my shapelessness, with all those written in your book, no day missing for those being formed."[6] This is the way you saw me, he is saying, before I was shaped and formed like those already born and made perfect, with not a day short, and enrolled in your books. Blessed Daniel also makes mention of these books: "The court sat in judgment," he says, "and the books were opened";[7] and the Lord in the sacred Gospels [says], "Even the hairs of your head are all numbered."[8] By *books* here is to be understood God's all-encompassing knowledge and God's unfailing memory.

(9) After thus outlining the divine attributes, he unveils his own purpose, not having recourse to ambition but proposing an example of utility. *To me your friends, O God, are extremely honorable, their powers made extremely dominant* (v. 17). History also teaches this clearly: he accorded the divine priests every privilege; they all heard, in fact, the promises which God made to Abraham, saying, "I shall bless those who bless you, and curse those who curse you."[9] The phrase, *their powers made dominant,* Theodotion rendered this way, "Their needy made dominant": those who once led a life of poverty and need on account of the transgressions of the impious kings enjoyed every honor from Josiah. *I shall count them, and they will become more numerous than the sand* (v. 18). In other words, to the piety of the king those once godless but now enlightened in mind sang a song of recantation and embraced the life according to the Law, and those whose numbers could once be counted [1941] proved more numerous. The word also prophesies at the same time the transformation of the world achieved after the Incarnation of our God and Savior: those attentive to the worship of God surpass in number every city and place. *I have risen, and I am still with you.* Symmachus, on the other hand, put it this way, "I

6. Though the verse is obscure enough, the failure of the LXX to read aright the Hebrew verb tenses disqualifies it as a basis of commentary, so Theodoret turns at once to his accustomed resource, Symmachus.

7. Dan 7.10.

8. Matt 10.30.

9. Gen 12.3. Theodoret is forced to rationalize inadequate versions by LXX and Theodotion of another difficult verse.

shall awake, and be always in your company": ever stirring my-self, I shall both expel the sleep of indifference and preserve the memory of you in my mind, thus enjoying your providence.

(10) *If you kill sinners, O God, depart from me, men of blood, be-cause you are given to controversy* (v. 19). It is characteristic of those who love good people to detest the opposite kind. Hence he says, Since you in your loving-kindness do away with the sin-ners, much more shall I avoid their company after recognizing their quarrelsome attitude: they have no patience with good ad-vice, but reject it in their unresponsive attitude. *They will take your cities to futility* (v. 20). You will kill them, he is saying, not unjustly but because they will inhabit the cities to no good pur-pose, reaping no benefit from your laws. *Have I not hated those who hate you, O Lord, and did I not waste your foes? I hated them with utter hatred, they became foes to me* (vv. 21–22): I depend on your love, O Lord. I want to love and to hate the same as you. For this reason I love and honor those clinging to your worship, whereas those hating you I not only hate, but I continue griev-ing at them and wasting away: as sinners I hate them, but as hu-man beings I pity them, obliged to mourn for them out of natu-ral fellow-feeling but in turn detesting them for their great wickedness.

(11) *Examine me, O God, and know my heart; test me and know my paths. See if there is a way of iniquity in me, and guide me in an everlasting way* (vv. 23–24): I presume this is the way I am, but I beseech you, the finest physician of souls, to observe my life carefully and scrutinize the movements of the heart. If there is something found in them that is opposed to your laws, I beg to be set aright by your wisdom and to be guided on the everlast-ing journey.

(12) While this was said by blessed David, it was in the form of a prophecy of the pious Josiah, and an occasion of salvation is set before all willing [to accept it].[10]

---

10. This is a brief summary of Theodoret's position on the authorship and application of the psalms as outlined in his preface, except for the possibility of a Christological sense, to which he has had brief recourse here. It has become clear that their general spiritual application receives least attention from him.

COMMENTARY ON PSALM 140

To the end. A psalm for David.

URSUED BY SAUL BLESSED David calls on the God of all for assistance. [1944] *Deliver me, O Lord, from a wicked person, rescue from an unjust man* (v. 1). Saul was unjust and ungrateful to the benefactor: he went to trouble to do away with the divine David, who, far from doing him any wrong, was even a source of many good things for him. *Who pondered injustice in their heart, waged war all day long* (v. 2): they not only had recourse to wicked thoughts, but also added works to thoughts. Symmachus, on the other hand, rendered *all day long* as "for the whole day."[1] *They sharpened their tongue like a serpent's; venom of asps is under their tongues* (v. 3): by recourse to deceit he often tried to do away with him; and often after taking oaths and adopting friendly words he broke the oaths. Hence it was right for the psalmist to compare the deceitful attitude and the hidden guile to the poison of serpents.

(2) *Protect me, O Lord, from the hand of a sinner, and deliver me from unjust people* (v. 4). The prayer becomes a just person, who requests not destruction for the foes but personal salvation. *Who have plotted to trip up my steps.* Driven out by Saul, blessed David took refuge with the Philistines; they were godless, however, and practitioners of every kind of lawlessness. On this score, therefore, he is admirable, for being everywhere a protector of piety, reluctant to be subject to necessities. Still, the man driving me out, he is saying, came close to tripping up the steps of my piety. *Arrogant people hid a trap for me, and with nets he laid a trap for my feet; they set stumbling blocks on my path* (v. 5). He calls Saul himself *arrogant,* and the various schemes, stratagems,

---

1. One wonders what Theodoret (or, in line with Dorival's thinking, a copyist) thinks this footnote achieves for his reader.

and wiles *traps, nets,* and *stumbling blocks.* He said this in a figurative manner, by analogy with hunters setting strings, traps, and nets.

(3) *I said to the Lord, You are my God* (v. 6). For my part, on the contrary, I scorned all human things and dedicated myself to you; I know you are Lord and God, and I await help from you. *Give ear, O Lord, to the voice of my supplication. Lord, Lord, might of my salvation* (vv. 6–7). The repetition comes from a person of faith and longing: In you, he is saying, I place the hope of salvation, you alone being strong enough to provide salvation. *You covered my head in the day of battle.* I learned this by experience: when I submitted to single combat with Goliath, and when I was engaged in battle with the Philistines, you protected me with your aid as with a shield.

(4) [1945] *Do not surrender me, O Lord, at the desire of the one sinning against me* (v. 8). Symmachus, on the other hand, put it this way, "Do not grant, Lord, the desires of the lawless one," and likewise both Theodotion and Aquila. Do not grant, he is saying, to the one hankering after my slaughter the realization of their desire. According to the Septuagint the sense to be taken is, May he not enjoy what he longs for in my regard: I desire to be saved, whereas he desires to do away with me; so do not grant him the desire in my regard.[2] *They plotted against me; do not abandon me lest they be puffed up:* they direct every thought to my murder; so do not strip me of your providence lest you provide them with an occasion for imposture.

(5) *The head of their circle, labor of their lips will cover them* (v. 9). From this point he foretells the evils to come to them. Symmachus, on the other hand, rendered it more clearly, "May the bitterness of those surrounding me, the effort of their lips cover them over": may they fall foul of their own schemes, he is saying, and suffer what they devised against me, and may the savagery hatched against me completely envelop those employing it. This resembles what is said in the seventh psalm: "He sank a

2. In a psalm characterized by many *hapax legomena* and archaic forms, Theodoret is predictably puzzled by some expressions. Unable to find light in the original, he can simply cite alternative versions and let them speak for themselves. His reluctance even to go to the Syriac is perhaps accounted for by its not being able to claim the inspiration he accords the Seventy.

pit and dug it out, and fell into the hole he had made."[3] *Coals will fall on them, and you will cast them into the fire* (v. 10): you will consume them with rage like a kind of fire. *In difficulties, and let them have no firm footing:* they will be beset with disasters and not survive them. This happened to Saul in the war against the Philistines: there he was cut down and reached the end of his life.[4] *A man of smooth tongue will not give guidance in the land* (v. 11). With this he hints at those who slandered him in Saul's presence, Doeg, the Ziphites, [and] others. They employed much flattery. And he teaches that those who used falsehood with a view to wealth and influence will fall short of their purpose and not attain what they long for. *Troubles will hunt down an unjust man to his ruin.* Saul suffered this fate as well, in fact: taken prisoner in war he received the death-dealing blow.

(6) *I know that the Lord will give judgment in favor of the poor and justice for the needy* (v. 12). I have learned the justice of the divine verdict, he is saying, and I know that he will not allow those deprived of all human help to be exposed to those waging war on them for their harm, but will exact due penalties of the wrongdoers. *But righteous people will confess to your name,* [1948] *and upright people will dwell in your presence* (v. 13). For this very reason the chorus of the righteous sing your praises on attaining this care from you; they love your eminence, with you always in their thoughts, and hoping to see your face. Such is the sentiment in the fifteenth psalm, "I foresaw the Lord ever before me, that he is at my right hand lest I totter."[5]

3. Ps 7.15.
4. In the war against the Philistines, of course, Saul was wounded but took his own life (1 Sam 31), not quite the fate described here and below.
5. Ps 16.8.

COMMENTARY ON PSALM 141

A Psalm for David.

HIS PSALM HAS THE SAME drift as the preceding one: pursued by Saul he petitions God, *Lord, I cried to you, hearken to me* (v. 1), calling enthusiasm of the soul a *cry.* Likewise, though Moses was silent, God said, "Why do you shout aloud to me?"[1] *Attend to the sound of my petition when I cry to you.* Kindly receive my petition, Lord, he is saying.

(2) *Let my prayer be directed as incense before you, the raising of my hands an evening sacrifice* (v. 2). He associated the practice of virtue with the prayer; the raising of the hands indicates this: the hands are entrusted with the task. He asks that the prayer arise like the vapor of sacrifice and resemble its fragrance; likewise that the spreading of the hands appear like an evening sacrifice. He made mention, of course, of the evening and not the morning one since it was amidst disasters and griefs, and disaster is like darkness and night.[2]

(3) *Set, O Lord, a guard on my mouth, and a door round about my lips* (v. 3). The Creator gave two walls to the tongue, one of teeth and the other of lips, to check its irrational impulses.[3] Nevertheless, the inspired author begs to enjoy other guards as well, afraid lest he utter something improper while lamenting

1. Exod 14.15. Enthusiasm, *prothumia,* which is one of the principal binomials of the spiritual life alongside indifference, *rhathumia* (mentioned in comment on the previous psalm), in Chrysostom's moral teaching as a preacher, has been conspicuously absent from this bishop's less moral treatment.

2. Weiser, ever sensitive to the liturgical dimension of the Psalms, observes that in the early Church this psalm was regarded as the appropriate evening hymn; but Theodoret is silent on this aspect, ideal though the occasion here would be for such comment.

3. This strikes us as a typically rabbinic comment: did Theodoret pick it up from the strong Jewish community in his area? Did some of the books of the Talmud stand alongside the Hexapla on his desk?

his lot. In fact, history witnesses to the fact that even when pursued by Saul he could not bring himself to say anything blasphemous at all; instead, when they were trying to kill [Saul], [David] referred to him as the Lord's anointed, and in addressing him he called himself his servant,[4] and the one who reported his death, bragging he had done it, he dispatched in the words, "Your blood be on your head for claiming to have done away with the Lord's anointed."[5]

(4) *Do not turn my heart in the direction of wicked words, to fabricate excuses in sins* (v. 4). He begs that not only his tongue be guarded [1949] but also the very movements of the mind lest any other thought beyond the divine laws be found in them. Symmachus, on the other hand, in place of *to fabricate excuses in sins* said, "lawless notions." According to the Septuagint it is to be taken this way: Blessed David could reason, Saul is foe and enemy, longing for my execution, so it is not unjust to do away with such a man, the Law being clear on this, "You shall love your neighbor and hate your enemy."[6] Foreseeing the evangelical way of life, however, he preferred to live by it, and he prays he will take no excuse for sin. *With people who practice iniquity, and I shall not mingle with their elect.* Those committing lawlessness do this, he is saying, but let me have no association with them, even if they have the utmost good fortune; he uses *elect* at this point of wicked people who enjoy success.[7]

(5) *A righteous person will correct me in mercy and will censure me; may oil of a sinner not anoint my head* (v. 5). The grievous things that come to me from the hands of righteous people for the

4. 1 Sam 26.

5. 2 Sam 1.16, a somewhat different account of Saul's death from the one given by Theodoret in the previous psalm—but then the Deuteronomist himself seems inconsistent, too.

6. In fact, though the frightening norm is cited by Jesus at Matt 6.43, it is done so there as a travesty of Old Testament morality (found textually, however, in Dead Sea codes); only the first half occurs in Lev 19.18. In this case, then, where he finds the LXX more suited to his theme than Symmachus, Theodoret (deliberately or more likely in error) is misrepresenting the biblical support for his hypothetical justification of Saul's slaying.

7. Theodoret gives an unlikely turn to this word, yet he is close to the sense modern commentators derive from the *hapax legomenon* in the Hebrew (such as appears in versions like the NRSV) by reference to other Semitic languages.

sake of correction and benefit, he is saying, are preferable to the pleasant things offered by the sinners, even if these provide me with an enjoyable life, like oil making the head glisten; I prefer to be corrected by the righteous than fawned on by the sinful. *Because my prayer is ever on their satisfaction.* Symmachus, on the other hand, put it this way, "But my prayer is ever within their defects": I am so far from envying their prosperity that I pray they be changed so as to undergo a conversion of their defects once their success is reversed.[8]

(6) *Their judges were swallowed up like things attached to rock* (v. 6). Within a short time, he is saying, they will be no more, and those clinging to the pinnacle of influence will be like drowning people clinging to the tips of rocks submerged by water—in other words, they will be consigned to oblivion. *They will hear my words because they have been made pleasant:* learning by experience the truth of my words, they will also feel their sweetness and benefit. *As thickness of soil is shattered on the earth, their bones were scattered in Hades* (v. 7). He gives the term *thickness of soil* to the solidity of soil, which is cut by the plough and divided into clods. Those now in existence, he is saying, will be dissolved in death like clods, and their bones will be scattered in the tombs; [1952] the phrase *in Hades* is used of the tombs.

(7) *Because towards you, Lord, Lord, are my eyes, in you I had hope that you would not bring my soul to naught* (v. 8): far from trusting in any human thing, I await your help and ask that my soul not be deprived of it. *Keep me from a trap they have laid for me and from stumbling blocks of the workers of iniquity* (v. 9). He made mention of these *snares* and *stumbling blocks* also in the psalm before this. He calls *snares* and *stumbling blocks* the plots from which he begs to be delivered. *The sinners will fall in his net* (v. 10), that is, God's: those who set traps for others will be caught up in divine retribution like a kind of netting, will have to bear whatever they commit, and will suffer what they inflict on others. *I shall be on my own until I pass on:* for my part, however, I shall remain separated from them until I reach the end of my life.

8. Another "sticky phrase" (in Dahood's term) in this psalm bearing Phoenician coloring. Theodoret without much help from the versions rationalizes his way around to come up with a respectable rendering.

COMMENTARY ON PSALM 142

*Of understanding, for David, when he was
praying in the cave.*

HE PSALM'S THEME IS clear. Pursued by Saul, the
divine David took refuge in the cave and hid himself in
its interior.[1] Then, perceiving Saul brought down into
it, he banished fear from his mind, called for the divine assistance, and attained it. *With my voice I cried to the Lord, with my
voice I besought the Lord* (v. 1). From this it is clear that he calls
his earnestness of mind *cry:* how could this man in hiding and
anxious to escape notice use his voice to cry out? So he means,
In all earnestness I implored God.[2] *I pour out before him my appeal, I report my tribulation before him* (v. 2). I made the trouble
clear to him, he is saying, and earnestly offered the petition
about it; he indicated by *pour out* the force of the request.

(2) *When my spirit failed me* (v. 3): this I did on perceiving the
extent of the evils, dwelling at the point of death as I was. *You
knew my paths:* everything of mine was clear to you, and nothing
of my doings escaped your eye. *In this path that I traveled they hid
a trap for me.* The hunters pick up the traces of the wild beasts
and set traps there. In imitation of them Saul continued his exertions against David, learned where he was living and focused
his schemes in that direction. This [1953] the devil also does:
for the one traveling the way of temperance he sets the trap of
pleasure, whereas for the one taking satisfaction in almsgiving

1. Cf. 1 Sam 24.
2. That *prothumia* again—but no attempt to urge the reader to adopt the
virtue as basic to the spiritual life, as Chrysostom so often does.

the net of vainglory, for the one scorning wealth the chances of avarice, for virginity pride, and for every single state of life the snare likely to catch them.[3]

(3) *I glanced to the right, and looked, and there was no one recognizing me* (v. 4). I espied no helper in any direction, he is saying, calling action of the better disposed *the right. Flight is no longer available to me, and there is no one looking after my soul:* I have fallen into nets from which there is no escape, I find no means of flight nor one to assist me. *I cried to you, O Lord, I said, You are my hope* (v. 5): so I beseech you, on whom my hopes depend. *You are my portion in the land of the living. Attend to my appeal, because I am brought really low* (vv. 5–6). Often the divine David called God his own *portion,* and in this case he did likewise. I have no other assistance, he is saying, you are my only helper, and through you I beg to attain life. He calls misfortune here *lowliness;* Symmachus indicated as much, "Heed my words, because I am really exhausted."

(4) *Rescue me from those pursuing me, because they are too powerful for me:* the enemies have become stronger than I, but through your aid I shall escape their clutches. *Bring my soul out of prison so that I may confess to your name* (v. 7). Aquila, on the other hand, put it this way, "Bring my soul out of confinement," in other words, it was as if he was held in a kind of enclosure and cell, with the enemies camped at the door of the cave. Yet he promises to repay the favors with hymns, once he attains salvation. *Righteous people will wait for me until you give me recompense.* Symmachus, on the other hand, put it this way, "The righteous will crown your name when you act in my favor": they will take the favor done to me as a pledge of salvation in their regard, and praise you as the just Judge.

3. A rare—and sage—application of the verse to the spiritual life of any reader, pithily inserted.

COMMENTARY ON PSALM 143

A psalm for David, when his son Absalom was pursuing him.

N SOME COPIES I FOUND "When his son Absalom was pursuing him." But I have not found this insertion in the Hebrew or the other translators; yet it bears on the facts, the psalm having this theme.

(2) *O Lord, hearken to my prayer, give ear to my petition in your truth,* [1956] *hearken to me in your righteousness* (v. 1). Paying the penalty for the sins he had committed, the divine David encountered troubles. Absalom, by contrast, was unjust, lawless, impious, and parricidal, and he desired the murder of his parent.[1] This is doubtless the reason why David makes his supplication to God that he hearken to his prayer in *truth* and *righteousness. And do not enter into judgment with your servant, because no one living will be justified in your sight* (v. 2). In truth and righteousness I petitioned you in my words, he is saying, not that I had confidence in my own righteousness but I knew the enemies' lawlessness. I know, in fact, that it is impossible that any innocent person should escape your tribunal: if you were to apply the norm of the laws passed by you to the life of human beings, no one would be seen to have lived according to it, whereas if you were also to make public your kindnesses and the good things you have provided to human beings, what human righteousness could in its turn be judged equivalent to your gifts?

(3) *Because the foe pursued my soul, humbling my life into the dirt* (v. 3): so I beg to attain your truth and righteousness, not for

1. Theodoret has a choice here of the way the psalm is to be interpreted. He concedes that the historical connection rests not on textual support but on an affinity of subject matter, and in fact he will not develop it at length. For the moment he is showing little interest in the psalm's inclusion among the early Church's group of Penitential Psalms.

you and me to be judged together, but for me and the enemies to have sentence passed on us; I have been expelled from the kingship by them, driven out of my country. History also teaches this humiliation: he took his leave unshod, skulking, and in tears.[2] *He sat me down in darkness, like those dead for an age:* I am no different from a corpse enclosed in darkness, driven out, and forced to pass my life in desert places. *My spirit fainted within me* (v. 4): for this reason I was filled with deep depression and distress, the soul here being called *spirit. Within me my heart was confused.* All my thoughts, he is saying, were stricken with confusion and turbulence.

(4) *I remembered days of old, I pondered all your works, meditating on works of your hands* (v. 5): I gave my mind, he is saying, to thinking how great were the calamities from which you delivered our ancestors without allowing them to be vulnerable to the enemies; and I recalled the fate of Abraham, of Isaac, of Jacob, of Joseph, of Moses, and I drew comfort from it. *I stretched out my hands to you* (v. 6), that is to say, I made supplication with complete earnestness. *My soul like land parched for you:* I thirst for your help just as the parched land looks forward to rain.

(5) *Hearken to me quickly, O Lord, my spirit has fainted* (v. 7). In these words he betrayed the extent of his depression; this feeling is typical of those in great distress. *Do not turn your face away from* [1957] *me, and I shall be like those going down into a pit:* if you abhor my supplication on account of the sin, I shall immediately be consigned to death. In figurative fashion he called death *a pit:*[3] just as it is not possible for someone confined in a pit to escape without assistance, so the dead cannot return to life unless God wills [it]. *Make your mercy known to me in the morning, because I hoped in you* (v. 8). Disclose your loving-kindness to me, he is saying, and let my hope not be disappointed; he used the term *in the morning* here for "promptly." *Reveal to me, O Lord, the path I shall travel, because to you I lifted up my soul.* Become a guide for me, he is saying, and give me a glimpse of the straight path:

2. Cf. 2 Sam 15.30.
3. We have noted on previous occasions Theodoret's failure to grasp the general Old Testament position on life after death and its doctrine of Sheol in particular (see Introduction, section 7).

turning my soul away from all human things, O Lord, I brought it to you.

(6) *Deliver me from my foes, O Lord, I have taken refuge in you* (v. 9): fleeing the enemies, I have a place of refuge in you, and beg to be delivered from their plot. *Teach me to do your will, because you are my God* (v. 10). This, too, I ask for, not only to know what you wish but also to put into practice what you wish, since I know you are my God and Lord. *Your good Spirit will guide me on the level land.* Here we learned the dignity of the Spirit: as God is good, so too is the Spirit called good; and as he begged God to guide him, so too he asks to enjoy the guidance of the Spirit so that nothing may be adverse or difficult for him, but that he travel the path that is level, smooth, and free of error.[4]

(7) *For your name's sake, O Lord, you will give me life* (v. 11): you made me king; I enjoyed your verdict and election, and I am afraid of being passed over by you and proving a source of blasphemy for your name. Do not have regard for my rank, therefore; instead, for the sake of your good name grant me a share in salvation. *In your righteousness you will bring my soul out of distress:* by deciding between me and the enemies you will in righteousness free me from the troubles inflicted by them. *In your mercy you will utterly destroy my foes and ruin all who distress my soul, because I am your servant* (v. 12). He said this also in the hundred and thirty-fifth psalm: "Who struck Egypt with its firstborn ones, because his mercy is forever";[5] and he said here, *In your mercy you will utterly destroy my foes:* mercy towards the wronged inflicts destruction on the wrongdoer. In like manner an excellent farmer cuts out the thorns at the roots, but waters and tends the plants.

4. Commentary on the verses has been confined to mere paraphrase before once again Theodoret finds in *pneuma* a reference to the Holy Spirit; and as was true of his similar comment on Ps 139.7, his Trinitarian terminology strikes us as in need of greater precision.

5. Ps 136.10.

COMMENTARY ON PSALM 144

For David. [1960]

N SOME COPIES I FOUND inserted in the title "Against Goliath"; but I did not find it in the Hebrew, in the other translators, or, in fact, in the Septuagint in the Hexapla.[1] [The psalm], on the contrary, has the following theme. Many of the prophets—the divine Ezekiel at greater length than the others—mention the nations making incursions against the Jews after the return from Babylon. [Ezekiel] has this to say along with many other things: "After many days you will become ready and will go to the land averse to the sword, populated with many peoples, to the land of Jerusalem, which was completely deserted. They emerged from nations, and they all will dwell in peace. You will go up like a shower of rain, you will advance like a storm, and like a cloud you will cover the land; you will fall, you and all those about you, and many nations with you." Then after many things he teaches also the manner of their death: "I shall summon against him on all my mountains fear of a sword, says the Lord Adonai. A man's sword will be against his brother, and I shall condemn him to death, to blood, to devastating rain, and to hailstones. I shall release divine fire on them, on all those with him, and on all the nations with him."[2] It is possible for the person reading the

1. Theodoret, whom we saw (in Introduction, section 3) getting good marks from Guinot as a textual critic, has certainly gone to a little more trouble than a modern commentator like Weiser, who says of this psalm simply that "the Septuagint and the Targum link (it) with David's fight against Goliath." As we have observed elsewhere, Theodoret is using his own Antiochene or "Lucianic" LXX text as a base, noting some variant LXX readings and checking them against what the Hexapla columns offer by way of Hebrew, a different LXX, and alternative Greek versions. He then rejects the variant reading also on the basis of content.

2. Cf. Ezek 38.8–9, 21–22. Theodoret had completed a *Commentary* on

prophecy to learn this more accurately if willing. This psalm prophesies it as well: *Bend heavens, O Lord, and come down; touch the mountains and they will smoke; make your lightning flash and scatter them; dispatch your arrows, and you will throw them into confusion* (vv. 5–6). Comment on individual verses will teach this more clearly.

(2) *Blessed be the Lord my God, who trains my hands for battle, my fingers for war* (v. 1). Having recently returned from Babylon, in other words, and being deprived of weapons and ramparts, they prevailed over the adversaries attacking them, thanks to divine aid. The words apply to us as well: freed from the tyranny of the devil, we are trained for warfare by God, practicing righteousness with our *hands,* and with our *fingers* putting the seal of the cross on our foreheads.[3] *My mercy and my refuge, my protector, my defender, my rescuer, in him I hoped* (v. 2). He gave the names from experience. You are *my mercy* he says: I received fountains of mercy from you. You are *my refuge:* taking refuge in you I was saved. You are *my defender:* enjoying your aid I proved superior to the enemies. You are *my rescuer* and *my protector:* you [1961] fortified me in battle and will rescue me when besieged. So I will have unwavering hope in you. *Who subdues my people under me.* This is applicable to Zerubbabel and the priest Joshua: they were in charge of the people at that time.

(3) *Lord, what is man that you have come to know him? or the son of man that you spare him a thought?* (v. 3). In place of *have come to know* Symmachus gave the rendering *learned:* I am in utter admiration of your immeasurable loving-kindness in that, though God and Creator of everything, you show such care for this lowly being. Then he shows its transitory nature: *Man is like futility, his days like a passing shadow* (v. 4). Theodotion says, "Man is like vapor," and Symmachus, "smoke": like smoke, that is formed and dissipated, the nature of human beings is easily corrupted, and their life moves like a shadow—hence your care for such transitory human beings.

(4) *Bend your heavens, O Lord, and come down* (v. 5). He uses

---

Ezekiel before coming to the Psalms, he tells us in the preface; but one wonders if this citation brings much light to bear.

3. A rare and pithy application of the verse to the life of the reader.

the expressions in human fashion, knowing the divine nature is not circumscribed by heaven, but calling on his helper to punish the enemies. *Touch the mountains, and they will smoke.* This in fact happened on Mount Sinai: "The mountain smoked,"[4] Scripture says. *Make your lightning flash, and you will scatter them; dispatch your arrows, and you will throw them into confusion* (v. 6). He gives the verses optative force. He foretells the future events, which God prophesied through the prophet Ezekiel, which was in fact the way he consumed all those people.

(5) *Send out your hand from on high* (v. 7), teaching that it is sufficient for you [merely] to nod to provide the petitioners with salvation; he called the operation *hand,* as we have often remarked. *Deliver me and rescue me from the mass of water.* He called the multitude of enemies *the mass of water.* He said this also in the hundred and twenty-third psalm, "Our soul passed over a torrent, the irresistible water."[5] And to teach that in figurative fashion he called the foes *waters,* he added, *from the hand of alien sons.* He gave them the name *aliens,* not for being foreign but for being godless. *Whose mouth uttered futility* (v. 8). They used blasphemies, he is saying, of your glory, Lord. *Their right hand a right hand of injustice.* The facts correspond with the words: as they were blasphemous in words, so they were unjust in deeds; their very right hand did nothing right, being only an instrument of injustice.

(6) *O God, I shall sing a new song to you, on a ten-stringed harp* [1964] *I shall sing to you* (v. 9): I shall not be ungrateful for attaining salvation; instead, by employing the customary instruments I shall respond with the hymn of thanksgiving.[6] *To him who gives salvation to the kings* (v. 10). In this way, he is saying, you also saved our forebears who were entrusted by you with the kingship and made them victorious over the invading enemies—David, Jehoshaphat, Hezekiah, and anyone else who sought your assistance. *To him who ransoms David his servant:* you take complete care of us on account of the covenants with

4. Cf. Exod 19.18.
5. Cf. Ps 124.4.
6. We look in vain for some comment of a liturgical nature on this verse that would seem to invite it (as Chrysostom felt).

them. *Rescue me from a wicked sword, and deliver me from the hand of alien sons* (v. 11). He called the frenzy and ferocity of the attackers *a wicked sword,* and the same people *alien sons* for being godless. *Whose mouth uttered futility, and their right hand a right hand of injustice.* It was not without purpose that he employed the duplication; rather, intending to describe their good fortune, he adopted the accusation of wickedness to prompt God to assistance. Those who blaspheme you in this way, he is saying, living a life of injustice and wickedness, meet with fair weather, and in receipt of an abundance of good things from you they have success as support for their injustice.

(7) *Whose sons are like young plants ripening in their youth* (v. 12). They enjoyed many healthy children, he is saying, and are surrounded by their sons, like fresh plants. *Their daughters adorned, attired in the manner of a temple:* not only does natural beauty lend them charm, but they are also invested with great adornment from art so as to resemble the temples beautified in honor of the idols, such being the manner of whores and courtesans. *Their storehouses are full, bulging with one thing and another* (v. 13): when they see their cupboards full to overflowing, they direct the excess to other things in turn, according to the one who said, "I shall pull down my barns and build bigger ones."[7] *Their sheep prolific, multiplying in their departures; their cattle fat* (vv. 13–14); their beasts are rich and prolific. *There is no collapse of walls, no outlet, no cry in their streets.* Symmachus, on the other hand, put it this way, "No gap, nor retreat, nor wailing in their streets"; and so did the other translators—in other words, on account of the great prosperity and the abundance of good things, [1965] they live in luxury and good cheer, not having the experience of the wicked. He said this also in the seventy-second psalm: "There is no denial in their death and strength in their scourge; they are not affected by human troubles, and will not be scourged along with [other] people."[8]

(8) We also find many things in harmony with this in the other inspired authors; but all provide a resolution of their

7. Luke 12.18. Theodoret seems to have lost the plot here, and is rationalizing furiously.
8. Ps 73.4–5.

doubts. The divine David also did so in this case, adding, *They declared blessed the people for whom this is true, blessed the people whose God is the Lord* (v. 15): those devoid of truth do not understand how to judge the nature of things, measuring good fortune by luxury, wealth, and influence, and classing those enjoying them enviable and blessed. The devotees of virtue, on the other hand, in receipt of divine wisdom, declare blessed the people for whom you provide, and they rank your care ahead of the whole of life. The Lord also instructed us in such beatitudes, saying, "Blessed the poor in spirit, blessed those who hunger and thirst for righteousness, blessed those who mourn, blessed those persecuted for the sake of righteousness: to such people belongs the kingdom of the heavens."[9] Those who prefer the pleasures of life, by contrast, enjoy them for a short time, and then feel the effects of protracted pain from the brief pleasure.

9. The Matthean Beatitudes (cf. Matt 5.3–10), incomplete and garbled. Modern commentators admit the presence of various threads of thought, and possibly different sources, in this psalm. Theodoret, unable to be so liberally critical, has struggled to find clarity and consistency, and this finally induces him to make a pastoral application of at least the final verse.

COMMENTARY ON PSALM 145

Praise, for David.

HE TITLE ALSO INDICATES the psalm's purpose: it is an exhortation to sing the praises of the God of all, recalling God's power, magnificence, kingship and majesty. The grace of the Spirit also made other such psalms to stir the people to gratitude. It also contains prophecy of the nations' calling and acceptance. This hymn is also arranged alphabetically,[1] and through the repetition it teaches the inspired author's desire.

(2) *I shall extol you, O my God, my King, and I shall bless your name forever and forever* (v. 1). By nature God is most high, not having elevation in addition. The devotees of piety proclaim it, and teach it to the ignorant. The saying of Christ in the Gospels is like this: "Father, I glorified your name on earth"; and a little later he teaches that he did not give him glory he did not have before, but revealed what he had; he said, "I made your name known to people." In like manner the Father also did not give the Son glory he did not have before, but taught the ignorant what he had: "Glorify me, [1968] Father," he said, "with the glory I had in your presence before the world existed."[2] So he did not take what he did not have, but what he had was made clear to those who did not know. Here the inspired author does not promise to make God elevated, but shows to people his elevation to the extent possible; he gives the God of all the appropriate names *God* and *King*, prompted by love to do so.

(3) *Each day I shall bless you, and praise your name forever and forever* (v. 2). I shall always continue singing your praises, he is

---

1. We recall that at the end of Ps 111 Theodoret had to rely on others for the information that it and the following psalm were alphabetic in structure; the same source is perhaps responsible in this case, too.

2. Cf. John 17.4, 6, 5.

saying, and shall allow no day to be without a role in hymn singing. *Great is the Lord and highly to be praised, and there is no end to his greatness* (v. 3). Since all size is perceptible, and can be seen to be great when measured by length, breadth, and depth, he was right to add, *there is no end to his greatness,* to show that the one being praised is bodiless and uncircumscribed. I know he is great, he is saying, though he is indeed incomprehensible and immeasurable: I find no beginning and no end of his greatness, as it is unlimited and surpasses all grasp.

(4) *Generation and generation will praise your works, and proclaim your power* (v. 4). At this point he announces in advance the divine acknowledgment on the part of the nations: not only ourselves, he is saying, those from Israel according to this generation, will sing the praises of the benefactor, but also another generation, the church from the nations, will proclaim the magnificence of your works.[3] *They shall speak of the magnificence of the glory of your holiness, and will recount your marvels* (v. 5). The nature of the one being praised surpasses the ability of the inspired author: searching for worthy and appropriate titles, he then fails in the effort, and links many names together at the same time, mentioning *glory* and *magnificence* of *holiness.* To be sure, he foretells these will be proclaimed by the other generation.

(5) *They will speak of the might of your fearsome things, and recount your greatness* (v. 6). While he seems to employ repetition, yet likewise he means different things: *marvels* means wonders worked as favors for some people, whereas *might of fearsome things* means the great deeds demonstrated in punishment of others, such as manifold plagues he inflicted on Egypt through the divinely inspired Moses: *might of fearsome things* is to be understood as those events. He provided the people with manna in the desert, snared quails, and deluged dry land; these things moved the tongues of grateful people to wonder. [1969] The divine Apostle also made this distinction: he said there were given by the all-holy Spirit not only gifts of healing but also opera-

---

3. It is interesting that Theodoret, as he has implied elsewhere, sees himself and his community in the church descended from Israel, not in the church of the nations. His comment on the final verse does not quite concur.

tions of power,[4] naming the gifts of healing as the mobility of the lame, the cure of the sick, the raising of the dead, and such like; and the operations of power—the blinding of Elymas, the death of Ananias and Sapphira,[5] those given over to Satan,[6] so that they might learn not to blaspheme.

(6) *They will give vent to the memory of the abundance of your goodness, and rejoice in your righteousness* (v. 7). The inspired author wishes to give a glimpse of the riches of both the divine goodness and power, but by using human language and by being incapable of attaining his desire, he has recourse to piling up many terms, and forecasts the gratitude of the generation to come, reveling in the divine sayings and uttering the account of the divine loving-kindness like a kind of belch.[7] The divine Apostle, to be sure, has the same problem: unable to describe adequately the divine [wonders], he makes an attempt with a series of terms: "The exceeding riches of his grace," he says, and elsewhere admits he is beaten, saying: "How unsearchable his judgments and inscrutable his ways."[8]

(7) *The Lord shows pity and mercy, he is long-suffering and rich in mercy* (v. 8). Here again the inspired author has the same problem: taking stock of the way he formed the human race, the degree of the dignity and providence he accorded them in legislating for all of visible creation's offering them the necessities [of life], in putting up with each of their daily faults, and making his sun rise on evil and good and the rain fall on just and unjust,[9] he calls him not only *piteous* but also *merciful, long-suffer-*

4. Paul does speak of both "gifts of healing" and "deeds of power" in 1 Cor 12.28, but without going into the gifts Theodoret lists.

5. Acts 13.8–11; 5.1–11. On this psalm, which has no title confining the commentator to one historical reference but allows an eschatological interpretation, Theodoret's freedom to follow his own line of thought is reflected in the relative abundance of Scriptural documentation.

6. Cf. 1 Tim 1.20 on Hymenaeus and Alexander.

7. Always alert to the figurative character of the Psalms, Theodoret here feels he has to apologize for the psalmist's use of the verb "belch, give vent," a term used at the opening of that Ps 45 which the Fathers—Chrysostom in particular—found fertile soil for developing their thinking on biblical inspiration; see my "Psalm 45: a *locus classicus* for patristic thinking on biblical inspiration". Theodoret showed similar delicacy at its occurrence in Ps 119.171.

8. Rom 2.4; 11.33.

9. Cf. Matt 5.45.

ing and rich in mercy. In fact, exercising his immeasurable goodness, he kept our sins as far from us as east is from west,[10] and
loved the world so much as to give his only-begotten Son for
it.[11] *The Lord is good to all, and his mercies are directed to all his works*
(v. 9): he not only exercised his providence in favor of Jews, but
poured out his loving-kindness on all human beings—and not
only human beings, but has a care also for the brute beasts and
provides necessities for all.

(8) *May all your works confess to you, O Lord, and your holy ones
bless you* (v. 10): not only do inanimate things sing God's praises
and irrational things utter a rational cry, but also in these ways
rational and God-loving people compose their hymn singing.
That is to say, observing what is done by him to each thing, and
[1972] perceiving the greatness of his wisdom, they move their
tongue to giving glory. *They will speak of the glory of your kingship
and tell of your power, to make known to the sons of human beings your
power and the glory of the majesty of your kingship* (vv. 11–12): these
holy ones, either Old Testament authors or apostles, and those
after them taking up the ministry of preaching will teach all human beings the eternal kingship and the ineffable power; they
will in fact offer this teaching not to Jews alone but also to the
whole human race. *Your kingdom a kingdom of all ages, and your
lordship in every generation and generation* (v. 13): the power you
have is boundless and your kingship everlasting, without beginning or end. *Faithful is the Lord in all his words, and holy in all his
deeds:* the truth of the words shines forth, confirmed by the
deeds, and these are adorned by the righteous one.

(9) *The Lord supports all who fall, and raises up all who are borne
down* (v. 14): he has care not only for the devotees of righteousness, but also for those who have lost their footing, are brought
down, and have suffered the wounds of sin; he supports them
and does not allow them to fall, while the fallen he raises up,
extending his right hand. *The eyes of all hope in you, and you give
[them] their food in due season* (v. 15). He did not use *hope* here in
the sense of disposition: those living a life of impiety do not
have this hope, nor do the species of brute beasts have a faculty

10. Cf. Ps 103.12.
11. Cf. John 3.16.

of reason; instead, he teaches that each develops a need appropriate to their own case. Then he also gives a glimpse of the ease of supply: *You open your hand and fill every living thing with satisfaction* (v. 16): once you wish it, everything enjoys the good things you supply; just as it is easy for us to contract and extend our fingers and open our fist, so it is simple for you to provide the supply of good things in a flash.

(10) *The Lord is righteous in all his ways, and holy in all his works* (v. 17): in all your arrangements righteousness shines through; he gives the term *ways* to his arrangements. *The Lord is near to all who call upon him, to all who call upon him in truth* (v. 18). The word *near* does not imply space: by nature God is present everywhere; after all, "in him we live and move and have our being," according to the divine Apostle.[12] Rather, he indicated in this way state and disposition. [1973] The addition of *truth* was commendable: he approaches those who not simply call upon him but choose to do it in truth; for "not everyone who says to me, Lord, Lord, will enter the kingdom of God, but the one who does the will of my Father in heaven."[13]

(11) Hence he added, *He will do the will of those who fear him, and will hearken to their appeal and will save them* (v. 19). Those who have the fear of God are the first to do God's will; so since their purpose corresponds with the divine will, the Lord necessarily fulfills their wishes, as they wish nothing opposed to his will. *The Lord guards all those who love him, and all the sinners he will destroy* (v. 20). He showed how righteous the Lord is in all his ways: it is characteristic of the righteous to assign everyone their due, for which reason he protects and guards those well-disposed to him and frees them from schemers, whereas those adopting the opposite way he gives over to punishment.

(12) *My mouth will speak the Lord's praise, and may all flesh bless his holy name forever and ever* (v. 21). Therefore I have written this hymn, he is saying. It behooves the whole human race always to celebrate in hymns of praise the Creator, and to offer due worship to the divine name. It should be noted, however,

12. Paul in fact is addressing the Areopagus (Acts 17.28), but quoting the classical author Epimenides.
13. Cf. Matt 7.21.

that here, too, he summoned not Jews to offer the hymn but all flesh to hymn singing. Accordingly, the prophecy becomes evident by confirmation from the outcome: in all nations throughout the world, in keeping with the prophecy, the praises of the God of all are sung.

COMMENTARY ON PSALM 146

Alleluia.

F HAGGAI AND ZECHARIAH" occurs in some copies; but I did not find it in the Hebrew, nor the other translators nor did I find it in the Septuagint in the Hexapla. This psalm bids them sing the praises of the God of all, as the title also indicates:[1] *Alleluia* means, "Praise the Lord," as we often have said.

(2) *Praise the Lord, my soul* (v. 1). The grace of the Spirit urges us all to bestir ourselves to giving glory to God. *I shall praise the Lord in my life, I shall sing to my God while I live* (v. 2). In the sixth psalm he said, "Because in death there is no one to remember you; in Hades who will confess to you?"[2] For this reason we are taught to sing God's praises all life long until we come to the end of this life.

(3) [1976] *Do not trust in rulers* (v. 3). Good advice: far from ruling forever, rulers have temporary authority, nor do all rulers esteem righteousness. To touch on both points, it was necessary to have regard of the impermanence of [human] nature; he adds just that, *In sons of human beings, in whom there is no salvation:* look at [human] nature, and place no trust in its power; "a human being has become like futility," and "man is like grass all his days."[3] *His breath will depart, and he will return to his earth* (v. 4). He calls soul here *breath;* when it departs, the body retires to its own kind, according to the divine saying, "Because you are earth, and to earth you will return."[4] *On that day all his plans will perish* with the soul parting company and the body dis-

---

1. Perhaps not yet conscious that all the remaining psalms begin with an Alleluia, Theodoret takes the word as part of the title, not the opening of the body of the psalm.
2. Ps 6.5. 3. Cf. Ps 144.4, 103.15.
4. Gen 3.19.

357

solving into dust, the figment of the imagination is shown to be in vain. The Lord also taught us this in a parable: introducing the rich man whose property was prosperous and who was planning to demolish his barns and build bigger ones, he added, "Fool, tonight they require your soul of you, and to whom will belong what you have acquired?"[5] With other people, too, some dream of government and influence, some of holdings of land and buildings, while others have thoughts of victories in war, and others plot overthrow of their foes; but death unexpectedly intervenes and leaves their dreams [a matter of] imagination.

(4) After thus showing the futility of hope in human beings, he gives evidence of the usefulness of trust in God. *Blessed is the one whose help is the God of Jacob, whose hope is in the Lord his God* (v. 5). It was not without purpose that he used the name *God of Jacob,* instead, to remind us how great a providence Jacob enjoyed with hope in God, and how many and how great the fruits [were which] he reaped from that hope, he urges [us] to hope in that man's God, calls him *Lord* and *God,* and proclaims his power through both. Then, from the creation of the works he teaches his goodness and power. *Who made heaven and earth, the sea and all that is in them* (v. 6). He concisely included in words the whole of creation, visible and invisible: he mentioned not only heaven, earth and sea, but also everything in them. In heaven are angels, naturally invisible things, sun and moon, and the multitude of the stars; on earth and sea are human beings and the kinds of brute beasts—such, he is saying, is the power of the Maker of all things. Consequently, you will notice the difference between corruptible rulers and the Creator of [1977] all things.

(5) After thus showing in person the Creator of all things, he shows him also exercising providence over what he made. *Who protects truth forever, delivering judgment in favor of the wronged, giving food to the needy* (vv. 6–7): he is reliable in his promises, and as a lover of truth he fulfills his promises. He also defends the wronged, judges justly, and as well provides appropriate food to

---

5. Luke 12.20. The psalm does not invite historical reference, and Theodoret can apply it generally; but he does not stop to moralize, as would a preacher like Chrysostom.

all the needy. Here he foretells as well the benefits done to us through the Incarnation of our Savior. *The Lord releases those in fetters, the Lord gives wisdom to the blind, the Lord raises up those borne down* (vv. 7–8). The God of all forecast this also through the prophet Isaiah: after saying, "I gave you as a light of the nations," he added, "to open blind people's eyes, to lead out shackled people from bondage and those sitting in darkness from a prison."[6] And elsewhere he spoke in the person of Christ the Lord, "The spirit of the Lord is upon me, for which reason he anointed me, he sent me to bring good news to poor people, to heal the contrite of heart, to proclaim release to captives, recovery of sight to the blind."[7] And elsewhere, "Then deaf people will hear words from a book, and eyes of blind people in the darkness and in the fog will have sight."[8]

(6) *The Lord loves righteous people. The Lord will guard the proselytes* (vv. 8–9): the Lord of all offers to each what is appropriate: righteous people who love him he repays equally, and gives them in return a father's love and affection, whereas those shunning ancestral impiety and approaching him in faith he regales with complete protection and providence. He calls the strangers *proselytes;* blessed Paul also spoke that way, "We were once without Christ, alienated from the commonwealth of Israel, strangers to the covenants of promise, having no hope, but we who were once far away have been brought near."[9] *Orphan and widow he will support, but sinners' way he will obliterate.* He brought the treatment away from the overall providence to the particular, saying the ruler of all neglects no one but even accords those bereft of human care complete attention, and defeats the schemes against them.

(7) *The Lord will reign forever, your God, O Sion, from generation to generation* (v. 10): he has everlasting power and eternal kingship, he who is now thought to be your God only, O Sion.

---

6. Isa 42.6–7.   7. Isa 61.1.
8. Isa 29.18.
9. Cf. Eph 2.12–13—but Paul, a Jew, could not have spoken in the first person, Theodoret either deliberately or by mistake changing the reference.

COMMENTARY ON PSALM 147

Alleluia.

ERE WE WERE TAUGHT clearly the meaning of *alleluia:* [1980] the Hebrew *alleluia* means *Praise the Lord* (v. 1), whereas Symmachus left it untranslated, saying "Alleluia, because a psalm is good." Theodotion, on the other hand, said, "Praise Yah."[1] So this psalm bids [us] praise, and prophesies the return from Babylon and the building of Jerusalem that happened afterwards. Jerusalem, in fact, will not be rebuilt, as Jews expect; instead, the inspired word prophesies the building done already by Zerubbabel.[2]

(2) *Praise the Lord, because a psalm is good; praise would be acceptable to our God* (v. 1). Hymn singing, he is saying, is advantageous, productive of good. Yet it is not the hymn that is pleasing to God, but the intention of the singers; he himself has need of nothing, rejoicing only in the salvation of human beings. *In building Jerusalem the Lord will bring together the scattered [remnants] of Israel* (v. 2). This is the reason it is necessary for his praises to be sung, he is saying, that he will build Jerusalem after destruction and accord return to those made captive. If not everyone returned, however, the divine word was not falsified; rather, their wickedness was established: while his orders through Cyrus were for everyone to return, they had a stubborn attitude and preferred the foreign country to their homeland.

1. Theodoret has made a couple of (feeble) attempts to explain the Hebrew term (cf. Ps 105 and Ps 135); this effort by Theodotion gives him his best chance to reduce the word to its elements, but—probably through ignorance—he can go no further.
2. Verse 2 has provided commentators with a possible clue to the historical circumstances of composition, the rebuilding of Jerusalem. Theodoret sees this event as prospective on the part of the psalmist, but curtails the viewpoint lest it encourage Jews of his day to think in terms of a rebuilt Jerusalem post-Titus.

(3) *Who heals the brokenhearted and binds up their brokenness* (v. 3). He related spiritual ailments to physical, and showed [God] not only granting freedom to the captives but also regaling with healing the sufferers of the wounds of sin. *Who counts numbers of stars and gives them all names* (v. 4). In every respect he proclaims God's power. By *Who counts* here he referred to knowledge, and by *names of stars* to the different kinds of stars, their position, array, and relationship to one another: the God of all does not call stars by their names—they are lifeless, after all, and devoid of reason. Human beings, on the other hand, adopting a godless attitude, assigned names to the stars on the basis of fairytales devised by themselves.[3]

(4) *Great is our Lord, and great his strength, and there is no measure to his understanding* (v. 5): they are all immeasurable—his greatness, strength, and praise; yet we sing his praises to the extent we manage. *The Lord lifts up gentle people, but brings down sinners to the ground* (v. 6). Symmachus said "recovers." This is characteristic of divine providence: he shows care for the victims of some people's schemes as a result of their own goodness, while dispatching to death those who assail them unjustly; the former he renders conspicuous and illustrious, while consigning the memory of the latter to oblivion. This was the way the chorus of the holy apostles was famous, this the way the ranks of martyrs were celebrated. The memory of those who warred against them, on the contrary, was given over to oblivion.

(5) [1981] *Begin [a hymn] to the Lord by way of confession; sing to our God on the lyre* (v. 7): so knowing this goodness, wisdom, and power of God, begin using the customary instruments of hymn singing. *Who surrounds the heaven with clouds, who prepares rain for the earth* (v. 8). Both are examples of power and goodness: in so far as he is good and loving, he shows providence for things on earth, and in so far as he is omnipotent, he raises the bodies of water on high and obscures the view of heaven, building the clouds into a kind of roof between heaven and earth, and watering the earth with their birth pangs. Then he shows the advantage stemming from this: *Who makes grass spring up on*

3. We can add astronomy to the range of sciences in which Theodoret displays an interest.

the mountains, and foliage for the service of humankind:[4] he waters
not only land farmed by human beings but also the mountains
and the desert places, providing the cattle with fodder grown
from them. This he does as a favor for human beings, while directing the cattle to be of service to human beings.

(6) *Who gives to cattle their food, and to ravens' chicks that call on
him* (v. 9). Ravens are not rational by nature, nor is it a fact that
they use reason to call on the Creator; rather, the cry arising
from need resembles a petition. I think it was on the basis of
this verse that Christ the Lord likewise omitted mention of the
other birds in referring to the ravens and saying to the disciples, "Consider the ravens: they do not sow nor gather into
barns, and your heavenly Father feeds them."[5] *His delight is not
in the power of the horse, nor is he pleased with a man's fleetness of foot.
The Lord is pleased with those who fear him, and with those who hope
in his mercy* (vv. 10–11). It is not strength of body, he is saying,
equine skill and fleetness of foot that God delights in, but fine
actions of which piety is the source. His providence is earnestly
bestowed not only on them but also on those who have fallen
into sin but had recourse to repentance and are confirmed in
the hope of loving-kindness. For he said that God is pleased not
only with the perfect practitioners of virtue but also with those
who look for the divine mercy.

Alleluia.[6] The inspired word here, too, bids [us] sing praise.
And it foretells the victory after the return. In addition to this,
it prophesies the preaching of the apostles, traversing the
whole world as quickly as possible. [1984] *Praise the Lord,
Jerusalem, sing the praises of your God, Sion. Because he strengthened
the bars of your gates* (vv. 12–13): on account of the invincible aid
of God, liberated from the enemies, and remaining free of

4. This second phrase has crept into some forms of the LXX from the similar verse in Ps 104.14. Theodoret does not notice its absence from the Hebrew,
or refer to the other versions.
5. A collation of Luke 12.24 and Matt 6.26.
6. The LXX here begins a separate psalm, a division Dahood defends on literary and exegetical grounds. Theodoret shows no awareness that the Hebrew
does not acknowledge the division, taking anew both historical and eschatological senses for the psalm.

siege, Jerusalem, repay your benefactor with hymns. By *Jerusalem* he refers not to the buildings but to its inhabitants. *He blessed your children within you:* in receipt of the blessing of many healthy children you developed into a multitude.

(8) *Who put peace as your outer limits* (v. 14): he presented you with peace on all sides; distraught with fear at those fallen in battle, others do not presume to attack again. *And fills you with the finest wheat:* he also lavished on you the good things of the soil. He called *the finest wheat* the abundance of fruits, naming the whole from the part: *wheat* is grain, and *the finest wheat* the best bread; he implied the other fruits, too, through mention of this. Jews, however, enjoyed this providence in the past; by resisting the Savior they were deprived of all good things. Hence, the inspired word, after recounting this about them, prophesies the salvation of the nations. *Who sends out his word to the earth, his word runs swiftly* (v. 15). Here he called the preaching of the Gospel *word*. He sent it not only to Jews but also to all the other people: "Go," he said, "make disciples of all the nations."[7] He also showed the swiftness of the movement: in a short time they filled all land and sea with the teaching. Foreseeing this the inspired author said, *his word runs swiftly,* which was not novel or surprising: everything gives way to the divine will. Accordingly, once he wills it, he straightway changes the waters, naturally united, into countless forms.

(9) *Who gives his snow like wool, sprinkling mist like ashes, hurling his ice like morsels* (vv. 16–17). From the one substance of water comes ice that is solid, snow that is porous and soft, resembling a flock of wool, and also moist dust, such being the character of mist. *Who can stand before his cold?* He changes the air easily, and shortly turns what was red-hot into ice-cold. *He sends out his word, and it melts them; he will breathe his breath, and waters will flow* (v. 18). In turn, by contrast, as soon as he wills it, he easily melts the solidified water, and makes it flow like a stream: once the south wind blows, snow and ice melt. It was not without purpose that he gave a description of these things:[8]

7. Matt 18.19.
8. Theodoret is a commentator on whom the listing of natural phenomena in these psalms is not lost.

it was to suggest other things through them. Just as snow [1985] falls and covers the mountains, but melts and moves to nearby rivers and provides irrigation for different places, so the supply of God-given goods was conferred on the Jews first; but when they renounced the grace, the irrigation of the teaching was offered to the nations by the sacred apostles, as though by some rivers.

(10) *Who sends out his word to Jacob, his ordinances and judgments to Israel* (v. 19)—the Law of old, and grace afterwards; but they were shown to be unworthy of both. *He did not act like this with every nation, nor show them his judgments* (v. 20): to none of the nations he gave the Law through Moses, nor did he offer the benefit of the inspired authors; to them alone he accorded such irrigation. But they proved ungrateful to their benefactor. The nations, on the contrary, received the illumination of the mind's light through the sacred apostles, recognized their own Creator, and constantly offer him worship.

COMMENTARY ON PSALM 148

LLELUIA, *Alleluia.*[1] The inspired author delivered the admonition twice to prompt souls to greater enthusiasm. This is a further hymn that stirs all creation—both with intellect and with senses, both rational and irrational, both animate and inanimate—to a single harmony of hymn singing. Heaven and earth, deeps, the lights of heaven, mountains, plants, and all other such things as share life and reason he urges to offer the hymn. But those with a share in reason he urges to have regard to them, and by learning the wisdom evident in them to sing the praises of the Creator.

(2) *Praise the Lord from the heavens, praise him in the heights* (v. 1). The great Moses taught us that two heavens were made by God: one was made along with the earth, and the second one, which he also called firmament, was bidden to be formed in the midst of the waters.[2] For this reason [the psalmist] gave orders for God to be praised *from the heavens* and *from the heights,* that is, the choruses of incorporeal beings both in the one and in the other. Since even the divine Moses taught us nothing about the creation of the intellectual beings, of necessity here the inspired author made mention of them as well. Hence he also recommends that the hymn be offered to the Creator: this debt is due to him from the creatures, and everything made by him and dignified with reason ought to discharge this debt continually. If, however, things with a created nature sing a hymn, but neither the Son nor the all-holy Spirit are linked with those that sing, it is clear that they have no share in created nature:

1. Theodoret finds the duplication in his form of the LXX, and easily rationalizes his discovery. A more likely reason, however, is that one Alleluia has drifted from the end of the previous psalm, where it occurs in the Hebrew as an inclusion, to join the initial one here. The same occurs with the next two psalms.
2. Cf. Gen 1.1, 6.

otherwise, they would sing the praises of the Creator before the others as [1988] fountains honoring the righteous quality of righteousness. But neither the Son nor the all-holy Spirit sings a hymn, and therefore neither the Son nor the all-holy Spirit shares created nature. Obviously praises are sung to him and to the all-holy Spirit: there is no other difference between those praising and those being praised than that the creation praises and the Creator is praised. If, however, someone does not sing the praises of the Creator, it is out of ingratitude that he does not sing. But we have discoursed on this at greater length in the sermons on the Holy Spirit;[3] so let us go on with the rest of the commentary.

(3) *Praise him, all his angels, praise him, all his powers* (v. 2). He calls the intellectual beings *angels* and *powers*—*angels* as transmitting the divine words, *powers* as free from bodily passions and capable of discharging commands: "powerful ones," Scripture says, "doing his bidding in strength."[4] While it is true that he included all intellectual beings in these names, very appropriately he summoned to hymn singing the heavenly choruses first.

(4) *Praise him, sun and moon, praise him, all the stars and the light* (v. 3). Symmachus, on the other hand, put it this way, "Sing his praises, all stars of light," and so too do the others. The Septuagint, by contrast, is to be understood this way: God created the light on the first day, and the luminaries on the fourth; hence he mentioned the light separately, not as existing of itself but as distributed in the luminaries. As we have already said before, it is not as animate and rational things that he summons them together; rather, he urges us to gain an insight into this, to learn the wisdom of God, and to compose hymn singing to him through them all. *Praise him heaven of heavens, and the water above the heavens* (v. 4). God separated the body of waters with

3. Theodoret has certainly hammered home the point of the uncreated nature of Son and Spirit, and implicitly their consubstantiality; and it is possibly a work of his, referred to by Severus of Antioch as "On the theology of the Holy Trinity and the Incarnation" (cf. Quasten, *Patrology* III, 547), (once thought two works, and even attributed to Cyril!), composed a decade or so earlier, that he refers to here, implying the reader either heard it as *logoi* or can access it.

4. Ps 103.20.

the firmament, in his ineffable wisdom devising for them the utmost separateness. He bade the unlimited fire of the luminaries to travel over the compacted waters; water and fire were [not eliminated] by one another, neither was the fire extinguished by the waters, nor the compacted water evaporated by the unlimited fire. These things reveal God's ineffable power. He spoke of *heavens* in the plural, not from a knowledge of many of them, but following Hebrew usage: they speak of them in the plural, as we say Athens and Thebes.[5] Of course, here he spoke of them as *heaven of heavens,* elsewhere he called them *heaven of heaven:* "The heaven of heaven belongs to the Lord,"[6] Scripture says.

(5) *Let them praise the name of the Lord, because he spoke in person and they were made, he commanded in person and they were created* (v. 5). It is proper to sing the praises, he is saying, of the one who formed all these things by his word.[7] [1989] *He established them forever and ever; he issued a command, and it will not pass away* (v. 6): he not only created but also continues to take care of them—hence they have continuity, as was his personal wish, and they will not be able to overstep the limits set by him. So the inanimate things, and of course the species of other things, respect the laws laid down; only human nature, endowed with reason, transgresses the laws. The sea knows the limits, and respects the sand, and night and day keep the measures laid down, whereas human beings scorn the divine laws.

(6) Having thus summoned beings of heaven and above heaven to share in hymn singing, he moves to the earth, the common mother of human and irrational beings. *Praise the Lord from the earth* (v. 7); then in detail, *dragons and all depths.* The sea is part of the earth, and the sea monsters are in it. Even

5. Has Theodoret, who is here suggesting that the plural term in the Hebrew is merely a morphological irregularity of the kind found also in Greek, forgotten that in commentary on v. 1 he claimed that the Torah distinguishes two heavens as an explanation of the plural form? Or do we have here a different form of Theodoret's text, unacknowledged by editor Schulze?

6. Ps 115.16.

7. That is Theodoret's (reasonable) comment on the accent on personal command in this verse. Dahood sees the nuance differently: "The psalmist rejects the tenets of neighboring religions concerning the origin of the universe."

the very providence of the Creator is admirable in creating the huge and immense beings and containing them in the unnavigable oceans, on the one hand revealing this by his creation [of them] and instilling fear into human beings by mention of them, and on the other proclaiming his goodness by preventing harm coming from them. *Fire, hail, snow, ice, stormy wind* (v. 8). These things have their source in water; but hail, snow, ice, and the strong winds—hence his term *stormy*—are formed in the air. Fire likewise is not only on earth, but can be seen appearing also in the air: lightning flashes, thunderbolts, and hurricanes come from the air.[8] *Those that do his will*. These, he is saying, yield to his wishes, not as animate and rational things, but as responding to his will: each of them is made as God decides.

(7) *The mountains and all the hills, fruitbearing trees and all cedars* (v. 9). These suffice to move our tongues to thanksgiving: it is not only their size that is amazing, but also the advantage stemming from them, great and manifold as it is. *The wild beasts and all the cattle* (v. 10). These too are itemized: he did not simply cite the four-legged [animals], but distinguished the fierce from the gentle. So he requires the Creator to be celebrated by both the former and the latter: there is nothing superfluous and idle, even if it is at variance with our knowledge.[9] *Creeping things and birds on the wing*. Creeping and swimming things are linked in this reference, the creeping one swimming in the waters. God called them that, too: [1992] "Let the waters bring forth creeping kinds of living beings," he said, "and birds flying across the firmament of heaven."[10]

(8) After all these he summons the one singing praise in all; after everything the human being was accorded the divine creation. He summons them group by group; first he introduces the choir of kings, then the hordes of subjects, saying, *Kings of the earth and all peoples* (v. 11). He does not relieve them of hymn singing, nor the leaders of second rank, nor the judges

8. Theodoret's manner as he discourses on these natural phenomena is magisterial; he feels he knows as much about them as the psalmist.

9. As an Antiochene Theodoret approves of the psalmist's precision; as a naturalist he faults him for accuracy (*akribeia*, as we noted in Introduction, section 5, requiring only the former).

10. Gen 1.20.

after them; instead, he here gives them a share in the benefit: *Leaders and all judges of earth.* Every age and kind, both male and female, he bids do this, in the first place men and women of mature age: *Young men and maidens* (v. 12); then each extreme: *Let elders along with youngsters praise the name of the Lord.* Let age, he says, both immature and over-ripe, celebrate God. Because his name alone is exalted: memory of the false gods is extinguished, and the name only of the true God is shown reverence.

(9) *His confession on earth and in heaven* (v. 13): no longer do things above heaven alone sing his praises; rather, "all the earth was filled with the knowledge of the Lord, like much waters covering seas."[11] *And will exalt the horn of his people* (v. 14). He will show his own people, he is saying, to be invincible, the cynosure of all eyes, calling their strength *horn* by analogy with horned animals, which pride themselves on having strength in them. *A hymn for all his holy ones:* he makes those who believe in him not only strong but also celebrated amongst everyone. *For the children of Israel, a people close to him.* Israel enjoyed this notoriety when it stayed close to God; but now its fame has disappeared along with its piety, and they are deprived of it, whereas the nations rejoice in the divine gifts.[12]

11. Cf. Hab 2.14. Theodoret seems to omit from comment two of the three clauses in this verse of the psalm.

12. Commentators (excluding Theodoret) notice the adoption of this psalm in the LXX expansion of Dan 3, the Benedicite.

COMMENTARY ON PSALM 149

LLELUIA, *Alleluia.*[1] Those after the return who triumphed through divine aid over those many nations urge that this hymn be offered. It also contains a prophecy of the achievements of the Maccabees.[2]

(2) *Sing to the Lord a new song, his praise in the assembly of holy ones* (v. 1): celebrating God is proper not for the lawless but for the holy ones. [1993] *Let Israel be glad in its Maker, and let children of Sion rejoice in their king* (v. 2). While the God of all things is everyone's God, he is styled *king* peculiarly of the Israelites. So once they were stricken with ingratitude and requested another king be made for them, God said to Samuel, "It is not you but me they have rejected from reigning over them."[3] *Let them praise his name in dancing, let them sing to him on drum and lyre* (v. 3). On every instrument, he is saying, let us sing the praises of our benefactor according to the Law.

(3) *Because the Lord takes pleasure in his people* (v. 4). He has regaled us with much loving-kindness, he is saying, and shown us his characteristic goodness. *And he will exalt gentle people with salvation:* those bereft of help and practicing good behavior he will make to appear illustrious and of high station. *Holy ones will boast in glory and be happy in their beds* (v. 5): those esteeming righteousness will have a good name and enjoy deep repose; he called repose *bed,* lying down implying repose.

1. For the likely transposition of one "Alleluia" from the close of the previous psalm, where it formed an inclusion, see note 1 there.
2. Weiser remarks: "From the fifth century AD up to the present day the psalm has constantly been interpreted as referring to Maccabean times, though the composition itself does not go beyond very general allusions which fit into every age." Theodoret is aware of such an interpretation, but like the moderns prefers to find an application of his own.
3. 1 Sam 8.7. With the end of the *Commentary* in sight, Theodoret is dispatching verses at a rapid rate, Scriptural documentation down to a minimum, no alternative versions on offer.

(4) *The high praises of God in their throat* (v. 6): they constantly proclaim the divine favors, celebrating the one responsible for them. *Double-edged swords in their hands for wreaking vengeance on the nations, reproofs on the peoples* (vv. 6–7). Conquest in war is not inconsistent with repose; conquest, in fact, is more satisfying than complete repose. In these words, then, he foretells the Maccabees' valor, exercised by them in subduing neighboring peoples and struggling against the Macedonians.

(5) *For binding their kings in fetters, and their nobles in iron manacles* (v. 8). History teaches that many things of that kind were achieved by those men, and for anyone willing it is easy to read the inspired composition to learn the truth. *For executing on them a judgment recorded* (v. 9). What they did in justice against [the enemies] was written down and to this day remained their unforgettable glory;[4] in fact, he added, *This will be the glory for all his holy ones:* holiness is the mother of good reputation, and its devotees become celebrated for it.

4. The reference is not patent, as Chrysostom admitted, as do modern commentators. Theodoret, not for admitting ignorance, and here in obvious haste, settles for an unconvincing application to the Maccabees.

COMMENTARY ON PSALM 150

LLELUIA, *Alleluia.* This hymn, too, is triumphal. It forecasts, however, the knowledge of God that will be [enjoyed] by all human beings.[1]

(2) *Praise God in his saints* (v. 1). This is, in fact, sufficient occasion for hymn singing: if on the basis [1996] of plants, wild animals, and reptiles we were bidden to find grounds for thanksgiving, much more should we consider the saints and with greater justice celebrate their God. After all, who ever learned the story of blessed Paul, the divinely inspired Peter, John the most divine, the other apostles, the triumphant martyrs, the other saints, or today's practitioners of virtue without moving the tongue to singing hymns to him who regaled human beings with such an abundance of good things? *Praise him in the firmament of his power.* Symmachus, on the other hand, put it this way, "Praise him in his indestructible firmament": he alone is firm, proof against destruction, and possessing everlasting might.[2]

(3) *Praise him for his mighty deeds* (v. 2): beyond words are the constant achievements of his saints. *Praise him according to the extent of his greatness.* This resembles what we have already commented on: "Because there is no limit to his greatness."[3] His

1. Theodoret, we have noted, is not sensitive to the liturgical origins and continuing application of the Psalms in worship, and so has not recognized this series of Hallel psalms, failing, for instance, to see the inclusion employed in the last five with "Alleluia" at beginning and end. He also does not acknowledge the conclusion this particular Hallel psalm makes to the series or the Psalter's fifth book. Yet he takes the opportunity to comment on at least the final verse as a fitting conclusion to the whole Psalter, though apparently not finding a closing "Alleluia" in his form of the LXX.

2. A closing tribute to Symmachus, on whom Theodoret has depended throughout the *Commentary* for some enlightenment, even when as here little if any refinement of the LXX is achieved.

3. Ps 145.3.

greatness is unlimited, he is saying, his power without measure; so continue singing his praises for everything.

(4) *Praise him with sound of trumpet* (v. 3). This instrument was a priestly one: the priests used trumpets, recalling the trumpets that were on Mount Sinai.[4] *Praise him with lyre and harp, praise him with drum and dancing, praise him with string and [musical] instrument, praise him with clanging cymbals, praise him with cymbals of jubilation* (vv. 3–5). The Levites of old used these instruments in celebrating God in the divine Temple, not because God took delight in their sound but because he accepted the intention of what was happening. For proof, in fact, that the deity does not take delight in songs and notes, we hear him saying to Jews, "Take away from me the noise of your songs; I will not listen to the sound of your instruments."[5] So he allowed these things to be done in his wish to rid them of the error of the idols: since some liked sport and play, and it was all conducted in the temples of idols, he allowed these things so as to draw them away through them, preventing the greater harm with the less, and teaching in advance the perfect through the imperfect.

(5) *Let every breath praise the Lord* (v. 6)—not only Jews but all human beings: he is God not only of Jews, according to the divine Apostle, but also of nations. Actually, in the hundred and forty-fourth psalm he said, "Let all flesh bless his holy name,"[6] and here, *Let every breath praise the Lord*. In the former case, however, he did not summon only flesh, nor in this case only breath; rather, through both the one and the other he urges both body and spirit to sing the praises of the God of all. [1997] The conclusion of the whole work of the Psalms is admirable, and in keeping with the purpose of inspired composition: inspired composition proclaims salvation to the nations, and the conclusion of the inspired composition urges those who have attained it to sing the praises of the benefactor. We do not, however, only hear the words, but here we also perceive the realization:[7] in each city and village, in fields and on bor-

---

4. Cf. Exod 19.13–19.   5. Amos 5.23.
6. Ps 145.21.
7. For Theodoret, at least at this point, the Psalms are sung prayer, a liturgy

ders, on mountains and hills, and in completely uninhabited wasteland, the praises of the God of all are sung.

I urge those reading this book, if it seems to be a fit and proper work of commentary, to reap benefit from them.[8] If, on the other hand, we have not in some cases arrived at the Spirit's hidden mysteries, do not be too hard on us: what we succeeded in finding we proposed to everyone without stint, and what we learned from the Fathers we were anxious to offer to posterity.[9] The labor undergone was ours; for others free of labor is the benefit we offer. I ask them to repay the labor with prayers, so that relying on them we may add actions to words, and reap the beatitude that arises from both; Scripture says, "Whoever practices and teaches will be called great in the kingdom of heaven."[10] May it be the good fortune of us all to attain this, through Christ Jesus our Lord, to whom with the Father belongs the glory, along with the Holy Spirit, forever. Amen.[11]

---

practiced universally in his time, as the psalmist desired. To grasp their full sense *theoria* is required, as the verb here indicates.

8. Having terminated the final psalm with comment on the psalmist's exhortation to all people to praise God, Theodoret pens a brief conclusion to his whole *Commentary*, speaking in the plural of a series of commentaries.

9. He is honest enough to admit his debt to his predecessors, while claiming modestly to leave posterity indebted to his own inspired contribution.

10. Matt 5.19. As he stated in his preface, Theodoret has been interested primarily in the *teaching* of the Psalms, disappointed though we may have been in his lack of attention to their liturgical dimension.

11. While Chrysostom as a preacher closed every individual commentary on a psalm with such a doxology, Theodoret as a desk theologian evidently thought such perorations out of place.

INDICES

GENERAL INDEX

adoptionism, 209
akribeia, 60, 141, 142, 286, 323, 368
Albright, W. F., 281, 314
Alexandria, 10, 112
allegory, 167
almsgiving, 65
anagogical, 126, 143, 190
Anomoeans, 53
anthropomorphism, 209, 302
antigrapha, 22, 146, 343, 346
Antioch, *passim*
Antiochus Epiphanes, 41, 329
Apamea, 64
Aquila, *passim*
Asaph, 3, 25, 31, 41, 279
Assyria, *passim*
Augustine of Hippo, 156
authorship, 3, 11, 20, 25, 30, 40, 84,
  97, 161, 245, 285, 334

Babylon, *passim*
baptism, 88, 90, 113, 334
Baptist, 69, 70
Beaucamp, E., 77

Caligula, 12
canon, 41
Chalcedon, 112, 207, 212
Christology, *passim*
chronology, 11
Church, 84, 180, 237, 352
communicatio idiomatum, 196, 206
conciseness, 5, 9, 40, 59, 122, 154,
  159, 202, 210, 278, 302, 304
Constantinople, 17, 61, 76
council, 17, 61, 76
crucifixion, 17, 112, 202
Cyril of Alexandria, 153, 366

Dahood, M., *passim*
dating, 250

David, *passim*
devil, 14, 201
Diodore of Tarsus, 10
dogma, 3, 25, 97, 161
Dorival, G., 232, 252, 304, 335

Ehrlich, A., 229
Eissfeldt, O., 49
eschatology, 4, 8, 68, 76, 77, 84, 94,
  114, 123, 130, 140, 168, 188,
  237, 239, 279, 353
eucharist, 33, 187, 233, 234
Eunomius, 53
Eusebius of Caesarea, 3, 10, 112
exegesis, 18, 42, 296, 321

Fall, 67, 82, 253
fifth edition, 19
flexibility, 21, 25, 97

geography, 36, 60, 312, 316
grace, 157, 199, 252, 270, 302
Guinot, J.-M., 232, 346
Gunkel, H., 24

Hebrew, *passim*
hermeneutics, 30, 31, 68, 84, 158,
  188, 195
Hexapla, 12, 19, 112, 137, 225, 231,
  301, 329, 346
Hill, R. C., 7, 161, 197, 257, 277, 353
history, 4, 34, 38, 64, 66, 97, 106,
  116, 120–2, 140, 147, 155, 180,
  199, 239, 306, 308
homoousios, 53
hypostatic, 153

Incarnation, 61, 97, 113, 151, 192,
  271, 366
inspiration, 11, 31, 52, 132, 186,
  197, 262, 277, 279, 328, 353

377

INDEX OF HOLY SCRIPTURE

379

New Testament